Administration of Criminal Justice

A MANAGEMENT SYSTEMS APPROACH

Alan R. Coffey

Director of Staff Development
Juvenile Probation Department
County of Santa Clara, California

•

Instructor, DeAnza College,
Foothill College, University of
California at Santa Cruz, California
State University, San Jose

Other books authored or co-authored by
ALAN R. COFFEY

PRINCIPLES OF LAW ENFORCEMENT
POLICE-COMMUNITY RELATIONS
HUMAN RELATIONS: Law Enforcement
in a Changing Community
POLICE AND THE CRIMINAL LAW
CORRECTIONS: A Component of the
Criminal Justice System
JUVENILE JUSTICE AS A SYSTEM:
Law Enforcement to Rehabilitation
CRIMINAL JUSTICE AS A SYSTEM: Readings
AN INTRODUCTION TO THE CRIMINAL JUSTICE
SYSTEM AND PROCESS
CORRECTIONAL ADMINISTRATION
PREVENTION OF CRIME AND DELINQUENCY

PRENTICE-HALL, INC.   ·   *Englewood Cliffs, N.J.*

Library of Congress Cataloging in Publication Data

COFFEY, ALAN
    Administration of criminal justice.

    (Prentice-Hall series in criminal justice)
    Includes bibliographical references.
    1. Criminal justice, Administration of.
2. Management.   I. Title.
HV8665.C57   364   73-19620
ISBN 0-13-005314-7

Printed in the United States of America

10   9   8   7   6   5   4   3   2

PRENTICE-HALL SERIES IN CRIMINAL JUSTICE
    James D. Stinchcomb, Editor

PRENTICE-HALL INTERNATIONAL, INC., London
PRENTICE-HALL OF AUSTRALIA, PTY. LTD., Sydney
PRENTICE-HALL OF CANADA, LTD., Toronto
PRENTICE-HALL OF INDIA PRIVATE LIMITED, New Delhi
PRENTICE-HALL OF JAPAN, INC., Tokyo

Contents

v

Preface

This is a book about managing the programs of criminal justice.

The management of programs in criminal justice necessarily differs from management in private industry or business. Moreover, the differences go far beyond the frequently cited profit index of industry, the fundamental nature of business and industry being entirely different from the nature of criminal justice.

But differences in nature notwithstanding, once the concept of management has been isolated, it has great similarities in all areas in which it occurs.

Against the background of a wealth of managerial principles developed in the private sector, this volume proposes a specific, concrete management model for criminal justice—a "systems model."

With great emphasis on clarification of managerial role and function, the proposed systems model seeks to combine successful management of the particular criminal justice organization with the coordinative management of *all* criminal justice organizations. Broadening the managerial scope to encompass all segments of criminal justice is based on the firm belief that ultimately no segment of criminal justice succeeds unless the entire criminal justice system succeeds.

Simply stated, then, this volume introduces a managerial approach with two related purposes: (1) successful management of an organization, and (2) successful management of a complex system of criminal justice through successful management of each criminal justice organization.

This book is dedicated to those who
seek to manage criminal justice
well enough to give it a *chance* to succeed.

ARC

Acknowledgments

With ever-increasing clarity, each new writing project demonstrates that appropriate acknowledgement can never be given to all those who have helped in developing ideas and notions that have crystallized in this book. The author has been the beneficiary of the realistic thinking of judges, district attorneys, police executives, probation and correctional administrators, and a host of criminal justice management personnel taking part in the writer's training programs.

The significant influence of California's Commission on Peace Officer Standards and Training ("POST") in creating an awareness of the need for managerial development no doubt facilitated many of the writer's efforts. In this same regard, the International Association of Chiefs of Police have been helpful beyond the many citations in this volume from the IACP journal, *Chief*. Successful compilation of this volume stems in part from experience gained through writing collaboration on other books with the most prolific author in criminal justice, Ed Eldefonso.

Successful development of the management model itself could not have occurred without the administrative commitment of the Chief Probation Officer of Santa Clara County, Richard W. Bothman, in whose managerial debt criminal justice increasingly finds itself. The timely analogies from football and medical analogies offered by his Chief of Operations, Mike Kuzirian, frequently replaced frustration with humor during development of the model.

Finally, for reasons possibly clear only to those who have written a book while directing a managerial development program, conducting training, teaching college, consulting on management systems etc., my very special and enduring gratitude to the finest ladies in the world: my mother, Margaret D. Coffey, for convincing me, and my lovely wife and daughters for keeping me convinced.

ARC

Administration of
Criminal Justice

PART ONE

MANAGING CRIMINAL JUSTICE: THEORETICAL IMPLICATIONS

CHAPTER 1

Criminal Justice as
a Manageable System

As suggested by the chapter title, this discussion deals with criminal justice as a system that can be managed; indeed, the concept of management can be applied to the entire system of criminal justice much as it is in the industrial/business world. In the process of exploring this possibility, it will be necessary to define the word "management"—a task that will be undertaken throughout most of this book.

Even without the benefit of this definition, it is possible to establish an appropriate context for criminal justice as a manageable system. To clarify this idea of context, consider the example of . . . a chief of police and a county sheriff with bordering jurisdictional responsibilities. The chief prosecutor advises both law enforcement administrators that much physical evidence will be required for any conviction in local criminal courts. Upon examination of the actual requirements, both administrators determine that either more resources (personnel and equipment) or fewer arrests are required. They further determine that this "management problem" is mutual and that sharing the costs of a mutual crime laboratory represents enough budget savings to increase the number of personnel to a desirable rather than a merely acceptable level.

On still closer perusal, they agree that the court's insistence on more physical evidence relates solely to unwitnessed burglaries. Statistically, it is determined that most of these burglaries occur in the sheriff's jurisdiction in the daytime and in the police chief's jurisdiction at night. With this awareness, each administrator directs that the detective division of the police department share with the sheriff all information on daylight burglaries (heretofore thought insignificant), and the sheriff's detectives share with police night burglary information (heretofore thought insignificant).

Of course, the concept of management is far more involved than the simple example just cited. It is increasingly clear that management is a virtual science that is vitally needed and is just beginning to emerge within the system.

Some initial consideration of this emergence might prove useful. The twentieth century appears to most observers to have already witnessed an almost unbelievable growth in the significance of management; quite literally, it has emerged as "the central activity of our age and economy."[1]

It is clear that the overwhelming majority of this expanded significance relates to the industrial nature of American culture. Probably the greatest single stimulant to the incredible development of managerial science is the ever-increasing complexity of transforming raw materials into competitive products. But regardless of the reasons, management in industry has indeed emerged as a central activity of our culture.

The pace at which management has evolved in private industry, however, has not been matched by managerial development in government. The management of the myriad agencies, bureaus, departments, and other organizational jurisdictions of government has proven far more resistant to constructive growth than in the private sector. Indeed, the management of local, state, and federal government is still considered by many to be a political issue, as viable for today's politician as for the politician of a century ago.

Criminal justice, as a broad concept, encompasses a great deal of the overall government organization. Not surprisingly, then, the growth of managerial programs for criminal justice has occurred at about the same pace as management growth within government; thus, to whatever degree government has fallen behind private industry in recognizing the distinct science of management, criminal justice has also lagged.

An approach to remedying this situation might best begin with the recognition that criminal justice is a *system*—a manageable system.[2] The policeman, the judge, the prosecutor, the defense attorney, the probation officer, the prison staff, and the parole agents all perform work that, when managed effectively, forms a viable, functional system. Effective manage-

[1] C. S. George, Jr., *The History of Management Thought* (Englewood Cliffs, N. J.: Prentice-Hall, Inc., 1968), p. 1.

[2] Eugene G. Columbus, "Management By Systems," *The Police Chief*, 37, No. 7 (July 1970), 14–16.

ment means, in the case of criminal justice, management in relation to all other segments of criminal justice toward some goal. This is the theme of this entire volume. Indeed, virtually all of the management models that will be presented in chapters four through eight will bear directly on effective management defined as goal-achieving administration.

Actually, there is little distinction between administration and management beyond noting the following:

> . . . if it were possible for the head of an organization to perform all of the work himself without the help of any additional personnel, it is conceivable that he would have to use only a small part of the administrative process. Once he had organized his own work, his administrative functions would be limited to a bit of planning and nothing else. However, for the most part, an organization run by one man is not readily conceivable because even the most hearty of men have their limitations as far as physical and mental capacity are concerned. However, the one-man operation would need little administration because that one individual would be in complete control of the situation. The need for the administrative function increases with the growth of an organization because the larger the organization the more the administrator will be out of actual touch with work situations.[3]

As related to all the segments of criminal justice, then, effective management is what an administration uses to achieve *goals*—to manage criminal justice as a system.

This chapter is addressed to criminal justice as a *manageable* system. Consideration is therefore given to the nature both of criminal justice and of systems.

THE NATURE OF CRIMINAL JUSTICE AND OF SYSTEMS

There has never been a civilized society that did not find itself continually coping with crime. It can be said that great differences exist between the crime philosophies and criminal theories and activities from culture to culture. But it cannot be said that any society, including our own, can avoid the necessity of coping with crime on a continuing basis.

The American method of dealing with crime is known as the "criminal justice system." In effect, the word "system" is the specific focus of this chapter. The actual word will be elaborated in considerable depth. Before moving into this elaboration, however, consideration of the "flow" of criminal justice—the overall operation and sequence of activities that are involved—might prove useful. Consider the following:

---

[3] *Principles of Civil Service Administration and Management* (Santa Cruz, Calif.: Davis Publishing Co., 1972), p. 1.

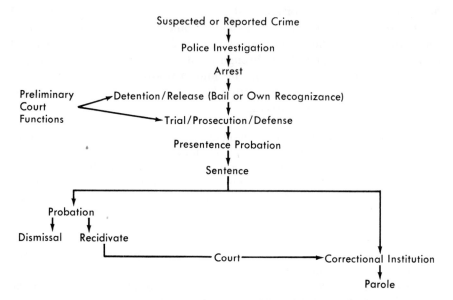

Of course a great number of variations routinely occur in this flow, and the functions of the various levels are far more complex than implied by this chart, but it reflects the essential activities involved in a proper recognition of the nature of systems and criminal justice.

The criminal justice system has many segments, all strategically important and interrelated. Police, courts, prosecution-defense, corrections, and the law itself interrelate in many crucial ways, and these interrelationships actually form the basis of developing a manageable system of criminal justice.

Chart of Criminal Justice as a System of Parts

Put another way, criminal justice can function systematically only to the degree that each segment of the system takes into account all other segments. In the absence of functional relationships between the various segments, the criminal justice system is vulnerable to fragmentation and ineffectiveness—perhaps becoming a "non-system."[4]

[4] Frederick W. Howlett, and Hunter Hurst, "A Systems Approach to Comprehensive Criminal Justice Planning," *Crime and Delinquency,* 17, No. 4 (October 1971), 345–54.

Fragmentation

Fragmentation and ineffectiveness can be measured simply in terms of crime rates that are not reduced and by law violators who continue to offend. In short, American society is not coping with crime when the criminal justice system is fragmented.

The precise manner in which the criminal justice system suffers fragmentation can vary from one part of the United States to another, or from one jurisdiction to another. Ineffective criminal justice that occurs through fragmentation between segments may be caused by many different things. When police operate without regard to the prosecution or when a court shows indifference to corrections or to police activities, the system is clearly not operating in an effective way.

The point is that when any segment of the system functions in isolation from the rest of the system, the fragmentation lends itself to reducing the system's effectiveness.[5] Effectiveness in this case is society's successful approach to crime in general.

By focusing on the broad definition of effectiveness as the overall society's success with crime, a background is provided for criminal justice *management* rather than *supervision*. Indeed, the systems approach being introduced is geared to the entire administrative and managerial concept within criminal justice—not merely to the supervisory functions.

For these and many other reasons that will be explored later, the systems approach—the *concept* of systems—will now be examined.

Systems, Criminal Justice and Otherwise

Later in this chapter and elsewhere throughout this volume, systems will be presented in terms of precise relationships, influences, and consequences. As a background, however, attention is first directed toward the general functions of systems. The systems approach has to do with integrating quantitative measures and human behavior toward specific goals. Through this integration, the systems approach focuses on causes and effects, which in turn have to do with interaction. All human interactions are effects of some kind; even the supposed absence of interaction has effect on those who notice its absence. The interaction of the armed robber with the victim results in the *effect* of the robbery, but it is also the *cause* of another interaction—with police (hopefully), prosecution, corrections, and so on. The interaction of police with prosecution, similarly, is a variety of both causes and effects, as are the interactions of corrections with courts and police.

The limitless effects also cause still other effects. Consider any possible reaction to police making an arrest. The arrest itself is an effect, but any

---

[5] *Ibid.*

reaction to this causes other effects. And so the endless cycles go.

A system, in short, is simply a chain of these effects and causes—manageable once a quantitative goal-oriented approach is integrated with behavioral considerations. The system may or may not cause favorable effects—indeed, many effects tend to cause unfavorable results. Managers, however, seem to tend to assume that policy alone eliminates unfavorable results, regardless of evidence to the contrary.[6] Thinking of an organization in relation to other organizations seeking to accomplish tangible goals permits a manager to recognize that policy frequently becomes both cause and effect in activities totally removed from achieving a goal. In the later discussion of the management model, both *behavior* and *policy* will be isolated in terms of their respective impact upon achieving criminal justice goals in both the entire criminal justice system and particular segments of it. But in terms of systems, the relationship of each segment to all other segments is significant enough to consider prior to either behavior or policy.

The need to relate each segment of the criminal justice system to all other segments has been noted. If fragmentation prevents such a relationship, it should not then be surprising that the system produces extremely *un*favorable results within the cause and effect chain in spite of policy. A system that produces unfavorable results may continue to work, but with little or no effective impact on the problem for which it is intended. And in terms of a system being manageable in relation to a specific goal, its consistent effective impact becomes the only measure.[7]

System Consistency

To clarify how a systematic chain of interactions can be designed to provide consistent effects that cause desirable results, the analogy of heating a house might be useful.

If a home is equipped with an efficient furnace that is controlled by a thermostat, it can be said that a heating *system* is available. The reason that this is a system is that it has a consistent chain of causes and effects which provides a desirable range of warmth on a predictable basis. In the case of this particular system, desirable results are produced on a "self-adjusting" basis. Complaints about excessive heat or cold are not required to get the furnace adjusted correctly; sensitivity to the problem for which the system is intended insures consistent and proper adjustment to the system on an ongoing basis. The thermostat measures the temperature inside the house

---

[6] Douglas McGregor, *The Professional Manager,* Caroline McGregor and Warren G. Bennis, eds. (New York: McGraw-Hill, Inc., 1967), pp. 32–39.

[7] See, for example: E. H. Schein, *Organizational Psychology* (Englewood Cliffs, N.J.: Prentice-Hall, Inc., 1965); also see, D. Katz and R. L. Kahn, *The Social Psychology of Organization* (New York: John Wiley & Sons, Inc., 1966); and J. W. Forrester, *Industrial Dynamics,* (Cambridge, Mass.: M.I.T. University Press, 1961).

and then controls the furnace accordingly—this interaction of causes and effects produces the desirable results of healthy indoor climate.

Compare this heating system with its sensitivity to temperature changes and its automatic correct adjustments to one in which the occupant must run to the basement to manually adjust the furnace every time a temperature change occurs. Also consider the overall system if any single part functions independently to the degree that it is not directly related to the overall *purpose* of the system. Clearly, the system that adjusts itself to change not only produces better results and requires less effort, it necessarily becomes the only desirable system.

Relating this analogy more specifically to criminal justice, recall the example at the beginning of the chapter that involved a police chief, sheriff, prosecutor, and court. Their individual functions were performed in a systematic manner to serve a common goal. Like the thermostat of the heating system, the prosecutor registered change and communicated this change to the police chief and sheriff. Like the furnace, the police chief and sheriff responded with what was needed. Moreover, the systematic manner in which they interrelated made possible the allowance for variations of many kinds. In other words, though the heating system responds to the single variable of heat, the criminal justice system can and does respond to a great number of variables. For example, social, legal, and economic change, along with many other changes, impinge directly upon police, courts, prosecution-defense, and corrections through a number of "thermostats."

The criminal justice system, then, must be flexible.

System Flexibility

Change itself is the significant consideration in flexibility. A brief glimpse at the significance of change (or more particularly, *social* change) may illustrate the need for flexibility in a workable system of criminal justice.

Tremendously oversimplified, changes during the history of the world might be thought of in terms of the thousands of years man has spent farming compared to the couple hundred years of "blue-collar era" that accompanied the Industrial Revolution. With this background of suddenly accelerated change, man now faces an uncertain future with automation, cybernation, and an explosion of knowledge having the effect of creating more knowledge almost daily than was created during thousands of years prior to the twentieth century.

The ever-accelerating pace of social change, because it has a direct impact on the causes and effects within the criminal justice system, requires incredible flexibility for the system to survive. The requirement of flexibility flows as readily from the systems approach as from the increasing criticism that criminal justice is long overdue for certain adjustments—one of which occurs in the area of management.

WHAT MAKES A SYSTEM SYSTEMATIC

Although the idea of considering a system merely a chain of interactions is simple enough, in reality, interactions number in the millions— possibly billions. Knowing which interactions are significant becomes the important consideration. More precisely, knowing *how* significant the interactions are—knowing to what degree they affect the system—is the important managerial consideration.

To organize all of the complicated possibilities, the idea of a system can be thought of as having three parts: *input, process,* and *output.*

Input, Process, Output

Before elaborating these components, it may be worthwhile to note that this particular configuration is *not* the only way to conceive of a system. For example, most dictionaries define system merely in terms of an arrangement that is in some way interrelated. Even technical definitions of *system* vary somewhat—for example:

> . . . general-systems [management] model is one that brings together in an ordered fashion information on all dimensions of an organization. . . .[8]

> . . . the term system covers an extremely broad spectrum of concepts. . . .[9]

> . . . *system* is a network of related procedures developed according to an integrated scheme for performing major activity. . . .[10]

> . . . system in general can be defined as an established arrangement of components which leads to the attainment of particular objectives according to plan. . . .[11]

Of course these and many other varying definitions are correct, and will be drawn on extensively in later discussions of a systems approach to management. They will also be used extensively in elaborating a management model. But in order to approach the concept of systems on a consistent basis, the three main components of a linear system will be used: input, process, and output.

Among the many advantages of this approach is the ease with which it can be adapted. As noted in the present context, the concept refers to criminal justice overall; later it will be adapted to management in general.

[8] Bertram M. Gross, "What Are Your Organization's Objectives? A General Systems Approach to Planning," *Human Relations,* 43, No. 4 (April 1964), 205.

[9] R. A. Johnson, F. E. Kast, and J. E. Rosenzweig, "Systems Theory and Management," *Management Science,* 10, No. 5 (January 1964), 368.

[10] R. F. Neuschel, *Management by System* (New York: McGraw-Hill, Inc., 1960), p. 10.

[11] L. J. Kazmier, *Principles of Management,* 2nd ed. (New York: McGraw-Hill, Inc., 1969), p. 349.

Eventually it will serve as the conceptual vehicle to introduce the management model.

Indeed, the single configuration of feedback as flowing from input → process → output will be utilized for consistency in every context in which *system* is used.

Input is *what* the system deals with, process is *how* the system deals with the input, and output represents the *results* of the process—results that may or may not be desirable.

In terms of desirability of results, the analogy of the heating system might again be considered. First, the heating system has an input of excessive changes in the house temperature, the process of registering the changes and adjusting the furnace accordingly, and an output of healthy inside climate. Of course this assumes that the process *is* to adjust the furnace downward when the house is hot and upward when the house is cold. But consider a heating process that works in the following manner.

If the thermostat were disconnected from the actual "control" of the furnace, a wrong response when the temperature change is signaled might occur—the thermostat might detect a *drop* in temperature and the furnace might receive it merely as a signal of temperature *change*. The furnace could then guess wrong on the direction of the temperature change and turn downward, causing the house to become even colder. Of course, someone outside the heating system will eventually insist on improving this unsatisfactory hit-or-miss process.

To the degree that any system achieves satisfactory output by chance, that system is poorly managed and in dire need of improvement.

CRIMINAL JUSTICE AS A SYSTEM

Using the distinctions *input, process,* and *output,* the criminal justice system can be seen in its major, systematic parts.

The input consists of selected law violations. The number of unreported crimes is mere conjecture, so selected law violation refers only to reported crime that brings one or more segments of the system into contact with either the victim or the violator, or both.

The process of the system consists of the many things then done by police, attorneys from prosecution and defense, judges, probation and parole officers, and prison staff. This then makes process the most significant part of the management of the system.

Why Include Output?

Of course, the output of the criminal justice system is comprised of the results—the success or failure of society to cope with crime. Recalling the heating system set up so that a thermostat merely signals change (without signaling *what* change), it can be seen that the system process may or may not respond appropriately to input. To the degree that the criminal justice system may also respond to signals of change in a random manner, the risk of intolerable malfunction remains. It is for this reason that output (or results) is presented as very relevant in any thesis that deals essentially with the management of process. For indeed, a system that is unable to provide a

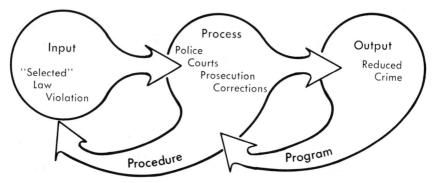

The Components of the Process of the Criminal Justice System

process that effectively changes input into desirable output is a system that needs changes made in its process. This reason alone suggests the main characteristic of the management model that will be presented in subsequent chapters.

Consider again the overall system of justice:

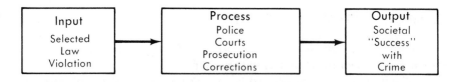

Now consider any one subsystem that makes up the process of criminal justice—the probation subsystem of corrections, for example:

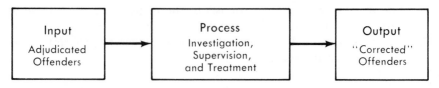

Of course, this does not simplify the system, but it definitely simplifies the concept of criminal justice as a manageable system.

The police or probation administrator manages the input, process, and output of his subsystem which in turn is *part* of the process of criminal justice. The very fact that it is the manageable outputs of each and all subsystems that form the process of criminal justice is the reason criminal justice is manageable—whether it actually is managed or not, it is manageable. Indeed, it is not only manageable, but it is manageable as an *effective* system.

Effectiveness Versus Efficiency

A key variable in the management model to be presented is the distinction between efficiency and effectiveness, as will be further elaborated in Chapter Five. But in terms of discussing the *effectiveness* of system output, some consideration of this distinction will prove useful here.

Consider an automobile as a total system. In terms of efficiency, the engine may be well-tuned, the transmission and power column perfectly synchronized, and the torque pounds of wheel turning power delivered to the rear axle—all in sufficient harmony to consider the automobile *efficient*. Suppose that this extremely efficient automobile becomes stuck in the mud. Regardless of its efficiency of operation, *effectiveness* is not forthcoming until such time as the automobile is extricated—assuming the intent is ultimately to move the passenger out of the mud.

This then, illustrates the justification of including output. Many systems, even when functioning without regard to output, can efficiently accumulate, store, and distribute records and other paperwork that may or may not have a favorable impact on accomplishing specific results.

CRIMINAL JUSTICE PROCESS

Having noted the implications of criminal justice input and output, the remainder of the chapter is directed to process. Noted earlier were the problems of possible fragmentation between system segments that make up process. Functional working relationships between all segments was presented as absolutely necessary for the success of the individual segments. Isolating any segment from any other is dysfunctional; this is a cold, hard, scientific fact.[12]

In reality, every segment of process is a subsystem—a system-within-a-system.[13] But to clarify the manageability of criminal justice as a concept,

[12] T. W. McRae, *Analytical Management* (New York: John Wiley & Sons, Inc., 1970), chaps. 1, 2, 8, 10, 18.

[13] Rocco Carzo, Jr. and John W. Yanouzas, *Formal Organization: A Systems Approach* (Homewood, Ill.: Dorsey Press, 1967), pp. 235–54.

the overall criminal justice system is being considered here. Though this may be necessary to insure clarity of the various roles and functions as they relate, the ability to recognize output (results) depends entirely upon the awareness of the interrelationships between each segment.[14] Continued awareness of these interrelationships and their collective goal orientation is a must, especially when the ultimate management context becomes in-depth consideration of its own functions and roles.[15] Functions and roles either *permit* or *prevent* management.

Functions and roles are strategically significant in managing the system of criminal justice, and the interrelationships between the segments that make up process are of crucial importance. For this reason, the functions and roles that constitute these interrelationships will be presented in Chapter Four as the *key* to the management model.

To further reduce the risk of ignoring the manageability of all segments of process, the reader is asked to ponder the implications of the following sentence: The primary responsibilities of law enforcement do not consist of technical legalities but the provision of personal safety and property security for members of society who conform to the law. This statement accurately introduces the *function* of the segment of process that deals with enforcement. But bear one critical factor in mind: the segments of process that *are* concerned with the legal technicalities actually have no immediate responsibilities for the personal safety and property security assigned as a responsibility to the law enforcement segment. Nevertheless, personal safety and property security, legal technicalities, and every other responsibility of *any* segment of the entire criminal justice system are crucial parts of a picture that is incomplete without any one of them. Every segment carries special responsibilities, but not to the exclusion of an awareness that successful discharge of the responsibility depends upon successful discharge of all other responsibilities in the system.

SUMMARY

In this introductory chapter, the criminal justice system of the United States has been presented as the American societal method of coping with crime. More specifically, criminal justice is presented as a *manageable system*.

The development of managerial science within government, and specifically criminal justice, appears to have lagged behind the industrial segment of American culture. As a background for later chapters that explore the

---

[14] Neuschel, *Management by System*, pp. 11–26.

[15] Don Fuller, *Manage or Be Managed* (Boston, Mass.: Industrial Education Institute, 1970), pp. 50–98. See also George E. Berkley, *The Administrative Revolution* (Englewood Cliffs, N.J.: Prentice-Hall, Inc., 1971), chaps. 1, 2, 3, 5.

various concepts of management, criminal justice and the concept of systems were reviewed.

Segments of the criminal justice system were dealt with in terms of interrelationships between police, prosecution-defense, courts, corrections, and the law itself.

The problem of system fragmentation was discussed in terms of continuity and effectiveness, with specific attention drawn to the contrast between *efficiency* and *effectiveness.*

The "systems approach" was introduced in terms of a synthesis between measurable and explicit goals with human behavior. The approach was elaborated in terms of input, process, and output—input defined as selected law violations; process as the function of police, courts, prosecution-defense, and corrections; output as results in terms of coping with crime within society.

Flexibility and sensitivity to social change were also presented as crucial to a functional system of criminal justice.

Contrast was made between the function of each criminal justice system segment and the respective relationships between its segments. The observation was made that the functions of segments are the theme of any specific managerial approach but not to the exclusion of consideration of the interrelationships among segments. Indeed, this chapter presented the interrelationships between segments as a virtual requirement to understanding the overall approach to crime in the United States in the interests of viable management of the criminal justice system.

QUESTIONS

1. Discuss the context in which a distinction was made between private industrial management and government management.

2. Discuss the general position that the overall criminal justice system is "manageable."

3. Discuss fragmentation within the criminal justice system in terms of efficiency, effectiveness, and continuity in dealing with crime.

4. How does human interaction relate to causes and effects?

5. How do causes and effects relate to systems?

6. Discuss system flexibility and social change.

7. Discuss social change and system management.

8. Define and relate input, process, and output to the management of criminal justice as a system.

9. What are the component parts of process in the criminal justice system?

10. Discuss any two managerial roles in any two segments of process in terms of continuity.

ANNOTATED REFERENCES

BARNES, H., and N. TEETERS, *New Horizons in Criminology.* Englewood Cliffs, N.J.: Prentice-Hall, 1960. Chapter One covers in great detail the concept of crime in society in the context used to introduce this chapter.

COFFEY, A., E. ELDEFONSO, and W. HARTINGER, *Human Relations: Law Enforcement in a Changing Community.* Englewood Cliffs, N.J.: Prentice-Hall, 1971. Chapter One presents a wide-scope picture of what this chapter isolated as system input.

COFFEY, A., E. ELDEFONSO, and W. HARTINGER, *Police Community Relations.* Englewood Cliffs, N.J.: Prentice-Hall, 1971. The first three chapters succinctly elaborate where system input and process interact outside the immediate sphere of reported crime.

COLUMBUS, E. G., "Management By System," *The Police Chief,* 37, No. 7 (July 1970). An exceptionally fine description of what this chapter briefly touched upon as a "subsystem."

ELDEFONSO, E., A. COFFEY, and R. GRACE, *Principles of Law Enforcement.* New York: Wiley, 1967. Chapter One embellishes the areas presented as criminal justice system input for the reader wishing extra clarity in this regard.

FULLER, D., *Manage or Be Managed.* Boston, Mass.: Industrial Education Institute, 1970. A good overall context for elaborating the position taken in this chapter that system modification is no longer an option. Further elaboration of the managerial role in system change is contained in George E. Berkley's *The Administrative Revolution.* Englewod Cliffs, N.J.: Prentice-Hall, 1971.

GEORGE, C. S., Jr., *The History of Management Thought.* Englewood Cliffs, N.J.: Prentice-Hall, 1968. A fine synthesis of all crucial influences in the evolution of sophisticated management.

HOWLETT, F. W., and H. HUNTER, "A Systems Approach to Comprehensive Criminal Justice Planning," *Crime and Delinquency,* 18, No. 4 (October 1971), 345–54. A good elaboration of what this chapter presented as the consequence of system dysfunction.

MCGREGOR, D., *The Professional Manager,* Caroline McGregor and Warren Bennis, eds. New York: McGraw-Hill, 1967. A good synoptic background for what will later be elaborated as the "Theory Y school" on systems—a particularly relevant subject to the management of criminal justice.

MCRAE, T. W., *Analytical Management.* New York: Wiley, 1970. In-depth exploration of methodologies for examining what this chapter presented as system interrelationships.

NEUSCHEL, R. F., *Management by System.* New York: McGraw-Hill, 1960. Elaboration of the science of what this chapter presented as output and results.

SCHEIN, E. H., *Organizational Psychology.* Englewood Cliffs, N.J.: Prentice-Hall, 1965. A good "systems" extension of the behavioral concepts implied by this chapter as a key issue. For deep elaboration, see also Katz, D., and R. L. Kahn, *The Social Psychology of Organization.* New York: Wiley, 1966; and Forrester, J. W., *Industrial Dynamics.* Cambridge, Mass.: M.I.T. University Press, 1961.

SCHODERBEK, P. P., *Management Systems*. New York: Wiley, 1967. Exceptionally good coverage of topic.

TAPPAN, P., *Crime, Justice, and Correction*. New York: McGraw-Hill, 1960. Chapters One and Two elaborate in greath depth the selected law violation presented here as input.

WINSLOW, R., *Crime in a Free Society*. Belmont, Calif.: Dickinson Publishers, 1968. Chapters 11, 12, and 13 clarify segments of the concept of process.

CHAPTER 2

Management as a Concept

Having considered criminal justice as a manageable system in the preceding chapter, attention is now directed specifically to management as a useful concept in criminal justice.

Until recently, much of what was referred to in criminal justice as "management" was at best merely "supervision"—supervision that all too often affords little distinction between administration and "line work." The fortunate trend accompanying an increased awareness of criminal justice problems is an increase in awareness of the need for management—a need for consistent systematic management that includes but is not dominated by supervision. The management model presented in chapters four through eight will elaborate the role and function that supervision plays *within* management, but significant though this role may be, it remains only one part of the overall concept of criminal justice management.

To many outside and, regrettably, to some inside the criminal justice system, the distinctions between managerial standards and "line work" standards remain more related to social distance and prestige variables than to what will later be discussed as managerial functions. Perhaps this accounts, at least in part, for some of the managerial development lag that has hindered the emergence of both the art and the science of management in criminal justice. Regardless of the specific line work involved, administration of any program is different from the work itself.

It is increasingly clear that management as a concept requires that such a distinction be made on the basis of functions—specific managerial functions that form the basis of all successful criminal justice administrations. Standards of measurement of managerial functions are different, then, than standards of measurement of line work, whether it be police, probation, parole or any other criminal justice process. No manager in any of these subsystems, whether police lieutenant, supervising probation officer, or prison warden, can measure his managerial effectiveness by the same standards applied to those who work for him. *Any person who is responsible for the performance of other staff is necessarily involved in management (to greater or lesser degree) and management therefore remains distinctively different.*

The distinction between line work and supervision may be vague, but even at this level of management the distinction remains significant. Some activities may "overlap" between a police patrol sergeant and his patrolmen, but in an *effective* overall patrol program, it is clear where the management lies. The supervising probation officer is often involved in the cases of his probation officers, but strictly as a *manager,* if his program is to remain effective.

At higher levels, the distinction gains clarity. Planning, program design, policy setting, organizational structure, comunication, fiscal matters, and a host of clearly administrative concerns help establish this distinction. Indeed, there is probably very little difference between the administrative activities of top executives from one criminal justice agency to another (if the agencies are effective). Although actual activities and operations may differ within different justice agencies, an increasing number of knowledgeable criminal justice administrators speculate that the *managerial* job is virtually the same, despite the fact that acknowledged "political differences" may exist. Whether or not such speculation is accurate, *there is a great deal about effectively administering public agencies that is the same regardless of the agencies.* It is this sameness that will be the subject of this chapter—the concept of management.

HISTORICAL DEVELOPMENT

It might reasonably be argued that the historical background of the managerial concept has very little influence on the pragmatics of modern criminal justice administration. However, within the context of approaching criminal justice management on the basis of picking and choosing that which *permits* management of both the individual organization *and* criminal justice as a system, some understanding of the background of what is chosen (for use in the management model) might prove useful. Understanding the background of what is *not* chosen, or is partially chosen, might also be useful. Thus, as a background for the later presentation of the management model, a brief history of management will now be reviewed.

Historians and anthropologists agree that early man began to merge families into tribes about 10,000 years B.C., forming organizations intended to provide mutual protection and effective production of the necessities for survival.[1]

Recognition of the value of adopting a "tribal management system" permitted man to evolve an organized agriculture. This in turn developed communities of agrarian people and heightened the requirement for managing the organization of human interaction. This increased need for systems of organization formed the earliest basis for not only the concept of management, but the concept of criminal justice as well.

Control of "business," rules for dealing with any violations, organization of taxation, establishment of status and role with any division of labor, all became solidified under the concept of early management.

The "ancients," who included the Sumerian kings of 5,000 years ago, refined management control systems to a level of reasonable sophistication.[2] The first Amorite Dynasty of the Babylonian Empire left considerable evidence of the growth of managerial refinement that grew in proportion to the emerging city-kingdoms of the time.[3]

Early Management of Criminal Justice

The relationship of management as a concept to the concept of criminal justice can easily be traced to the ancient role of societal punishment.

> With the rise of kings and potentates in the Middle East, the Sumerian rulers Lipitishtar and Eshnunna standardized what would constitute an offense. Some 100 years later, the Babylonian King Hammurabi standardized for his kingdom not only the offenses, but also codified the accompanying penalty. Although the penalties remained as brutal as those specified by the unwritten Lextalionis, the very fact that the relationship between offense and penalty was standardized is considered significant by criminologists. The Mosaic Code was still over 1,000 years in the future when these laws were written.[4]

---

[1] James Mellaart, *Earliest Civilizations of the Near East* (London: Thames and Hudson, 1965), p. 11.

[2] V. G. Childe, *Man Makes Himself* (New York: The New American Library, 1951), p. 143.

[3] George Contenou, *Everyday Life in Babylon and Assyria* (London: Edward Arnold, Ltd., 1954), p. 86.

[4] E. Eldefonso, A. Coffey, and R. Grace, *Principles of Law Enforcement* (New York: John Wiley & Sons, Inc., 1968), p. 40.

Perhaps the Great Code of Hammurabi had the greatest influence on the development of management and criminal justice in history. The codified statutes of Hammurabi covered labor, wages, market activities,[5] and penalties for everything from construction to medical practice—penalties enforceable by the "management" of the Babylonian society.[6] The later Babylonian rule of King Nebuchadnezzar refined this combination of statute and penalty to cover virtually all human society.[7]

The Chinese paralleled much of the managerial development of the Babylonians. Over 1,000 years before Christ, a civil service "constitution" was prepared for the Emperor of China, with explicit managerial policies elaborated.[8]

Of course the Hebrews, especially through Moses, crystallized many of the earliest concepts of management. Greeks also developed "principles" of management. For instance, Plato's *Republic* elaborated an explicit division of labor theory.[9]

Indeed, by the time of the medieval era, managerial concepts were an integral part of all civilized cultures. So also was a clearly defined system of criminal justice. The feudal society of this period was organized and managed in a fashion that had the effect of solidifying some of the earlier Roman principles of delegating managerial authority—in the case of the feudal era, proving that *delegation* of management cannot include release of control without dire consequence to the manager who is delegating.

The merchants of Venice rounded out the early historical background for the concept of management. Their nearly legendary commerce afforded a kind of legitimacy for the civilized world's approach to the Industrial Revolution to follow.

Limited Historical Context

Of course it should be remembered that management as a concept is necessarily limited in the scope of historical perspective to that part of history most germane to it. Whatever may be lost in continuity by not presenting detailed elaboration of history is hopefully regained through cogency. Nevertheless, to clarify the background and underpinning of the management model to be presented, further consideration of the historical develop-

[5] Robert F. Harper, *The Code of Hammurabi, King of Babylon* (Chicago: University of Chicago Press, 1904), pp. 104–57.

[6] Wallis E. A. Budge, *Babylonian Life and History* (London: Religious Tract Society, 1925), pp. 126–218.

[7] L. P. Alford, *Laws of Management* (New York: The Ronald Press Co., 1928), p. 37.

[8] Kuo-Cheng Wu, *Ancient Chinese Political Theories* (Shanghai: The Commercial Press, Ltd., 1928), pp. 40–41.

[9] Jules Toutain, *The Economic Life of the Ancient World* (New York: Alfred A. Knopf, 1930), pp. 133–34.

ment of management is called for—not history per se, but the highlights of some of the main contributions. Though somewhat fragmented through this special purpose selectivity, the relationship of the various contributors to be discussed will emerge later in the presentation of the management model.

Merging Art and Science

Perhaps the unifying concept within this discussion is the idea of merging the art of management with the science of management. This is particularly useful in clarifying the criminal justice application of management principles within the systems model.

In much the same manner that the Industrial Revolution was preceded by many stages of development, so also was the emergence of scientific management. For example, Frederick W. Taylor's 1913 publication, *Principles of Scientific Management*[10] is considered by many to be the main landmark in managerial literature. But nearly 100 years before the Taylor work, an English factory known as the Soho Foundry adopted the practice of purchasing *and* maintaining the tools of the workmen—a radical departure from the "art" of management that had required since the introduction of factories that laborers use their own tools.[11] This same factory also modified the art by adopting flow-charts, work distribution methods, and many other techniques of standardizing managerial practice, which proved to be a managerial prelude to Eli Whitney's use of interchangeable parts.

Perhaps a comment on the distinction between art and science would clarify this concept. For purposes of this discussion, art refers to the kind of intuitive approach utilized in producing employee effort prior to the Industrial Revolution; scientific refers to what will be discussed as a measurable approach to managed production.

But even before the popularity of managerial standardization associated with Whitney's interchangeable parts, standardization had been established as a managerial principle that was accepted even where the traditional managerial art prevailed over science.[12]

With the establishment of standardization as a management principle, along with other principles, the "science" of management began to merge with the "art" of management.

As noted early in the preceding chapter, the management of government (and of criminal justice as a system) gradually fell behind management in the private sector. Perhaps this began with the merging of the historically

---

[10] Taylor, *Principles of Scientific Management* (New York: Harper and Bros., 1913).

[11] Erick Roll, *An Early Experiment in Industrial Organization* (London: Green and Co., 1930), p. 172.

[12] W. F. Durfee, "The History and Modern Development of the Art of Interchangeable Construction in Mechanism," *J. of the Franklin Institute*, 137, No. 2 (February 1894), 122.

developed art of management with a newly emerging science of management
—government tending perhaps to retain more of the art than of the science.

SCIENTIFIC MANAGEMENT

Although Taylor's *Principles of Scientific Management* established him
as the "father of scientific management" to many, there is a virtual host of
early writings that undergird his principles.[13] Taylor, however, occupies the
status in criminal justice management that Darwin occupies in pure science.
Put another way, Taylor crystallized enough of the fragmented "art" in management for the "science" to take shape.

Although this scientific influence of Taylor and others being considered here is from the private sector, the implications for bringing the concept of management to bear on criminal justice are overwhelming. Consider
the overall level of managerial sophistication in the *system* of criminal justice. Can it be honestly declared that programs of police services, court process, and corrective rehabilitation are managed at the level of sophistication
that is increasingly required of private industry? Are the management functions of criminal justice performed as well as generally is required in programs
with profit measurements? Indeed, is the simple awareness that management
is a separate organizational function as clear in criminal justice as it is in
private industry?

One context for considering this would be to examine the relative managerial skills available to most business executives in isolating purely administrative problems as compared to those available to most police chiefs, chief
probation officers, or prison wardens providing a sophisticated analysis of a
private business problem. The answers to these questions justify that serious
attention be given both the art and the science of management within the
area of criminal justice. Whether developed in the private sector or not,
managerial concepts are far too valuable to be ignored.

Taylor Influence

To Taylor, management needed identity—a kind of managerial recognition of two primary concerns: (1) *what* constitutes a day's work, and (2)
development of managerial skills to insure that a day's work occurs for a day's
wages. Taylor proposed four activities for managers:

1. Develop a "science" of relating each element of work to each other element.
2. Select and train appropriate workmen for the appropriate element of work.

[13] Claude S. George, Jr., *The History of Management Thought* (Englewood Cliffs, N.
J.: Prentice-Hall, Inc., 1968), pp. 64–76, reviews much of the earlier management literature—pp. 2–63 also elaborates the material presented earlier in this chapter, but in terms
of early writings.

3. Develop continuity of management with labor in terms of the new science.

4. Management assume greater proportion of labor division as the new science clarified specific management functions.

Taylor anticipated the systems approach adopted by this text in that the organization (or system) would accept responsibility for continuity, instead of the traditional method of one generation of labor passing along task knowledge to the next generation. The approach he chose was centralization of planning, implementing, evaluating, and above all else, maintaining standardized continuity.

Taylor's ideas proved as frustrating to management as they proved rewarding. Taylor's own charismatic charm and the practices of his day permeated his writing and tended to obscure rather than clarify the scientific element of the science that he proposed. Nevertheless, his systematic elaboration of the managerial prerogatives virtually shaped modern management theory around planning, organizing, directing, and controlling, as well as cooperation.

Even before Taylor's impact, Henry L. Gantt elaborated what many call "the humanistic approach," which includes task/bonus systems, training responsibilities, and his widely used "Gantt-charts."[14]

Henri Fayd, shortly after Taylor, elaborated a complete theory of management; in 1927 came the sociological concepts of Elton Mayo, soon followed by Mary Elliott's "individual motivation" theories of management.

Prior to Norbert Wiener and Claude Shannon's systems analysis in the late 1940s, Max Weber, Rensis Likert, and Chris Argyris were making a separate impact on management from the same area—that of human relations. Each emphasized the psychological variables in organizational theory that lead to the open-system concept of management. Although the contributions of all three are cogent, Argyris best clarifies the essence of this position.[15] Likert's "grid" contributions will be presented in a different context later in this chapter.

Argyris saw formal organizations as having an incongruence between the needs of the worker and organizational goals. In effect, this inconguence was seen as a barrier to scientific management—a barrier existing because the better the science of management, the greater the conflict with the individual's need for independence and growth. The individual employee, in this theory, is pictured in terms of Maslow's theory of human motivation.[16]

---

[14] Henry L. Gantt, "A Bonus System for Rewarding Labor," *Transactions of the American Society of Mechanical Engineers*, Vol. 23, 1901.

[15] Argyris, "The Organization: What Makes It Healthy," *Harvard Business Review*, 36, No. 6 (November–December 1958), 107–16.

[16] See, for example Abraham H. Maslow, "The Authoritarian Character Structure," *J. of Social Psychology*, No. 18 (1943), 401–11. See also his *Principles of Abnormal Psychology* (New York: Harper & Row, Publishers, 1941), and *Motivation and Personality* (New York: Harper & Row, Publishers, 1954), chaps, 4, 5, 8.

Maslow Influence

Maslow's concepts of human personality, motivations, and need systems has had a great influence on most modern management theory. If individual behavior is a reflection of needs, it can be seen that these needs must be understood as they affect performance. Employees, having different levels of needs, will function individually, but always in reference to management and its understanding as well as its expectations of them. For example, if an employee has a need for independence, it may conflict with management's attempts to seek conformity in employee behavior and performance.

Specifically in terms of the criminal justice management area, human needs and motivations must also be dealt with. How does probation management develop program continuity while at the same time meeting the probation officers' needs? What must the prison warden know to both program and meet the needs of guards and treatment personnel, as well as of prisoners? What are the implications of human motivation when measurable (concrete and relevant) methods and results are being sought by criminal justice management?

McGregor: Managerial Assumptions[17]

The incongruence between the needs of the employee and the goals of scientific management were dealt with by the late Douglas McGregor, but within a different conceptual framework than that of Argyris as he worked in terms of Maslow's theories. Later chapters will clarify the relevance of this incongruence in prisons, jails, and probation-parole, but in terms of McGregor's influence, the dilemma of management goals conflicting with individual employee needs (at least the need for independence) led to a redefinition of managerial assumptions. McGregor saw this redefinition as the key to a solution. Beginning by challenging certain managerial errors about the kinds of employee motives that exist, he went on to challenge the validity of the philosophy of virtually all scientific management, which he referred to as the philosophy of Theory X. The cogency to the chain-of-command structure of many criminal justice organizations is striking: but whether or not criminal justice in general is subject to McGregor's concerns, it is nonetheless noteworthy that he took on all "command" managerial thinking in a grand manner.

THEORY X

The conventional conception of management's task in harnessing human ener-

[17] Douglas McGregor, *Leadership and Motivation: Essays of Douglas McGregor,* Warren G. Bennis, Edgar Schein, and Caroline McGregor, eds. (Cambridge, Mass.: M.I.T. University Press, 1966).

gy to organizational requirements can be stated broadly in terms of three propositions. In order to avoid the complications introduced by a label, I shall call this set of propositions "Theory X":

1. Management is responsible for organizing the elements of productive enterprise—money, materials, equipment, people—in the interest of economic ends.

2. With respect to people, this is a process of directing their efforts, motivating them, controlling their actions, modifying their behavior to suit the needs of the organization.

3. Without this active intervention by management, people would be passive—even resistant—to organizational needs. They must therefore be persuaded, rewarded, punished, controlled—their activities must be directed. This is management's task—in managing subordinate managers or workers. We often sum it up by saying management consists of getting things done through other people.

Behind this conventional theory there are several additional beliefs—less explicit but widespread:

4. The average man is by nature, indolent—he works as little as possible.

5. He lacks ambition, dislikes responsibility, prefers to be led.

6. He is inherently self-centered, indifferent to organizational needs.

7. He is by nature resistant to change.

8. He is gullible, not very bright, the ready dupe of the charlatan and the demagogue.[18]

McGregor goes on to point out that from the framework of Theory X management has outlined various means of accomplishing its task by either reward or punishment. As he saw it, management was confronted with two alternatives inherent in the concept of accomplishing work "through other people": the "hard management approach"—relying on coercion and threat with stringent control as the mode of directing employee behavior; or the "soft management approach," which included satisfaction of employee demands through permissiveness and focus on harmony, hoping that people managed in this manner would accept organizational direction.

Placed in the context of criminal justice, many examples verify this part of McGregor's reasoning. Two state prisons may be nearly identical in terms of structure, size, design, programs, resources, and so forth. The management style of each warden may flow from Theory X. But, one warden may operate on the "hard" principle, the other on the "soft" approach, each functioning from the framework of Theory X but with very different results. The guards and treatment personnel working under the administration of the "hard" warden may report that "a man always knows where he stands on this staff." The personnel under the "soft" warden may report that "the staff really count in here."

[18] McGregor, *Leadership and Motivation*, pp. 5, 6.

But McGregor nevertheless conceived of both these extremes as flowing from the same management position. Moreover, he saw them as presenting major management problems.

The "hard management" approach appears to be related to such counterforces as restricted output, unionism, and antagonism toward organizational objectives. On the other hand, "soft management" has produced harmony characterized by an abdication of management with an ensuing reduction in performance or production. McGregor suggested what amounts to a third alternative beginning with a reevaluation of managerial assumptions—inclusion of behavioral science which in turn became the basis for McGregor's Theory Y. And as in the case of X, Theory Y also has great relevance to much of criminal justice management.

As McGregor developed Theory Y, the premises and assumptions of management emerged in terms of creating opportunities, removing obstacles, providing guidance rather than control, releasing potential, and above all else encouraging growth. McGregor interpreted research findings as evidence that Theory X assumptions were in error to the degree that Theory X management is dysfunctional. In this regard, Theory Y differs from Theory X in much the same way that Peter Drucker's "management by objectives" theory, to be discussed later in the chapter, differs from "management by control."

Theory Y management, according to McGregor, is not the "soft management" indicated by one extreme of Theory X. Instead, as an approach to accomplish work through others, it must take into account the employee's desire to "do meaningful work" when given the opportunity. Various difficulties involved in Theory Y were acknowledged by McGregor, but primarily in terms of the violation of managerial tradition—violation of the expectation of both management and employees. Centuries of tying employees to jobs that utilized small proportions of their capabilities have, according to McGregor, accustomed employees to ignore the possibility of work providing ego-need satisfaction of any kind. Although McGregor conceded difficulties generated by a history of Theory X management, he nevertheless maintained the position that managerial ingenuity and innovation could prevail.

Hertzberg Influence[19]

An embellishment on what will soon be discussed as "production and people concerns" along with "grid" influences, Frederick Hertzberg's research evolved the notion of "dissatisfiers" and "satisfiers"—noting that management typically depends on "dissatisfiers" to motivate people. Not surprising-

---

[19] Frederick Hertzberg, Bernard Mausner, and Barbara Snyderman, *The Motivation to Work* (New York: John Wiley & Sons, Inc., 1959). p. 81, and related matter on "dissatisfiers and satisfiers" of the Hertzberg study.

ly, Hertzberg found that management experiences low yield while in pursuit of motivation through "dissatisfiers." He found that the "satisfiers" are in reality the high satisfactions available when high peformance and high motivation are made possible by management.

The Hertzberg study also raised the question of whether or not sophisticated management might not in reality be approaching excessive control of human behavior—at least within the framework of a democratic society.

The management model to be elaborated later reflects considerable attention to the delicate balance between organizational integrity through control and expression of individual talent in achieving optimum managerial yield. In this particular regard, the Likert influence, discussed next, is germane. (Probation, parole, and correctional administrators may well find this "delicate balance" extremely cogent in the quasi-military organizations that typify these facets of criminal justice.)

Likert Influence[20]

Beyond the "human approach" with which this chapter identified Likert earlier, he developed a conceptual method to blend organizational morale and productivity, suggesting that two important trends have been instrumental in improving employee performance and are exercising a major influence on current trends of "human relations" in management. The two trends are known as "production-centered" and "employee-centered" management, respectively.

Production-centered management is, according to Likert, characterized by placing emphasis on production almost to the exclusion of concern for the employee. Managerial concern is for seeing that workers are using correct procedure to insure adequate production volume. The relatively tight management is underpinned by an assumption that it is only necessary to buy an employee's time and that he will willingly and effectively pursue managerial direction.

Consider, for example, a police officer assigned to traffic. The chief and his management team may assume that by *paying* this officer they can expect a certain number of traffic citations. If the officer differs philosophically on this point, he may write citations for previously ignored violations of the local bankers, business leaders, city council members, and mayor. Of course, tight management can "handle" such a problem, but Likert's concerns probably emerge in the process of an employee's willingness (or lack of it) to pursue managerial direction.

Employee-centered management, conversely, emphasizes teamwork and, more specifically, employee needs. Likert noted that major responsibility in

[20] Rensis Likert, "Motivational Dimensions of Administration," *America's Manpower Crisis* (Chicago: Public Administration Service, 1956); also, *New Patterns of Management* (New York: McGraw-Hill, Inc., 1961).

this approach remains production but it is characterized by a more "diffused" management (as opposed to production-centered management). Employee-centered managers try to build a spirit of teamwork among employees rather than generate methods of control.

Likert conducted a great deal of research attempting to determine which of the two orientations had the greatest production yield. In general, he found that the production-centered management was less successful than employee-centered management. To reinforce the point, he conducted additional research indicating about a 20 percent increase in production was experienced after a change from production-centered management to employee-centered management. In this sense, he verified empirically what many managers and social scientists had claimed for some time.

Participatory Management. Although wide and at times diversified managerial approaches are labeled "participatory," Likert developed an excellent scale for isolating an organizational system's operating characteristics in terms of either *authoritative* or *participative,* which in turn could be subdivided into (1) exploitive authoritative; (2) benevolent authoritative; (3) consultative; or (4) participative group. In a later discussion, the various "families" of managerial approaches will be discussed as command, human resource (or relationship), or results. Although these categories tend to lump participatory management approaches into the human resource (or relationship) classification, Likert's research concern with "employees as opposed to production" provides the basis for many managerial programs—human resource and otherwise.

As early as 1955, Likert formulated a schema for conceptualizing the "employee as opposed to production" notion.[21] This, along with other managerially valuable facets of the Likert influence, will be discussed as at least part of the base of emerging managerial concepts in criminal justice, participatory and otherwise.

In essence, the Likert influence focuses around the idea of blending morale and productivity—his two prime requisites of successful management. In the illustration below, it can be seen that the relationship between morale and production is somewhat complex. Note that it is possible for low morale to correlate with low production (Area A); high morale with low productivity (Area B); low morale with high productivity (Area C); and high morale with high productivity (Area D).

Area C of this schema, as well as Area A, reflect the kind of situation that might occur under what Taylor envisioned as the scientific approach. Area B, however, reflects the situation in which high morale is accompanied by *low* production—a situation that Likert contends is merely evidence that emphasis was placed on morale to the exclusion of production. The ob-

[21] Likert, *Developing Patterns of Management,* Part I, General Management Series No. 178, American Management Association, N.Y., 1955 Exhibit No. 7.

servation is that management programs which overemphasize the human relations approach can generate as much dysfunction as improvement. Area
D reflects high morale accompanied by high productivity and this, according
to Likert, is evidence, in effect, of the value of McGregor's Theory *Y*—a refinement and modification of the assumptions inherent in the managerial
tasks.

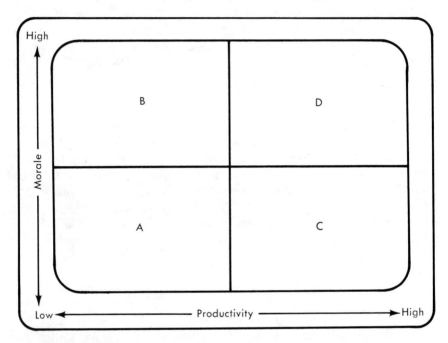

Morale Production Schema by Likert

*Reprinted by permission of the publisher from General Management Series No. 178, Strengthening
Management for the New Technology, © 1955 by the American Management Association, Inc.*

With particular regard to the establishment of management as a legitimate and separate function within the realm of criminal justice, a number
of variables intervened to combine the "Likert influence" with the "Blake
and Mouton influence" next to be considered. Though no effort will be
made here to survey the entire range of these intervening variables, an example may serve to clarify a part of the sequence in which these particular
concepts from the private industrial sector began to arrive in criminal justice.

The excellent managerial institutes and workshops conducted during
the mid-1960s by Drs. Vincent O'Leary and J. Hall on behalf of The National Council on Crime and Delinquency drew heavily upon the works of Likert
and the managerial grid of Drs. Blake and Mouton. Facing a task that virtually amounted to a "conceptual retooling," O'Leary and Hall introduced

the notion of "people and production" from two reference points: the Likert views just discussed, and the incredibly useful Blake/Mouton Grid.

Within this text, the interest in isolating managerial training as a legitimate activity within criminal justice began, in large measure, as a result of the clarity with which O'Leary and Hall related Likert's "quadranted" concepts on productivity and people to the managerial grid devised by Blake and Mouton.

Blake and Mouton Influence[22]

It would be difficult to overestimate the significance of the managerial grid devised by Robert Blake and Jane Mouton for both industrial and criminal justice management. In essence, they conceive of production and people as *independent* of each other—measurable on separate axes. Put another way, the Blake and Mouton idea was that a manager could virtually retain one concern to the exclusion of another. Thus, production-centered concern does not necessarily have to be accompanied by people-centered concern.

Examination of the grid that follows will indicate that people or "concern for people" is placed on the vertical axis in a scale of 1 to 9. The scale position of 1 indicates extremely low interest in people, 9 reflects a high managerial concern for people. The horizontal axis, also scaled 1 to 9, is an index of the managerial interest in production. Again this scale reflects a position of 1 as low interest in production, 9 as extremely high interest in production.

This conceptual frame affords virtually endless analytical possibilities, particularly in terms of shades and degrees. Regardless of the nature of the organization structure, the style of management in the organization can be plotted.

Of course the theoretical ideal is depicted in the upper right corner as 9,9—full commitment to both people *and* production. Excessive concern for harmony raises certain problems with the 1,9 (a kind of "country club"), just as excessive concern for production to the exclusion of concern for people poses management problems for the 9,1 (a kind of "I'm boss"). A sort of "split-the-difference" approach to balancing people and production is the 5,5—a particularly tempting managerial position in the public limelighted administration of most criminal justice organizations. Of course the 1,1 manager is in effect "pre-retired."

In essence, three of the approaches depicted on the grid rest on the assumption that production concerns and people concerns are incongruent.

[22] Robert R. Blake and Jane S. Mouton, *Group Dynamics: Key to Decision Making* (Houston, Texas: Gulf Publishers, 1961); also *The Induction of Change in Organization* (Austin, Texas: Scientific Methods, Inc., 1962); and *The Managerial Grid*, Addison–Wesley Series, Reading, Mass., 1969, p. 10.

THE MANAGERIAL GRID

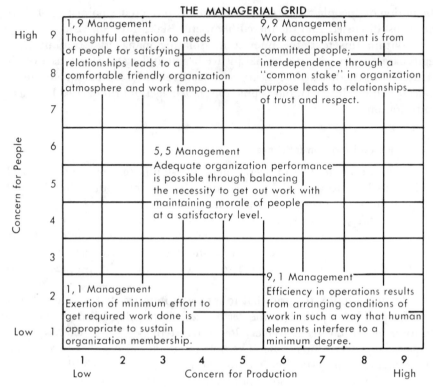

The Grid®.

(*Source:* R. R. Blake and J. S. Mouton, The Managerial Grid. Houston: Gulf Publishing Company, 1964, p. 10. Reproduced by permission.)

The 9,1 depicted in the lower right-hand corner is the type of management Argyris spoke of in evolving incongruence as a concept; the 9,1 manager relies heavily on formal authority and appointive power.

The upper left-hand corner 1,9, or "country club manager," reflects the opposite extreme referred to by McGregor. Conflict is denied (or stifled) in the managerial activities that focus totally on harmony—to the virtual exclusion of concern for production.

The lower left-hand corner of the grid is impoverished by virtue of the fact that 1,1 is in reality without concern for production or people. The ability of this manager, of course, depends upon his ability to appear interested in both while remaining interested in neither. Buck-passing and defensive procedures, along with other nonproductive features, characterize this particular style.

The mixture of the first three approaches occurs with the 5,5 "middle-of-the-road-manager," operating what is hoped will remain a live-and-let-live organizational climate. This was conceptualized by Blake and Mouton as ineffective in dealing with organizational problems—an inherent weakness in "split-the-difference" management.

The upper right-hand corner 9,9 grid position is the ideal of team management—"ideal" in the sense that optimum production is forthcoming as a result of optimum concern for people. This theoretically perfect mixture has been presented by Blake and Mouton as being dependent on behavioral sciences. Fuller elaboration of the managerial potential of the grid is reflected in the later Blake-Mouton publication, *Building A Dynamic Corporation Through Grid Organization Development* (Reading, Mass.: Addison-Wesley Publishing Company, 1969).

APPROACHES TO APPLIED MANAGERIAL CONCEPTS

Thus far this chapter has presented management as an emerging concept of significance to the criminal justice system. Many applications of this concept have also developed. The theory of organizational development for example, has evolved into a virtual school of thought.[23] The incorporation of the management grid is one of many features of this concept that clearly delineate it as a distinctive application of management.[24] As mentioned earlier in this chapter, Peter Drucker's "management by objectives" theory is bounded by scientific applications of management as a concept—a particularly significant application of management within the criminal justice system.[25]

In addition to Peter Drucker, the names associated with the "management by objectives" theory include McGregor, Argyris, and Likert (along with Odiorne, Kellogg, Hughes, Mahler, Kindall, McConkey, and Schleh). There appears to be no evidence that the positions of *any* of these men is substantively different than the contributors to the organizational development theory. Similarities between these two schools of thought and between most modern concepts of management seem to exceed the differences. Indeed, except for a different philosophy on the use of "sensitivity training" for managerial development, the management model to be presented has a great deal in common with both theories.

The police chief who successfully develops his organization with specialist-consultants of organizational development orientation probably obtains the same level of potential to achieve criminal justice results as the chief probation officer who is successfully developing his managerial team

[23] See, for example, the Addison-Wesley Series on Organizational Development, Reading, Mass., 1969; Edgar H. Schein, *Process Consultation;* P. Lawrence and J. Lorsch, *Developing Organizations: Diagnosis;* W. Bennis, *O. D.: Its Nature, Origins and Prospects;* R. E. Walton, *Interpersonal Peacemaking.*

[24] Blake and Mouton, p. 4 (beginning "The Excellence Gap").

[25] See also Carl Terwilliger and Stuart Adams, "Probation Department Management by Objectives," *Crime and Delinquency,* 15, No. 2 (April 1969); also considerable unpublished curricula effort by Dr. Harry More, Chairman, Department of the Administration of Justice, California University at San Jose.

through the consultation of management by objectives consultants. Both forms of successful managerial development, moreover, afford as much as the successful yield of the management model, except perhaps in the area of systematic relationships with other segments of criminal justice.

However, as will be noted in many different contexts throughout this volume, the difference in philosophy on the need for sensitivity training leads to further differences on the need to change attitudes or to change any other personality variable. The management model depends on accountability for performance of specific functions assigned to clearly defined managerial roles, rather than seeking personality or attitudinal changes.

In spite of these differences, there nevertheless remain many common grounds between the management model and managerial approaches seeking attitudinal change. Perhaps the most popular of the approaches seeking attitudinal change, "transactional analysis," best illustrates at least one of these similarities.

> Alvin Toffler in *Future Shock* predicts that traditional formal organization cannot exist in our changing world and we will see bureaucracy more and more replaced. . . . In problem solving only the traditional approach was formerly used. Today creative problem solving such as brainstorming has been added as another dimension . . . an opportunity to combine both methods into a synergetic problem solving. . . . There is still much research to be conducted. But transactional analysis is already a part of management training. . . .[26]

Reference to "synergetic problem solving" in the above quotation specifically isolates the common grounds between the management model and managerial approaches, such as transactional analysis, that seek changes in attitude. Chapter Five elaborates synergetics (i.e., synthesis of organizational resources) in depth—although presented from the frame of reference of roles and functions rather than attitude, the outcome of effective organizational growth is the goal of both approaches, and hopefully *all* managerial approaches.

Dealing with the applications of management concept, then, will not be from the premise that great differences exist between the various approaches. Instead, applications of the managerial concept will be from three categories, or approaches: (1) *command management;* (2) *human-resource management,* also referred to as *relationship-oriented management;* and (3) *results management.*[27]

---

[26] Thomas C. Clary, "Transactional Analysis: An Innovative Technique in Management Training and Organizational Development," *Training and Development Journal,* 26, No. 10 (October 1972), 18.

[27] Based upon the unpublished training materials developed by the author in his capacity as training director in a large criminal justice agency, and as management consultant.

Comparative applications of these three approaches will be in terms of *organizational system* that is either functional, dysfunctional, or transitional.

Functional System. The term "functional system" means an organization that has greater managerial concern for *what* gets done than for *who* does it, or *how* it gets done. (Management in these terms is functional to the degree that what gets done takes priority over who does it, and how.)

Dysfunctional System. An organizationally "dysfunctional system" is the opposite of a functional system; in it, management is more concerned with *who* gets things done and *how*, than with *what* gets done. (Management, then, is dysfunctional to the degree that priority is given to who and how over what it is that gets done.)

Transitional System. The term "in transition" means simply that top management in a *dysfunctional* system has become aware of the dysfunctional management priorities on *who* and *how*. (In other words, once top management becomes aware of who and how taking priority over what gets done, this awareness is the definition of "transition"—no matter how long the duration of the transition.)

COMMAND, HUMAN RESOURCE, RESULTS

These three approaches, considered against the background of functional or dysfunctional system, are defined as follows:

Command. Command management is essentially what Douglas McGregor considered Theory *X*—whether "soft" or "hard." The command manager assumes responsibility for motivating and/or directing the activities and behavior of employees. Beyond the implications of McGregor's Theory *X*, a command manager also operates on the premise that continuous orders produce continuous achievement of organizational goals *independent* of concerns for production or morale.

Human Resources. The Theory *Y* that McGregor described also delineates a great deal of the human resource management style. Concern for the frustrations, anxieties, and personal adjustments of employees goes beyond either the "soft *X*" or the ineffective *Y* manager. Human resource approaches include integration of personal problems in the task of management, whether or not such concerns can be directly related to organizational goals of any kind. Although similar to the 1.9 "country club" management style of the grid, human resource styles establish happiness as a legitimate management task beyond the concept of employee morale.

Results. The approach to management referred to here means simply a reduction of *all measurements* used by management to predetermined, clearly defined, measurable results. The *only* measurement in this approach is the *accomplishment* of such results.

By accomplishment is meant the prison warden's success in programming early release through proven rehabilitation; the chief probation officer's success in programming a reduction in recidivism; the police chief's successful reduction of assaultive crimes—all presumably desirable criminal justice *results.*

Theoretical Effectiveness

Recalling the distinction made in Chapter One between *efficiency* and *effectiveness,* some theoretical speculation is possible regarding the possibility of the comparative effectiveness of the three approaches. Consider the following chart:

	Functional System	System in Transition	Nonfunctional System
Command	Poor	Poor	Good
Human Resource	Poor	Good	Poor
Results	Good	Poor	Poor

Functional Systems and Management Approaches

The reasoning for labeling *command* management as "good" in dysfunctional systems is the probability that "productivity potential" is increased when the measure of management success is simply *who* and *how* rather than *what* gets done. Put another way, with minimized concern for *what,* a manager willing to impose his influence and power on the limited context of *who* and *how* presumably is effective—at least by such limited measures. The human resource manager, in contrast, is probably seen as grossly disorganized when so limited a context is conceived for management. The poor performance of results management is also based on the limited context in which results might be considered superfluous.

The transitional system deprives either a command manager or a results manager of the anxiety reduction of the human resource approach. Giving up old tested managerial approaches affords the human resource manager ample opportunity to embellish the anxiety-reducing advantages of his particular style.

The functional system in which management gives top priority to *what* gets done, rather than *who* and *how*, affords the results manager his opportunity to shine. The assumption here is that employees aware of organizational goals are singularly responsive to a manager who measures nothing beyond achieving results, thereby allowing for great creativity in *who* and *how*—considerable role support for intermediate and first-line management.

In the following chapter, the further advantages of results management are presented in two frames of reference: first, from the implicit difficulty of management operating on the premise that "if you don't know where you're going then you can't get lost," and second, the great managerial advantage of permitting all employees at all levels to focus their unique abilities on accomplishing results.

SUMMARY

In this chapter an attempt has been made to isolate management as a unique concept. The historical development of management was traced to ancient human efforts to organize human endeavor and this endeavor was in turn presented as both resulting from and developing into a combination of management and criminal justice.

Various strategic influences throughout history were presented in the context of isolating management as a unique concept. Babylonian, Egyptian, Chinese, Hebrew, Greek, and Roman influences were presented as the background for the managerial styles that emerged in the medieval period. The ramifications of management were discussed in terms of such influences as the merchants of Venice.

The evolution of the concept of management was discussed as being "art" or a kind of intuitive approach to management used prior to the Industrial Revolution, shifting to the inclusion of "science" or measurable management concepts thereafter. The influence of contributors to the "science" were reviewed in terms of the emerging principles—primarily the principle of standardization. Particular significance was given to Taylor's planning, organizing, directing, controlling, and cooperation tasks for management.

As a part of the evolution, the tempering of scientific management with human relations influences were reviewed as a background for the modern management theories and contemporary management practices.

McGregor's Theories X and Y were discussed in relation to the emergence of the managerial grid and such managerial practices as implied by organizational development or management by objectives theories.

As a background for the chapter to follow, three approaches to management were presented: command management, human resource management, and results management. These different approaches were discussed in terms of concern for *what* gets done as opposed to *who* does it and *how* it is done. Further elaboration of these approaches was in terms of functional versus dysfunctional systems, functional defined as managerial priority given to what gets done rather than who does it or how it is done.

QUESTIONS

1. Discuss the relationship between the history of management and the history of criminal justice.

2. In what way did the Great Code of Hammurabi solidify the role of management in government?

3. Contrast the managerial concepts of ancient Egypt, Greece, and Rome with the managerial concepts that emerged following the Industrial Revolution.

4. Discuss the concept of standardization as a scientific principle.

5. Discuss the "art" of management and the "science" of management in terms of historical development.

6. Elaborate the implications of this chapter's position that management in government may have fallen behind management in the private sector during the merging of art and science.

7. Contrast Taylor's scientific management to any common position between Argyris (and Maslow), McGregor, Likert, and Weber.

8. Contrast the Likert concept of productivity and morale to the Blake and Mouton concept.

9. Discuss the five main positions on the Blake and Mouton managerial grid.

10. Elaborate the three approaches to management discussed toward the conclusion of this chapter (command, human resource, result).

11. Discuss the definition given functional and dysfunctional organizational systems in terms of *what* gets done versus *who* and *how*.

ANNOTATED REFERENCES

BERKLEY, G. E., *The Administrative Revolution*. Englewood Cliffs, N.J.: Prentice-Hall, 1971. Chapter One reviews the historical evaluation of management in different context than is used in the present chapter, enriching expansion of the notion of management flowing from history.

COFFEY, A., E. ELDEFONSO, and W. HARTINGER, *Human Relations: Law Enforcement in a Changing Community*. Englewood Cliffs, N.J.: Prentice-Hall, 1971. Chapter Eight elaborates the author's views on attitudinal considerations referred to in this chapter under the discussion of Theory *Y*.

COFFEY, A., E. ELDEFONSO, and W. HARTINGER, *Police Community Relations*. Englewood Cliffs, N.J.: Prentice-Hall, 1971. The author's views on the role of government are elaborated in Chapter Three within the context of what was discussed here as government management.

COLUMBUS, E. G., "Management By System," *Police Chief*, 31, No. 7 (July 1970). An excellent "transition" embellishment between the first two chapters of this text and the chapter that follows.

ELDEFONSO, E., A. COFFEY, and R. GRACE, *Principles of Law Enforcement*. New York: Wiley, 1968. Chapter Seven isolates the author's views on administration as a concept within the overall context of one criminal justice subsystem.

GEORGE, C. S., Jr., *The History of Management Thought*. Englewood Cliffs, N.J.: Prentice-Hall, 1968. The first six chapters of George's outstanding book elaborate in depth the history presented in this chapter.

LIKERT, R., *New Patterns of Management*. New York: McGraw-Hill, 1961. In-depth exploration of much of what this chapter dealt with as occurring in management following the Industrial Revolution.

MCGREGOR, DOUGLAS, *Leadership and Motivaiton: Essays by Douglas McGregor*, Warren Bennis, Edgar Schein, and Caroline McGregor, eds. Cambridge, Mass.: M.I.T. University Press, 1966. A singularly fine embellishment of the concepts reviewed in the second half of this chapter.

* ALSO RECOMMENDED:

ARGYRIS, CHRIS, "The Organization: What Makes It Healthy," *Harvard Business Review*, 36, No. 6 (November–December 1958), 107–16.

BLAKE, R. R., and J. S. MOUTON, *Building A Dynamic Corporation Through Grid Organization Development*. Reading, Mass.: Addison-Wesley, 1969.

HERTZBERG, F., B. MAUSNER, and B. SNYDERMAN, *The Motivation To Work*. New York: Wiley, 1959.

HOWLETT, F. W., and H. HUNTER, "A Systems Approach to Comprehensive Criminal Justice Planning," *Crime and Delinquency*, 17, No. 4 (October 1971), 355–72.

** PARTICULARLY RECOMMENDED:

PERT, L. E., "Motivation: An Operational Staff Presentation," *Law and Order*, August 1971.

CHAPTER 3

Systems as an Approach
to Management

Making the transition from the vitally needed science of management to the actual practice of the criminal justice system is a most difficult task. Relating sound managerial concepts to police, to courts, and to corrections is the actual goal of the management model.

Of value in this regard is a clear understanding of the distinction between "line work" and management, as discussed in the preceding chapter. But of even greater value is the clear understanding that managerial concepts permit *continuity* of good police work and of good probation work, and do so in a systematic manner.

Because of the importance of insuring good criminal justice work in a systematic manner, attention is turned to what is often called "systems theory." But once again, the unique context of criminal justice is worth recalling before exploring still another valuable management tool—the general systems theory. Criminal justice *as a system* is relatively new in terms of history, whereas the study of systems is ancient:

> the ancient Assyrians collected data and facts in the hope of compiling a cause and effect encyclopedia. . . . surely they could produce results at will by merely doing the appropriate things . . .[1]

Perhaps even more to the point is the serious question criminal justice must first resolve regarding the potential usefulness of any given managerial approach:

> the management philosophers who bring these terms to prominence and popularity are often either so vague or so impenetrable *that their real meaning cannot be detected.* This is partly protective. In any discipline the man who comes up with a new concept or a new approach to things first surrounds the concept with a defensive *network of jargon.* While this makes it difficult for rivals to steal the idea, it also makes it equally difficult for anyone else to grasp the idea too readily. If this is not done—if the concept is instead transmitted in plain English—there is a real danger that the acolyte will quickly see the whole thing (the Gestalt) and exclaim, 'But that's just common sense!' Worse, he might even observe that the emperor has no clothes on and cry out, 'But that doesn't mean anything!' The latter reaction is of course worse than the former, but neither is welcomed by the progenitor of a new management concept.[2]

Once this question is answered in favor of applying systems theory to criminal justice management (as opposed to mysterious processes without measurable outcome), the *unique context* of criminal justice can be examined as a prelude to exploring systems theory. Perhaps an example from correctional institutions might clarify this unique context.

Recently many state jurisdictions have shifted correctional emphasis away from the prison and toward the probation kind of program. Not surprisingly, offenders who are committed to prison in these states are committed for crimes that are more severe than has been the case in the past. In other words, prison populations are likely to be increasingly comprised *in total* of offenders who in the past made up only a small proportion of "maximum security risks."

Because prison administrators find themselves with fewer and fewer of those who once made up the "trustee-staff" (because these same offenders are being placed on probation instead of being committed to prison by the courts), the administrative problems of staffing immediately increase, and problems arise in terms of security—the more high risk, the more need for security.

The warden of a prison confronting this problem can scarcely ignore the fact that criminal justice is indeed a *system*, each subsystem of which influences another subsystem—in this case, the court subsystem and the probation subsystem profoundly influencing the prison subsystem's management. In the context of this and similar examples involving the systematic relation-

---

[1] Brian Rothery, ed., *The Art of Systems Analysis* (Englewood Cliffs, New Jersey: Prentice-Hall, Inc., 1971), p. 4.

[2] O. William Battalia and John J. Tarrant, *The Corporate Eunuch* (New York: Thomas Y. Crowell Company, 1973).

ship between police and courts, courts and prosecution, prosecution and probation, and prison and parole, further understanding of systems and systems theory is most desirable.

There are a number of facets of systems application to be covered, however, in understanding the systems approach in criminal justice management. We will begin with a discussion of the development of the systems approach.

Systems Development

There has been a considerable increase in the managerial interest in systems and systems theory during the past two decades.[3] The momentum toward various systems approaches such as the one presented in Chapter One may have began right after World War II—possibly as a result of that war.

The war left most organizations of any kind around the world either under severe economic stress or in radical transition to peacetime economics. Japan and the Far East approached economic collapse as the war ended. Western Europe was all but exhausted. France lost more than half of her industrial potential, and the war reduced Germany even more. England fared slightly better but felt most of the severe European post-war shortages of housing, schools, hospitals, transportation, and, above all else, the serious depletion of manpower resulting from the bloody conflict.[4]

From the perspective of the managerial concepts discussed in the preceding chapter, Western Europe faced further difficulties. Communism as Karl Marx had proposed it 100 years earlier emerged as a distinct possibility among masses of people disillusioned with a failing capitalism—disillusionment heightened by the presence of a seemingly successful Russian Communism.[5] The post-war Asian picture was no less bleak.

The willingness of American management to respond to the influences discussed in Chapter Two may have been facilitated by the complexities of world economic recovery, the role of American aid in this recovery, and the combined impact of these factors. At this juncture, criminal justice management was virtually unaware of systems.

Different schools of thought exist on the factors that relate to the American culture and those ultimately producing systems awareness. But certainly the strain of depleted foreign markets, combined with returning domestic competition, had some bearing on any willingness to examine management. Even before the depleted foreign markets were transformed into formidable competitors, most progressive American organizations were examin-

---

[3] See, for example, Richard T. Neuschel, *Management by System* (New York: McGraw-Hill, Inc., 1960), chaps. 1 and 2; Peter P. Schoderbek, *Management Systems* (New York: John Wiley & Sons, Inc., 1971), chaps. 1–4; Rocco Carzo and John Yanouzas, *Formal Organization: A Systems Approach*. (Homewood, Ill.: Dorsey Press, 1967), Part One.

[4] George E. Berkley, *The Administrative Revolution* (Englewood Cliffs, N. J.: Prentice-Hall, Inc., 1971), pp. 36–65.

[5] Ibid., p. 37.

ing the managerial concept from the frame of reference of McGregor and those who followed. To the degree that management accepted new concepts following World War II, systems also gained increasing consideration and acceptance in management. In this regard, criminal justice can scarcely ignore the apparent value of the managerial effectiveness of the systems approach as it began to develop.

Consider the confusion necessarily generated when the input of a police or probation department is not distinguished from the managerial output or the activities that make up process. *Even with this simplified conceptual tool, the use of highly trained technical consultants* (as presented in Chapter Fourteen) *is required.* But *without* the concept of systems as part of the concept of management, activities that pass as managerial functions rarely if ever relate to each other in a goal-oriented manner in the police department or the prison or any other criminal justice organization. Even when a relationship does occur, it is frequently not on the basis of administrative goals, and is definitely not *systematic* in nature.

However foreign a managerial approach based on systematic programming may seem, the value to criminal justice cannot be ignored.

ELEMENTS OF CRIMINAL JUSTICE AND THE SYSTEMS APPROACH[6]

In the opening chapter, the systems approach was presented in terms of input, process, and output. The input of criminal justice as a system is selected law violation, the process is whatever is done about crime, and the output is the consequence of process—hopefully an output consequence of less crime.

Further consideration might be given the notion of *systems.* Technically, a system is what Webster's Dictionary defines as a "set of things so related or connected as to form a unity." "Unity" will gain a particular definition later in this chapter. But from the general systems theory viewpoint, systems are simply all relationships that can be abstracted from any form of empirical evidence.

Although many scientists question the validity of the general systems theory,[7] studying the elements of a whole in terms of the relationships of the parts remains valuable not only for research of the whole but for the management of the parts—the elements or subsystems.

[6] Taken from unpublished management training materials developed when the author was training director for a criminal justice system agency, and from materials developed by the author for management consultation and college instruction.

[7] See, for example, Walter Buckley, *Modern Systems Research for the Behavioral Scientist* (New York: Aldine Publishers, 1968), p. 21; also Ludwig Von Bertalanffy, "An Outline of GST," *British Journal of the Philosophy of Science,* I (1950), 139–64; D. C. Phillips, "Systems Theory—A Discredited Philosophy," in *Management Systems,* Peter Schoderbek, ed. (New York: John Wiley & Sons, Inc., 1967), pp. 55–64.

In the chapters that follow, the various subsystems of criminal justice as a whole (police, courts, prosecution-defense, and corrections) will be presented in terms of specific management programming. As further and ultimately valuable background for discussing the systems approach to criminal justice management, some consideration will be given the *nature* of the systems approach.

The Nature of the Systems Approach

The complex nature of management systems has to do with human behavior with some quantitative variable that is measurable within a manageable structure. Another way of putting this is to state that *the systems approach is the placing of significant human interaction into a logical design that permits measurable results.*

There is an implied definitional requirement that human interaction be *significant*. By "significance" is meant simply that behavior must be relative to the results being sought. Later in this chapter considerable discussion will focus on human behavior that is not directly related but is nevertheless influential. For purposes of defining "significant behavior," however, the systems approach deals only with human interaction and behavior related to measurable results.

This particular systems approach, then, is a *results management* approach as described in the preceding chapter. Top management considers the system's output, or results, to be the main priority of management.

This is in contrast to *human resource management,* in which virtually *all* human interaction within the organization is of managerial concern. The results-oriented systems approach to management also differs from *command management,* in which top management assumes that continuous orders produce a continuous compliance as discussed in Chapter Two. Results management makes no such assumption, as will be seen in the chapters that follow.

When a *functional* system is assumed in terms of the definition presented in the last chapter, the systems approach to results management emphasizes *what* gets done rather than who does it and how it is done.

Systems and Criminal Justice Pragmatics

The systems approach to management permits concern for what the system does rather than for the management philosophy held by the administrator. Put another way, emphasis on well-defined results and systematic determination of what is needed to achieve these results can become significant enough to virtually replace concern for the administrator's management philosophy—and is likely to become that significant with the systems approach. Excellent literature is beginning to emerge that isolates the system relation to managerial situations instead of the theory X or Y relation to situations.[8]

As will be noted throughout the four chapters that present the management model, this distinction between management philosophy and systematic results is vital to criminal justice administration, whether the administration relates to police, courts, prosecution-defense, or the correctional subsystems.

The example cited early in this chapter referring to prison administrators is worth considering here. The prison administrators' management philosophy probably has no influence on the courts, whereas the systematic results achieved (or not achieved) have considerable influence.

This then represents the criminal justice pragmatic of the results-oriented systems approach to management—a pragmatic awareness that the influence of one subsystem upon another relates to results rather than to managerial philosophy. Nowhere else in the range of management application is this reality so devastatingly true as in the widely varied system of criminal justice. For this reason, further discussion of philosophy in terms of Theories X and Y may be useful.

As already noted, by emphasis on *what* is done to achieve results, rather than who does it and how it is done, and on accomplishment of predetermined results as the *only* success measurement, top management can avoid being restricted to a particular managerial theory. Just as important, separating input from process and process from output makes possible the recognition that Theory Y activities discussed in the preceding chapter are *process* activities. Moreover, these activities are *permitted* by Theory X managerial decisions from the system's output—X decisions made sooner or later—at least to the degree that certain segments of Theory X might possibly be correct. Indeed, the very decision to permit Theory Y to start or continue is at least in part an X decision—resentment of the Theory Y manager notwithstanding. And all this tends to reinforce a determined emphasis on results instead of philosophy.

The results-oriented systems approach, then, acknowledges the value of management style *only* in terms of results, no effort being given to change the style of the manager. Focus on the style rather than on results is, from the systems approach, likely to obscure either output, results, or what it is that the organization does (as opposed to who does it and how).

Recalling the impact of the results of the court subsystem, obscuring either the output or results is precisely what must be avoided at all costs if American criminal justice is to become less fragmented and is to become a genuine *system*. This is true not only with the court subsystem relating to the prison subsystem in terms of results rather than philosophy but also

[8] See, for example, Phillip B. Crosby, *The Art of Getting Your Own Sweet Way* (New York: McGraw-Hill, 1972), especially preface and pp. 8–156.

with police relating to prosecution, probation to courts—in short, to all relationships within the system.

From the frame of reference of the various elements of criminal justice, the systems approach requires the setting and achievement of goals to take priority over any particular style of management. In other words, styles are simply a means to achieve goals, assuming management can set worthwhile goals. Without these goals—without clearly defined, predetermined results—the style of management is likely to receive not only inordinate attention, but also inappropriate priority that fragments criminal justice.

From this frame of reference, attention is now directed to the description of the systems approach used earlier in the chapter: *the systems approach is the placing of significant human interaction into a logical design that permits measurable results*—behavior and quantitative measure combined.

BEHAVIOR AND SUBSTANTIVE MEASUREMENT

To this point it may appear that human behavior is taken for granted—that the systems approach assumes responsive behavior in much the same way the command manager does. To the contrary, an individual is always the final expert on his productivity. This in effect means that the behavior to be integrated into quantitative measure is behavior either offered or withheld by employees. As a background for the systems technology of the management model, it is worthwhile to consider the concept of *motivation* at this point.

Behavior and Motivation

As already noted in the discussion of Maslow's theory of human motivation, getting employees to "offer" certain behavior may be related to satisfying certain human needs.[9] But before further consideration is given behavior, some attention will be directed toward motivating employees. In discussing organizational behavior in terms of developmental research, Mason Haire optimistically states, "Both the social scientists and the managers have been too modest in their hopes for the results from the application of new concepts."[10]

It must be emphasized that this context for a discussion of motivation is *not* an implicit endorsement of what was discussed earlier as management

[9] In addition to the preceding discussion of Maslow's influence on management as a concept, see also Maslow, "A Theory of Human Motivation," *Psychological Review,* 50 (1943), 370–76.

[10] Haire, "The Social Sciences and Management Practices," *California Management Review,* 6, No. 4 (Summer 1964).

by relationship (as contrasted with command management and results management). On the contrary, *human relations* remains in the managerial position suggested by William Fox: "Many mistakenly regard it [human relations] as an 'end' toward which the organization should endeavor rather than as what it should be—a 'means' for achieving the organization's primary service objectives."[11] In this regard, Clark Kerr has written, "They [the human relations advocates] begin by saying that man dislikes isolation and end by consigning him to the care of the managerial elite for his own salvation,"[12]—in other words outlining a lethal component to the philosophy of human relations within a frequently accepted *theory* of human relations. Motivation, or more specifically, motivating employee behavior, is instead a matter of retaining *productivity* as the main priority in managerial effort to combine satisfactory production with the fulfillment of human needs. In this regard, Herbert Zollitch, the noted authority on administering wage and salary, sums up both the human needs and more particularly management's needs succinctly:

1. Understand the complicated factors involved;
2. Constantly analyze and be aware of the individual needs of the workers hired and the ever-changing state of the conditions which affect motivation and job performance;
3. Communicate the goals of the company and what the worker can expect with the company; and
4. Show sincerity and integrity in carrying out personnel policies which are designed to attract, select, hire, train, motivate, reward and retain competent employees.[13]

Although these four observations were made with reference to the private sector of business, the relevance to management in criminal justice is unmistakable. What police chief, chief probation officer, or any other criminal justice manager can afford to administratively ignore any of these observations? In terms of undertaking the difficult task of combining productivity with the fulfillment of human needs while retaining productivity as the main goal, it would appear that criminal justice administrators can not afford to ignore any of these observations. Moreover, the observations provide a context in which motivation can be managerially related to behavior. This context is clarified by the comments of Harold Leavitt:

[11] W. M. Fox, "When Human Relations May Succeed and the Company Fails," California Management Review, 8, No. 3 (Spring 1966).

[12] C. Kerr, *Labor and Management in Industrial Society* (Garden City, N. Y.: Doubleday & Company, Inc., 1964), p. 57.

[13] Herbert G. Zollitch, "Motivation for Productivity," *Proceedings of the 7th Annual Midwest Management Conference* (Carbondale, Ill.: Business Research Bureau, Southern Illinois University, 1964), p. 68. See also *Wage and Salary Administration* by Langster and Zollitch (Cincinnati: South-Western Publishing Co., 1961).

. . . motivation is so much in the limelight these days that some of us have come to believe motivation *is* management. I submit that motivation is a large *part* of management. An important part. But not the only part.[14]

Within this context, attention is again directed specifically to employee *behavior*.

Behavior is process in the same sense process was discussed in Chapter One. As noted there, criminal justice process involves the activity of policemen, judges, prosecutors, defense attorneys, and correctional personnel. In human terms, these activities are the process of people relating to an individual—in this case a person accused of a crime. This relationship is an extremely significant consideration to management. Indeed, perhaps one of the more crucial concerns of management may be the accuracy with which the relationship between the employee and the organization can be understood. The *ultimate* management measure may not be the understanding of the relationship between the individual and the organization, but certainly such understanding is critical to integrating behavior with quantitative measure.

Perhaps such understanding begins with considerations of the individual personality. Though this is essential in understanding the managerial integration of behavior and measurement, later discussions will elaborate the position that personality change is *not* required for effective management. *Consideration of personality is for the sole purpose of understanding the administrative task of integrating human behavior and criminal justice results measurements—not* for the purpose of "change." Regardless of how significantly related personality may be to successful police work, management priority must remain with measurable results that are being accomplished.

Personality

There are many uses and definitions of the word "personality." (Perhaps this relates to the many uses and definitions of the word "person.") The psychiatrist, when he speaks of "personality disorder," means something different than the definition given "personality" by a charm school. Prison inmate classification systems introduce still other definitions, as do police modus-operandi files.

The meanings given the word range far from the original Greek word *persona*, which means "theatrical mask." But in terms of managerially integrating behavior with quantitative measures, "personality" will be considered as including both that which is seen and that which is not seen. The idea of a theatrical mask may imply a conscious choice to hide "the real face." However, in contrast to this conscious choice, the analogy of an iceberg presents the notion of only one-eighth showing above the surface, the remainder being

---

[14] Leavitt, "It's a Valuable Management Tool, But . . . Motivation Is Not Enough," *Stanford Graduate School of Business Bulletin*, 35, No. 2 (Autumn 1966), 21.

hidden because of the nature of an iceberg rather than because of the conscious choice of the iceberg itself. For the manager, this points out the necessity of exploring the "seen" and "unseen" segments of personality, even though the systems approach dictates only that which is seen and, further, that which relates to results. Such exploration is appropriate to the degree that the analogy of an iceberg remains consistent—the one-eighth that shows remains connected and influenced by the seven-eighths that does not show.

The writings of Sigmund Freud help clarify the relationship of early life experience to the behavioral concerns of the manager.[15] Freud conceptualized the child as being born with virtually no conscious awareness of others, or even of himself. The segment of personality known in psychoanalytic theory as the "id" functions in terms of hunger, thirst, and a wide range of physical comforts or discomforts. Awareness of discomfort stimulates particular behaviors, some of which produce a reduction of discomfort (crying results in getting diapers changed, being fed, etc.). Once a behavior consistently produces satisfaction, an "ego" begins to develop, as well as a way of perceiving—this aspect of particular concern to managers. The ego connects conscious awareness of what behavior led to satisfying id needs, and further reinforces the relationship between growing perception and behavior —of ultimate consequence to managers. Finally, social training begins to impose a "superego"—an awareness of the restrictions imposed on the individual (conscience). Perception of these restrictions and behavioral reactions to such control again emerge as managerially significant.

Were it possible to be aware of complete and total satisfaction of all needs at one time, the possibilities of what Freud called the "oral stage" might become clear. The oral stage of personality development is essentially the first stage of development. As the name implies, an infant in this period of growth experiences only needs for nutrition and affection. The loving, breast-feeding mother theoretically provides 100 percent of the infant's perceived needs and, in doing so, provides powerful inducement to the infant to accept whatever "control" is imposed. Once conscious awareness of other controls occurs, much of the baby's continued personality development is accomplished through "learning." This is an extremely involved process, and there are a variety of learning methods.[16] Many of these methods are relatively simple, such as in the case of conditioning (of singular importance to the command manager, but also to the results manager more interested in what gets done than who does it).

Conditioning has the advantage of relating most directly to personality development in terms of evolving a relationship between *perception* and *behavior*—ultimately the same "behavior" to be integrated by management

[15] A. A. Brill, *The Basic Writings of Sigmund Freud* (New York: Random House, 1938).

[16] See E. R. Hilgard, *Theories of Learning* (New York: Appleton-Century-Crofts, 1956).

with quantitative measurements (behavior of police officers, parole agents, and so forth). One of the three varieties of conditioning that relate more directly to behavior from a managerial perspective is called *operant*. Experimental psychologists consider as fundamental the classical conditioning of Pavlov's salivating dogs and the contiguous conditioning of Guthrie's "cued-stimulus-response."[17] But the "operant conditioning" of Skinner's "positive and negative reinforcements"[18] bear directly on criminal justice management.

In terms of the relationship between perception and behavior, operant conditioning is likely to be nonverbal at first. Mother may provide a positive reinforcement with smiles and caresses for good behavior and negative reinforcement with wrinkled forehead and narrowed eyes for bad behavior. Of course the roles of ice cream and spankings are obvious. Supervising prison guards or police watch commanders may unconsciously influence behavior in much the same way.

Soon the positive and negative reinforcement power of other family members enter the learning process. Once the influence of other persons outside the family is felt, personality development in terms of *socialization* is well under way. But as noted earlier, relating perception and behavior is a part of the child's development—they become a part of the socialization process.

For purposes of discussing management's interest in perception and behavior, a *folkway* may be thought of as merely a standard of individual behavior for which only mild negative reinforcement (punishment) is meted out if violations occur. (Being late for a movie violates the "on-time" folkway and the punishment is missing the first part of the movie.) On a much broader scale, criminal justice also "punishes." *Mores* are simply higher expectations with greater punishment for violation. Violating "late-for-school" mores generates stronger negative reinforcement than the movie folkway. Virtually all folkways and mores, when instituted, relate in some way to the general needs of the people forming the society or organization—at least *at the time* they evolve. From this frame of reference, individuals who are unaware of, indifferent to, or opposed to folkways and mores actually inhibit their potential to have their own needs met within the society. Consider this observation in the context of the McGregor position discussed in the preceding chapter.

To clarify the role of folkways and mores and a criminal justice manager's efforts to integrate behavior with quantitative measurements, consideration might be given a hypothetical group of prehistoric clansmen. In this instance, a folkway might be the mutual responsibility to gather firewood. The punishment for violation might be the loss of a position near the fire on a cold night.

[17] Ibid., pp. 48–81.
[18] Ibid., pp. 82–120.

Mores of this group might be restrictions regarding the use of another individual's weapons, animal skins, or women. Violations might generate a painfully aggressive punishment from the owner, sanctioned by the entire organization. In this sense, management of criminal justice is merely a smaller scale of managing society. In instances in which the rule of behavior was deemed so important that these informal penalties would not be adequate, a kind of social institution would likely be formed and organizational management emerge.

Perhaps here the question should be posed: What has all this to do with managing a criminal justice organization? Such a question is singularly cogent within the context of results having managerial priority over philosophy—the criminal justice pragmatics discussed earlier.

Recalling that our rationale for exploring personality is to understand the administrative task of integrating human behavior and criminal justice results, it is now possible to see that the organization and society both impinge upon the criminal justice employee in terms of how he perceives, and this in turn relates to his early life experiences—the *only* reason for managerial interest. Individual perception is influenced by all early life experiences in general, plus several specific influences such as social change.

Social Change

Consideration of social change is then necessarily relevant, but only in terms of managerial efforts to integrate human behavior with quantitative measurement. Social change, however, more than any other variable, impinges directly on individual willingness to participate in the accomplishment of organizational goals. Criminal justice—being a system of insuring that the population "participate" in behavior acceptable by societal standards—can scarcely ignore social change in either the population or the personnel who "operate" criminal justice.

Until recent times, most young adults were reasonably certain about their agrarian future. Whether or not farming was preferred, farming was in most cases certain. Powerful social controls evolved through "everybody knowing everybody" in the small rural communities that constituted most of the early American culture. These social controls, buttressed with the security of a predictable future, afforded more than adequate support for the willingness of young people to participate in achieving cultural (if not organizational) goals. Indeed, this powerful control of behavior provided society far greater control of crime, for instance, than would be reasonable to expect from the most sophisticated modern criminal justice system in the automated, urbanized, cybernated twentieth century—an observation that will be examined in depth in later chapters. For now, merely consider this in terms of managerially integrating behavior and results.

The Industrial Revolution, bringing urbanization and anonymity, was quickly followed by automation, cybernation, and a host of other variables that greatly weakened the powerful control of behavior that once existed in rural America. This weakening was accelerated by major wars combined with international economic upheavals and an ever-increasing exposure to the major social problems that relate to poverty.

In short, the individual's willingness to permit his behavior to be regulated by society, or to participate in achieving organizational goals, has been steadily modified since the Industrial Revolution—both for the young people employed and those served by the criminal justice system. Indeed, from a managerial point of view, the individual's willingness to have his behavior regulated can no longer be assumed in any instance, frequency of criminal justice preferences for command management notwithstanding.

Family Influence

Managerially, determining to what degree there is administrative interest in why behavior does not achieve results should prove easier whenever the influence seems to flow from family experience. With this in mind, family influence will now be considered. If a family is thought of as a group of individuals, it becomes possible to examine the impact of one individual upon another and, more managerially important, of the group upon the individual.

In terms of the impact of individual family members on one another, consider the cultural American belief in the honesty of very small children —at least when the distinction between fantasy and reality is considered. Contrast this to the "flexible" honesty of many older children, and a somewhat stereotyped disparity emerges, the source of which deserves further consideration in terms of an analogy to managerial efforts to integrate behavior and quantitative measure.

On a common-sense basis, it is abundantly clear that a small child's motive to be honest is jeopardized by the punishment of honest response to such parental questions as "Who left this bike in the driveway?" Multiply such subtle training a millionfold during a child's pre-teen years, and it would be surprising if his honesty had not become flexible. Managerial procedures that "punish" employee integrity in systematic efforts to align behavior with results relate to this concept.

However, a child's honesty is only one of many facets of family dynamics that suffer during such training. In a family that depends on this approach to child-rearing, a kind of emotional equilibrium develops around the "dishonesty"—an equilibrium that may be brought to his criminal justice involvement later.

Consider parents who for their own reasons fear open expression of anger or hostility—who in effect have a rule (sometimes secret) against the expressing of anger within the family. Consider the parallel of criminal justice administrators, who, for managerial reasons, fear open expression of creative or innovative alternatives to achieving results—who in effect have a rule (sometimes subtly disguised) against expression of alternatives. Family, and sometimes organizational, rules may or may not be known to the person following them. Family groups frequently establish rules for behavior in terms of their earlier experiences or, in some way, to modify what appears to be threatening. Individual employees bring to the organization their experience of dealing with rules within the family. In the case of the mother and father establishing a rule against the expression of anger, earlier life experiences of each parent contribute to the enforcement of this family rule. Perhaps the prison warden or police chief hoping to generate optimum yield from the systems approach might reflect on earlier managerial experiences when attempting to integrate behavior with quantitative measure—this would be much more than a mere personnel consideration.

As the children of a family group are subtly punished year after year for expression of any kind of anger, a system homeostasis, or emotional equilibrium, occurs even though considerable family tension is present at all times. All criminal justice "families," though larger, also develop homeostasis, but may also develop it around a kind of continuing tension that mitigates heavily *against* managerial efforts to integrate behavior and quantitative measure and against results needed to weld criminal justice into a *system*.

A younger child in the family, unaware of the rules that have been increasingly reinforced through the years and having experienced less of the tension that the rest of the family feels may still be the target for both parental punishment and great redress from his siblings. Such scapegoating may occur both within families and organizations, to the detriment of the systems approach to management. Few criminal justice organizations are without some form of internal blacksheep.

Personnel But Still Management

Although most, and in some cases, all of the problems of organizational scapegoats and black sheep are dealt with managerially within the personnel context to be presented later, it should be remembered that resources lost to a manager are lost to the achievement of results as well. Indeed, every police officer bearing the organizational label of "dink," every probation officer regarded by peers as a "schnook," every parole agent seen as an "eightball," and every prison guard seen as a "dud" becomes a *major* reduction in the potential impact of criminal justice as a system.

For this reason, integrating human behavior with achievement of quantitative results remains crucial even in a systems approach—an approach that holds results more managerially important than philosophy, and more important than past experience. This all managerial programs of the systems variety have in common. Overshadowing any technical differences are the major similarities in managerial programs in which general systems theory forms the basis of administrative function. One such similarity, of course, is the need to integrate human behavior with quantitative measurement; another is the recognition that an organization *is* a system. The system may either be functional in terms of desirable outcome or nonfunctional and fragmented—and still be an organizational system. Moreover, the common definition of a system remains a complex of variables that collectively form (or systematically fail to form) a *whole*. It may be hopelessly fragmented by excluding results in favor of philosophy—nevertheless it is a *system*. The axiom of success in systems management is *that combination of science and energy that achieves desirable outcome.*

In the systems model that follows in the next four chapters, it will be noted that the most significant segment of this combination is *taxonomy*: the science of *classification*. The "laws and principles of classification" are also a part of taxonomy, and collectively form the basis of other significant segments of science within a systems model such as research, experiment, mathematical principles, and so forth.

The most significant part of the human behavior half of the combination of science and energy is *ergometrics*: the measurement of energy expended for the amount of work accomplished, again, solely in terms of criminal justice results.

In what will be described as the function of first-line supervisors in an organization using the systems model, separation of task definitions from the potential energy required for accomplishing tasks is one primary use of ergometrics—a use that permits a sophisticated assessment of organizational resources—making possible what will be discussed as *system energy assessment*. Stated more simply, this is the actual integration of human behavior and quantitative measure—the systems approach.

In the broader context of management overall, combining taxonomy with ergometrics is the prime requisite in achieving an administratively desirable outcome. Other scientific segments incidental to effective classification, along with other behavioral considerations incidental to ergometrics, remain incidental; achieving measurable criminal justice results systematically is the idea. Virtually all reasonable results are possible once taxonomy and ergometrics are administratively combined—once human behavior and quantitative measure are integrated systematically.

The main administrative application of taxonomy has to do with classifying the ingredients of success. In the case of the systems model to be presented, the success ingredients will be presented as the definition of results that are to be achieved; of defining what is operationally needed to achieve these results; who is most effective in achieving the desired outcome; how the outcome is to be achieved; and measurement of all of these managerial functions in order to provide what will be presented as "interface accountability"—in other words, what various criminal justice managers "do" to achieve results.

The main administrative application of ergometrics in the management model has to do with two critical managerial concerns: (1) optimum use of energy resources; and (2) establishing "interfaces" between managers that permit communication without distorting the vital role definitions that form the basis of the systems model overall. Another way of expressing these two concerns is in terms of the integration of criminal justice personnel behavior with quantitative measurements of success. The relationship of behavior and quantitative measurement is crucial to the management model. Combining these quantitative measurements in such a way that results are achieved emerges as the role of all levels of management.

The frequent obscurity often surrounding the actual activity of management in criminal justice presents a formidable challenge. This challenge can be met, at least in part, by conceiving of criminal justice management in terms of the unit blocks depicted in the following diagram.

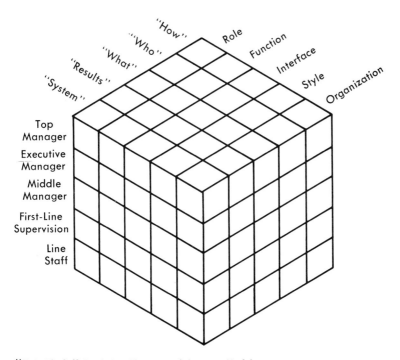

"Unit Blocks" Depicting Elements of Systems Model

This, then, concludes the discussion of the theoretical implications of criminal justice as a manageable system made up of manageable subsystems. Part Two, A Management Model, will explore the specific roles, functions, and applications of the management principles selected on the basis of their relevance to criminal justice.

SUMMARY

This chapter has discussed systems as an approach to management within the criminal justice system. A *system* was discussed as a unified set of related parts or components in a logical configuration of input, process, and output that permits some kind of quantitative measure. Input, process, and output were discussed in the same context as elaborated in Chapter One.

The systems approach to criminal justice management was presented as the integration of significant behavior with the quantitative measures needed by a system—significant behavior defined as behavior related to achieving predetermined results. Unlike the command management, in which an assumption is made that continuous orders produce continuous employee participation in organizational programs, the systems approach stressed that results are forthcoming only to the degree that the employee's behavior is recognized as a choice of the employee.

Also considered was the relationship of behavior and motivation within the systems approach to management. With emphasis on the limited role of human relations in systematic managerial success, motivation of employees was elaborated in the context of management needs for certain varieties of employee behavior. This point was discussed within the managerial context of concern for employee behavior as strictly limited to the administrative task of integrating behavior with quantitative measures and achieved results.

Within this same context, early life experiences that influence personality, along with social change and family influence, were presented as managerial areas related to personnel functions and management of organizational resources.

In addition to picturing the systems approach as integrating human behavior and quantitative measurement, the systems approach of the management model was discussed as being results-oriented in the context of the preceding chapter. It was also presented as functional in terms of priority being given *what* is done to achieve results, rather than *who* does it or *how* it is done.

Emphasis was placed on the absence of requirements for particular management theory or style if results are appropriately defined in advance. Theories X and Y were discussed as less significant than results in the systems approach to the management model to be developed in ensuing chapters. Any given position on the managerial grid was similarly placed in lower priority than results.

Consistency and continuity were also discussed as more amenable to results priority than to priorities on theories or style—further clarification of this point to be reflected in the discussion of managerial role and skills presented in the following chapter.

The appropriateness of the methods used to develop definitions of results and other managerial goals was presented as the safeguard against evolving an "end justifies means" management system—again to be developed in the three chapters that follow.

QUESTIONS

1. Discuss the relationship of World War II to American management.

2. Discuss the nature of the systems approach to management as presented early in this chapter.

3. Discuss the relationship of the quantitative measures to employee behavior.

4. In what way does command management differ from results management in terms of employee behavior?

5. Distinguish between significant behavior and behavior in general in terms of results management.

6. For what reason is a results manager interested in behavior and interactions that are not directly related to quantitative measure in the systems approach?

7. Discuss the rationale for placing results in a higher priority than either managerial theory or style.

8. Discuss functional system in terms of the systems approach.

9. Relate organizational consistency to managerial flexibility and style.

10. Relate personality and socialization factors as presented in this chapter to family influences.

11. Relate personality, socialization, and family to the managerial concerns of the systems approach.

ANNOTATED REFERENCES

ACKOFF, RUSSEL L., "Systems, Organization and Interdisciplinary Research," *General Systems,* V (1960), 1–8.

——, *Scientific Method: Optimizing Applied Research Decisions.* New York: Wiley, 1962. Excellent reading in the methodological relationship of the systems approach in this chapter to Chapter VI on the management information system.

ARGYRIS, CHRIS, *Interpersonal Competence and Organizational Effectiveness.* Homewood, Ill.: Dorsey, 1967; also Argyris, *Organization and Innovation.* Excellent transition reading between the concepts present in the preceding chapter and this chapter.

BUCK, R. C., "On The Logic of General Behavior Systems Theory," in Herbert Feigal and Michael Scriven, *Minnesota Studies in Philosophy of Science,* Vol. 1. Minneapolis: University of Minn. Press, 1956. In-depth elaboration of what this chapter introduced as the integration of behavior and quantitative measure. Particularly valuable in exploring the rationale of the management model.

CARZO, ROCCO, JR., and JOHN N. YANOUZAS, *Formal Organization: A Systems Approach.* Homewood, Ill.: Dorsey Press, 1967. Chapters 3 and 4 afford in-depth consideration of the relationship between the theories presented in the preceding chapter and this chapter.

GREBSTEIN, L. C., ed., *Toward Self-Understanding.* Glenview, Ill.: Scott, Foresman, 1969. Over forty outstanding articles by authorities on human interaction as discussed in the latter part of this chapter.

MILLER, JAMES, "Towards A General Theory For the Behavioral Sciences," *American Psychologist,* X (1955), 513–31. Further clarification of what this chapter referred to as integrating behavior and measure.

NEUSCHEL, RICHARD F., *Management by System.* New York: McGraw-Hill, 1960. Part I, "The Case For A Systematic Ordering of Operations," makes a good case for systematic ordering per se.

SCHODERBEK, PETER P., ed., *Management Systems.* New York: Wiley, 1967. Part One ("The Systems Concept") covers virtually every ramification of general systems theory, cybernetics, and all relevant material from them as related to the management model.

WOHLKING, WALLACE, "Management By Objectives: A Critical View," *Training and Development Journal,* April 1972. Same issue: HARRY LEVINSON, "Management by Objectives: A Critique"; GEORGE STRAUSS, "Management by Objectives: A Critical View"; WALTER R. MAHLER, "Management by Objectives: A Consultant's Viewpoint." Collectively, these articles deal with a great deal of the rationale used for the modifications of Peter Drucker's MBO to what this and the previous chapter presented as a results-oriented systems approach.

WRONG, DENNIS H., and HARRY L. GRACEY, eds., *Readings in Introductory Sociology.* New York: MacMillan, 1968. Sixty-two sociological articles dealing with the entire range of behavioral subjects presented in this chapter.

PART TWO

A MANAGEMENT MODEL: CRIMINAL JUSTICE SYNERGETICS AND RESOURCE EFFECTIVENESS

CHAPTER 4

Management Roles and Functions: Key to the Model

GLOSSARY

RESULTS—administratively defined department goals ; **WHATS**—operational determination of what is needed to achieve results along with precise measurement ; **WHO**—managerial determination of operational staffing ; **HOW**—supervisory determination of methods.

Part One covered the theoretical implications of managing criminal justice, and the general managerial context in which the management model will be presented was also considered. Part Two will cover the critical areas of the model, including roles, functions, styles, and skills in this chapter, and efficiency and effectiveness through synergetics, management information, decisions, planning, budget, personnel, labor unions, managerial communication, and training in the three chapters that follow. Of great importance, the critical management areas within the unique framework of criminal justice will be discussed.

The management model will be referred to interchangeably in the chapters of this section as the "systems model." This of course is because the model is systematic in terms of a consistent distinction between the input, process, and output of the criminal justice system and subsystems.

The part of the management model that will be introduced in this chapter is actually a combination of several considerations, including managerial interfacing of roles, functions, styles, and skills. Great emphasis will be given the clarification of managerial roles, and this will in turn require considerable concern with managerial functions.

Although emphasis is given to clarifying managerial roles and functions, it must be noted that such clarification tends to remain extremely complex, especially in terms of the great subsystem variation within the criminal justice system. The purpose of this chapter, is, therefore, to clarify and hopefully simplify this complexity in managerial role and function.

Programming, organization, personnel, budget, and many other managerial considerations will be given high priority in the chapters that follow. But in the final analysis, having and utilizing clear definitions of the various managerial roles and their related functions either permits or prevents successful, continuous, and, above all else, *systematic* management.

SYSTEM INFLUENCES ON ROLES AND FUNCTIONS

Of course, the problems of clarifying managerial roles and functions are made more complex because of the variations in organizational criminal justice systems and subsystems. These organizational concerns, along with system analysis, however, will be dealt with in other context later in the volume. Without minimizing the significant influence of both organizational and system influence on the clarification of roles and functions, then, the immediate problems confronting management role clarification will now be considered.

The Problems of Role Clarification

As already noted, one of the significant difficulties in clarifying managerial roles in criminal justice has to do with the diversity of organizational structure. Although organizational considerations will be dealt with later in this volume, it will be useful here to briefly discuss the relationship of organizational structure to role clarification.

Consider, for example, the great variety of police organizations that exist in the local, county, state, and federal jurisdictions. Then, bearing in mind that there are many subsystems in criminal justice, consider the great variety of services provided any *one* police jurisdiction that may not be provided by other jurisdictions. Role definition could plainly become an unnegotiable problem; to prevent this, the strategy adopted here begins with separating the organizational considerations (see Chapter Nine) and further separating the technical systems analysis influences (see Chapter Fourteen).

The beginning point for a discussion of role clarification of this model will, then, start with acknowledgment of the problem of public identity. This simply refers to the fact that many, if not most people involved in criminal justice management are not known by their appearance to the general public. What is more important, neither are their specific roles. Public expectations definitely impinge on defining managerial roles in criminal justice.

Still another problem in defining managerial roles in criminal justice has to do with how criminal justice managers *become* managers. The police lieutenant, for example, was once a police patrolman; the supervising probation officer was once a line probation officer; the supervising prison guard was once a guard—the same common denominator exists in the background of all criminal justice managerial staff. Chances are that the same kind of common denominator exists at the very highest administrative level—chiefs of police, of probation, of parole, and wardens of prisons usually started their careers as line workers in the field. Indeed, even the elected positions of sheriff or district attorney in many jurisdictions are filled by former line workers.

Understandably, criminal justice managers frequently feel (whether rightly or not) that promotions are evidence that lower-level line skills gain administrative promotions—a kind of rationale to continue doing line work at a higher level. Also understandably, these managers are not always anxious to relinquish such skills—skills that not only gain promotions but probably were the very things that attracted them to the field in the first place.

But line skills are different from managerial skills. The retention of working skills nevertheless remains one of the major problems in attempting to clarify managerial roles. A probation officer, for example, trained in modern sophisticated treatment methods, may never become fully productive because his supervisor, unclear on his managerial role, continues to vicariously do line work through his subordinate—a subordinate frequently told "the old ways are the best ways." A patrolman trained in modern methods of dealing with the public[1] may never bring his training to bear if his superior is so unclear about his managerial role that he continues to be involved in line work to the point even of competing with the patrolman.

The complexities of overlapping functions also pose problems in clarifying managerial roles in criminal justice. In short, there are many problems in defining managerial roles that suggest the need for a strategy.

The strategy of this chapter will be, first, defining "role," second, isolating and defining functions that are required for successful managerial styles, and, third, relating both function and role to "managerial interfaces" (overlapping) which in turn can be related to managerial styles and skills.

[1] Coffey, Eldefonso, and Hartinger, *Police-Community Relations* (Englewood Cliffs, N.J.: Prentice-Hall, Inc., 1971). See also their *Human Relations: Law Enforcement in a Changing Community* (Englewood Cliffs, N.J.: Prentice-Hall, Inc., 1971).

DEFINING MANAGERIAL ROLES AND FUNCTIONS: PRELUDE TO SUCCESSFUL INTERFACING

Regardless of the particular "management package" (i.e., management by objectives, organizational development, "pure" applied general systems theory, and so forth), managerial role is the prime ingredient of continuity in successful administration. Of course the successful utilization of clearly defined managerial roles requires an equal clarity of managerial functions— functions that "interface" or "overlap" to form the actual basis of management continuity.

Although few would argue that role and function do not occupy a strategic position in successful management, the late Douglas McGregor cautioned against the frequent impulse to oversimplify.

> One might say that a manager's role is defined by a position description which states his responsibilities and authority, and a title which locates his position in an organizational hierarchy. In the purely formal sense this is true, but such a definition is gross oversimplification of reality.[2]

In criminal justice, such oversimplification is regrettably all too common. The "position description" approach to managerial roles is so consistent in many jurisdictions that it is regarded by management personnel as natural.

Those seeking a relatively simple explanation of "role" might turn to the theater, where the dramatic definition is "a part or character performed by an actor in a drama."[3] Another way of conceiving of this word when simplification is desired might be the sociological definition: a role is defined by a *status* which is simply a position in or obligation to a group— this is further elaborated to mean that the role is simply expected behavior in a particular group.

With the assistance of these two definitions, perhaps the somewhat oversimplified position description referred to by McGregor may be used in successful role definition for criminal justice managers.

Managerial role includes behavior that is "expected," taking into consideration the *status* of manager—a status specified by a *position description*. In the sense that the actual expectation is for this "performance" to be played, the *position description* of a management status is also related to the theatrical definition of role.

Role then can be defined simply as *the performance of expected managerial functions*.

---

[2] McGregor, *The Professional Manager,* Caroline McGregor and Warren Bennis, eds. (New York: McGraw-Hill, 1967), p. 46.

[3] *Webster's New Collegiate Dictionary*, s.v. "role."

Managerial *functions*, then, become the most significant feature of managerial role. This suggests that comprehensive understanding of managerial roles requires understanding of managerial *functions*.

Managerial Functions

The wide variety of definitions for the word "function" suggests the value of immediately relating the model to functions. The dictionary defines function as "special purposes, office, duty."[4] This definition goes on to define the word "office" as relating "to work to be performed by a person" because of his "position or the like" The word *duty* is then defined as applying "not only to tasks required by one's occupation but to which is imposed by one's rank, status" etc. The "rank or status" concept, although defined in the dictionary as a part of *function*, has more to do in management with *role*— with being chief, captain, sergeant, warden, etc. Consider the following table:

MANAGEMENT

Roles	Functions
Sergeant	Defines results
Inspector	Defines what is needed to achieve results
Chief	Defines who is needed to achieve results
Director	Defines how results are to be achieved
Captain	Planning
Lieutenant	Budget
Supervisor	Personnel
Senior	Programming
Coordinator	Control
Commander	etc.
Warden	
Attorney General	
etc.	

The systems model approaches rank or status as a role to which functions can be assigned systematically. The "tasks required by one's occupation," on the other hand, are the *functions*.

By dividing the definitions of function to place "rank or status" with role and "tasks required" with function, it becomes possible to apply the systems model to large and small departments as well.

The number of roles (rank/status) involved determines how many functions will be performed by any given role—larger departments assigning a single managerial function to a single managerial role, smaller departments assigning several managerial functions to each managerial role.

[4] Ibid., s.v. "function."

But though a relatively simple concept emerges, the actual clarification of a function remains anything but easy. As McGregor puts it in terms of the expectations involved in role,

> The role pressures arising from the expectations of others makes a mockery of the neat, logical, formal statements of what he [the manager] *should* do.[5]

As it relates to function, this inherent conflict between expectations on the basis of role is compounded by the obscurity of the typical managerial position description.[6] Of course, this obscurity is because role has little to do with the actual functions in many cases—particularly among criminal justice subsystems.

Another difficulty in establishing the clearly delineated managerial role as opposed to the managerial function has to do with the tendency to identify one with the other—to equate role with function. This juxtaposition frequently occurs in terms of the classical management functions of planning, organizing, directing, controlling, and coordinating. Just as frequently, confusion flows from other variations of "standard management functions";

> There are four basic functions in management: (1) To determine; (2) To communicate; (3) To do; and (4) To control.[7]

Further confusion many emerge in attempting to clarify roles when clear distinctions are not made between managerial functions and managerial styles.

Managerial Styles

Recalling the previous chapter's discussion of the management grid, the various styles of performing function can be seen. A management function, defined in relation to "tasks" in contrast with role, which is defined as the status, can be performed by any of these styles.

For example, if one style can actually achieve results that include morale even though morale is not a part of that style, then the managerial function is being performed just as well as by another style that includes great emphasis on morale. Indeed, *any* managerial style or combination of styles can continually achieve managerial results in the presence of the managerial skills to be discussed later in this chapter.

In effect, this suggests that specific concern with managerial style may not only be *secondary* in priority to functional achievement of results but may also be all but irrelevant if results are being achieved systematically.

[5] McGregor, *The Professional Manager*, p. 48.

[6] Ibid., p. 49.

[7] Don Fuller, *Manage Or Be Managed* (Boston, Mass.: Industrial Education Institute, 1970), pp. 63–64.

Although this may indicate, at this point, a kind of "end justifies the means" approach, the nature of the functions to be used in the model preclude such a dangerous managerial philosophy from emerging. (This will be clarified in depth in the remaining chapters on the systems model.) It will be seen that the use of interfacing (overlapping) management functions that produce consistent results simply remove style from administrative concern, thereby allowing each individual manager to achieve results in his *own* style.

Another popular managerial tool is known as the Johari Window.[8] From this frame of reference, the confusion between styles and functions can be divided along an axis of what is known and what is not known. Though it may not appear likely that results can be achieved with managerial style that permits a reduction in what is known, the only requisite in terms of managerial knowledge is that which relates to the specific managerial functions assigned to any managerial role.

	Known to Self	Not Known to Self
Known to Others	1 Open	2 Blind
Not Known to Others	Hidden 3	Unknown 4

The Johari Window

Reprinted from Group Processes by Joseph Luft by permission of National Press Books.

When confusion exists between styles and functions, examination of the degree to which knowledge is appropriate can be judged on the defini-

---

[8] J. Luft, "The Johari Window," *Human Rights Training News*, 5 (1961), 6–7. See also Luft, *Group Processes* (Palo Alto, Calif.: National Press Publications, 1970).

tion of "interface" that will be presented later in this chapter: *function, interface is of value when it affords enough overlap to permit the exchange of management information* (not merely knowledge for the sake of knowledge), *but not so much overlap that roles are distorted.*

From this frame of reference, management styles can be the individual prerogative of each manager—of concern to administration only insofar as the manager fails to interface his functions successfully in achieving results. This further affords the unrestricted use of individual creativity and innovative talent in achieving results through the overlapping of managerial functions.

With reemphasized acknowledgement that clarification of both role and function must include organizational considerations (to be considered in Chapter Nine) and systems analysis (to be considered in Chapter Fourteen), attention is now turned to the specific application of roles in the management model.

APPLIED MANAGERIAL ROLES

Roles have been defined as performance of expected functions, and functions defined as duties that can be assigned to virtually any role—a single function to a single role in larger departments, several functions to a single role in smaller departments.

This in effect states that the performance of functions is of great importance to the application of managerial role; knowing all of the managerial functions would explain at least a major segment of all managerial roles, regardless of how the functions were distributed among the roles.

In approaching the actual *application* of managerial role, however, some concern must necessarily be directed to the level of the role. In terms of role level, it is important to relate to the actual criminal justice applications—to the police chiefs, chief probation officers, prison wardens, directors of institutions, sheriffs, district attorneys, and so forth—all examples of managerial level in criminal justice. To clear up any remaining confusion about variations in function, it should be noted that the managerial functions of defining results—of planning what is needed to achieve results, of implementing plans by selecting *who* is needed, and of achieving results by determining *how* things are done—are managerial functions and are the key functions of the management model. They are the *same* functions whether performed collectively by one top administrative role in a small department or by several role levels in a large department.

Role Level: Responsibility Versus Accountability

Role level retains considerable significance even though the four key functions remain consistent. This significance relates, primarily, to organizational *responsibility* as opposed to *accountability*. In the preceding chapter, the functional system of organization was discussed as administrative concern for results over and above managerial concern for who achieves them (as well as exceeding managerial concern for how they are achieved). In other words, what happens is more important than who does it or how it is done.

This of course refers to top administrative roles such as directors of institutions or chief probation officers. This stratification is appropriate because even in the smallest criminal justice organization, administrative responsibility divides into these four areas (who, what, why, and results).

Although this is by no means the only way to conceive of managerial priorities,[9] it is the most appropriate conceptualization of managerial priority in criminal justice.

Clarification, then, of managerial levels is to specifically isolate the concept of responsibility versus accountability within criminal justice.

Consider the example of a prison organization that employs between 300 and 600 total staff—personnel that includes guards, counselors, medical specialists, clerical, administrative, and ancillary staff. Imagine that responsibility for results is 100 percent vested in the office of the prison warden. Responsibility here is in the broadest social sense—the context of society in general—a society no longer indifferent to the possible absence of accountability, an idea that is beginning to emerge in the literature.

> We speak of the criminal justice system as if it were an integrated, functionally flourishing operation. Yet, it is a non-system, a failure. The reasons? There are many, but one is its unaccountability—except to itself. The so-called system is not a corporate entity. Its only allegiance is to itself. It has no moral conscience, no need to report to its immediate neighbors, let alone external agents. Thus it has become an index of our decadence, of our failure to treat each man as a part of humanity, of the pressures of numbers upon a bureaucracy that becomes bereft to emotion.[10]

In contrast to the warden's virtually complete responsibility, managerial accountability emerges in terms of the functions assigned to the managerial roles operating under the warden's direction. In this regard, there are three levels of managerial roles that are accountable (as opposed to his own responsibility) to the warden. But though they are increasingly accountable in a functional system, only the warden himself remains ultimately responsible. (As an aside, some theorists consider the warden's responsibility actually an *accountability* to the overall criminal justice system.)

---

[9] See, for example, John Senger's Spring 1971 *California Management Review* (Vol. 5, No. 5) article, "The Co-Manager Concept." See also any of the popular "matrix-management" literature, especially the seven books comprising the Addison-Wesley series on Organizational Development (Reading, Mass., 1969).

[10] Marvin E. Wolfgang, "Making the Criminal Justice System Accountable," *Crime and Delinquency* (January 1972), pp. 15–16.

In terms of the management model, however, the three levels of management below the warden have no responsibility for the subsystem but do have varying proportions of accountability (division commanders, middle-managers, and supervision). Ideally, knowing this is enough to determine level of managerial role. It also suggests the number and kinds of functions to be assigned to a particular role level. In other words, the warden holds his managers accountable to him, but only to the degree of their role level. Although these levels may have a great impact on determining which functions can be assigned to given roles, level and function are not synonymous.

Imagine that the four key managerial functions (*results, what, who,* and *how*) are disproportionally distributed among two relatively low-level managerial roles, leaving higher-level managers virtually free of specific functions. Such a plan for the redistribution of functions might make it possible for the warden to more successfully discharge his total responsibility for the prison—i.e., if he were to: (1) assign the definition of results to his own role; (2) conceive of division directors and commanders as executives and assign to their roles the definition of *whats*—an assignment that may well provide him an approximate index of 50 percent proportion of all managerial accountability; (3) distribute the remaining 50 percent of managerial accountability on the basis of 35 percent to middle managers and 15 percent to the first-line supervisory staff.

ACCOUNTABILITY BY ROLE LEVELS

	Responsibility %	Accountability %	Functions %
Role I (Warden)	100	0	1
Role II (Division Commanders)	0	50	2
Role III (Middle Managers)	0	35	3
Role IV (Supervision)	0	15	4

Although this example may serve to introduce the concept of various role levels, it fails to clarify the relationship of one level to another. For this reason, relationship between levels, already referred to as functional interfacing, will be considered.

FUNCTION INTERFACE: ENOUGH OVERLAP FOR COMMUNICATION

The words *what, who, how,* and *results* (for definitions, refer to the Glossary at beginning of chapter) have been used thus far for the purpose of conceptually isolating those functions that permit greater managerial yield. They are also useful in isolating the precise point at which managerial functions interface or overlap.

As for the word "interface," managerial consultants tend to disagree on its definition. That used for the management model is suggested in part by the 1971 Third Edition of the International Business Machines Data Processing Glossary (GC 20–1699–2), which defines *interface* as a "shared boundary." Another common definition of the word is that used by organizational development consultants, which suggests a sort of confrontation between groups of people within an organization.

For purposes of examining the relationship of one managerial function to another, however, "interface" will be defined here in these words: *function interface is of value when it affords enough overlap to permit the exchange of management information, but not so much overlap that roles and role levels are distorted.*

Put another way, managerial functions must be connected for communication, but distinct for *accountability*.

Interfaces hold (or fail to hold) the department together at the points where criminal justice management meets criminal justice "labor." Although the concern of this volume is *management*, it must never be forgotten that the results are ultimately achieved by those who are "managed."

Function interface then, by the definition used in this chapter, focuses directly upon the relationship of distinct managerial functions to other distinct managerial functions.

Perhaps the manner in which these interfaces occur will emerge through careful consideration of the following diagram:

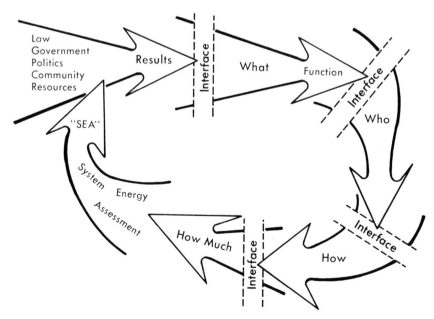

Role and Function Relationships

In terms of function interface, then, the definition of "results" is only one of many of the ingredients of success. Indeed, later chapters will clarify that its definition depends in large measure upon the definition of existing staff resources available to achieve results—a kind of participatory management to be discussed in subsequent chapters.

"Participatory management" of course refers to the variety of considerations covered in Chapter Two, particularly under the discussion of the Likert influence. In addition to the following chapter's elaboration of the *how* function as participatory, the ramifications of this concept in criminal justice administration will be considered in many other contexts throughout this volume, with particular attention to the frequency of quasi-military organizational structures.

Returning to specific concern for the actual interfacing of functions, *results, what, who,* and *how* functions will now be elaborated.

To be certain that these words do not lose their connection with criminal justice, an example of the *how* function is a policeman directing traffic (a routine part of police operations). An example of the *who* function is a captain who staffs the operation and distributes command power. The *what* function is exemplified by the duties of a division director in a probation department designing plans for managerial programs. With this in mind, results will now be considered, and ultimately, closer consideration given to the other functions as well.

Results

In terms of role level, the managerial function of defining results is necessarily a part of top administration. For one thing, results include integrating government and community expectations as well as support. They are also what is to be achieved in the future on behalf of the staff, clientele, and the government and community as well.

Results are functions of top administration because they must be defined in advance. The complexity of this requirement is suggested in consideration of interfaces involving the managerial function of *what*, which begins with an interface between the results function and the *what* function.

What

In small criminal justice departments, this interface cannot occur because both the *results* function and the *what* function may be integrated into a single managerial role. In larger departments, however, the *what* is customarily assigned to an executive level role that interfaces with the top administrative role.

For purposes of clarifying both the interface and the previously discussed accountability, some consideration of the component parts of a managerial *what* function might be useful.

There are four main parts, the first of which is a specific statement of what is specifically planned for—what the *objective* is in terms of beginning to achieve long-range results. The second part is the time available, or the date when completion is expected. This date is by no means an estimate as will be noted in the following chapter, where the scientific nature of determining the time variable will be discussed in terms of synergetics that include concern for the third and fourth parts of a what: the measurement of success by specific criteria, and the alternatives available to management to achieve results should these criteria not be met.

Specific, tangible measurements with clear definitions of success and failure constitute the third part of a what. This measurement is by no means guessed at, either. Indeed, measurement emerges as the most critical aspect of administrative planning. Police chiefs, captains, chief probation officers, directors of corrections—criminal justice administrators in general can find a great advantage in utilizing it to influence all major management decisions.

As the systems model is elaborated, it will also become clear that the measurement segment of the *what* function relates to managerial function interfacing in two ways: *implementation whats* and *cost benefit whats*.

For purposes of this discussion, an *implementation what* is simply the getting started and measuring how well the starting activities move ahead. The *cost benefit whats* include measurements of the criminal justice programming that is already under way in an organization. (Considerable attention will be given this subject in later discussions—particularly budget discussions at the conclusion of Chapter Six.)

The fourth part of a *what* consists of the managerial alternatives available if completion date and/or measurement are not met for the purpose of continuing to achieve results regardless of unforeseen difficulties.

One method of systematically producing these four *what* components is through a modified "decision tree," which will be explored in several other contexts throughout this volume. A fairly rich literature exists on the concept of decision trees.[11] For purposes of discussing managerial function interfacing, the decision tree concept is seen in terms of (1) A start, (2) A finish, and (3) A route.

From this frame of reference, it can be seen that results definitions are a kind of starting point. *What* it takes to start is not a part of the results, but a separate managerial function. Consider the following diagram:

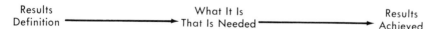

Results Definition	What It Is That Is Needed	Results Achieved

[11] See, for example, E. Dale, *Management Theory and Practice* (New York: McGraw-Hill, Inc., 1969), pp. 551–57. See also "Decision Trees Offer Clear Alternatives," *Administrative Management,* (November 1967), pp. 30–31; F. S. Drechler, "Decision Tree and the Second Law," *Operational Research Quarterly* (December 1968), pp. 409–19; R. A. Flinn, "Decision Tree Analysis," *Research Management* (January 1970), pp. 27–34, and p. 181 of the May issue.

But the *what* can take many forms, depending on department size, organizational structure, existing resources, and so forth. One approach can assume the availability of everything needed, another can assume the virtual absence of everything needed, and a third can fall in between.

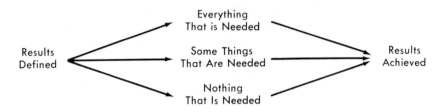

Moving a step further, even the route can be greatly influenced by considerations such as changing community needs.

But because the *what*, like the objectives in the management by objectives theory, are intermediate goals subject to regular measurement, a great deal of flexibility remains possible while keeping results (long-range goals) constant. This is vital in terms of the interface between the *what* function and the *who* function when they are assigned to different managerial roles.

For one thing, the *who* function performs in terms of an awareness of the alternatives produced by the modified decision tree. It further permits operational management to occur in the context of various staffing priorities which in turn are related to administrative planning.

The decision tree itself, in addition to proving of great assistance in the interfacing of managerial functions, also provides a source of considerably greater precision in determining completion dates and success measures that are essential to the *what* definition. Moreover, the same alternatives used to facilitate the function interface between *what* and *who* affords a graphic configuration of organizational planning that clarifies alternatives "never starting from scratch."

For example, a chief of police defining the reduction of traffic accidents as the results to be achieved might see his executive staff (in a large department, or himself in a smaller department) begin with a choice of two *whats*. The first alternative might be to establish a working agreement with the press for an intensive public relations program. The second might be transferring officers from his patrol division to his traffic division for intensive traffic programs. The options beyond these two *whats* will of course guide the selection and are clearly delineated on the elaboration of decision trees to be covered in subsequent chapters.

Hypothetically, should the measurement of success not be met by the first alternatives, the managerial change to the option involving staff transfers would be pursued. Such alternatives are continually available as various *what* objectives are met until results are accomplished.

Measurement. With regard to measurement, the concept of a linear system (i.e., input, process, and output) offers a great deal of clarification. Specifically, the *what* measurements occurs just prior to *process* becoming *output.* In later discussions of managerial decisions as they relate to decision trees, it will be noted that the requisite measurement can easily be coupled to a planned managerial alternative in a program that achieves results even when the current program fails.

Measurement is either quantitative, qualitative, or both. But above all else, it is *explicit.*

One area in which concrete quantitative measure is readily available in most instances is the budget. In later discussions of the fiscal process of the systems model, it will be noted that cost benefit analysis affords managerial leverage. Costs and costing procedures also provide a tangible index on one facet of accomplishment, accomplishment remaining the prime priority of the model.

In the discussion that follows regarding the *who* function, it will be noted that ongoing or reflexive measurement is available within the system process through the interfacing of management functions, as illustrated in the following diagram:

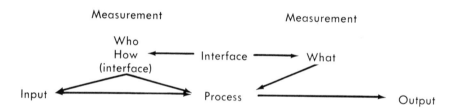

As in the case of a *what* measurement, the *who/how* measurement can be either quantitative, qualitative, or both, but also must be explicit.

Recalling the modified decision tree concept discussed earlier, measurement can be clarified diagrammatically. Consider the following:

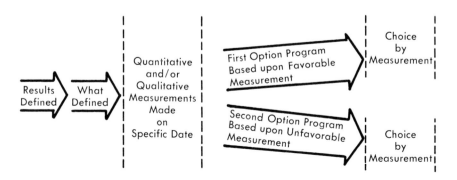

Looking at the use of measurement in terms of the interfaces, managerial functions establish a kind of direction-oriented system—a system that never raises the question of whether or not results are being sought, but instead focuses on *how* they are achieved. In other words, the inability to achieve results the ideal way merely means that they will be achieved in some less ideal way (instead of meaning they won't be achieved at all).

From this frame of reference, the *who* function and its interfacing process will now be considered.

Who

In terms of impact, the position is taken here that at least in departments large enough to include middle management in the staffing pattern, the greatest influence on successful managerial operations occurs at that role level. Because of this, it appears to be a natural level for assignment of the *who* function—the managerial function of "staffing" managerial plans. Interfacing as this function does with the *what* and the *how*, the middle is extremely strategic.

The literature of criminal justice began to acknowledge this strategic personnel function of middle-management role some time ago. As Harold Butterfield said more than a decade ago, "Middle management has a greater impact on working relationships than anywhere else in the hierarchy."[12] The increasing significance of this role has, in part, related to the steady emergence of electronic data-processing programming. But by far the most significant variable in middle management is this impact on staff—a strategic personnel or who function.

Some definition of middle management may prove useful to clarify the position taken that this level of management is "natural" for the *who* activities. *A middle manager is one who supervises other supervisors but does not direct a major division of department programming.*

In smaller departments, of course, the managerial *who* function may well be performed within the same role as performing the functions of defining *results* and *whats*. In any event, whoever performs this strategic *who* function emerges as a strategically critical manager in terms of the *who/how* measurement.

Who/How Measurement

One of the more pragmatic reasons for insisting on the *who* function interfacing with the *how* function has to do with measurement of the same variety already discussed in terms of the *what/who* interface. Results definitions presumably establish the end result. Implicit in these end results are

---

[12] F. Harold Butterfield, "Middle Management's Responsibility for Employee Development," *California Youth Authority Quarterly* (Winter 1960).

certain broad definitions of success. Rensis Likert eloquently sums up the problems involved if limitations are placed on measurement:

> The only measurement provided [supervisors and managers] . . . are measurements of such end-result variables as productivity and cost. . . . If managers are to make the best use of their experience, they need measurements which will paint for them a full and accurate picture of their experience . . . an organization's need for accurate measurements increases as it increases in size. . . .[13]

Although Likert elaborated these remarks in a managerial context somewhat different than the systems model, the concept of measurement and attendant problems is essentially the same. Measurements discussed thus far will hopefully retain the same broad-based success definition developed in the *results/what* interface when approaching the end result through the measurements of the *who/how* interface. In this context, the *who* function provides measurement beyond simple end-results to insure the depth of *results* definitions that are involved. Indeed, insofar as attendant problems of measurement are concerned, the *who* function affords managerial measurement on a much broader base than the relatively explicit quantitative and qualitative measurements accompanying the *what/who* interface.

In what will be discussed as "reflexive synergetics" in the following chapter, the wide range of measurements are described as generated by the relationship of the *who* function to the *how* function long before the *what* measurements are taken. Each of these "premeasurements" is geared to the problem inherent in what Likert referred to as "inadequate measurements" and "erroneous decisions":

> Working from seriously inadequate measurements, the different levels of management today are expected to guide and change the causal variables—including their own behavior—so as to maintain the end result.[14]

As the managerial *how* function is considered, particular attention will be given the specific activities involved—presumably activities of the role of first-line supervisor—whether he is a supervising probation officer, a patrol sergeant, or any number of other first-line managers in criminal justice.

How

The *how* function is of course the final key managerial function of the model—it is the "how it's done" management function.

The distinction between what is to be done and who is to do it focuses

---

[13] Likert, *New Patterns of Management* (New York: McGraw-Hill, Inc., 1961), pp. 69–70.

[14] Ibid., p. 73.

on this final distinction of *how* it is to be done, provided administrative and executive management have retained more concern for what gets done than for who is doing it and how.

In small departments, this function can be included in some managerial role that may also include the *who* function. But just as in the case of combining *results* and *what* being easier than combining *what* and *who*, the *how* function is more productive when *interfaced* with a *who* function than when combined.

This is true for a number of reasons relating to the synergetics to be presented in the following chapter, but more fundamentally, it relates to the problem of direct supervision of plans that are constantly in stages of development beyond the immediate activities being supervised. Put another way, a supervisor who is "on top" of what is going on retains the *how* function with ease, but may be hard-pressed to back off and examine the managerial implications of the program.

But whether the *how* function is merely one of others in a broader managerial role of a small department, or the entire role of a single supervisor in the large department, it remains management's influence over how things get done—the things to be done having already been managerially determined. Again it is stressed that this determination, as will be seen in subsequent chapters, is not a process of continuous orders or command management.

In this regard, some degree of self-motivation may be assumed, but the purpose of the systems model is to produce a method of interfacing various functions in such a way as to enrich the probability of self-motivation, which is defined as follows:

> Self-motivation is the highest and most desirable type of motivation. It is always operative. It does not depend upon the pressures of any *particular* set of internal circumstances for its operation. . . .[15]

But while the systems model may avoid functioning as a command management method partially through self-motivation, the *how* function frequently emerges as the managerial source of a wide range of stimulation, from the most altruistic and ideal to such things as criticism cast in a positive philosophy. "The goal of criticism is to leave the person with the feeling he's been helped."[16]

In the context of this extremely wide range of getting things done as a functional responsibility, the managerial *how* function is seen as virtually the same whether assigned to a high-level person or a first-line supervisor.

---

[15] P. Ecker, J. MacRae, V. Quellette, and C. Telford, *Handbook for Supervisors* (Englewood Cliffs, N.J.: Prentice-Hall, 1963), p. 49.

[16] *Bits and Pieces*, Vol. C., No. 2, p. 16.

With this in mind, consider the *how* function implications of the following supervisory questionnaire:[17]

Answer affirmatively in the "Hit" column and negatively in the "Out" column. When you are finished, add up the number of hits and divide into the number of times at bat to get your supervisory batting average.

At Bat	Hit	Out
1. Do you give employees reasonable deadlines?		
2. Do you plan your work so that it is always completed on time?		
3. Do you thoroughly understand the work of each person under you?		
4. Do you make it easy for employees to talk with you?		
5. Do you personally see to it that people in your department work under good conditions?		
6. Are you sympathetic with workers' problems?		
7. Do you always give clear and understandable instructions?		
8. Do you compliment employees when they do a job well?		
9. Are you considered even-tempered?		
10. Do you make every effort to keep grievances from arising?		
11. When complaints do arise, do you try to handle them honestly and objectively?		
12. Do you have a good worker trained to be a back-up man to yourself?		
13. Do you always reprimand in private?		
14. Do you encourage suggestions and ideas from your people?		
15. Do you avoid passing the buck on mistakes?		
16. Do you always give credit where credit is due?		
17. Are you cooperative with other department heads and foremen?		
18. Do you always set a good example yourself?		
19. Do you make efforts to improve your ability in human relations and technical skill?		
20. Can you take constructive criticism?		
21. Do you keep employees posted on their progress?		
22. Do you keep your promises?		

[17] Edward B. Gale, *What a Foreman Should Know About Constructive Discipline* (Chicago: Dortnall Corp. Press, 1971), pp. 12–13.

23. Do you avoid jumping to conclusions? _____ _____
24. Do you give reasons for changes, or lack of changes, when needed? _____ _____
25. Do you avoid sarcasm? _____ _____
26. Do you give employees the real facts to cut down rumors? _____ _____
27. Do you make an effort to remember names and faces? _____ _____
28. If someone disagrees with you, can you usually argue the point without getting irritated? _____ _____
29. Do you make special efforts to fully indoctrinate new employees? _____ _____
30. Do you avoid a "superior" attitude? _____ _____
31. Do you avoid favoritism? _____ _____
32. Can you make decisions promptly? _____ _____
33. Do you help employees work toward advancement? _____ _____
34. Are you impartial in making assignments? _____ _____
35. Can you accept change without getting upset? _____ _____
36. Do you have confidence in yourself? _____ _____
37. Are you a self-starter? _____ _____

AVERAGE _____ percent   TOTAL _____ _____

The nature of "hits" and "outs" tends to emerge as a cogent rationale for allowing great flexibility in the measurements involved in *who/how* interfacing. With this flexibility in mind, attention is now turned to the managerial skills suggested for achieving results on the basis of interfacing the functions just discussed—"skills" as opposed to "styles." Though these skills (like styles) are secondary to achieving results, they are nonetheless, necessary to systematically achieve results even when function interfaces are well-designed and assigned appropriately to managerial roles.

THE MANAGERIAL SKILLS OF THE MODEL

Perhaps one way to introduce this final consideration clarifying managerial roles is through what McGregor called "the manager's view of reality: cosmology."[18] In defining cosmology as "the theory of the universe as a whole and the laws governing it," he developed a conceptual tool in which managerial skills can be brought to bear on criminal justice. It is this "managerial cosmology" that forms the background against which managerial skills either succeed or fail to make the performance of functions possible. The context of this background is clarified best in McGregor's comments:

[18] McGregor, *The Professional Manager*, pp. 4–30.

In some sense every individual's cosmology is unique. In other respects all individuals share common beliefs about reality. However, no cosmology *is* reality; it is human perception of reality.[19]

Stressing both individual uniqueness and common beliefs in terms of perception of reality, the managerial skills needed to perform the managerial functions of the model might be thought of as *conceptual skills, program skills, human skills,* and *political skills.*

Conceptual Skills

Isolating various skills and distinguishing them from other skills may suggest a belief that skills operate independently. The manager's "reality" is that frequently the skills that will be discussed as program do not get off the ground without the skills discussed as *human,* or *"political"*—regardless of how well the function interfaces may be working. But to relate each of these managerial skills directly to function and role, each must be distinguished enough so it is possible to determine its individual presence or absence; the problems of interfacing frequently trace directly to the absence of one or more of the skills.

Conceptual skills are frequently the underpinnings of the other three managerial skills. Separated from the other three, however, conceptual skills emerge as the manager's ability to integrate theoretical abstractions and possibilities with the pragmatics of experience, tradition, and resources limitation. (It is here noted that these are to the absolute exclusion of concern with managerial *style.*) Many consider the conceptual skills to be simply "imagination"; others claim a great deal of semantic difference by calling them "creative."

Program Skills

Program skills are those required once theoretical possibility has been integrated with practical reality through use of conceptual skills. Program skill, then, is actually managerial skill needed in translating a concept into specific plans. At this point it is worth noting that on a broad scale, criminal justice administrators defining results draw heavily on conceptual skills followed, in large agencies, by executive determination of the *whats* that draw on the program skills. But also noteworthy is the need of human and political skills for definitions of results and whats.

Human Skills

A story is told that illustrates the essence of what is referred to here as

[19] Ibid., p. 4.

human skills. A troubled father was called into a high school principal's office and told that his two teenage sons were about to be expelled if they did not stop swearing at the teachers. Desperately concerned, the father decided to implement a drastic program the following morning.

At the breakfast table, he confronted his oldest son with the question, "What would you like for breakfast?" and received the answer, "Give me some of those God-damned corn-flakes."

Enraged, the father knocked his son to the floor and turned to the second boy, asking, "And what would you like for breakfast?" The second son, having observed the sequence, quickly responded, "You can bet your sweet ass I don't want any of those God-damned corn-flakes!"

Much more than *communication* is involved in this story. A judgment of the father that the message he "sent" was the message his son "received" would show the absence of what is referred to her as *human skills*. Hopefully, the presence or absence of such skills is clearly relevant to successful interfacing of managerial functions.

Political Skills

Specific consideration of the relationships between criminal justice management and "politics" will be the subject of Chapter Fifteen.

In terms of *political skill*, the definition used here is somewhat different in that it relates directly to a manager's ability to weigh consequences— to distinguish between a "solution" per se and a "feasible solution." (Some decisions might solve fewer problems than they create.)

The political skills needed by managers in the model being presented focus conceptual skills on pertinent theory, on pertinent pragmatics, or on both. These same political skills then would influence program skills toward consequence-oriented managerial behavior—arranging the function interfaces toward achieving results.

Perhaps of even greater yield is when political skills combined with human skills guide a manager's judgment through functional interfacing toward combinations of innovation and productivity.

Though results achievement retains priority, the plan and purpose of the management training that will be presented in Chapter Eight is actually the development of all four of these managerial skills.

SUMMARY

Chapter Four has introduced an output-oriented management model in terms of interfacing roles, functions, styles, and skills. Acknowledging the inherent problem of attempting to clarify the complexities of management role (particularly in criminal justice), a strategy of isolating *functions* was pursued. Further acknowledgement was made of the inability of line men promoted to managerial positions to stop functioning in terms of line work and perform in a managerial capacity.

Role was discussed and defined as the performance of a "position-description" combined with expectations of a given managerial *status*—this status was later discussed in terms of *level*. *Function* was discussed as a significant variable in role definition and defined as a "duty having special purpose." Interface was defined as enough overlap of function to permit exchange of management information but not so much overlap as to distort roles. Managerial *style* was reviewed from previous chapter discussions and related as a significant variable in the managerial role definition. Style itself was discussed in terms of the various positions on the managerial grid. The relevance of managerial style was minimized in relation to the achievement of results, style being presented as of no managerial concern unless demonstrably related to failure to achieve results.

Emphasis was placed on *measurement* of results achievement in several contexts, but particularly quantitative as opposed to qualitative measurement.

The technical difficulties involving development of sophisticated measurement, along with other scientific methods for developing the systems model itself, were discussed in the context of consultants and other specialties (a subject to be further discussed in Chapter Fourteen). Other variables such as organizational considerations were related to management role but postponed for elaboration to Chapter Nine.

Management roles were discussed in terms of *responsibility* and *accountability*, which in turn were related to role levels. Accountability was translated into *proportions* and stratified along lines of role level.

The key functions of the systems model were presented in terms of interfaces between results achievement (*what* is required to achieve results, *who* will do the achieving, and *how* the achieving is to occur). The relationship of these specific functions to roles and role levels was further elaborated.

Finally, the managerial skills necessary to obtain maximum achievement of results from the management model was contrasted with managerial skills, defined as *conceptual skills, program skills, human skills,* and *political skills.*

QUESTIONS

1. Discuss the problems involved in attempts to clarify managerial roles.

2. Discuss the advantages of role clarity.

3. Contrast a manager's former role to his present role after at least two managerial promotions
    (a) in terms of function,
    (b) in terms of style.

4. Contrast and define managerial roles, functions, and styles.

5. Relate "level of responsibility" to managerial role

   (a) in terms of function,
   (b) in terms of status or rank,
   (c) in terms of proportion of accountability.

6. Define the functions of

   (a) results
   (b) whats
   (c) who
   (d) how.

7. Define role-interface.

8. Discuss the relationship of managerial skills to managerial roles.

9. Define the following skills:

   (a) conceptual
   (b) program
   (c) human
   (d) political

10. Distinguish between political skills as discussed, and overall managerial skills involved in criminal justice dealings with real politics.

ANNOTATED REFERENCES

BERKLEY, GEORGE E., *The Administrative Revolution, Notes on the Passing of Organization Man.* Englewood Cliffs, N.J.: Prentice-Hall, 1971. Chapters One and Two prove of singular interest to the reader retaining doubts that management is surviving well without explicit, goal-oriented, functional roles.

BOSTICCO, MARY, *Creative Techniques for Management.* London: Business Books, 1971. This entire volume elaborates the overall implications of what this chapter presented as managerial skills.

LUFT, J., "The Johari Window," *Human Rights Training News,* 5, (1961), 6–7. A good general context for what was discussed in this chapter as functions, styles, and role-interface.

McGREGOR, DOUGLAS, *The Professional Manager,* CAROLINE McGREGOR and WARREN BENNIS, eds. New York: McGraw-Hill, 1967. (See also his *Leadership and Motivation,* Cambridge, Mass.: M.I.T. Press, 1966.) An in-depth elaboration of the implications of dealing with management as a profession.

WOLFGANG, MARVIN E., "Making the Criminal Justice System Accountable," *Crime and Delinquency,* January 1972, pp. 15–22.

CHAPTER 5

Effectiveness Versus Efficiency: Synergetics

GLOSSARY

RESULTS—administratively defined department goals ; **WHAT**—operational determination of what is needed to achieve results along with precise measurement ; **WHO**—managerial determination of operational staffing ; **HOW**—supervisory determination of methods ; **TASK FORCE DEVELOPMENT LAB**—a middle management group performing the who function ; **SYSTEM ENERGY ASSESSMENT**—managerial determination of staff capability through the how function ; **SYNERGETICS**—managerial synthesis of resources and defined results.

Against the background presented in the preceding chapter of the complexities of role and function, this chapter will deal with the managerial distinction between *efficient* and *effective* function interfacing by elaborating the actual activities of the managerial interfaces involved in the model.

But before exploring this useful distinction a case example might prove enlightening.

Imagine a relatively large probation department that has become experienced and sophisticated in developing programs not typically associated with the programs of a traditionally administered probation department—programs involving such things as crime prevention, delinquency prevention, community centers, drug abuse, family crisis centers, and a host of similar criminal justice projects. Further imagine that the administration of this department is able to supplement pertinent programs with a federal grant (budget) that permits the coordination of some fourteen different law enforcement jurisdictions participating in a program intended to divert children who are not delinquent (but merely family problems) away from the juvenile justice system.

Because of the experience and sophistication in previous innovative criminal justice programming, the probation department experiences relatively no managerial problem in bringing representatives from the many police agencies together for training in family theory, and consultation on program implementation.

From this perspective, there is virtually no doubt that the probation department is unquestionably *efficient* in terms of its management function interfaces.

1. *Results* defined—probation administration interfacing with all police subsystems of the region to develop the consentient goal of reducing the number of nondelinquent children in custody.

2. *What* defined—probation executives interfacing first with administration, then with the *who* function, then planning and executing a federal grant proposal along with peripheral managerial programming.

3. *Who* defined—probation middle managers interfacing with the *how* function and devising an outstanding task force to implement the *what*.

4. *How* defined—an exceptionally qualified first-line supervisor interfacing with the probation officers assigned to the task force and designing a program for training and assisting participating police officers.

In spite of the extremely efficient functional interfacing just described, it soon becomes clear that three of the fourteen agencies are still bringing children who are obviously family problems into custody. Informally, it is made clear by the administration of these three police jurisdictions that there is a general awareness of the nature of the problems of most of the children being booked, but it is clear that, to them, booking is easier than getting involved in family hassles.

Independent of the regrettable problem of involving nondelinquent children in a process geared primarily for delinquency, the sequence just describes illustrates a thoroughly efficient probation department that is only partially effective.

Of course the breakdown in effectiveness cannot be attributed to an inadequacy on the part of the probation department. On the contrary, effectiveness in eleven of fourteen jurisdictions is outstanding—particularly when many conceive of law enforcement as being isolated from the remainder of the system of criminal justice. Nevertheless, this program serves as still another example of criminal justice efficiency exceeding effectiveness—and this is the theme of this chapter and the core of the whole management model.

At this point we have established that differences between efficiency and effectiveness are possible and may in fact determine the usefulness or value of procedures and policies, and that policy-setting is part of the management model being presented when such differences occur.

With this in mind, consider the following quotation:

> A policy is a settled course to be followed. Actually, a policy may be laid down by anyone in supervisory authority over another, so long as it does not conflict with a policy enforced by a higher authority. A policy may thus pertain to any aspect of the business over which the policy maker has authority.
>
> It is a responsibility of the top executive to distinguish between the important policies and those of lesser importance, and to leave the lesser ones for determination by his subordinates.
>
> In other words, it is a responsibility of the top executive, within the limits of his authority, to lay down the most important policies under which the business is run. Successful top executives in their policy decision-making usually seek the recommendation of their principal subordinates.[1]

This definition permits a distinction between efficiency and effectiveness to specifically determine the value of policy-making.

What will be referred to as "synergetics" later in this chapter is actually an effort to guide the momentum of the organizational system by systematic function interfacing instead of by policy. "Synergetics" is an effort to bring out the most creative, innovative, and *effective* methods of achieving goals through the use of functional interfacing.

The management model is designed to gain participation of all managers in the actual operation of the organization. And beyond effectively utilizing all managerial talent, it stresses a fuller involvement of staff in developing the resources of the organization. To a degree, synergetics involves staff in the development of some of the programs in which resources are to be managerially programmed.

This relatively flattened pyramid needs some clarification before moving on to a discussion of synergetics.

The Flattened Pyramid

The very nature of police work defies organizational structure that does not retain elements of chain authority. Flattening this particular pyramid

---

[1] George W. Peak, "Policy-Making and Organizing Responsibilities," *Michigan Business Review* (November 1971), p. 1.

can achieve a great number of advantages for an administrator seeking results and distinguishing between efficiency and effectiveness, but the *degree* to which this is done is crucial in criminal justice.

Of course the notion of participatory management is anything but unique. By some standards, the retention of any form of pyramid or command structure leaves the administrator vulnerable to clogged communication, staff rebellion, inefficient and ineffective work processes, and a very clear image of a plantation overseer. Moreover, some rather compelling literature suggests that the era of managerial influence through typical bureaucracy has nearly ended.

> To replace the crumbling pyramid, a new organizational structure is emerging. I say emerging, not emerged, for what took thousands of years to evolve will not vanish in a night or in a year. However, the contours of this new structure are already beginning to appear.[2]

The author of this statement goes on to elaborate a managerial concept substantially removed from the systems model. Nevertheless, the cogency of the quote is valid wherever the organizational pyramid structure is considered.

For example, urban problems related to ethnic, juvenile, and drug, and even traffic factors may suggest modification of the way many police departments are organized. Whether or not a police chief, prison warden, judge, or any other criminal justice administrator agrees with the future being forecast in this quotation, he must at least consider the suggested implications in relation to the current need for changes in the criminal justice system. Whether or not a criminal justice organization is structured as a command pyramid, the plain truth is that executives who manage to achieve results do so with the planning, sensor-matrix information, and fiscal procedures that will be the subject of later chapters.

Removing the "giving and following orders" focus from the system of criminal justice can probably be traced to the increasing areas of specialty and expertise that twentieth-century technology has brought to bear on the complexities of a rapidly urbanizing society and on all segments of the pyramid.

In terms of the pyramid, the managerial approach discussed briefly in Chapter Three as organizational development also flattens the command structure—in some ways similar to the management model.

Organizational development is widespread as well as diversified, and therefore difficult to isolate. Many, if not most, OD consultants, however, would probably agree that the six books comprising the original Addison-

---

[2] George E. Berkley, *The Administrative Revolution* (Englewood Cliffs, N.J.: Prentice-Hall, Inc., 1971), p. 24.

Wesley Series on organizational development (cited in Chapter Three) fairly well cover the highlights of OD.

One of the authors in that series, Warren G. Bennis, sums up the OD position succinctly:

> Organizational Development does not prescribe any particular [style of leadership] other than an open and confrontive one, which is anything but [permissive]. . . . The basic value underlying all organizational development theory and practice is that of *choice*. Through focused attention and through the collection and feedback of relevant data to relevant people, more choices become available and hence better decisions are made.[3]

In this particular regard, there is an extremely significant similarity between our systems model and organizational development.

But the style of management remains directly related to how flat the managerial pyramid can become. In this regard, a significant difference between the systems model and organizational development exists: the systems model retains a specific degree of command structure, and there is enough structure to insist that style adjust whenever results are in jeopardy in any way.

Recalling the previous chapter discussion of the prison warden having total responsibility (as opposed to the accountability of his managers), McGregor's philosophy is useful in understanding the rationale underpinning the systems model. Writing on what he regarded as a conviction that "the boss must be the boss," he stated:

> It took a couple of years, but I finally began to realize that a leader cannot avoid the exercise of authority any more than he can avoid responsibility for what happens to his organization.[4]

The implications of this statement, even though isolated somewhat out of context, nevertheless bring into focus the continuing relationship of managerial style and fuller utilization of management functions within the configuration of a pyramid. And from this same frame of reference, a position on leadership as well as style within the pyramid can be adopted for the systems model. Regardless of the individual manager's personal style, the function-interface cannot permit any more accountability for management functions at lower levels than is permitted by the top administrator's responsibility for what happens to his organization.

Stating this position on leadership and style within the pyramid an-

---

[3] Bennis, *Organizational Development: Its Nature, Origin and Prospects* (Reading, Mass.: Addison-Wesley Publishing Co., 1969), p. 17.

[4] McGregor, *Leadership and Motivation;* Warren G. Bennis, Edgar H. Schein, and Caroline McGregor, eds. (Cambridge, Mass.: M. I. T., University Press, 1966), p. 67.

other way, any combinations of "styles" limit the use of participatory management approaches to flattening the pyramid—especially in terms of McGregor's definition of "responsibility for what happens to his organization."

Although the purpose of the management model is to systematically utilize a fuller, richer range of managerial and staff talent, the model *at no time* suggests that the impact of subordinates on the organization is anything but the top administrator's direct responsibility.

In effect, when the synergetics of function interfacing occurs, the top administrator is still responsible for the impact of these interfaces—even though he may be holding various managerial role levels accountable. The accountability is to top administration, whereas the top administrator is accountable to both government and community as well as responsible for what happens to his organization.

One of the more dramatic and succinct approaches to drive home this point would be to place upon the desk of all top administrators a sign reading *THE BUCK STOPS HERE.*

Any negative implications may be further tempered by the emphasis that is placed on clear role and function definition in the model, combined with clear accountability connections between the various functions through interfacing.

Within this context of criminal justice, attention is turned to "reflexive synergetics," a term that describes a very valuable management concept. It also refers to the process of combining those specific interfacing activities that will be discussed shortly.

REFLEXIVE SYNERGETICS THROUGH FUNCTION INTERFACE

As with many other managerial terms, "synergetics" is a combination of derivations and contractions from related words such as "synergestics" and "synergy." All such terms tend to vary in meaning with the individual using the term.

To complicate the definitional process even further, some relatively common managerial terms are not defined in some common sources. For example, many consider the *1971 IBM Data Processing Glossary* as carrying an extremely comprehensive list of terms related to programs that lend themselves to automation and computerization, but it does not list the word "synergy."[5] For purposes of the model, however, we will include a useful term defined there that relates to synergetics: "synthesis," meaning "the combination of parts to form a whole." From this point it can be noted that Synergy, a California-based management consulting firm, defines its name as

---

[5] *IBM Data Processing Glossary*, 3rd ed., Poughkeepsie, N.Y. (GC 20–1699–2).

meaning "To work together; combined or cooperative action or force." Abraham Maslow's further definition is also cited by the Synergy firm: "Synergy is the state which exists when the institutions of an organization are so arranged that an individual by attempting to meet his own needs also meets the needs of the organization."[6]

From the following elements, then, we can see our definition of function interfacing emerging:

1. Synergetics are a synthesis of organizational resources
2. Synergetics are a cooperative action or force
3. Synergetics represent the expression of individual talent toward organizational results

The final definition of synergetics is then: *Results-oriented action and force as resources cooperatively synthesized through expression of individual talent.*

Reflexive Synergetics

Before proceeding into the model's use of role interfaces between management functions, some consideration will be given to the nature of the synergetic process. Perhaps the word "responsive" would serve the purpose of the function interface just as well as "reflexive." But because such great emphasis is placed upon the reduction of wasted effort or lost resources, reducing redundance, and focusing staff energy, the choice of "reflexive" is an attempt to show that the nature of the function interfaces should be as automatic as possible but in a specific direction. The word is intended to imply that synergetics consists of a *systematic* sequence of function interfaces that are productive because of the inner relations of subsystems within a main system.

From this it can be seen that the synthesis of resources is unlikely if timing is not correct. If it can be assumed that staff members who *prefer* program participation will outproduce those who do not want to participate, it is obvious that management must make participation available at the time the eagerness occurs. But this timing, however critical it may be, is only one part of the interfacing process. Another critical factor involves the judgment involved in managerial determinations regarding the use of existing resources—the "appled managerial skills" concept discussed earlier. Managerial judgment, then, can be conceived of in terms of the reflexive synergetics that emerge when function interfacing occurs. Hence, the trick is for management to first discover resources, then, without losing time, use function-related judgment to synthesize these resources into goal achievement.

---

[6] *Synergy Basic Skills Course,* 2nd printing (Synergy, 4242 Manuela Court, Palo Alto, Calif., 1970), p. 1.

The functional definitions of managerial judgments can be understood better if the diagram on p. 71 is consulted. It can be seen that bringing managerial judgment to bear ultimately depends upon a clear understanding of the function of each manager. In combining administrative goals with staff resources, the range of judgments for any given manager is obviously simplified in terms of his specific function.

In terms of reflexive synergetics through functional interfacing, consider the position of managerial judgment in the following diagram:

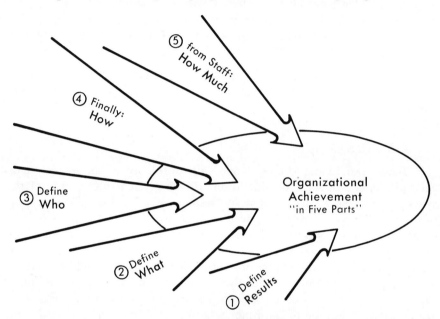

The way in which function interfacing will be considered for the re mainder of this chapter is in terms of the actual application of reflexive synergetics—the specific activities of criminal justice managers involved in interfaces that create a very productive "cycle."

SPECIFIC ACTIVITIES AS A PRODUCTIVE CYCLE

Having considered the reflexive synergetics of function interfacing, the specific activities involved in these interfaces will now be considered in terms of the cycle they form.

The supervisory determination of methods to be used begins the productive cycle in the sense that organizational resources are first determined in this function, and this is the determination upon which results are based. This, then, can be considered the initial point in the managerial cycle of synergetics.

The *How* Function

With the assumption that has already been made in terms of the *how* function being ideally suited for a first-line supervisory role (although possibly in another role level in a smaller department), the interface between *how* and the staff function of *how much* readily lends itself to the kinds of activities likely to occur in a typical staff meeting. Of course, against the background of management functions, "how much" refers to the degree of staff willingness to provide resources. In addition to whatever routine business might be accomplished at this meeting, the supervisor might post the following chart:[7] This chart may be understood better by reference to Appendix A at the conclusion of this chapter.[8] The various procedures are worth skimming if for no other reason than to relate this process to the participatory management already discussed and the crucially needed resource assessment for results definition.

TASK OR PROBLEM _____

Staff Options	Solves	Possible	Appropriate
1.			
2.			
3.			
4.			
5.			

In essence, the meeting process functions on a format that combines staff participation and various changes in department procedures in such a way that enthusiasm and commitment emerge in a way that can be reported, for the purposes of correlating definitions of *results, what,* and *who.*

Even without becoming involved in the details of this procedure, however, it is hopefully clear that such an approach permits a supervisor to recognize the availability of staff resources at the critical managerial time—the time that the resources exist. Moreover, when the procedures are followed as outlined in Appendix A, other managerial advantages exist:

1. The managerial role of the supervisor is clarified through the dramatic demonstration of his functions that the procedures call for.
2. The managerial willingness—indeed insistence—that staff participate in at least that part of the managerial process that impinges most directly upon them is their immediate supervisor's functional judgment relating to their jobs.

[7] A procedural device used by the author in training supervisory-level staff on the *how* function in relation to middle management.

[8] Printed instructions used by the author in training supervisory staff in this segment of the *how* function.

3. The managerial evidence that staff influence is *real*.
4. There is system of judging what kinds of programs generate the greatest staff enthusiasm.
5. Training staff to distinguish between notions that solve problems, and notions that cause problems.
6. There is an index of "staff energy" that increases the effectiveness of the Task Force Development Lab.
7. There is generated a more creative atmosphere for still other activities at a staff meeting.

Managerially, the most dramatic advantage occuring probably relates to No. 5—the staff learning that many solutions cause more problems than they solve.

Once this segment of the *how* function has been performed, the assessment of staff enthusiasm and energy is the supervisor's next activity. First he must decide whether or not the enthusiasm exists in areas already a part of his supervisory assignment. Second is the question of whether or not staff enthusiasm is in areas unrelated to the supervisor's assignment but nevertheless related to the departmental goals. A part of the *how/who* interface is the prompt reflexive transmission of this resource assessment to the task force development lab.

The instrument the supervisor uses to standardize this systematic weekly reporting of resource assessment might be a form such as the one appearing as Appendix B at the back of this chapter.[9]

The complexity of resource gathering is greatly simplified by certain "TFDL" procedures, even though they may at first appear somewhat complex. Above all else, these simplifications occur without loss of the managerial yield.

Thinking of "resources" as what are technically referred to as "ergometrics," (or energy) these "TFDL" procedures permit the constant assessment of the available resources for what is transmitted to middle management—in effect, results achievement based on accurate assessments of available resources.

Even when simplified, the concept of energy, like all valuable management concepts, remains somewhat involved. The main idea is to establish clear communication between the staff function of *how much* through the interface with the managerial function of *how* and the managerial function of *who/how*.

The value of this assessment is discernable if consideration is given to middle management unwisely attempting to distribute resources to implement a plan of action without an accurate assessment of existing activities throughout the agency. For, as will be seen shortly, the middle manager's

---

[9] Training material used by the author in criminal justice management development programs.

judgment is whether or not sufficient resources exist to staff a given plan in the most ideal manner.

Of course, the timing already mentioned remains particularly crucial because the activities and enthusiasms of agency personnel change from time to time. Adjusting managerial program on the basis of resources available requires critical timing.

The Who Function

The specific activities of reflexive synergetics involved in the managerial determination of operation staffing relate to two separate interfaces, the first being the *what/who* and the second the *who/how* function interface.

The *middle* managerial position affords an ideal position to place a number of vital criminal justice activities:

1. The staffing and personnel activity.
2. The cross-divisional base of what will be discussed in the next chapter as the management information system.
3. The operational base of resource utilization through what will be discussed as the Task Force Development Lab.
4. The corrective leverage for adjusting disparity between administrative planning and staff capability.
5. Sensitivity to the requirement that constant adjustment in the parameters of assignments be made for an optimum yield.

The main advantage of placing these activities within middle management has to do with the "fail-safe" system balance design of the model. In this regard, the first consideration is the strategically significant implementation activities implicit in the *who* function.

Another facet of the fail-safe segment also relates to the middle management responsibility for accountability. In this context, accountability refers to the *who* function being performed at a managerial role high enough to be removed clearly from process but low enough to insure sensitivity to administrative influence. In other words, middle management is just right for the *who* function as introduced in the preceding chapter.

Still another argument in favor of the *who* function being placed with middle management has to do with the "task environment," defined as "environment coupled with a goal, problem, or task—one for which the motivation of the subject is assumed."[10] *The managerial who function, when made part of middle management role, permits within a fail-safe model the systematic effort to keep the organizational environment coupled not only with the goal of results and tasks, but with assumed motivation as well.*

[10] Allen Newell and Herbert A. Simon, *Human Problem Solving* (Englewood Cliffs, N.J.: Prentice-Hall, Inc., 1972), p. 55.

Great value, then, is placed on conceiving of *implementation* as a part of this function, which is ideally suited for the middle management role. Control of the task environment flows to middle management because of the natural relationship to the strategic managerial position of supervisors who are in charge of other supervisors but do not direct major departmental programs.

Returning to the clarification of specific activities of the function interfacing introduced in the preceding chapter, attention is turned to group functions. When middle managers who control the task environment do so as a collective function, a great deal of agency-wide advantage emerges.

TASK FORCE DEVELOPMENT LAB

In a large probation department, as a helpful example in understanding this concept, the chief probation officer defines the goals that the organization is to achieve. His division directors translate these goals into plans that state what is needed to achieve these results. The second-line supervisors or middle managers comprise the "task force development lab" because they *collectively* determine *who* it is that will achieve the results.

As will be noted shortly, all middle managers must participate in the TFDL for it to be organizationally successful. In theory, this eliminates the possibility of redundance in staffing. The chance of having pockets of activities around the department diminishes as the goal orientation of TFDL focuses the entire department on results.

Tasks Versus Energy to Perform Tasks

The ergonetic principle emerges as a valuable managerial tool most readily when a distinction is made between tasks and the energy needed to perform tasks in programs to be implemented. Conceiving of staff energy as a managerially precious resource makes possible this valuable distinction for the TFDL.

The overall process involving ergonetics is by no means easy, but the managerial payoff more than justifies the effort—at least in results-oriented programming. One way to simplify the conceptualization of this approach to using the managerial activities of reflexive synergetics to achieve results is to conceive of three separate categories: operations, projects, tasks.

Operations, Projects, Tasks

One way to relate resource utilization (the TFDL goal) in terms of staff energy is to think of the sequence of operations, projects, and tasks in terms of reflexive synergetics. Administrative *results* and executive *whats* draw on the total department resource potential in each case—at least in theory.

This is so because every *what* is examined by TFDL for possible cross-divisional task force implementation as opposed to simply assigning it to an existing division.

These operations translate into either task forces or divisional projects, and thence into tasks. In an organization structured with TFDL handling the *entire who* function (including the personnel activity of hiring and firing) top administration in effect can establish absolute accountability links to all operations, to all projects, and to all tasks. This is in no way mitigated by the problem of middle management having its programs staffed by those not directly accountable for implementation.

In any event, conceiving of TFDL in terms of operations that develop projects out of tasks simplifies the concept of utilizing of resources whether or not complete accountability for such utilization is structured.

Resource Availability

In terms of middle-management "assessing personnel resources," many criminal justice agencies have adopted a procedure often referred to by such names as "THE AVAILABILITY/RELIEF FACTORS."

Although primarily for "post-positions" that must be "filled" 24 hours a day, seven days a week (i.e., police patrol, prisons and other institutions, etc.), it is nevertheless of value in managerial planning overall.

In their simplest form, Availability Relief Factors can be computed for a week, a month, or a year. Consider the following:

There are many approaches to computing staff availability, the most popular and simplest being an integration of these factors:

1. Regular days off per man per pay period ("average" including holidays for your HOW and HOW MUCH staff);
2. Vacation days off per man per pay period (again the average);
3. Average sick days per man per pay period;
4. Average injury days (IOD) per man per pay period;
5. Average days training per man per pay period.

The following is an example of the method used to obtain the availability (and relief) factors:

1. Regular days off per man per pay period, including holidays.
   4 days
2. Vacation days off per man per pay period.
   2 days
3. Average sick days per man per pay period.
   1 day
4. Average injury days per man per pay period.
   1 day
5. Average training days per man per pay period.
   1 day

$$\frac{\text{Pay Period} - A + B + C + D + E}{\text{Pay Period}}$$

Example: $\dfrac{14 - A(4) + B(2) + C(1) + D(1) + E(1)}{14 \text{ days}}$

(see 1 through 5 above)

$$= \frac{14 - 9}{14} = \frac{5}{14} = .36 \text{ Availablility Factor}$$

Relief Factor $1.00 - .36 = .64$

$$\frac{.64}{.36} = 1.9 \text{ Relief Factor}$$

Continuing with the example, a position which must be manned constantly on a given shift and which requires one man present at all times will require one man *plus* 1.9 men for the position. This formula will work for any number of positions. For example, 3 positions require $3+(3 \times 1.9)$ *or 8.7 men*—a horrible management problem.

Of course, the "reason" the RELIEF FACTOR is "smaller" than the AVAILABILITY FACTOR is twofold:

1) AVAILABILITY refers to the percentage of time a policeman, prison guard or other "POST POSITION" is available for duty in a *SEVEN-DAY-WEEK.*

2) RELIEF refers to the percentage of "another man" that it takes to keep the position "filled" *SEVEN DAYS A WEEK.* But the "other man" is no more "available" than the first man—hence the RELIEF FACTOR is "smaller."

Returning to the concept of staff as "resources," an important consideration is noteworthy.

The most important principle is a managerial perception of staff energy as *the most precious of all managerial resources.*—Consider the staff energy concept in terms of police work, including the demands on the policeman, the ever-present risks and hazards, and of course the public reaction to his work. Consider staff energy in terms of the probation or parole officer diligently trying to protect the community and rehabilitate the offender at the same time. Staff energy can be seen to be the most precious resource in the criminal justice system.

The *What* Function

Consider the following distinction between control staff authority and functional staff authority.

Control authority [is] the responsibility for controlling certain aspects of line performance . . . functional authority [is] decision-making authority outside formal chain of command and for specified purposes only.[11]

As the reflexive synergetics involving the *what* function relates to authority, both of these definitions apply.

A *what*, it will be seen, relates directly to certain aspects of line performance, but it is also related to lateral cross-divisional considerations that are outside the formal chain of command—at least if command is vertical rather than lateral.

Recalling the last chapter's definition of the *what* function in terms of a modified decision tree, the relationship between the top administrator's total responsibility for the organization and for goal definition (which determines what happens to his organization) can be linked to accountability for devising what is needed to achieve these results.

This forms the source of both control and functional authority to direct what is needed to achieve results whether or not it is vertical or lateral. In other words, the *what* function has a similar activity to the *who* function in that cross-divisional concerns are integrated into the process.

By using the decision tree methods as shown in the diagram above long-range plans can be delineated in terms of various sequences of *objectives,* which relate to the impact of all department operations upon each other; a *what,* then, is a given objective to be achieved before a further managerial decision is required.

But this objective must be much more than implied on this simplified version of a decision tree if the task force development lab is to develop the high yield discussed in terms of resource utilization. Actually, it has four parts:

1. A specific short-range expectation in relation to the cross-divisional long-range plan;
2. A specific and realistic completion date;
3. A specific, realistic, and concrete measure of success; and
4. A specific alternative if either measure or date is not met.

Of course, authority of the *what* function is diminished by the absence of any one of these criteria, and this in turn diminishes the accountability of the TFDL inasmuch as it can be accountable for no more than is made systematically possible through the delineated objectives.

By equating *what* authority with the adequacy of *what* definition in terms of four specific criteria, system pressure is placed on adequate planning and programming. The object, from an administrative point of view, is to

---

[11] Leonard J. Kazmier, *Principles of Management, 2nd ed.* (New York: McGraw-Hill, Inc., 1969), pp. 136–37.

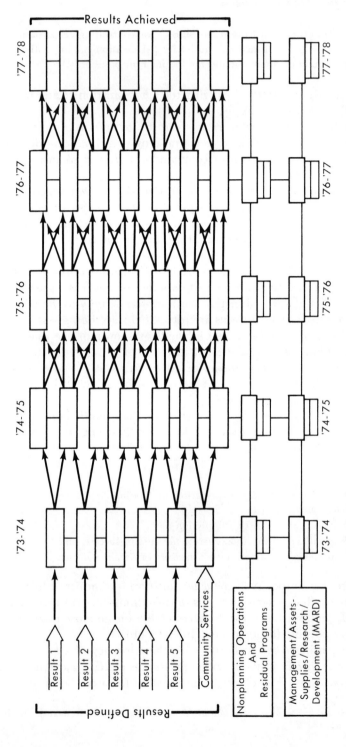

Once the decision-tree method of planning has been completed, a kind of visual "map" of management options, alternatives, and even consequences becomes available. Major program "modules" can then be displayed in relation to each other, as in the method shown here. This method was developed by the author to focus attention upon the planning potential to "bounce back" to more favorable positions after each year that measurements are not met. Each arrow represents a primary or alternative program.

bring virtually *all* departmental resources to bear on achieving results through adequate planning and programming; in other words, the *what* segment of reflexive synergetics is intended to gain cross-divisional as well as line direction through adequate planning and programming.

The Scope and Updating of Whats

As will be noted in the discussion of planning in the next chapter, *the systems model always plans five years ahead*—i.e., there is constant updating. This updating tends to widen the scope of the decision tree to include *all* departmental programming. In addition to the reasons already discussed for cross-divisional *what* reflexive synergetics, still another crucial part of the updating process is the assessment of both efficiency and effectiveness of programming through full utilization of measurement as introduced in the preceding chapter.

The technicalities of the actual methodology for updating is somewhat complex and is dealt with in other literature.[12] This complexity, however, is of little consequence to an administrator because design of a locally appropriate system of updating is best handled by the outside consultants, which will be elaborated in depth in Chapter Fourteen in this and other contexts deferred in previous chapters.

The main point is that once the model is being systematically updated on a regular basis, the top administrator has a chance to manage continuing results, in contrast to the unpredictable programming of either command or relationship management.

Although the strategic *who* function is crucial to the overall balance of the synergetic system cycle (particularly through the TFDL), the impact of the *what* function emerges as even more significant in retaining the accountability of each functional interface involved in achieving results. Even the first-line supervisor's ability to retain his classical line leadership status depends almost entirely upon the *what* function.[13] With this in mind, the concluding discussion of specific activities of interfacing synergetically is turned to the "boss"—results defined.

The *Results* Function

The activities involved in defining the results a department is to achieve include many considerations outside the organization, some of which will be elaborated in depth in Chapter Fifteen.

[12] See, for example, T. W. McRae, *Analytical Management* (New York: Wiley & Sons, Inc., 1970), chaps. 4–9, 19–21; and William King, *Probability For Management Decisions* (New York: Wiley & Sons, Inc., 1968), chaps. 3–6, 11.

[13] Classical in the sense as depicted in much of the supervisor literature—see, for example, J. J. Famularo, *Supervisors in Action* (New York; McGraw-Hill, Inc., 1961); and George D. Halsey, *Supervising People* (New York: Harper & Row, Publishers, 1953).

Any administrator in the criminal justice agency must include in his results definitions more than organizational considerations, regardless of how significant organizational considerations may be. But top administrators using the systems model to achieve results must integrate these external influences into a total program module that includes all of the following influences:

1. System Energy Assessment,
2. Five-Year Updated Administrative Plan,
3. Fiscal and budgetary government support,
4. Community sensor-matrix (an array of intelligence concerning trends within the community).

(A total program module that reflects these four considerations must of necessity move into the political world and it will be in this context that outside influences are discussed in Chapter Fifteen.)

In the long run, achievement of results depends on a top administrator's ability to integrate all four considerations. In effect, his subsystem *input, process,* and *output* with corrective feedback produces results only when the definition of long-range results effectively integrates the four considerations.

The planning and use of managerial information from roles responsible for the *what* function are of great assistance in this regard and will be one of the subjects of the following chapter.

SUMMARY

The management model introduced in the preceding chapter was further elaborated in this chapter by exploring efficiency and effectiveness in terms of a relationship with policies and procedures. The position was taken that procedure and policy manuals are functional only to the degree that managerial functions are not performed at any given level. Efficiency was distinguished from effectiveness with the goal of integrating both within the model, but retaining priority for effectiveness.

The fuller participation of all managerial levels in the management process was discussed as releasing greater ranges of creative talent systematically focused on *results* achievement through managerial functions and roles.

Leadership was discussed as critical even though the "flattening of the pyramid" was presented as necessary for effective synergetics (synergetics defined as a synthesis of force and resources in a system of reflexive managerial process).

The various managerial functions were related to the model in terms of specific interfacing activities, *how* being the activity of determining how results are achieved, *who* being the activity of determining who will achieve results, *what* being the activity of determining what is required for results, and *results* being the activity of determining what results are being sought on a broad base of government and community in addition to organization-wide programming.

Factors influencing effective synergetics through interfacing functions such as timing, managerial judgment, and a consideration of the most effective roles for the various managerial functions were discussed in the context of the ability of smaller departments to integrate several functions within one role. It was also emphasized that in larger agencies there is great advantage to relating *one* managerial function to *one* management role in the same context as presented in the preceding chapter.

Distinctions were made between task definition and task energy—elaboration of the concept of "ergonetics" introduced as "staff energy." Emphasis was placed on the managerial value of energy. A motivational program was presented using the interface between *how* and *who* functions, interface defined as "enough role overlap for communication but not so much to cause role distortion." The motivational approach discussed included redefinition of tasks to permit staff energy to be expended toward results without losing staff enthusiasm—enthusiasm systematically assessed through procedures that were also presented. The *reflexive* nature of these procedures, just as in the case of managerial judgments in role interfaces, was emphasized.

The concept of cross-divisional optimum resource utilization was discussed in terms of the *who* function within a task force development lab made up, in the ideal, at least, of all departmental middle managers. One of the numerous advantages of the TFDL presented was the *base* of the management information system to be discussed as a major part of the following chapter.

QUESTIONS

1. Distinguish between efficiency and effectiveness.

2. Discuss the role of leadership in this management model.

3. Discuss four organizational and managerial limitations of pyramid flattening.

4. How is creative talent released by role and function clarification?

5. Discuss the activities of the *how, who,* and *what* functions.

6. Discuss the activities of the results function.

7. Describe the activities of the task force development lab.

8. Describe this managerial model.

ANNOTATED REFERENCES

BECKHARD, RICHARD, *Organizational Development: Strategies and Models.* Reading, Mass.: Addison-Wesley, 1969. An excellent elaboration of other approaches to a management model than presented in this and the previous chapter—particularly of interest in the area of strategies.

FAMULARO, JOSEPH J., *Supervisors in Action.* New York: McGraw-Hill, 1961. Chapters Seven through Ten elaborate a number of the traditional supervisory activities that may well remain within the *how* function.

HALSEY, GEORGE D., *Supervising People.* New York: Harper & Row, 1953. Chapters One through Six elaborate a number of activities associated with the *how* function.

KAZMIER, LEONARD J., *Principles of Management,* 2nd ed. New York: McGraw-Hill, 1969. Chapter Two on management functions and Chapter Seven on staff relationships are an excellent context for what was discussed here as interface.

LAWRENCE, PAUL R. and JAY W. LORSCH, *Developing Organizations: Diagnosis And Action.* Reading Mass.: Addison-Wesley, 1969. Chapters Three and Four on interface afford a contrast with the role approach to interface used in this model.

LUTHANS, FRED, *Cases, Readings, and Review Guide to Principles of Management.* New York: Wiley, 1969. Within the format context of the book, Chapters Seven and Eight on staff relationships and centralization are excellent background for this model.

McRAE, T. W., *Analytical Management.* New York: Wiley, 1970. For those interested in the technicalities of systematically updating the model, this book provides most of the principles involved. Also highly recommended is W. R. KING, *Probability for Management Decisions.* New York: Wiley, 1968.

NEWELL, ALLEN, and HERBERT A. SIMON, *Human Problem Solving.* Englewood Cliffs, N.J.: Prentice-Hall, 1972. Again, for those interested in the technical aspects of the model, virtually all of the principles underlying the role interfaces of the model are covered in this excellent volume.

APPENDIX A

Part I   The Participatory Task/Problem Option Chart

A. Select a task or problem that you consider relevant to
   1. the assignment of your unit,
   2. the interests of staff under your supervision.

B. Print this task or problem at the top of the chart.

C. Print the alphabetically arranged last names of staff under your supervision and include your own name.

D. Allow as much time as you deem necessary to discuss the task or problem.

E. Stressing the possibility that the option selected by the group (*whether or not it is yours*) will be adopted, collect an option for every name on the chart.

F. Rate each column (Solves - Possible - Appropriate) stressing distinctions— particularly the facts that certain solutions may not be feasible and that feasibility alone can be too expensive.

G. Total all options and officially adopt the collective choice.

Part II Post-Meeting Analysis of Staff Options

A. Recognizing that clear communication in this specific area will probably require over six months to develop, use your second-line supervisors' function analysis as the first guideline to placing staff energy into categories.

B. Combine categories whenever possible and select terms agreeable with your second-line supervisor.

C. Use these mutually acceptable terms; list them under "nature of staff energy or capacity" on your weekly form (with the understanding that the terms may modify as your second-line supervisor gains cross-divisional experience in the Task Force Development Lab.).

D. Using your total staff schedule knowledge as a basis, determine the number of hours this particular energy probably exists this week by

  1. judging degree of staff commitment implied through their voting on the option(s) involved,

  2. relating your first judgment to an additional judgment of how much staff time is available

  a. via present schedule, and/or

  b. via modifications in present schedule made possible through enthusiasm of staff to expend this particular energy.

E. Ascertain the percentage of this staff time that is already committed to existing programs.

F. Ascertain the percentage of increase or decrease in this energy over last week (or note that this energy was not detected previously).

G. Comment briefly on any matter relevant to this energy.

Part III Staff Motivation Via Task Force Activity

After at least six months' practice with energy assessment, negotiate through your second-line supervisor further training to

A. utilize these procedures to permit the Task force development lab increased sophistication in selecting task force members from the framework of

  1. motivation,

  2. morale,

  3. unused talent.

B. Increase the awareness of top management of unused staff potential.

C. Facilitate your own managerial impact on your *how* responsibilities.

APPENDIX B

SYSTEM ENERGY ASSESSMENT FORM

WEEKLY SUPERVISOR ANALYSIS OF STAFF'S PROBLEM OPTIONS

TO: _____
(Second Line Supervisor)

FROM: _____
(First Line Supervisor)

For Week of ____ / ____ / ____ to ____ / ____ / ____

Nature of staff energy or capacity	Total amount of this energy available in hours, programs and/or other measures	Percent of this energy already committed to existing programs	Percent of increase or decrease in this available energy (energy beyond existing programs)	Comments
1.				
2.				
3.				
4.				

CHAPTER 6

Management Information, Decisions, Planning, and Budget

GLOSSARY

RESULTS—administratively defined department goals ; **WHATS**—operational determination of what is needed to achieve results along with precise measurement ; **WHO**—managerial determination of operational staffing ; **HOW**—supervisory determination of methods ; **MIS**—Management Information System.

Consider the following remarks in terms of those criminal justice subsystems attempting to attain effectiveness (as opposed to efficiency) as presented in the preceding chapter:

> The difficulty today is that we do not know specifically for what we stand—in structure, in personnel, in method, or even in basic concepts. What is needed is not a restatement of fundamental principles, most of which are as applicable now as they were 100 years ago, but rather a formation of precise, operational, down-to-earth concepts by which we can guide the course of twentieth century corrections.[1]

[1] Howard B. Gill, quoted in *Federal Probation*, 36, No. 2 (June 1972), 46.

This particular reference is to the prison (corrections) subsystem of criminal justice, but there appears to be considerable applicability to *all* subsystems—at least among those that recognize that criminal justice is a total system (functional or not).

But regardless of the applicability, the "formulation of precise, operational down-to-earth concepts" remains anything but easy. (Some of the problems involved are suggested by the complexities presented in the preceding two chapters on results definitions and reflexive synergetics through managerial role interfacing.) Even in those fortunate instances in which it does occur, there remains the equally difficult task of *retaining* the cogency of such formulation in spite of the accelerating pace of social change, which affects criminal justice as never before. Sustained relevance of concepts is, in the long run, every bit as important as any other facet of the systems model.

For this reason, an information system is needed to aid managers in critical decisions. Managerial decisions must be made on the basis of pertinent information; planning must underlie these decisions; and finally, an adequate budget system must be developed if the effectiveness of the reflexive synergetics combined with information, decisions, and planning are to be sustained.

Adequate information, sound managerial decisions, specific criminal justice planning, and a budget provide the systems model with a cohesive force that both reflects and sustains those "formulated, precise, operational, down-to-earth concepts" that emerge with good results.

The cohesive force that systematically produces effective management is developed through a combination of these four elements. By "cohesive force" is meant a system of reinforcing the function interfaces in order to provide a sense of purpose and direction—a formulation of precise concepts.

THE MANAGEMENT INFORMATION SYSTEM

The first variable, crucial to the cohesive force of all four variables, is the system whereby management gets its information. The concept of MIS is by no means restricted to the systems model; indeed, it is becoming a prime requisite of all managerial programs, particularly those having access to electronic computers.

Information and Time

Sadly, much of what is thought of as criminal justice administration and even management is sometimes little more than mere supervision. Good supervision is admittedly an integral part of management, but if a distinction between administration and supervisory management is made on the basis of "time orientation," most supervisory management is oriented to "today," and most administrative orientation is, or should be, oriented to "tomorrow." Because of this, there is a genuine difference in the type of information needed for the various levels of managerial functions (an example is stolen car reports, and a host of other crime data or records needed to "perform" rather than to "manage").

A management information system, furthermore, does not require automation, which merely aids in providing decision aiding data to managers. In large departments, to be sure, an MIS is likely (and fortunate) to have automated data processing and data retrieval systems.

At this point a specific definition of MIS is necessary.

MIS Defined

Anything as general as "information" covers a broad scope—even when restricted to management information. In terms of how MIS relates to the systems model, its definition never encompasses that which is not directly related to management functions of *how, who, what,* and *results*.

Although this restriction of scope is still admittedly broad, it nevertheless confines MIS to the specific functions of the systems model. To the degree that functions and roles are clear within an organization, regardless of the width and breadth of information, the complexity of information is never greater than any given function to which it is directed. A well-designed MIS systematically provides specific decision aiding data to specific functions—sorting relevant from irrelevant data.

> Most MIS's are designed on the assumption that the critical deficiency under which most managers operate is the *lack of relevant information.* I do not deny that most managers lack a good deal of information that they should have, but I do deny that this is the most important informational deficiency from which they suffer. It seems to me that they suffer more from an *over-abundance of irrelevant information.*[2]

Providing criminal justice managers with enough information to perform the functional interfaces thus includes the removal of extraneous information along with the provision of useful information.

Managers, confronted as they are with ever-increasing mountains of information, simply cannot find the time to sort relevant from irrelevant information. The amount of information that confronts not only the criminal justice manager but everyone living in the second half of the twentieth century is a growing problem.

> . . . there are limits on just how much sensory inputs we can accept, there are inbuilt constraints on our ability to process information. . . . Whether we are submitting masses of men to information overload or not, we are affecting

[2] Russell E. Ackoff, "Management Information Systems" (Chap. 15), in Peter P. Schoderbek, *Management Systems,* 2nd ed. (New York: John Wiley & Sons, Inc., 1971), p. 179.

their behavior negatively by imposing on them still a third form of over-stimulation—decision stress. Many individuals trapped in dull or slowly changing environments yearn to break out into new jobs or roles that require them to make faster or more complex decisions. But among the people of the future, the problem is reversed. Decisions, decisions, they mutter as they race anxiously from task to task. The reason they feel harried and upset is that the transience, novelty and diversity pose contradictory demands and thus place them in an excruciating double bind.[3]

Whether or not we agree with this drastic assessment of information overload, it is clear that the potentially overloaded manager could well be ineffective in an otherwise functional interface.

MIS then, in addition to sorting relevant from irrelevant information, has the additional task of narrowing information to specific functions to reduce the possibility overload; an MIS must distinguish between the functions of reflexive synergetics to be useful.

Although the concept of denying information continues to threaten many criminal justice managers, no manager is capable of digesting the full range of criminal information system even when it is reduced to legitimate relevance.

Information and Criminal Justice

Managerial staff in the many subsystems that make up the criminal justice system have a greater need to "narrow" incoming information than managers elsewhere. Take, for example, a police department information system overall. Police officers are line workers who require a great deal of information to perform well. They require radio information, teletype information, and a host of other types of information to perform their duties. Additionally, they also operate on the basis of information from superiors. The initial task in this case is to separate information needed to *cope* with crime from information needed to *manage* a program of coping with crime.

Complexities emerge with even the simplest teletype message about an armed robbery. Information about the cost of the teletype service, the salary of the operators, the number of operators needed, the training required, and the necessary supervision is *management* information, and as easy to separate as the allocation of resources, organizational structure, and other managerial matters that may permit the teletype to operate. The difficulty emerges when the line police officer requires teletype information on a specific armed robbery in order to perform, and the manager requires teletype information on the number of armed robberies overall in order to manage.

Continuing with the example of complexity in separating managerial from line-work information, consider a radio dispatch of a patrol car to a

---

[3] Alvin Toffler, *Future Shock* (New York: Bantam Books, 1971), pp. 351 . . . 355.

burglary in progress as police information. The cost of the insurance of the police car, the cost of the car and radio, and the number of cars needed is clearly within the context of management information. What is not so clear is that the radio dispatch needed by the line police officer is also needed by the manager to determine "service effectiveness" measurements.

Further, information must be more than mere facts, whether it is police information or management information. Additionally, discrimination between facts is needed before groups of facts become *information*.[4]

Perhaps an example of a specific information system within a criminal justice system might clarify many of these confusing considerations.

The following excerpt from an actual federal grant application illustrates how criminal justice information and management information can be combined within a single system. The letters CJIC refer to Criminal Justice Information Control.

Structure of CJIC

CJIC is an inter-governmental, computer-based information system being developed by and for all of the City and County criminal justice agencies in Santa Clara County.

CJIC was proposed because all agencies within the region needed decision-aiding information about an individual's prior, current and scheduled involvement in the total criminal justice process. Management and planning staff needed information to identify, plan, control and evaluate programs, organizational changes and policies.

CJIC is a prototypical system that can be used by other large or medium-sized counties. Inter-agency coordination and support of transferability have been priority considerations. Santa Clara County has had previous success in designing a Welfare EDP System now shared by six other counties.

CJIC is conceived as two functional groups of data. The first group, the Person–Case Information Subsystem, is concerned with the information required for the processing of persons through the criminal justice process. (Examples: booking information, charges, future court appearances, jail release dates, notification to Probation Department of arrested probationer.) The second group, the Management–Information Subsystem, provides the decision-aiding information needed for planning, for organization structuring, for staffing and allocation of resources, for direction of activities, and for the control of, and feedback from, these activities. (Examples: statistics for resource allocation, command/control, probation recommendations, crime prevention models, program evaluation.)

A management information system, then, sorts the relevant from the irrelevant facts and translates the results into decision aiding management

[4] Leonard J. Kazmier, *Principles of Management,* 2nd ed. (New York: McGraw-Hill, Inc., 1969), p. 365.

information that has been narrowed into specific categories of relevance in terms of specific management function.

Any managerial determinations of what is needed to achieve certain results are received by the task force development lab—the middle managers —and are routinely examined for the possibility of using cross-divisional staff resources for implementation. If nothing else, this information affecting any part of the department is clarified, but beyond that, the discussion of various middle managers regarding the available resources under their direction provides still more information, directly related and narrowed to the staff who will implement managerial programs. This requires an exchange of sophisticated narrowed management information.

Similarly, reporting the various resource/energy assessments provides managerial information on the reflexive synergetics of all department activities.

Of course, as discussed before, in the larger agencies such information reaches volume levels of complexity that virtually demand electronic processing. But the point here is that TFDL reflexive synergetics, in and of itself, form an MIS as soon as the function interfaces of *what/who/how* are established.

Decision Aiding

By conceiving of the management information system as a method of sorting relevant from irrelevant information and narrowing it to a specific management function to prevent overload, the MIS and the reflexive synergetics are readily combined in the interest of what was quoted in the opening of this chapter as a need for "precise, operational, down-to-earth concepts" that retain relevance.

This means that MIS information is related to managerial decisions on results definitions such as community desires, governmental controls and law, pertinent fiscal and budgetary information, and of course system energy assessment. In keeping the criminal justice concepts relevant, MIS will provide decision-aiding information on long-range plans, their updating, and pertinent measurement data.

In general, MIS is intended to aid the police sergeant, for example, to direct the implementation of patrol procedures, and the supervising probation officer to direct the interviews with offenders. The MIS aids the police lieutenant to determine who is best suited to direct particular activities, and aids the captain in determining what is called for to achieve the chief's definition of results.

The MIS also aids the effort to interface these managerial functions systematically enough that command management does not replace results management—i.e., reflexive synergetics prevail.

The MIS can be a valuable tool for all criminal justice managers—provided they are able to see it only as a tool. Managers frequently do not—some may even fear MIS. This may be because it is often associated with computers, even though a computer is not actually necessary for MIS to function.

Electronic Data Processing program designers as a group probably have one of the greatest ranges of technical jargon and exotic terms of all managerial consulting specialties (a point to remember in the discussion of consultants reflected in Chapter Fourteen). This is not to say that this and Automated Data Processing jargon is dysfunctional. More often than not, the terms used by these specialists fit the process they are discussing very accurately. Moreover, COBOL, standing as it does for Common Business Oriented Language, also stands for recognition that the exotic language of programming has become a bit too exotic for many managers.

As will be elaborated in Chapter Fourteen, most criminal justice personnel are without an EDP background, except perhaps for experience in sophisticated record systems or automatic criminalistic data retrieval programs. The exotic computer language can rarely communicate to the administrator without considerable translation, which does little to aid managers and administrators in conceptualizing MIS as a tool. The unfortunate part of this is that it makes possible a "tail wagging the dog" effect, in that the EDP at times controls the manager rather than the manager controlling the EDP.

As police and other criminal justice subsystems increase the use of electronic "record retrieval methods," the problems involved in separating linework information from management information could increase also. The trick is to know before an MIS is designed that it *is* a tool designed to provide information needed by police, probation, parole, prisons, courts, and the prosecution-defense.

For example, a computer can be programmed with criminal record information *and* management information in a way that separates information *in advance*. In other words, the police MIS can remain a tool even when combined with a very complex law enforcement information system as long as it is designed to differentiate management information from line work information.

GARBAGE-IN-GARBAGE-OUT

GIGO is the only technical term needed in order for the concept of decision-aiding data to be programmed into the "hardware" and "software" —a goal sometimes overlooked when dealing with the "hardware" salesman (programmer). GIGO, though a term derived from automated systems, is also valuable in nonautomated systems. To a manager, it suggests that the MIS gives back only what was put in—that is, processed data. It also means that only management knows what to give the MIS—MIS cannot meaningfully ask.

If exotic language, confusing print out formats, electronic technology, and other confusing variables tend to confuse those seeking information, a GIGO system of information is desirable. Recalling that the task of MIS is a sorting of facts into relevant information, a GIGO system is necessary when an MIS simply gives facts instead of information (a pitfall more apparent with the computer MIS but also possible with a nonautomated MIS approach). GIGO can be relevant in both automated and nonautomated information systems.

To a manager, GIGO suggests that MIS is designed to provide him *only* with information relevant to him.

MIS Design

The configuration of a system has been presented thus far in this volume as being linear in nature and comprised of *input, process, output,* and *feedback.* Technically, a great number of criminal justice organizations, and the overall criminal justice system itself, may *not* be completely linear in nature as depicted in the diagram below. Indeed, as will be noted in Chapter Fourteen, one of the consultant specialist's more complex jobs is to ascertain whether or not the system is linear through analysis of some such complex variables and standards as the following:

> . . . we cannot say that a system is non-linear if it contains a multiplication or division of variables or if it has a coefficient which is a function of a variable. . . .[5]

This level of sophisticated analysis, however, is of little direct value to criminal justice administrators beyond the involvement of consultants (the subject of Chapter Fourteen). For the sake of continuity and clarity, then, retention of the linear idea of a system will be applied to MIS, which can function on the "GIGO principle" with or without electronic data processing.

In considering the precise application of GIGO in a linear system, it is noteworthy that process is where GIGO is usually heeded. When the data fed in or the data that comes out is *isolated,* few if any managers have difficulty determining whether or not it is relevant to results. It is usually when managerial concern and activities mistakenly drift to process that irrelevant facts are palmed off as management information. The reason for this is that *process* is where most of the complex activities occur. When the mistake is made of equating complexity with priority a GIGO system should operate. GIGO, as "garbage-in-garbage-out," continues to remind management that MIS can be no more useful than the quality of it's input.

In design of the MIS for the systems model, there are four main con-

[5] Jay Forrester, "Industrial Dynamics—After the First Decade," *Management Science,* 14, No. 7 (March 1968), 404.

cerns in avoiding an equation of complexity and priority and in designing an MIS that provides decision-aiding data for managers:

1. All management information must relate to results—results being simply the output of the overall subsystem.

2. Management information never should be divided on the basis of process, but instead on basis of managerial functions (*how, who, what, results*).

3. All functions should participate in input in terms of each function interface. Managerial style, as has already been noted, is not relevant to the systems model unless it relates to results. Reflexive synergetics through function interfaces crucially relate to results and for this reason must be an integral part of the input of a management information system.

4. The final consideration in MIS design is that information be managerially decision-aiding and clearly distinguished from information that is vital to the department's mission but not to the management of the department. This concern may not be as complex as it seems in that the problem is at its greatest where MIS influence is the least: functional interface between the managerial *how* and the staff *how much* presents the greatest problem, but in the context of having the least MIS influence.

Beyond these four initial concerns, no two criminal justice departments can have precisely the same MIS design, at least if the MIS is functional. For example, administrators differ from one police agency to another if for no other reason than variations in city council or community variables. Yet the *principles* of MIS remain consistent through even the widest variation of legal restrictions, budgets, jurisdictions, staffing patterns, population sizes, and so forth.

Timing

Timing is vital to any MIS. How often information is available is just as crucial as the information itself in the reflexive synergetics of the model. Ideally the middle management group will meet together at least a full day a week, and on the following day take steps to insure that every manager throughout the organization is equipped with the strategic management information they have developed.

This, in the ideal, is part of the reflexive synergetics of the model. Results newly defined or modified through plans that are updated and translated into distinct plans of action are made a part of the task force development lab sessions in such a way that the interfaces tend to knit together. The implementation of plans, balanced against the resource assessments involved in analyzing the staff availability in all divisions and sections, creates a process from which *all* management information can be synthesized in such a way that it is easily narrowed to specific functions.

A wide range of variations and formats can develop in managerial decision-aiding data—formats ranging from computer printouts to department management newsletters that carry the fiscal, personnel programming, control and feedback implications to all those involved in various function interfaces within the framework of specific managerial functions. This, indeed, is a management information system when enough decision-aiding information is made available to perform each function of the model.

In terms of understanding the nature of an MIS, consider the following:

> One characteristic of most MIS's which I have seen is that they provide managers with better current information about what other managers and their departments and divisions are doing.[6]

But the MIS is far more than an ongoing informational briefing.

> Organization structure and information requirements are inextricably linked. In order to translate a statement of his duties into actions, an executive must receive and use information. Information in this case is not just the accounting system and the forms and reports it produces.[7]

If the distinction between efficiency and effectiveness made in the preceding chapter is to be of value, management information that goes *beyond* the efficiency of shuffling forms and reports is sorely needed make *effective* management decisions.

MANAGEMENT DECISIONS

Continuing the concern introduced at the beginning of this chapter in terms of formulating precise, operational concepts that can be retained on a continuing basis, consideration is now given the actual managerial decisions aided by the management information system.

Recalling that managerial judgments were discussed in the preceding chapter as relating to prompt assessments of resources and staff energy, a distinction between *judgments* and *decisions* is necessary.

In terms of criminal justice management, the main difference is that a *judgment* is a prompt personal assessment. A *management decision,* however, involves a more complex array of criteria, is far less personal, and has consequences beyond the reflexive synergetics of the function interfaces. This difference flows from the fact that management decisions relate to planning and to budget, which in turn are inextricably connected to results:

---

[6] Ackoff, "Management Information Systems," p. 181.

[7] D. Ronald Reniel, "Management Information Crisis," *Harvard Business Review* Vol. 2 (September–October 1961), p. 112.

. . . decision-making is basically a process of abstraction—of first solving simpler problems than the ones presented. Except in the most trivial decisions, how many times do decision-makers solve the problem *exactly* as it was given to them—without assumptions or simplification? This happens very infrequently indeed. . . .[8]

In terms of relating judgment to decisions, the prompt personal assessment involved in a judgment has more to do with the trival decisions cited in the quotation above.

Although this necessarily increases the magnitude of consequences of decisions over judgments, the manager nevertheless is not without methods of coping.

In recent years, a quiet revolution has been taking place in management. This revolution has involved the recognition that the decision problems of management may be subjected to explicit analyses by using the basic methods and techniques of science. This approach to management—alternately called "management science; operations research; or systems analyses"—views management as consisting of two essential functions: planning and execution.[9]

This observation clarifies the context in which management decisions can be considered.

Management decisions, like management information, are separate from decisions made by line workers (policemen, probation officers, parole agents, correctional counselors) and the decisions of both are based on separate and different information.

The criminal justice context for information and management decisions, then, is in part the distinction between record or enforcement information, and in part the implications of the graph on page 118.

In terms of management decisions, information is vital to insure that coping with crime is systematic and continuously effective. Managerial decisions do indeed relate to MIS.

And because they flow from MIS, another characteristic of decisions is (or should be) a correlation with *relevant* information—the virtual basis of managerial success.

The basic input which guarantees success is no longer labor or capital but information. The complexity and rate of change of modern life places a high premium on information. The success or failure of modern management de-

[8] Robert K. Jaedicke, "Current Analytical Techniques Useful in All Decisions," *Stanford Graduate School of Business Bulletin,* 34, No. 2 (Autumn 1965), 4.

[9] W. R. King, *Probability For Management Decisions* (New York: John Wiley & Sons, Inc., 1968), p. 1.

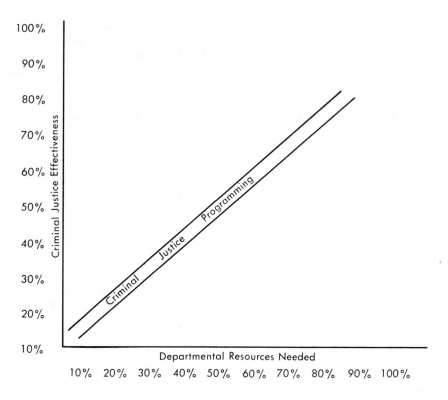

pends upon its ability to organize the efficient collection and distribution of information.[10]

Of course this quotation refers to the management of private industry, but the context of information is extremely relevant to criminal justice—at least if decisions are to be made by managers instead of computers.

Relating managerial decisions so strongly to the management information system may imply to many that they can be automated much like the MIS sometimes is. On the contrary, regardless of how automated the MIS, the actual managerial decision (and of course judgment) cannot be effectively accomplished in the systems model by a computer.

> Computers can't replace people in the management process; they may be fantastic devices but not for management control.
>
> Computers have been oversold as the way to make decisions. The story goes that if you have all the data on your organization at your fingertips, you will know as much as your managers and can detect all problem areas, bad value judgments, as cover-ups.

[10] T. W. McRae, *Analytical Management* (New York: John Wiley & Sons, 1970), p. 163.

That sounds great, but it doesn't work. No one has the ability or the time to assimilate the masses of data that a computer can churn out. And Program Managers need to know right away where they stand; they can't wait for a computer read-out. That's why Aerojet-General Corporation of El Monte, California, took the computers out of its decision-making process.

Computers are not magic tools. You get out of them only what someone else has put in, and it takes a lot of manpower to introduce information into the system and to analyze what comes out.[11]

Returning to the significance of information in managerial decisions, however, the focus is of necessity on appropriate decisions—decisions that can create, alter, or scrap criminal justice programming.

The Mechanics of Deciding

From time to time the old saying that "not to decide is to decide" emerges to confuse top level administrators. On the one hand, it *is* true that the failure to administratively react to cogent information is a kind of decision. It is also true that not reacting to certain information, at times, is administratively wise. Some indecisive managers use these two variables to disguise their reluctance to take definitive administrative positions when definitive adminstrative positions are called for—kidding themselves and other.

These and other considerations suggest clarification of the "not to decide" influence on the decision mechanics being discussed. For purposes of the systems model, *every* decision made by a manager, including his decision not to managerially react to information, is subject to whatever organizational system is designed to meet the model's requirement for decisions and planning.

From the frame of reference that *all* managerial decisions relate (or should relate) to the subsystem being managed, the activities and mechanics of decisions can be examined, beginning with risks.

Risks. One way of looking at decisions is in terms of risks.

A dozen times a day when we come to street crossings we must choose between alternative actions—cross now or don't cross now. In making the decision to go ahead, we are visualizing the risk of being hit as minimal. Thus, we believe that the odds favor our reaching the other side safely and we bet our lives on that belief.[12]

Translating the decision on street crossing into managerial activities, decision-making might be thought of as a system of determining the odds

[11] John D. Nichols, "Computers Don't Make Our Decisions Any More," *Management Review* (August 1972), Vol. 5–2, p. 31.

[12] H. J. Roy, "Using Computer-Based Control Systems for Decision-Making," *SAM Advanced Management Journal* (January 1971), Vol. V-2, pp. 57–62.

for and against alternatives reflected by the management information system. Perhaps the idea of crossing the street could be paraphrased to clarify the concept within the confines of criminal justice:

> A dozen times a day a patrolman chooses between alternative actions—stop a suspicious vehicle, or don't stop it. In deciding to make the stop, he is visualizing the risk of being confronted with a suspect in a recent but unreported armed robbery as a minimal risk because it hasn't happened in all his previous car stops. He bets his life on that belief.

The management-level decisions of the police department are also a matter of risks—far less dramatic, but nevertheless using the same principles —risk principles worth learning.

In addition to the isolation of risk as a concept, decisions are significant in terms of their consequence, and consequence is always in terms of the future—at least at the time of the decision. From this frame of reference it can be seem that, because no one knows the future, managerial decisions are on the basis of "odds interpretations":

> Arriving at odds requires looking at a large body of history. For example, if we're talking about credit, the history would include everything that was known at the time of decision about an appropriate sample of people who later turned out to be good (paid as agreed) or to be bad (failed to pay).[13]

Moving further into the mechanics of decision-making, setting odds and examining risks present the first logical step—that of the focus of management information on a large body of history.

First Step. Hopefully, this large body of history structures the odds for and against various alternatives and options. The management literature is rich in its coverage of the technology of using odds and probability in managerial decisions.[14]

But the top criminal justice administrator is, hopefully, far more concerned with priorities than the technology of odds-setting—the technicalities of a sophisticated system are available at any time to consultation to the manager who can clearly define by priority the odds he wishes to set. (Specialty consultation will be elaborated in depth in Chapter Fourteen.)

---

[13] Ibid.

[14] See, for example, S. Blumenthal, *Management Information Systems* (Englewood Cliffs, N.J.: Prentice-Hall, Inc., 1969); R. J. Brown, "Systems Approach to Management Development," *Financial Executive* (April 1970), Vol. X-2, pp. 20–25; N. Churchill, *Computer-Based Information Systems for Management* (New York: National Association of Accountants, 1969); J. Diebold, *Business Decisions and Technological Change* Vol. VII-3, (New York: F. A. Praeger, 1970); R. Fenstermaker, "Management Systems Engineering," *Management Review* (October 1969), pp. 2–14; W. King, *Probability for Management Decisions* (New York: John Wiley & Sons, Inc., 1968); T. W. McRae, *Analytical Management* (New York: John Wiley & Sons, Inc., 1970).

The first step, then, is not only focusing upon a large body of history, but focusing in such a way that a priority of determining odds can be established.

Second Step. Moving to the next step in the mechanics of decision, priorities for odds-setting logically relate to the future inasmuch as managerial decisions relate to planning and budget, both of which are future-oriented in the systems model. The role of "history" is nothing more than an effort to profit by past experience in dealing with the future.

The ability to relate decisions, plans, budget, and odds to speculation about the future is vital because the four become *less speculative when combined*—a laudable goal for management.

The decision tree introduced in previous chapters again proves a valuable tool in clarifying a process that at times can appear complex. Just as the literature on odds-setting is very rich, so also is the literature on the technology of decision trees.[15]

Similarly, just as the technicalities of odds-setting are of relatively little importance to the actual managerial decision, so also are the technicalities of decision trees; of much more importance is the potential for combining managerial decisions, plans, and budgeting with a knowledge of the odds— a combination made possible by reference to the same simplified decision tree discussed in previous chapters.

The second step can be seen as actually setting the odds.

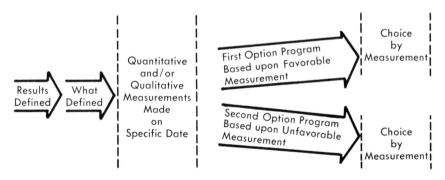

Still another valuable decision aid in executing the actual managerial decisions involved in the systems model is the program evaluation review technique, also known as PERT:

[15] See, for example, E. Dale, *Management Theory and Practice* (New York: McGraw-Hill, Inc., 1969), pp. 551–57; "Decision Trees Offer Plan Alternatives," *Administrative Management* (November 1967), Vol. VIII-3, pp. 30–31; F. S. Drechler, "Decision Trees and The Second Law," *Operational Research Quarterly* (December 1968), Vol. IV-2, pp. 409–19; R. A. Flinn, "Decision Tree Analysis," *Research Management* (January 1970), Vol. XXX-2, pp. 27–34, also the May 1970 issue, p. 181; J. A. Parsons, "Decision Trees," *Systems and Resources Journal* (November 1967), Vol. IX-1, p. 8; C. R. Warson, *Understanding Quantitative Analysis* (New York: Appleton-Century-Crofts, 1969), pp. 78–85.

Basically PERT is a managerial tool employing networks. The networks used are but flow diagrams consisting of the activities and events which must be accomplished to reach the program objectives, showing their logical and planned sequence of accomplishment, inter-dependences and interrelationships. The idea to be underscored is that the PERT network depicts not only the many and varied components making up a system or subsystem, but also the all-important intricate interrelationships that prevail among these.[16]

The PERT approach lends itself to a number of programming activities in large organizations but is readily adaptable to the managerial trained administrators of small departments as well.

Very few if any criminal justice programs could not be delineated in a PERT format with many of the decision-making advantages depicted in the decision tree.

Third Step. The third step in the mechanics of decision-making is the establishment of a precise system of odds-setting—necessary in relating decisions to *plans.* A wide variation in the establishment of this system is possible, but an example of one approach is reflected in Appendix A located at the back of this chapter.[17]

Regardless of the system devised, some of the advantages of odds-setting of course relate to simplifying the great complexities of meaningful ongoing decision-making. But of considerable importance is the common meeting ground provided managers of differing philosophies and styles. Indeed, the core of the rationale for holding managerial style as far less significant than the achievement of results relates directly to the common meeting ground provided managers of differing philosophies and styles on the basis of such weights.

The odds of success, then, and particularly the system of weights used in making the critical decisions through success-odds, are extremely important variables in the systems model, and of no small value in effective management everywhere.

Fourth Step. The final step in the mechanics of decision-making is to translate decisions into action. One action, of course, is the *what* definition forwarded to the task force development lab, which meets the following four criteria:

1. What is expected in relation to results,
2. When this is expected,
3. How it will be measured,
4. The decision tree alternatives if time and measures are not met.

---

[16] Ackoff, "Management Information Systems," p. 445. See also chaps. 38–45, in the volume from which this came: Schoderbek, *Management Systems.*

[17] Training material used by the author in managerial development programs in criminal justice.

The other action from decisions, just as important, is the adjustment in the long-range planning, the five-year plan of a systems model. This of course, relates decision-making directly to planning.

PLANNING

Long-range planning, or what was referred to earlier as "module planning," is an integral part of the systems model. Essentially, the five-year plan referred to in previous chapters is not actually a plan but rather a *method* of planning.

Recall in previous references to long-range planning the idea that the systems model is always thought of in relation to results in *five years* rather than in the next month. Of course this relates to the dynamic nature of reflexive synergetics, and to the philosophy that a truly effective management is always attempting to utilize *existing* resources instead of dealing with resources as they appeared to have existed in the past. So planning is a way of thinking about the future *now*—and *now* keeps changing.

But regardless of changes, an effective management is always thinking five years ahead of the month in which plans are being made, and adjusting and updating through an MIS signalling the need for decisions.

Though constant updating of the plans that influence the entire organization may at first appear chaotic in nature, the updating process is actually tranquil in comparison to the radical adjustments that are forced to occur when there have been no prior changes in plans.

Few, if any, probation, parole, or prison administrators have not felt some degree of pressure of this kind—and felt it even when they were administratively involved in the updating process. Indeed, so severe are some social changes and so accelerated the pace that even the most sophisticated updating process occasionally lags.

Planning and Success Components

Recalling previous discussions of the systems approach to management as "a combination of behavior with quantitative measurement," planning can be thought of in still another way—the development of "components of success"—development of things required to succeed.

Recalling also the brief discussions of what was identified as *ergonetics* (i.e., the laws and principles relating energy to work), planning can be placed in a technical context that involves an additional scientific principle: *taxonomy* (i.e., the laws and principles of classification).

In reality, the assistance of independent consultants or systems analysts are frequently required to utilize these two scientific principles to identify success components. Nevertheless, it may be very useful to consider the kind of information available for planning through the use of ergonetics and taxonomy.

Once results have been isolated and defined, and particularly when they have been translated into *whats*, a definition of success is already available. Put another way, accomplishing results within the systems model *is* success. The taxonomy of the ergonetics, or "classification of the energy that relates to work," is useful in determining influences that impinge on accomplishing results. Again emphasizing that technical consultation is needed to elaborate the actual process of this managerial tool, it is nevertheless worth noting that the process can in fact produce the components of success.

Of equal complexity to the taxonomy and ergonetic analysis is the complex process in which "valences" of all influences in the organization are assessed as either "positive" (helping accomplish results), or "negative" (preventing accomplishment of results).

A profile of these valence variables can emerge in terms of the taxonomy and ergonetics of a criminal justice organization and, though extremely complex to develop, emerge as tremendously useful in administrative planning.

The following list is typical of the kinds of success components that can be derived from such an approach.

1. Interface with administrative government
2. Interface with political government
3. Interface with immediate judiciary
4. Interface with secondary judiciary
5. Interface with law enforcement
6. Interface with prosecution
7. Relationship to public
8. Systematically weighted management information
9. Anticipatory information and sensor matrix
10. System energy and resource assessment
11. System development
12. Interface counterpart administrators prime jurisdiction
13. Interface counterpart administrators secondary (state)
14. Synergetic objectives
15. Accountability measurement
16. Planning alternatives
17. Fiscal timing
18. Resource timing
19. Planning
20. Procedural energy utilization
21. Feasibility and resource reserve

22. Research methodology and parametric consistence
23. Research execution and analysis
24. Research integration with sensor matrix and MIS
25. Ancillary finding and costing (grant and pilot)
26. Measurement and analysis
27. Adjustive corrections via planning after measurement
28. Sensor matrix and MIS countervalence for system homeostasis
29. MIS and planning update
30. Employee development
31. Training and education
32. Managerial function analysis
33. Managerial program analysis
34. Managerial interface analysis
35. Malfunctional interface corrections

Planning, then, can also acquire the ability to anticipate, to include, and to develop the components of success—to develop, in effect, a certain degree of insurance that planning will succeed by weighing virtually all the impinging influences.

By including these requisite components of success that are needed to succeed *within* program plans, the managerial measurement and accountability that were emphasized earlier as part of the systems model tend to emerge as functional in the same sense that the interfaces are functional (functional enough to isolate dysfunction if it occurs). In a sense, this permits planning to enhance rather than to merely guide organizational operation.

Returning to the less complex variables in planning in general within the systems model, the idea of success components can now be related to planning at any given time—even in between cycles of reflexive synergetics.

Organizational Plans at Any Given Time

By looking at managerial planning "in between" cycles of reflexive synergetics, the planning process is no different than good planning wherever it occurs.

One of the early descriptions of criminal justice planning is contained in the early work of O. W. Wilson.[18] In the early 1950s, he defined planning as "the process of developing a method or procedure or an arrangement of parts intended to facilitate the achievement of a defined objective.[19] After classifying police planning in a variety of categories, Wilson commented on the scope of planning as it then existed, as follows:

[18] Wilson, *Police Planning* (Springfield, Ill.: Charles C. Thomas, 1952), chaps. 1, 2.
[19] Ibid., p. 3.

The planning effort may be directed at a very small segment of the total organization or operation, or it may involve a complete survey of the whole with a view to developing new plans throughout.[20]

In this regard, planning in our systems model is more narrow than Wilson's concept of scope. Specifically, *all* plans of the model "involve a complete survey of the whole with a view to developing new plans throughout" because plans, related as they are to decisions, occur at a high level. In the model, plans referring to what Wilson identified as those "directed at a small segment of the total organization" are the functions of *how* and *who*, and in the context of implementation *after* planning. This seemingly slight difference is amplified by the comment "Planning must be in operation at every level and every functional unit of the organization."[21]

The planning referred to at "every level" is very similar to the function interfaces in between the times these interfaces are actually occurring. In other words, the managerial activities between the function interfaces best fit what Wilson refers to as "planning . . . in operation at every level."

During the actual interface processes discussed in the two preceding chapters, even greater differences exist. But differences notwithstanding, the five steps in planning established by Wilson remain relevant to the most modern sophisticated managerial approaches. These steps are simply the recognition of planning needs, stating objectives, gathering and analyzing data, developing details of the plan, and obtaining congruence between organizational units.[22] Although they are integrated into a larger scale functional interface arrangement of reflexive synergetics, compare these five steps to five considerations of the systems model: the rationale presented for establishing results-oriented management; the *results* and *whats* definitional process; MIS; TFDL operations; and the emphasis placed on cross-divisional accountability—all considerations that presumably relate planning to a reliable system.

Planning a Reliable System

Beyond the simple definitions of what planning is lies an equally useful definition of what planning *does*—to the system of management.

One thing it does in the systems model is to put managerial decisions in the context of the future—in the context of consequences. But hopefully, planning does even more; it increases the reliability of the system.

In order for a system to function properly, it is necessary that certain of its individual components function properly. One way of improving the probability that a system will function properly is to duplicate or add parallel com-

---

[20] Ibid., p. 7.
[21] Ibid., p. 9.
[22] Ibid., p. 10.

ponents to the system. However, by adding components, we also increase the probability that the system will function inadvertently.[23]

Thinking of planning as one of the components that must function properly, the *reliability* of the planning component is actually the reliability of the entire system. Placing organizational planning in such a crucial role is by no means an exaggeration of the importance of planning in the model. Consider, for example, results definitions alone, or results definitions in terms of the *whats*, either or both without reliable planning. To whatever degree planning is reliable, the particular criminal justice subsystem is reliable. Conversely, to whatever degree planning is unreliable, the criminal justice subsystem is unreliable.

The *results/whats* actually must combine to provide systematic planning in the model. But in terms of the technicalities of planning, it is the *what* function that creates the actual plans.

By continuing the core of the organizational planning within the accountability of the *what* function (combined with the *results/what* interface), some certainty is offered that plans are both reliable *and* updated. And because not only the accomplishment of results depend on planning, it would not appear to be an overstatement to say that *all* managerial activities of the model depend on production of reliable functional plans in terms of *whats*, which serve as the actual translation of goals into programs.

Planning Strategy

Having considered the relationship of the management information system to decisions, decisions to planning, and planning to a reliable subsystem, a *strategy* for planning—a kind of *master planning strategy*—is necessary.

> Every enterprise needs a central purpose expressed in terms of the services it will render society. And it needs a basic concept of how it will create these services.[24]

Although in a substantially different context than the initial reference in this chapter to the "formulation of precise, operational, down-to-earth concepts," the point of both references is essentially the same: methods of clarifying the concepts within which the system operates. This is, perhaps, another way of calling for a master planning strategy.

Recalling the activities in the managerial function of defining results,

---

[23] Rocco Carzo, Jr. and John N. Yanouzas, *Formal Organization: A Systems Approach* (Homewood, Ill.: Dorsey Press, 1967), p. 442.

[24] Fred Luthans, *Cases, Readings, and Review for Principles of Management* (New York: John Wiley & Sons, Inc., 1969), p. 115.

it is hopefully clear that when *all* the internal and external considerations have been effectively integrated, the central purpose of the organization will have, in effect, been stated. The definition of results states the central purpose, and, moreover, the services to be rendered to society have also been stated.

In terms of these services to society, criminal justice includes a fairly wide range. Police efforts alone encompass all that is implied by the concept of personal safety and property security within a democratic society. In addition to the humane implications involved in rehabilitation, correctional services also include security with respect to dangerous offenders. All that is implied by the concept of "justice" is the potential of the courts, probation, and of prosecution-defense. Criminal justice indeed provides the potential of tremendous services to society.

The plans to create these services, then, have in effect a master strategy suggested as soon as the results are defined.

The first part of the suggested strategy is the use of reflexive synergetics to place the resources for implementing plans into a logical and effective array. Inasmuch as the functional interfaces involved are the basis of most of the input of the MIS, and because MIS is most of the basis of decisions that affect planning, a master planning strategy that constantly integrates the results definitions into these interfaces is likely to find output of MIS already related to results.

Further, such strategy has the results influence in the managerial process even before crucial decisions are made and plans adjusted.

Consider these advantages in the following context:

> We can spot some of the weaknesses without difficulty. One of them is planning. Much planning is done unilaterally, with little thought about how the proposed change will affect other parts of the system. An increase in police manpower in a city will mean a rise in the caseloads of prosecutors, courts, defender services and jails. When the police make many more arrests and see that cases are stalled for months and years, that offenses are knocked down in plea bargaining, that criminals slip through the fingers of the law, their attitude toward the court tends to become negative and uncooperative. Other parts of the system are similarly affected and the whole system, fragile to begin with, is weakened.[25]

Planning that takes into account a system of criminal justice along with the administrative concerns of the individual organization is, in the final analysis, the only meaningful planning in the sense that the future certainly holds change whether planned or not. Criminal justice management depends upon planning just as the individual organization depends upon planning.

---

[25] T. M. Thompson, "The Criminal Justice System: A View From Outside," *Crime and Delinquency* (January 1972), XXXIV-2, p. 25.

If both are remembered, both then have a relatively simple, even traditional, concept of planning.

The primary purpose of criminal justice planning is to provide direction for goal-oriented action. Consequently, an integral part of planning is stimulation and facilitation of such action. In the case of criminal justice planning, the purpose is directed toward action that yields a high level of protection for the community.[26]

"Protection of the community" may then be thought of as the results from which plans can be made for the entire system of criminal justice, provided that the entire system is integrated into the organizational planning of the individual subsystems.

Viewed as a managerial function, the process of planning includes the identification of organizational objectives and the selection of policies, procedures and methods designed to lead to the attainment of these objectives—the overall objective of the protection of the society being served.[27]

From this frame of reference for planning in criminal justice, still another vital consideration (whether preferred, favored, appreciated or not) will now be considered—the fiscal budget.

BUDGET

Managerial processes involving information, decisions, and planning, although at times complex, are relatively simple in comparison to the fiscal procedures to which many criminal justice administrators are subjected.

Budget and Cost Benefit

A frequently ignored budget consideration is cost benefit. By this is meant "how much" in the way of planned results the budget will buy—how expensive achieving results is.

Even when cost benefit is considered, still another factor is often overlooked: the cost of building and maintaining the organization in addition to the cost of operating it.

Although sophisticated cost benefit analysis is complex and consulting specialists are usually required to assist the administrator, there is a relatively simple way of conceptualizing the task so as to avoid the problem of overlooking major cost factors such as building and maintaining the organization.

[26] Frederick W. Howlett and Hunter Hurst, "A Systems Approach to Comprehensive Criminal Justice Planning," *Crime and Delinquency*, 17, No. 4 (October 1971), 532.

[27] Kazmier, *Principles of Management*, p. 41.

Recalling the system components of *input, process,* and *output,* the frequent oversight in procedures such as cost effectiveness or cost benefit is *output*—the process of output is frequently ignored in the "process" of determining costs of process and input. Extremely sophisticated measurement of all costs of process and/or input can ignore the costs of the management process that makes the effectiveness of spending possible.

In later discussions of module programs as part of budget and political interfaces that prove effective between government and administrators, the power of fiscal practice will be presented as directly dependent upon the total cost relating to total effectiveness—actual value for each dollar spent.

To whatever degree fiscal procedures function without regard to the cost of *any* facet of the total system the powerful "dollar's-worth" influence is removed and weakened. Although this weakening is subtle and difficult to detect, the criminal justice administrator choosing to ignore this principle usually pays a very tangible price at budget time each year.

With this total systems approach to costs, the cost benefit might be conceived of in this manner administratively:

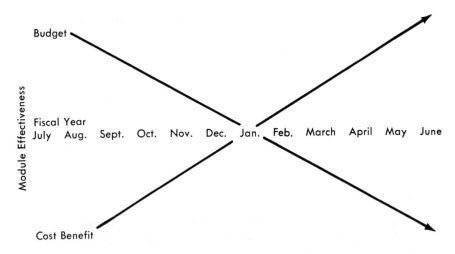

Note that as the budget funds are expended and hopefully cost benefits from the systems model increase, the module effectiveness also increases— cost benefits are thus one measurement of module program effectiveness. But of even greater administrative significance is the obvious loss that may occur each year if the entire fiscal cycle is repeated at budget time.

New budget parameters influence a repeat of at least part of the lower cost benefit during the buildup period of expending monies on relatively new programs—new in the sense that the constant updating of the systems model avoids a great deal of the "business as usual" programming that permits service compatible with annual budgets.

In other words, the systems model creates programs in relation to the results that are to be achieved rather than only to as much service as the budget allows—more service some years than others depending totally on the new budget each year.

By demonstrating how effectively money is spent in achieving concrete, tangible results, the administrator also develops evidence that budget, like planning, improves with length of span—the longer the range, the greater the effectiveness.

Regardless of how unrealistic this radical budget idealism may seem, the pressure to lengthen the budget span begins with the first shred of evidence that starting all over again every year is all an administrator can do— a kind of "re-invent the wheel" process obscured somewhat by simply doing more, or less, of the same old thing.

And in this context, the overall budget process of the systems model will now be considered.

The problems inherent in an interface between administration and the political world are significant enough to be isolated and dealt with in a special context later in this book. But with specific regard to the budget process, attention is now directed to the fiscal approach of this management model— a fiscal approach acknowledging the reality of an interface between administration and politics.

Information, decisions, and planning, when combined with budget, do indeed create the cohesive force that was pointed out early in this chapter. However, the advantage of bringing about the cohesion of the reflexive synergetics, and the TFDL operations go well beyond the continuity that was cited.

In effect, the very process of continuity in achieving predetermined and measurable results suggests a streamlining of fiscal approach that includes fiscal process of both routine budgetary functions and grants from federal and state sources as well. For purposes of the model, the approach will be referred to as "module programming."

Module Program and Program Budget

Module programming as it relates to criminal justice can be thought of as a variety of combinations of systematic efforts to cope with crime and delinquency.

For example, laws are enforced selectively by police if for no other reason than there are more laws to be enforced and more potential law violators than there are police.

In devising various strategies to cope with law violation, police administrators may well consider the homicide, robbery, and burglary a far more significant variety of crime with which to cope than vagrancy, public drunkenness, and traffic violation. Given any severe restriction in budget or personnel resources, they necessarily place priority on spending department funds on dealing with the more significant crimes—perhaps not to the exclusion of lesser crimes, but certainly with emphasis on the most serious crimes.

Module programming is, in effect, an administrative effort to once again discharge the responsibility implicit in the graph found on p. 118. Its relationship to the program budget can be illustrated in a hypothetical case.

Suppose a criminal justice administrator poses a question to the body responsible for his budget, whether it be a city council, county administration, state legislature, or the U.S. Congress.

> If I were able to establish program standards and measures as concrete as the equipment standards of program budget, could I budget on the basis of program modules?

In anticipation of the reaction that this question will stimulate, the administrator quickly adds:

> My administrative program is such that I have reason to believe that my organization will consistently provide far more service than you could reasonably expect for the total amount of the budget.
>
> In each area of service, I have a number of managerial activities and service activities that combine with the equipment standards of program budget.
>
> Collectively, the managerial activities, service activities, and standard equipment form a program module as soon as measurable results are included.
>
> Of course it would be necessary for you to engage in an independent study to establish what level of service is reasonable to expect. This is necessary for us to be absolutely certain that the program module actually achieves more than you could reasonably expect.

Then, with as much selectivity as possible, the administrator directs his summary to whatever level of fiscal criticism exists:

> Without such a constant measurement, none of us could be certain that we were actually saving the tremendous amount of time, effort, and money that the module program appears to promise—of utilizing the principle of program budget to its fullest.

Notwithstanding the gross oversimplification of the tremendous array of fiscal obstacles involved, this budget approach is every bit as feasible as the original program budget—although probably suspect to many experienced administrators on first sight.

Moreover, in the context of a results-oriented, reflexive synergetically enriched, function-interfaced systems model, success with this budget approach is not only possible, it emerges as downright likely!

Notwithstanding a nightmare of initial work facing budget specialists in establishing the fiscal measurements to correspond with program measurements, the ensuing cycle, becoming as it does all but automatic, clearly justifies the effort.

SUMMARY

As a continuation of the initial discussion of the management model, Chapter Six has dealt with four related processes in terms of what was introduced as a need for consistent formulation of precise, operational, down-to-earth concepts: systematic management information, management decisions, management planning, and the budget process. Management information was defined as relevant facts that are sorted into relevant information—information defined as much more than facts alone. Information was further discussed as a crucial influence on the reflexive synergetics of the model because of the relationship between information and managerial decisions.

For this reason, the management information systems (MIS) was discussed in terms of sorting information not only from facts into relevance, but into specific relevance for specific management functions.

The activities of the task force development lab was presented as part of the management information system regardless of automation, which was presented as desirable only to the degree that MIS remains a managerial tool.

Problems relating to reluctance to use MIS were presented primarily in terms of the exotic language of electronic data processing. Other problems such as the "garbage in-garbage out" principle were also discussed but in the context of a linear system in which process considerations usually are the source of any confusion.

Design of MIS was discussed in terms of priority on results achievement through reflexive synergetics.

The managerial decisions to which MIS is geared was discussed in several contexts as a prelude to relating decisions to planning.

From the reference point of "not to decide is to decide," the mechanics of decisions were presented in the context of risks and probabilities, or odds. With emphasis on the future, these mechanics were presented in four steps: priorities for odds-setting, actually setting the odds, relating decisions to plans, and translating decisions into actions.

Various decision-making avenues were discussed involving the previously introduced decision tree along with another frequently used decision-aiding device—the program evaluation review technique.

Also discussed were the success components of criminal justice administration in terms of managerial planning. Taxonomy and ergonetics were presented as rather complicated scientific concepts that were worthy of consideration because of their ability to lead to strategic portions of success components for criminal justice subsystems.

Budget and cost benefit were elaborated in terms of dollar effectiveness at the output stage of a linear system (comprised of input–process–output), noting in particular those problems involved in gearing cost effectiveness to either input or process instead of output.

Also elaborated was the favorable cost benefit outcome in terms of lengthening the budget span to coincide with the length of the planning span.

Planning, in the context of updating the model (as discussed in the two preceding chapters) was presented as a way of thinking ahead, always planning five years from the present month rather than simply in terms of the immediate future

The similarity to traditional administrative planning was discussed as existing in between cycles of reflexive synergtics.

System reliability was equated to the reliability of planning, and planning strategy was placed in the context of the function interfaces of the model.

QUESTIONS

1. Discuss the distinction between facts and information.

2. Discuss managerial information.

3. Describe a system of managerial information (i.e., MIS).

4. Discuss the task force development lab operation as a management information system.

5. Relate role interfaces to management information systems.

6. Distinguish between managerial judgment and managerial decisions.

7. Describe the relationship of MIS to decisions; to planning.

8. Discuss the differences between traditional planning and the planning proposed for the model.

9. Relate system reliability to planning.

10. Discuss planning and impact on the overall system of criminal justice.

11. Describe the program module approach to budget.

ANNOTATED REFERENCES

CARZO, ROCCO, Jr., and JOHN N. YANOUZAS, *Formal Organization: A Systems Approach.* Homewood, Ill.: Dorsey Press, 1967. Chapters 11–14 elaborate the entire context of the system reliability discussed here as relating to planning.

HOWLETT, FREDERICK W., and HUNTER HURST, "A Systems Approach to Comprehensive Criminal Justice Planning," *Crime and Delinquency,* 18, No. 4 (October 1971). An excellent perspective for what was discussed here as the impact of organizational planning on the overall system of criminal justice.

KING, WILLIAM R., *Probability to Management Decisions.* New York: Wiley, 1968. The first five chapters elaborate the technical premises on which "odds setting" are based in the model.

MCRAE, T. W., *Analytical Management.* New York: Wiley, 1970. Chapter 4, "Quantifying Risk," along with Chapters 7 and 8, affords good technical background for the discussion of both the management information system MIS and management decisions.

SCHODERBEK, PETER P., *Management Systems,* 2nd ed. New York: Wiley, 1967. Elaboration in depth of the management information system in Chapters 15–24 (see also this chapter's footnote 10). Chapters 41–45 elaborate what was discussed in this chapter as PERT.

WILSON, O. W. *Police Planning.* Springfield, Ill.: Charles C. Thomas, 1952. An excellent background for consideration of any administrative planning in the criminal justice system—considered by many administrators a classic.

APPENDIX A

Improving Decision Odds

I Define subsystem effectiveness
  A. General system or goals
  B. Subsystem or objectives

II Separate solutions from feasibility by MBO option chart
  A. Some decisions would solve problems but are not feasible
  B. Some decisions are feasible but solve nothing

III List subsystem programs that both
  A. Solve problems in terms of effectiveness
  B. That are feasible as well

IV Make a "good/poor odds table"
  A. Accumulate a thorough list of attributes of the programs chosen by MBO option chart
  B. Divide list into "good" and "poor" in terms of subsystem effectiveness
  C. Put attributes in rank order of significance by "weighing" each 1–5 (5 is very good or very poor; 1 is not so good or not so poor)

EXAMPLE

	Program attributes	Division
	1. Expensive	Poor
	2. Fast	Good
	3. Cumbersome	Poor
Step 1	4. Complicated	Poor
	5. Technical	Poor
	6. Popular	Good
	7. Relevant	Good

	Good	Weight	Poor	Weight
	1. Fast	5	Expensive	5
	2. Popular	3	Cumbersome	4
Step 2	3. Relevant	4	Complicated	3
	4.		Technical	2
	5.			
	6.			

	Good	Weight	Poor	Weight
	1. Fast	5	Complicated	5
Step 3	2. Relevant	4	Cumbersome	4
	3. Popular	2	Expensive	3
	4.		Technical	2

V Use decision odds-table on all decisions in program

   A. Make a "yes/no" dichotomy out of every decision

      1. Complicated decisions are reduced to a series of dichotomies, all of which must be "yes" to gain favorable odds for overall decision

   B. List the attributes of a "yes" decision

   C. List the attributes of a "no" decision

   D. Add the appropriate weights from the decision odds table

   E. If "Good" outweigh "Poor," the odds are favorable for "yes" decision (and vice versa)

CHAPTER 7

Personnel, Labor Unions, and Managerial Communication

GLOSSARY

RESULTS—administratively defined department goals ; **WHATS**—operational determination of what is needed to achive results along with precise measurement ; **WHO**—managerial determination of operational staffing ; **HOW**—supervisory determination of methods

The presentation of the management model is concluded in this Chapter. The context in which personnel, labor unions, and managerial communications occur should by now be one that includes clear role and function definitions within a system that acknowledges the interactions and relationships between all the subsystems that ultimately make up criminal justice.

PERSONNEL

Little change has occurred in the governmental concept of personnel since the late 1930s and early 1940s—except perhaps for an increasing awareness that training and career development are hampered when dealt with as simple personnel services.

The government concept, reflecting a wide range of significant managerial concerns, usually includes the areas of recruiting, screening, testing, indoctrination-orientation, performance evaluation, discipline, job description, classification, promotion, transfer, up and downgrading, and in some cases, hiring and firing. Of less concern to criminal justice management, but nevertheless often associated with personnel activities, are the areas that deal with health and safety, employee services such as insurance and retirement, records, badges, and I.D. cards, and soon. All of these activities are, in the ideal, a part of the interface between the operational staffing and the methods used to attain goals.

Perhaps this point is significant enough to justify elaboration before moving on to further consideration of personnel services.

Perhaps the reason the Who function in criminal justice organizations rarely influences personnel activities is the virtual absence of a *functional* definition of personnel in relation to the *functions* of management.

Take, for example, a departmental personnel officer who is respected as a "trouble shooter"—a "guy that solves problems." While this *role* may be played well, it may also obscure the *function* of *preventing* the personnel problems in the first place. By *prevention* is meant the function of determining such things as good typists who fear meeting the public and making this personnel information available to the Who function *before* the typist is assigned to a task force that requires public contact.

Recalling that a Role Is Evaluated and a Function Is Measured, the functional use of personnel activities is established when the presence of personnel problems proves the absence of personnel functions. And in addition to bringing accountability to personnel activities, connecting the personnel function to the Who function, accountability also increases in middle-management.

The WHO Function and Personnel

In order to hold the Who function accountable for "who-is-chosen" to staff criminal justice programs, *all* organizational control over determining "who there is to choose from" must be given the managerial role carrying the Who function. This is necessary regardless of the "role level" to which the Who function is assigned.

A Human Relations Orientation

In terms of the specific relationship of personnel to the systems model, Wilbert E. Scheer's excellent Personnel Director's Handbook gives an appropriate orientation:

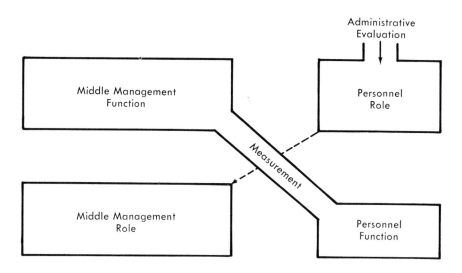

There is much more to personal management than the day-to-day administrative duties involving people. Applying scientific, or at least systematic procedures to the area of human relations calls for a different understanding from that used in the materialistic realm. Here we are dealing with human values, blood-bought souls, divinely created and eternally destined beings. We are not dealing with human machines.[1]

This orientation is one of building the personnel segment of the system's model around *people.* Although it may seem obvious, this focus is justified in private industry, with which Scheer is concerned, but it is *demanded* in criminal justice where not only the *process* but the *product* is people. All personnel matters, without exception, relate to what was discussed in Chapter Three as managerial human skills.

The Personnel Services

In a sense, the highly sophisticated and complex managerial effort to distinguish task definitions from the energy needed to perform tasks is a personnel matter for no other reason than that it relates to "classification"— recalling the technical discussions of *taxonomy* (the science of classification) within the context of *ergonetics* (task and energy). However, later discussions of the role of technical consultants will clarify the source of expert assistance in the task/energy managerial functions. With regard to personnel services not directly involved in ergonetics, there are several that are common to virtually all criminal justice organizations. Recruiting, screening, testing, indoctrination-orientation, performance evaluation, discipline, classification,

---

[1] Scheer, *Personnel Director's Handbook* (Chicago, Ill.: Dartnell Press 1969), p. 22.

job description, promotion, transfer, up- and downgrading, and of course hiring and firing cover a wide range even without the inclusion of employee services.

When specific goals are decided upon as well as the methods to attain them, two personnel services that form a natural pairing for the middle management are job description and performance evaluation. By "natural pairing" is meant the necessity of having descriptions of existing jobs and evaluations of the performance of those doing the jobs, in order to focus departmental resources on implementing and achieving the goals.

The next activity involves the cross-divisional assessment of resources and energy relating to transfers. These services tend to flow naturally where the *who* function is coordinated well. Personnel and management run into more difficult problems at certain times, however, in classification, reclassification, upgrading and downgrading.

Any differences of opinion between the personnel specialist and the manager may not be easy to resolve, but there is a frame of reference from which both can negotiate:

> . . . position-classification adheres strictly to the view that current duties of a position are the sole basis for its classification, and recognizes at the same time that these may be changed in character, difficulty or scope by reason of capabilities or deficiencies of the employee occupying the position. . . .[2]

Often, if not usually, the differences of opinion regarding classification relate to what might be called the importance of a job.

Another effective method of removing classification from the argumentative arena is to focus on *standards*.[3] This is singularly useful in the model because the measurements built into the methods decided upon are in effect standards readily adaptable to classifying positions.

The final method of achieving a clear understanding of classification is by relating the systems model to the source of personnel resources.

Personnel Resources

The widely used and respected *Municipal Personnel Administration* comments on personnel organizations in the city as follows:

> In the United States, cities carry on personnel administration in four ways: (1) There is no formalized program. Sometimes this means "patronage" is the system for filling jobs; sometimes it simply means that there is a stage of confusion. (2) There is a civil service program for some city employees. A limited

---

[2] Ismar Baruch, *Position Classification in Public Service,* Civil Services Assembly, c. 1941, ed. 1942.

[3] O. Glenn Stahl, *Public Personnel Administration* (New York: Harper & Brothers, 1956), function #5, p. 525.

program usually covers fire and police personnel. (3) There is a civil service program for all employees except officials and certain specified appointments. (4) There is a "merit" program under the chief executive instead of a civil service commission.[4]

This statement, when expanded along the jurisdictional boundaries of country and state, pretty well covers the range of centralized personnel resources to which the criminal justice administrator must turn for services.

In larger criminal justice departments, decentralized personnel services are often available through a departmental personnel officer. The Federal Civil Service requires such decentralization:

The Personnel Officer

(1) Executive Order 9830 requires the head of each agency to designate a director of personnel, or other similarly responsible official, to provide advice and assistance to him in carrying out his personnel management responsibilities. This director or other official represents the agency head in personnel matters; consults with him on personnel policy matters; develops, implements, and reviews the agency's personnel programs; and participates in all personnel management activities. As a part of the management team, the appropriate personnel officer at each agency level has the basic responsibility of helping both managers and firstline supervisors carry out their personnel management responsibilities. The personnel officer generally has such specific responsibilities as:

(a) Representing and advising agency management in relating substantive program requirements to manpower requirements and program decisions to manpower decisions.

(b) Establishing and maintaining an up-to-date manpower information system to provide timely and appropriate information on the agency's human resources, as needed for basic management decision-making purposes as well as for planning and administering an effective personnel program.

(c) Initiating and actively participating in all elements of personnel management essential to the achievement of the objectives listed previously.

(d) Developing technically competent personnel staffs to advise, assist, and train agency managers and supervisors at all levels to carry out their personnel management responsibilities, to meet the needs of managers and supervisors arising from daily agency operations, and to help employees resolve work-related and other problems which may affect employee job performance.

(e) Advising or representing management on labor relations matters.

(f) Facilitating the full participation of managers, supervisors, employees, and recognized employee unions in appropriate personnel management activities, including the formulation and implementation of personnel management objectives, policies, guides, and standards.

(g) Insuring that government-wide and agency personnel management

[4] International City Managers Association, *Municipal Personnel Administration,* 6th ed., Chicago, Ill., 1960, p. 19.

goals, policies, and practices are communicated to and understood by managers, supervisors, employees, and employee groups and that, to the extent possible, the support necessary to make them effective is achieved.

(h) Taking timely personnel actions, promptly processing the necessary paperwork, and efficiently establishing and maintaining required personnel records.

(i) Evaluating the effectiveness of agency personnel programs at each level of organization and management, and providing top agency management with the information needed to evaluate the success with which subordinate managers and supervisors are carrying out top management's objectives and decisions.

(j) Initiating appropriate planning and research to support personnel management programs; informing top management of promising new personnel management concepts; and recommending appropriate changes in agency policies and practices.

(2) The personnel officer must advise agency managers on how the many features and flexibilities provided in the Federal personnel system may be best used to accomplish agency program and manpower decisions. He must make sure that the manager fully understands how personnel management is carried out in his agency. When problems arise in personnel management, whether they come under the primary jurisdiction of the agency itself, of the Civil Service Commission, or some other central government agency, the personnel officer has an obligation to determine the underlying cause and practical effect of such problems, and to propose appropriate action to resolve them, including the revision of statutory law, policies, regulations, or administrative procedures.[5]

Although this wider scope of personnel responsibility does not fit the managerial role and function interfaces of the systems model, it does emphasize the significance of personnel services and the largest management system of them—the federal government. Indeed, in federal government, management and personnel seem at times to be interchangeable terms:

Manpower needs. A public service of high quality, and one which is fully capable of carrying out all the complex modern programs of the various Federal agencies, is essential in maintaining good government and in meeting the demands of the changing world. Such a public service must be composed of people who are competent, loyal, responsive, impartial, strongly motivated, and well led. This requires that the executive branch of the government must continually seek, attract, select, develop, and retain, on the basis of merit and fitness, the best persons available from the standpoint of knowledge, skills, integrity, and suitability.

Management requirements. Management of people is of primary importance because only through their efforts are the objectives, missions, projects, and work of an organization accomplished. Personnel management is an integral part of over-all management and is not accomplished separately from other

---

[5] *Federal Personnel Manual,* chap. 250, "Personnel Management in Agencies," Inst. 121, Nov. 29, 1968, pp. 250–56.

management activities. Those activities which primarily relate to the employment and supervision of people are encompassed under the general term of personnel management. Personnel management is the responsibility of all the officials, executives, managers, and supervisors who participate in the planning and accomplishment of the work of the executive branch of the government from the President of the United States through the heads of departments and agencies to firstline supervisors. The creation and maintenance of a flexible, productive, efficient, and proud career public service is the basic objective of Federal personnel management.[6]

Recruiting and Performance Evaluation: Good Man Mythology

In an article entitled *How Effective Executives Use Their Time,* Peter Drucker, the "father" of management by objectives, stated: "First of all, there is no effective type."[7] Though this statement refers to executives, it might also apply to any employee if it were modified to state: "First of all, there is little agreement on what is meant by 'good man.' "

The word "effective" is specifically defined in the systems model in terms of results achieved. But "good man" is not defined. And because it is used so frequently by so many managers (whether or not involved in the systems model), a definition is necessary.

An exercise used by some management consultants asks administrators to list terms that describe a "good man." Then the administrators are asked to list terms that describe a poor employee. Ten or more items are encouraged for each list. When the lists are compared, an interesting phenomenon sometimes occurs; frequently terms that one uses to describe a "good man" are precisely the same terms used by another administrator to describe a "poor employee"—both administrators having frequently communicated with each other using the term "good man."

Another unexpected phenomenon sometimes occurs in these comparisons—even among administrators making major decisions on the basis of "good man," most of them differ in describing what a good man actually is. In other words, very little similarity exists in the remaining descriptions of either good or poor employees.

For these reasons, the personnel services involving recruiting and performance evaluation appear better off entirely within the realm of results achievement, or potential to achieve specific results. Personnel services in general appear far better off without intuitive "good man" criteria. And because in criminal justice, recruiting and performance evaluation are per-

[6] Ibid., chap. 230, "Organization of the Government For Personnel Management," 230–33.

[7] Peter F. Drucker, "How Effective Executives Use Their Time," *Hospital Administration,* Vol. XX, No. 5, October 1967.

formed as often by managers as by personnel specialists, it should be relatively easy to integrate the results orientation through the middle management.

By approaching the evaluation on this basis, an additional advantage quickly becomes clear: An employee evaluated on the basis of results he either did or did not achieve is far more likely to hear constructive criticisms as suggestions for improvement—at least more so than the employee who is told subtly that he isn't "good man." This appears true whether the evaluation is formal and structured or informal and spontaneous.

Once evaluation is free of the "good man" mythology, freeing the recruiting service of this distortion becomes easier, with results achievement continuing as the measurement.

Of course results can be defined to include *any* pertinent variable, but once defined, results achievement is the total measurement—at least if effectiveness outweighs efficiency.

One additional concern in the recruiting area deals with "professionalism" in criminal justice. There is a healthy trend toward increasing the standards and hopefully the competence of criminal justice personnel.[8] Disagreement exists, however, on "credentialism." An increasing administrative concern flows from the following philosophy:

> What should be done to reduce credentialism? This question does not imply that the road toward the reduction of credentialism will be easy. But it does seem imperative that we begin to talk much more seriously than before of various stratagies to reduce credentialism—the mythology that educational certificates really designate the possession or absence of the appropriate abilities for a job.[9]

Efforts to establish a more professional standard in criminal justice specialties can scarcely ignore the implications of this warning. But any idea of excluding college preparation altogether is obviously wrong. Besides specific "course content" provided at college, there is also the vital element of *learning how to learn*. A learning discipline increases the potential productivity of personal learning to the point where it can be assumed that an earned degree equates with the ability to learn. The reflexive synergetics, deliberately geared to flexibly integrating radical changes in the realities of criminal justice, require personnel capable of *continually* learning—of learning new realities on virtually a daily basis.

The problem, of course, is that learning how to learn is difficult to either measure or explain—a problem indeed for a model based largely on clarity.

[8] See, for example, the outstanding work of Harry W. More, *Critical Issues in Law Enforcement* (Cincinnati: W. H. Anderson, 1972), pp. 373–422.

[9] S. M. Miller, "Strategies For Reducing Credentialism," *ACTION: Action For Change In Public Service Careers*, Summer 1970.

LABOR UNIONS

For purposes of this chapter, "labor union" refers not only to a formal union but to all employee associations or organizations that participate in collective bargaining within the criminal justice system.

"Collective bargaining" means different things depending upon who is using the term (and sometimes *how* it is being used). However, in this systems model, it implies the formal negotiation between an employee organization and management, either the administration or government.

Participatory Management

In Chapter Two's discussion of the Likert influence, the notion of *participatory management* was introduced. Translating this directly into a criminal justice context, it refers to police officers, probation officers, and other criminal justice personnel who participate in the management of the organization for which they work.

As was noted in the earlier discussion, at least some of the facets of employee-oriented management have great potential. Recalling the discussion of the *how* function, collective bargaining is necessarily a participatory management procedure. The weekly supervisorial activities and the immediate managerial adoption of a staff preference in terms of procedure not only *permits* but *requires* staff participation in that part of management that affects employees most directly—management by immediate supervisors.

With or without participatory management systematically integrated in the model, however, collective bargaining nevertheless remains a fact of life for management. And as a fact of life, it requires further personnel service: i.e., labor negotiations.

Labor Negotiations

Collective bargaining does not usually involve those matters for which organizational management is responsible. Instead, salary and working conditions are most frequently the subject of labor negotiations, and are outside this sphere of organizational control.

For the criminal justice manager, labor negotiations are more likely to be related within the frame of reference of participatory management as just discussed, or the personnel services also discussed in relationship to the managerial functions of the model. Employee grievances relating to these functions exhaust the *direct* involvement of criminal justice management in labor negotiations.

But limited though direct labor negotiations may be in criminal justice administration, the significance of labor unions and other employee groups is enormous—even when the participatory function is performed well. Perhaps police unions might serve as the best example of this significance. The public impact of unions representing law enforcement is more immediate and dramatic than unions representing probation, parole, prisons, and other correctional organizations. Further, there are more law enforcement employees than any other criminal justice segment.

President Woodrow Wilson reacted articulately to the well-known Boston police strike of 1919:

> . . . leaving the city at the mercy of an army of thugs is a crime against civilization. . . . the obligation of a policeman is as sacred and direct as the obligation of a soldier. He is a public servant, not a private employee . . . he has no right to prefer advantage over the public safety. . . .[10]

In the time that has elapsed since Wilson's observations, a number of influences have of course influenced the various philosophies on a policeman's "rights to prefer." Administratively, however, a chief of police or any other criminal justice administrator cannot administer an effective program when his personnel are even *thinking* about a strike.

The salary and working conditions, then, are of administrative concern although both are outside the control of the administrator and therefore outside the control of the administration. For even when assuming that the motivational components of the model's reflexive synergetics eliminate employee grievances *organizationally*, the grievances generated by dissatisfaction with salary or working conditions remain just as detrimental to managerial effectiveness. Moreover, the steady increase in the formation of police employee organizations participating in collective bargaining[11] does not suggest that complete satisfaction exists in salary, working conditions, or even in other areas of personnel services.

However, a hopeful trend appears to be developing. If the police administrators can be used as a measure of criminal justice management in general, there is evidence that they are recognizing the need to integrate the unions and employee organizations into managerial process.[12] Although such a trend may not directly influence the unrest related to salary or working conditions, it may at least establish that salary and working conditions are the source of the unrest (when and if they are.) And because working conditions in particular have rarely concerned city councils,[13] focus on this source

---

[10] Carl E. Heutis, "Police Unions," *The Police Yearbook*, (Washington, D.C.: International Association Chiefs of Police, 1958), p. 45.

[11] Hervey A. Juris and Kay B. Hutchison, "The Legal Status of Police Employee Organizations," *Center for Law and Behavior Science*, University of Wisconsin, pp. 4–21.

[12] "Report of The Special Committee on Police Employee Organizations," *International Association Chiefs of Police* (mimeograph), Washington, D.C. (September 1969), pp. 23–24.

[13] V. A. Leonard, *Police Organization and Management*, 2nd ed. (Brooklyn, N.Y.: Foundation Press, 1964), p. 39.

of unrest appears to be in the best interests of an administrator—particularly if those who control the budgets of county, state, and federal criminal justice entertain a similar indifference to working conditions.

Administrative interests are served whenever city councils, county boards, or state legislatures are able to focus directly on the source of unrest in such a way that problems cannot be simply dismissed as poor administration.

Little comfort is provided by the absence of strikes to settle grievances in criminal justice. Technically, eliminating the strike option within police unions, for example,[14] is of little consequence because the impact of various slow-down substitutes are just as detrimental to achieving managerial results.

Employee organizations are already a reality in criminal justice administration. What remains to be seen is whether or not the labor union movement and managerial programming are to move in the same direction. Part of the answer lies in managerial communication.

MANAGERIAL COMMUNICATION

Later in this chapter, managerial communication will be discussed as being restricted to a relatively narrow definition, which relates to the achievement of results within the model. To provide a context for this discussion, however, the broader scope of communication will first be explored from several perspectives, beginning with the complexity of numbers.

Only three communication combinations are needed to trace all possible communication connections in a three-man department. But with only four more department members, twenty-one connections are necessary. Imagine 500 employees—1000—5000; the number of connections, it can be seen, increases geometrically according to the number of people within a department.

The relative clarity of a geometric progression is clouded by differences in status, age, sex, emotions, and so forth, of department members. These considerations, combined with sheer numbers, compound the complexity of communication.

Many other complexities exist and will be explored later in this chapter. But in terms of managerial communication, the primary complexity for the time being has to do with human relations. Moreover, this complexity exists within the important requirement that feedback exist.

Management Feedback: A Key to Communication

One of the very few axioms in the many approaches to organizational communication is the requirement that management feedback exists. The

[14] Robert Sheehan, "Lest We Forget," *Police* (September–October 1959), p. 1.

word "feedback" itself has an axiomatic definition: The feeding back of part of the output to the input at the proper phase (proper phase meaning the time at which greatest influence is exerted toward achieving results). Ideally, this feedback is accomplished through the organizational system— but recall the complexities arising with increased numbers.

The systems model must acknowledge not only the feedback axiom but also the requirement that feedback be produced systematically on an ongoing basis. In the case of the systems model, feedback is produced as a requirement of the role interface and reflexive synergetics.

Before examining the structure of the feedback mechanisms that are built in to the model, some consideration will be given the rationale used in *not* isolating feedback—of not viewing it separately from the other component parts of the model.

Structuring feedback within the functional role interfaces and reflexive synergetics, instead of separating it as an isolated function, has a number of reasons, not the least of which is the similarity of feedback to a certain philosophy of happiness. Like *happiness*, it becomes most elusive when sought for its own sake. Consider a paraphrase for the philosophy "Happiness is not a destination but a daily way to travel"—*"feedback is not a destination but a daily way to manage."*

"A daily way to manage" does not mean a simple philosophical direction. Behind the idea is a systematic, ongoing structure that requires feedback as part of *measurable functions*. At no point is a function of the systems model performed to the exclusion of feedback—at no time is the statement "We're working on feedback" an acceptable substitute for measurable performance. The function, which includes feedback, is either performed or an evaluation of needed improvements is called for.

Precise accountability exists for the consequences of poor or inadequate feedback within the management function for which a specific manager role is accountable.

Sensitivity. Temporarily opened feedback channels accomplished through T-groups, encounter retreats, and a host of sensitivity approaches tend to isolate not only feedback but all managerial communication as well. Once isolated, communication per se, and feedback specifically, may in fact emerge as excuses or at least as explanations of *why* results are not achieved. Isolating feedback as something that requires special preparation in effect shifts emphasis away from achieving results rather than directly toward achieving results.

Entrusting accountability for feedback to the capricious variables of "sensitivity level" is in reality removing accountability—at least *specific measurable accountability*—for this vital managerial tool. Noteworthy in this regard is the observation that *stress* frequently increases the need for feedback, but it may reduce sensitivity as well. To whatever degree this is true, dependence on sensitivity is dependence upon that which is least available when most needed.

Of course the complexities of organizational communication may require training to be perfected. When roles and functions are not clear and this brings about a lack of communication, it is possible that sensitivity training may have a distinct value. Indeed, in larger organizations, communication training is likely to emerge as a primary goal of managerial development. But at no time in the systems model is accountability for functional feedback removed because of training; nor is the absence of functional performance excused because of insensitivity.

Against this background of the rationale for structuring feedback within managerial role interfaces and reflexive synergetics, the mechanism of feedback will now be examined.

FEEDBACK MECHANISMS

Once a result has been defined by top administration within the organization, the next step is to decide on what is to be done to achieve desired goals. In smaller organizations, both functions (i.e., both results and whats) may be within one managerial role, thereby resolving the need for feedback. In larger organizations, however, the *results* function is ideally within one role and the *what* function in another. In this instance, accountability for specific achievement serves as motivation to share prompt feedback on at least those organizational programs that may hamper further ability to achieve results.

Of a much more positive nature is the feedback that a *what* function is motivated to provide top administration in terms of staff resources and energies. Enhancing the motivation to provide feedback on this avenue to influence further results definitions is the continuing awareness that resources in fact determine the degree of accountability for the *what* function.

Recalling the definition of role interface, *enough overlap of function to permit communication but not enough to distort roles*, feedback mechanisms of this nature tend to reinforce rather than distort roles. More important, feedback, when structured on this basis, is ultimately of value to both the method of achieving the results and the results themselves.

Moving on to the next interface, the definition of specifically what is to be done is followed by a determination of who is to do it. There are four criteria for deciding upon goal-achieving methods:

1. A description of any one branch of the managerial decision tree—the program required to move from one point in the organizational plan to the next.

2. The precise measurement to be used in determining whether or not results were accomplished.

3. The exact date the measurement is to be made.

4. The decision tree alternatives if the measurement is not met.

The absence of any one criterion of the four tends to remove staff accountability for function and performance, but it is also the technical source of unfair expectations with regard to performance—further motivation to insure feedback within the interfaces and within the reflexive synergetics.

The interface between middle management and the supervisory determination of methods develops feedback in several ways. First, the accountability for how the results are to be achieved is no more valid than the managerial program that makes achievement possible. A first-line supervisor may be asked to devise managerial methods for achieving results, but he is not accountable until achievement is possible—until policy permits it, until staff are available, until budget is provided, until equipment is purchased, and so on. Feedback, then, is in the interest of both *who* and *how* functions in this regard in much the same way that feedback is in the mutual interest of all interfacing managerial roles of the model.

Additionally, the system energy assessment tends to generate further feedback. Those who carry out the managerially determined methods must have accurate resource assessment to utilize organizational potential, for which they are accountable. Resource assessments must be made and communicated to place realistic limitations on what is expected of any given task force.

The mechanisms of feedback within the interfaces and reflexive synergetics are designed to focus on the value of feedback in terms of accountability—so clearly that personality clashes and similar problems become too costly to the organization as well as to the individuals involved. Indeed, the unreasonable expectation that all managers like each other is itself deemed expensive in our systems model.

Accountability for function and performance makes it possible to gear the feedback mechanisms of the organization to specific value that is related to the specific accountability of each manager. It thus becomes possible to gain completely productive interfaces between managers who personally dislike each other—*enough functional overlap for communication but not enough to distort roles.*

Ideally, all managers should "like" all other managers. Ideally, systematic and ongoing accomplishment of managerial results should include great bonds of personal affinity between all of those managers participating. Realistically, however, it may well be that the most that can be hoped for is a system in which all managers respect the need for feedback from all other managers and know that it is a prime requisite of managerial success. In effect, this would be a system in which the personal relationship between managers is totally divorced from the accountability for feedback. Inclusion in the function interfaces of that part of managerial communication known as *feedback* provides just such a system.

Communication and Human Relations

Human relations in criminal justice falls into two related categories. First, it is obviously the nature of criminal justice to be involved with human relationships.[15] Second, in addition to the contact made by criminal justice with people, is the human relations involved between management and staff of the organization. Both criminal justice dealing with people outside the organization and criminal justice management interfacing with personnel within the organization depend on *communication*. Good communication, in this case, can be assumed if good human relations exist, and vice versa.

The Bureau of Better Business Practice *Training Director's Handbook* covers "human relations" as thirteen topics:[16]

1. Employee Needs
2. Improved Morale
3. Successful Discipline
4. Managing Women Workers
5. Handling Trouble-Makers
6. Grievances
7. Motivation
8. Know Your Men
9. Marginal Employees
10. Leadership
11. Supervisory Discipline
12. Goldbrickers
13. Training in Human Relations

The *Training and Development Handbook* of the American Society For Training And Development focuses on human relations in another way, but no less emphatically:

> . . . the leadership development program should be put to this test: Does it bring about improvement in the way the manager, the supervisor, the foreman, the top executive usually behaves on the job. . . .[17]

[15] Coffey, Eldefonso, and Hartinger, *Human Relations: Law Enforcement in a Changing Community* (Englewood Cliffs, N.J.: Prentice-Hall, 1971). See also Coffey, Eldefonso, and Hartinger, *Police Community Relations* (Englewood Cliffs, N.J.: Prentice-Hall, 1971).

[16] Staff, *The BBP Training Director's Handbook* (Waterford, Conn.: Bureau of Better Business Practice, 1970), pp. 129–60.

[17] Leland P. Bradford and Dorothy J. Mail, "Human Relations Laboratory Training," *Training and Development Handbook*, R. L. Craig and L. R. Bittle, eds. for American Society for Training and Development (New York: McGraw-Hill, Inc., 1967), p. 251.

Careful review of the topics covered by the BBP handbook indicates that the model has already dealt with these to the degree that the role interfaces are actually functioning. With regard to the ASTD handbook, the position taken for this model is that a manager's personal style—his *behavior*—is not involved in management unless and until it relates directly to results.

Moreover, even when unrelated to results, behavior is the responsibility of the individual manager who remains, in the model, accountable for a particular function and the achievement of results. His behavior never becomes the responsibility of the organization. *Nor, it is emphasized, does his personality configuration become the responsibility of the organization under any pretext.*

The approaches to changing behavior and personality in organizations may be utilized by any administrator. But in this systems model, there is neither a requirement nor even a suggestion that the risk of these controversial approaches be tried:

> Sensitivity training is a novel and controversial form of education which goes under a variety of names: laboratory training or education, encounter groups, "T" groups, "L" (for Learning) groups, self-analytic groups and many more.[18]

The "novel and controversial" assessment is borne out by the author's years of experience as a training director utilizing virtually all known group processes. Results ranging from dramatic improvements in a manager's ability to get along with people through apparently permanent breakdowns in interpersonal relationships have been witnessed. Some of the more serious breakdowns have occurred during or immediately after group processes directed by foremost names in group work—an extremely significant consideration each time "therapeutic treatment process" is tried on managerial staff.

Of course this assessment of communication training relates to management—it does not relate to working staff dealing with the community or with other clientele who are without well-defined roles and functions that in turn produce well-defined interfaces. This does not endorse communication training for working staff without regard to the form it takes, however. Indeed, the questions raised about sensitivity training for criminal justice managers are valid also with regard to line policemen, probation officers, parole agents, and institutional staff.

In this regard, the Johari Window presented earlier may be of value:

In areas in which effective criminal justice depends upon the "open" position, the communication training that may be required is in the interest of achieving results. When the "blind," "hidden," or "unknown" positions do not relate to effective criminal justice, policemen, probation and parole officers, and institutional staff can spend their training time more profitably. In making the determination of whether or not these positions relate to ef-

---

[18] Warren G. Bennis, *Organizational Development: Its Nature, Origins, and Prospects* (Reading, Mass.: Addison-Wesley Publishers, 1969), p. 61.

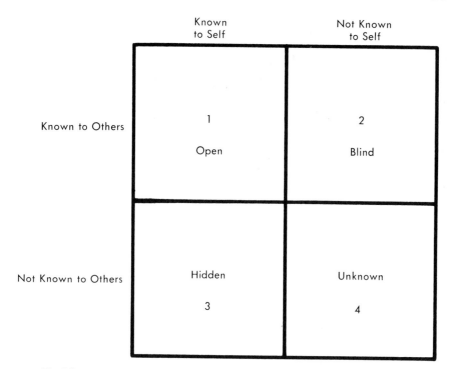

The Johari Window

Reprinted from Group Processes by Joseph Luft by permission of National Press Books.

fective management, it might be useful to consider the relationship of the GRID® presented earlier, to the Johari Window.

Because a window can be open or closed, the relationship of the GRID® to the Johari Window is simplified (see illustration on page 154).

Thinking of each of these five diagrams as a window, each of the five GRID® positions can then be thought of as a particular view.

Although this by no means eliminates the need for a management decision about the relationship of a Johari Window to a particular program, it nevertheless clarifies the specific considerations involved.

Returning to the specific managerial context of communication training, it is worth noting that there does not appear to be evidence that even nonmanagerial goals are achieved. (This point will be elaborated in later chapters, particularly Chapter Sixteen.) But within the context of management communication, it is worth exploring briefly here—particularly in the context of changing managerial personality or behavior.

Managerial Personality and Behavior Change

Beyond the implications of the model itself, sensitivity training geared to change of behavior or personality of managers raises other questions beyond simple controversy.

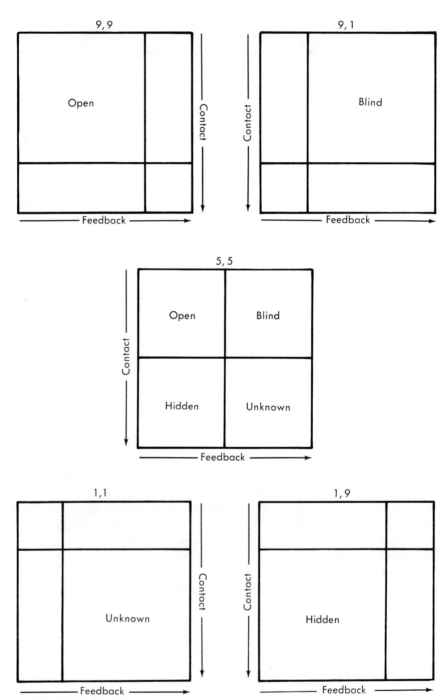

Too frequently sensitivity training is essentially experience for experience sake. Imagine, Schwartz suggests, spending an intensive encounter weekend exposed to all kinds of intimate physical and psychological exploration. Come dusk, the marathon folds, each participant says "good-bye," expecting never again to see one another, never to pursue their involvement with one another. Each of the participants knows that the experience is anonymous and time-limited. This, unlike psychotherapy, Schwartz suggests, "encourages not depth of feeling, not seriousness (in intent) and meaningful involvement, but more hollowness, more emptiness in relating to others."[19]

Those who have experienced this in the weekend marathon "stranger groups," hoping that the longstanding and continuing relationship of managers in such groups would eliminate this problem, have in general been sorely disappointed. In this regard, the impressive work of psychiatrist Irvin Yalom of Stanford University raised still further managerial questions about improving these problems simply on the basis of charismatic or well-known group leaders.[20]

Within the context of criminal justice, managerial sensitivity training will be elaborated in later chapters, particularly the final chapter.

But in terms of managerial communication, the position is being taken here that police chiefs and their managers, along with chief probation officers and their managers, can learn and effectively utilize the systems model without sensitivity training.

In any event, this model does not suggest the risks of such controversial methods, however popular they may appear to be at times in certain areas.

Returning to human relations, the fact remains that good managerial communication can be assumed with good human relations—human relations defined only in areas covered by the model. Actually, the model *requires* good communication, but not in every area of human relations. Indeed, it is doubtful that continuous communication between all people and large groups is even possible unless confined completely to roles and functions; continuous, predictable, reliable communication in at least a minimal level is a requisite of successful management and of successful managerial communication.

Some specific definition of what is meant by managerial communication is, therefore, indicated at this point.

Approaches to Defining Managerial Communication

One approach to what managerial communication *is* might be found in a consideration of what managerial communications *does*:

[19] Carl Goldberg, "An Encounter With the Sensitivity Training Movement," *Canada's Mental Health* (September–October 1970).

[20] Irvin D. Yalom, M.D., *Theory and Practice of Group Psychotherapy* (New York: Basic Books, 1970).

A breakdown in communication is the beginning of many human relation conflicts. Somewhere along the line, the sender's message becomes warped and the receiver reacts to unintended distortion. When, for example, you ask your secretary, "Is the XYZ report finished yet?" you simply want information—but she thinks you're chiding her for not having the report ready and she becomes defensive.[21]

This reference to the *content* of a message will prove useful in defining managerial communication shortly.

Another approach to defining managerial communication is offered by analyzing the components of communication—for instance, the component of *listening*:

1. Find area of interest
2. Judge content, not delivery
3. Hold your fire
4. Listen for ideas
5. Be flexible
6. Work at listening
7. Resist distractions
8. Exercise your mind
9. Keep open mind
10. Capitalize on thought spread[22]

Still another approach to a definition is consideration of what encourages communication:

If the superior's control over the personal goals of subordinates were decreased, their fear of receiving a penalty for disclosure would undoubtedly decrease. It is perhaps unrealistic, however, to expect this to be a feasible alternative, given the kind of organizational structure prevalent in our society; it is a fact of organizational life that a superior has a fairly high degree of control over subordinates. He can often fire, lay off, block promotion, block salary increase, or hold back developmental assignments if he doesn't like what he hears from a subordinate. These threats, whether enacted or not, are enough to discourage an employee from disclosure.[23]

Managerial communication, where this approach is to be pursued, would likely emerge as an exploration of coercive control of employees through selective communication.

[21] Jack H. Grossman, "Are Your Messages Provoking Conflict?" *Supervisory Management* Vol. 10, No. 2, (November 1970).

[22] Ralph G. Nichols, "Listening Is A 10-Part Skill," *Nations' Business*, Vol. 3, No. 3, July 1957.

[23] Gary Gemmill, "Managing Upward Communication," *Management Review*, May 1970.

Actually, there are in the literature a host of approaches to defining communication.[24] But probably the one unifying variable—the *context* in which any communication occurs—suggests still another approach. This is reflected in a quote from three of the most gifted students of communication —Watzlawick, Beavin, and Jackson:

> . . . a phenomenon remains unexplainable as long as the range of observation is not wide enough to include the context in which the phenomenon occurs. . . .[25]

In other words, the *context* of anything communicated is important. The context is perceptible when there is a sufficient range of observation. The context of a message, when combined with the content of a message, has the potential of becoming communication.

Content and Context

The manager who states that the world is flat may find many who disagree with the *content* of his message. But assuming that there exists an otherwise healthy working relationship within his organization, even those disagreeing with the content of his message will hopefully agree on the *context* of the message—that of an individual's right to express whatever content he believes.

Communication Defined

For the model, then, managerial communication is only possible *when the context for the sender permits the content of the message to be received.* In other words, when meaning has been conveyed it does not matter whether or not agreement on the meaning has been reached.

This definition, by design, restricts managerial communication to the model itself. By removing the complexities of negotiating matters not related to results, managers are not asked to adjust their personality or behavior to circumvent or produce consentient agreement on anything other than communication directly related to results achievement. Removing the requirement that managers agree on *all* content, it becomes possible to either agree or disagree on all communication except that directly related to results achievement, which has clearly defined roles and functions that interface in a manner that mitigates against disagreement.

[24] See, for example, S. I. Hayakawa, *Semantics Et Cetera: A Review Of General Semantics*, 9 (4) (1952), 243–57 (also available as Bobbs-Merrill Reprint "Language 43"); D. D. Jackson, ed., *Therapy, Communication and Change* (Palo Alto, Calif.: Science and Behavior Books, 1968); A. Nehrabian and A. Weiner, "Non-Immediacy Between Communicator And Object," *Journal of Consulting Psychology*, 30 (1966), 420–26; Paul Watzlawick, *An Anthology Of Human Communication* (Palo Alto, Calif.: Science and Behavior Books, 1965).

[25] Paul Watzlawick, Janet H. Beavin, and Don Jackson, *Pragmatics Of Communication* (New York: W. W. Norton, Inc., 1967), pp. 20–21.

The value of removing the burden of agreement on irrelevant matters is much more significant than appears at first glance. Consider for example the gross variation in individual perception: two people looking at a glass of water may "see" two different things—one sees a glass half full, the other sees one half empty—and *both are right.* If each acknowledges a context that permits to the other his own perception, undistorted communication can continue—i.e., neither person will feel obliged to adjust his perception to fit the needs of the other and thus to filter and distort.

Communication Filters and Distortion

A frequent training exercise in communication illustrates the ease with which distortion can occur in communication. A group of people sitting in a circle is asked to whisper a message secretly from one to another until the originator has the secret he started whispered to him. Even with explicit, emphasized instructions to repeat the message verbatim, the message almost invariably returns to the originator at least distorted, and in some cases completely changed. This experiment might be thought of as a natural distortion that becomes grossly compounded when there are further distortions in the concepts of *self* and the *other* as discussed in Chapter Three. A "yes-man" counts himself out, the other in. This context filters and distorts information so he hears nothing about Indians on the warpath, but instead sees Indians inside the fort. This can lead to a discontented, argumentative organizational atmosphere.

But situations allowing the possibility of disagreement permits unfiltered, undistorted communication that is sorely needed by a manager seeking results. And this context for counting both *self* and *other* occurs primarily in face-to-face communication.

Face-to-Face Communication

Unfiltered and undistorted communication, regardless of its value, is unlikely if information is processed totally by the management information system discussed in the preceding chapter. Face-to-face communication remains the very core of an informational system.

Perhaps the absence of this awareness within some organizations accounts in part for the way sensitivity training seems to improve information flow in some instances. Perhaps sensitivity training sometimes provides the only approach to simple recognition of how complex human communication remains even when clarity of roles and functions permits simpler definitions of managerial communication.

Edgar H. Schein, one of the more sophisticated organizational process analysts, has written:

> One of the most important processes in organizations and one of the easiest to observe, is how the members communicate with each other, particularly in

face-to-face situations. Many formulations of communication depict it as a simple problem of transfer of information from one person to another. But, as all of us know, the process is anything but simple, and the information transferred is often highly variable and highly complex.[26]

Pointing out this "highly complex" process of human communication in general is what permits the use of an uncomplicated definition of managerial communication—uncomplicated as long as the context permits content to be unfiltered and undistorted.

Even the fact- and data-derived MIS content communicates very little if the face-to-face communication used with MIS has a context in which either *self* or *other* is discounted. Avoidance of any credibility gap is by far the most significant variable in the design of the systems model.

Communication and Model Design

The design of the model is such that if difficulty exists with content and/or context, it probably indicates that at least some roles and functions are not being performed. In other words, communication within the design of the systems model is a kind of index or thermometer for gaining additional measurement of role and function performance.

Managers need the *content* of the communication of other managers in order to perform role and function—at least when it is content that relates to the achievement of results. Communication content not related to results can be considered within the area of permissible disagreements.

When roles and functions are not performed in criminal justice because of failure in communication, there is a much greater social loss than when the same managerial problem occurs in private industry. The price tag on unperformed criminal justice management functions is inadequate police service and inadequate justice—with all the social consequences these entail.

Communication, then, can assist in determining when roles and functions are not being performed. Communication can also be the method of bringing to bear the managerial motivation for performing the roles and functions to the tremendous satisfaction of knowing what is expected, knowing how expectations relate to consentient goals, and knowing the measurements of success. An even greater motivation is the satisfaction of personal judgment interfacing with the talents of other managers in the actual achievement of results.

This systems model begins with clearly defined roles and functions in the first place and focuses communication on performance of these roles and functions—not on the improvement of personal communication between managers. Then, by emphasizing the profound complexity of human communication in general, the model promotes managerial process by restricting

---

[26] Schein, *Process Consultation: Its Role in Organizational Development* (Reading, Mass.: Addison-Wesley Publishers, 1969), p. 15.

managerial communication to areas related to results achievement.

The model frees the manager of the responsibility of sorting various inputs from other managers; most management suffers not from too little communication but too much. In other words, it attempts to relieve the police chief and his managers, along with the chief probation officer and his managers, of the unbearable burden of knowing everything.

Placing communication in this context for the systems model is by no means intended to discredit the efforts of consultants who use T-Groups successfully in organizations—it simply points out that the handling of communication problems can start at turnpike speed if roles and functions are clear in the first place and do not need to be interpersonally negotiated.

The model, of course, comes no closer to pleasing everybody than any other managerial approach—the purely consentient management approach will offend those with a strong preference for privacy, and the purely command approach will offend those with a preference for group involvement. But it certainly comes closer to achieving results than managerial approaches concerned more with who does things and how they do things than with what things get done. Similarly, the model avoids defining communication in such a way that *how* things get done becomes more important than *what* is actually done.

> The process of communication, that is, the passing of information and understanding, is a prerequisite for attaining changes in the behavior of subordinates and others in the organization.[27]

This model shares the position that communication remains a prerequisite. But the *amount* of communication is determined by the relevance of communication to results and not to any capricious individual variations in preference for communication.

The systems model, then, unlike other approaches, provides an answer for concerns about too much or too little communication—just enough openness in communication to achieve managerial results.

This approach admittedly forces the manager seeking overall communication improvement through changes in his personality to search *outside* the organization. But when results are involved, this approach also demands that managers who may not *like* the communication process participate sufficiently to insure performance of role and function—to insure the achievement of results.

SUMMARY

This chapter concluded the section in which the managerial model was

---

[27] Leonard J. Kazmier, *Principles of Management,* 2nd ed. (New York: McGraw-Hill, Inc., 1969), p. 176.

presented, with consideration of personnel, labor unions, and managerial communication.

Personnel was introduced in categories of recruiting, screening, testing, indoctrination-orientation, performance evaluation, discipline, job description, classification, promotions, transfers, up- and downgrading, and in some cases hiring and firing. Health and safety, along with typical employee services were also discussed.

The distinction was made between centralized and decentralized personnel services available to criminal justice managers on the basis of the relative size and complexity of the organization involved.

The problems of inconsistent use of "good man myths" in recruiting and performance evaluation were stressed. "Credentialism" was defended insofar as it relates to college preparation and professionalism—college preparation presented as an effective method of learning how to learn in addition to the content of some of the increasingly relevant criminal justice courses.

Labor unions and other employee groups involved in collective bargaining were discussed as relating to government "outside the department" in terms of salary and working conditions; and "inside the department" related to administration on all other grievances. It was noted, however, that even when all other grievances are remedied, unrest from salary and working conditions have a significant impact upon administration.

The fact was discussed that removing the threat of strikes fails to mitigate the unfavorable impact of unresolved unrest. Steady increase in the formation of employee organizations was observed.

Communication was presented in the context of human relations. Through emphasis on what communication "contains," the "content" of communication is discernible. Through consideration of the "situation" in which communication occurs, the "context" of communication in discernible. Then, through emphasis on *content* and *context*, managerial communication can narrow to specific managerial concerns. Managerial and organizational feedback was discussed and elaborated.

Sensitivity training and similar approaches in management were presented as unnecessary when roles and functions are performed adequately. It was acknowledged that sensitivity training might be of value in bringing about clarity of roles and functions in organizations where neither are clear.

The position was taken that management suffers more from too much communication than too little—that sorting input, no matter how skillfully, is not as functional as designing input.

QUESTIONS

1. Discuss the relationship of personnel, labor unions, and managerial communication.

2. Name the personnel services presented.

3. Relate each personnel service to the management model.

4. Discuss task force development lab operation in terms of personnel.

5. How is accountability related to the *who* function in terms of personnel?

6. Which of the four managerial skills (conceptual, program, human, and political) discussed in Chapter Three were presented as significant to personnel services?

7. Distinguish between centralized and decentralized personnel services available to administrators.

8. Discuss the "good man mythology."

9. Relate labor unions to the systems model.

10. Define labor negotiations in terms of personnel services.

11. Why is the administrator concerned with salary grievances even though they are beyond his control?

12. What is managerial communication?

13. How and why is management communication different from general communication?

14. Relate content and context to managerial communication.

15. Relate communication filters to the model; to sensitivity training.

16. What is meant by "managers suffer from too much rather than too little communication?" By "sorting communication input?"

ANNOTATED REFERENCES

BARUCH, ISMAR, *Position Classification in Public Service.* Civil Services Assembly, c. 1941, ed. 1942. This volume thought by many personnel specialists to be a classic of the title subject, affords in-depth elaboration of classification when managerial results have not been articulated.

HEUTIS, CARL E., "Police Unions," *The Police Yearbook.* Washington, D. C.: IACP, 1958. Provides good context for title subject as discussed in this chapter.

LEONARD, V. A., *Police Organization and Management,* 2nd Ed. Brooklyn, N.Y.: Foundation Press, 1964. An interesting managerial approach that clarifies the employee organization relation to criminal justice administration.

Municipal Personnel Administration, International City Managers Assoc., 7th Ed., Chicago, Ill., 1960. Although geared for the municipal personnel services, this comprehensive volume is respected by many personnel specialists as the most relevant literature in all public employment on the subject matter.

SCHEER, WILBERT E., *Personnel Director's Handbook.* Chicago, Ill.: Dartnell, 1969. Embellishes the entire range of the personnel services presented in this chapter.

SCHEIN, EDGAR H., *Process Consultation: Its Role In Organization Development.* Reading, Mass.: Addison-Wesley, 1969. An extremely well-done synopsis of the organizational development approach to communication analysis and group approach to organizational process consultation—contrasts in many areas with this model.

STAHL, O. GLENN, *Public Personnel Administration*. New York: Harper, 1956. Good elaboration of personnel services in the managerial context.

WATZLAWICK, PAUL, JANET H. BEAVIN, and DON JACKSON, *Pragmatics of Communication*. New York: Norton, 1967. By far one of the most sophisticated books on the impact of communication. See also Watzlawick's *Anthology of Human Communication* (book and tape). Palo Alto, Calif.: Science and Behavior Books, 1964.

YALOM, IRVIN D., *Theory and Practice of Group Psychotherapy*. New York: Basic Books, 1970. Strongly recommended reading for any administrator planning the group approach to managerial development. See also JOSEPH LUFT, *Group Processes: An Introduction to Group Dynamics*. Palo Alto, Calif.: National Press Books, 1970. Chapter Three is devoted entirely to the Johari Window.

CHAPTER 8

Managerial Training, Education, and Development

GLOSSARY

RESULTS—administratively defined department goals ; **WHAT**—operational determination of what is needed to achieve results along with precise measurement ; **WHO**—managerial determination of operational staffing ; **HOW**—supervisory determination of methods

Probably one of the most profound observations ever made about contemporary management training in public service was contained in the remarks of a top executive meeting with the heads of other large departments and agencies. He solemnly told his prestigious colleagues:

> Gentlemen, I submit to this group that, in all seriousness, the main administrative problem with most management training that comes down the pike is the inordinate amount of "B.S."

Though unaccustomed to profanity at these executive meetings, those present lost no time in using the same term to assess a great deal of their earlier experiences with management training. Most, if not all of the negative assessments focused on "sensitivity" or related training experiences. But the theme of the criticisms tended to fault training more for failure to integrate the overall career of the executive than for being unpragmatic.

Most of the management training for our systems model requires the assistance of a specialist. In large measure, then, the integration of executive career through management training becomes a function of administrative dealings with the training consultant.

But reducing the validity of any criticisms of management training is also a function of administrative understanding of managerial development —sufficient understanding to demand and get career integration from training specialists, and even exert influence over management education.

Furthermore, understanding managerial development is in part understanding managerial knowledge, or, more precisely, understanding the role of managerial knowledge. As Harold Koontz puts it:

> . . . there is ever the danger that management knowledge will not be used to obtain results in practice. It must be operational and it must be for reality since managing, as an art, is a matter of using knowledge to solve real problems to develop operating systems or environment in which people can perform. This means several things. Knowledge of management is not enough. There is always the danger in any field of developing a science aimed at elegance and polish, rather than *results*. Every science has its "educated derelicts" who know but cannot apply this knowledge to gain useful results . . . moreover, the reality with which a manager must deal is always tomorrow. . . .[1]

But integration of knowledge that will be used within an executive career is not management training alone. It is training and education for the purpose of managerial development, which relates in the systems model to administrators of statewide correctional systems, chief probation officers, federal directors, court administrators, and police chiefs.

Attention is now turned to managerial education and training as it relates to the administrators and managers of the widely diversified criminal justice system.

MANAGERIAL EDUCATION AND TRAINING

The education, training, and development of managers are three closely related but separate program considerations—both are necessary for successful development of managerial potential.

---

[1] Koontz, "Management and Challenges of the Future," *Advanced Management Journal*, 33, No. 1 (January 1968), 22.

Educational theorists have categorized and strongly supported the merits of education versus those of training. Each school of thought has offered substantial support for its views. What has become apparent is that complete and comprehensive educational programs have included training activities. Conversely, a sound training program will include much education. If either education or training is being presented properly, each will have a substantial amount of the other included in its curriculum.[2]

From this frame of reference, managerial development consists of programs including both education and training that create the managerial potential to achieve results needed in the systems model.

For purposes of this discussion, managerial *education* is broadly inclusive of academic and theoretical principles of applied behavior science and general systems; training is restricted in nature and scope to methods, strategies, techniques, and systems of applying managerial education; and managerial *development* is that combination of education and training that produces the managerial capability to achieve results within the systems model. Any format that successfully combines the required training with the required education is a managerial development program by definition.

Perhaps as the role of training is clarified within the criminal justice system, a clearer picture of how it relates to education will emerge, and a format will develop.

> Establishing departments in organizations that are specifically designed to train supervisory and non-supervisory personnel is a concept which has emerged only within about the past twenty years. Consequently, principles and guidelines for effective management of the training function have not yet been fully explored or established. In fact, the development of theory applicable to the management of training is sorely lacking.[3]

Evolving a theory of managing training may be facilitated by a sophisticated inclusion of both training and education in college courses. Consider the following course outline from the Department of Administration of Justice, California State University, San Jose:[4]

A. *Course Description*

A survey of the principles of law enforcement administration with emphasis upon their application toward the solution of current problems.

---

[2] Denny F. Pace, James D. Stinchcomb, and Jimmie C. Styles, *Law Enforcement Training and Community Colleges: Alternatives for Affiliation* (Washington, D.C.: American Assoc. of Junior Colleges, 1970), p. 5.

[3] Robert L. Minter, "Mismanagement of Training Programs," *Training and Development Journal* of the American Society for Training and Development, 26, No. 7 (July 1972), 2.

[4] Syllabus used by the Department of Administration of Justice at California State University, San Jose; similar to an increasing number of course syllabi used in administrative police courses, such as courses at Michigan State, Berkeley, and Indiana University.

B. *Student Requirements*

 1. Seminar paper

 a. Length, 20–35 pages
 b. Annotated bibliography
 c. Style—Campbell's Thesis Guide
 d. Topics must be approved by the instructor

 2. Assigned chapters will be read prior to scheduled discussions.

 3. An outline (1 or 2 pages will be prepared on each assigned article review —copies for each student). Each student will select an article appropriate to the subject.

 a. Synopsis
 b. Principal contribution
 c. Author

 4. Mid-term oral progress report by each student on the term project (copies for each student).

 a. Title
 b. Statement of the problem
 c. Importance of the study
 d. Methodology

 5. Final Oral Report by each student on the term project (copies for each student).

 a. Summary
 b. Conclusion

Although this course outline would provide a fine syllabus for most college courses related to criminal justice at any level, the point is that this outline is taught as a management course. Students fortunate enough to enroll in the course find themselves exposed to not only the theoretical basis of management but also the pragmatics of managerial (not "supervisory") application.

A theory of managing a combination of training and education may be further facilitated by the inclusion of both training and education in departmental training programs as in the case of the following introductory overview:

SANTA CLARA COUNTY PROBATION DEPARTMENT COMPREHENSIVE TRAINING PROGRAM

The departmental development program has three main parts :(1) skill and concept training programs in each of the four divisions and the ancillary functions, (2) a cross-divisional comprehensive managerial development/implementation program, and (3) a program of overall system development.

Skill and Concept Training

Staff Development programs are provided each division and ancillary function on an "in-service" or "on-the-job'" (OJT) basis. These programs are supplemented by tuition-reimbursed college courses that range from the Chapman

Master's curriculum taught virtually "in-house' 'to courses taken at nearby colleges.

The in-service programs range from orientation series for new staff that includes such areas as drug training and minority group coursework along with intensive in-depth treatment/classification methods (i.e., I-Laval, Conjoint Family Therapy, Brief Paradox Therapy, Behavior Modification, etc.) through a host of techniques directly related to job activities. These programs are taught primarily by the training division but are also offered in some instances by other staff or outside consultants.

Specialized training bulletins and materials are continually published in support of the in-service program. An agency library emphasizing professional literature is also maintained.

Managerial Development

Perhaps the best starting point for sketching the JPD [Juvenile Probation Dept.] management package is with the classical criticism of public agency management: "If you don't know where you're going then you can't get lost." This means that our managerial training is goal-oriented—geared to determining when "we're lost" in relation to long-range planning.

Goal-oriented management is results-oriented management, and effectively achieving results depends on clearly defined managerial roles for each level of the management team: first-line supervisors, second-line supervisors, division directors, and office of chief. Creating ego satisfactions for each of these managerial levels permits not only the effective achievement of results without role interference between managers but also permits the ego satisfaction of excellence in line work that is unencumbered by managers who forget they are managers.

Each managerial role is defined by the degree of responsibility for achieving results—results determined in advance on a long-range basis. The office of chief, of course, negotiates these long-range results politically, fiscally, and socially. Division directors determine operationally what part of the results must be accomplished on a priority basis and turn these duties over to second-line supervisors.

Second-line supervisors make a determination of who will assume management responsibility for how tasks are accomplished. To ensure agency-wide, cross-divisional opportunities for staff to express individual talent, this who function is also performed collectively in the second-line supervisor group now known as the task force development lab.

First-line supervisors develop the capability to assume absolute and total managerial responsibility for how defined results are achieved.

The management program stresses sensitivity to staff desires, interests, and capabilities in order to provide program opportunities for staff to express talents that might otherwise go unnoticed. The actual procedures for gaining the staff's participation in the managerial process tend to flatten the pyramid.

The training required for effectively implementing so comprehensive a program is admittedly complex. Fortunately, we are over half way. In brief, these training areas are the core of the program: classical "X" and "Y", managerial grid, matrix management and certain other OD derivatives, MBO, cybernated information systems, synergetics, and those fundamental managerial skills related to general systems theory.

Implementation is by stages as well as phases of managerial level. Function analysis of management scope, the management information system, five-year planning, and many other component parts make up the implementation cycle. Of course, the most vital part remains the systematic assessment of staff interests and talent.

System Development

The training design for the system development segment of the program includes the gradual assumption of control over skill and concept training to ensure optimum yield in terms of systematic effectiveness.

Adjustments in the existing management system that relate to the managerial development program are also a function of system development. As managerial competence increases, advanced levels of sophistication in programming are implemented.

Training Philosophy

Organizing training efforts into effective programs can be justified only when training content is well ahead of current practice. *Effective* training cannot be an academic version of the status quo—staff can and do learn the status quo without professional trainers.

Though there is great complexity in continually adjusting programs to function ahead of current practice, there is nonetheless a simple measure of training effetciveness: whether or not training leaves perceptible results that complement the long-range mission of the agency.[5]

In any case, successful managerial development programming includes that combination of training and education producing the managerial capability to achieve results required by the systems model. Moreover, it includes what Greenlaw has referred to as "the manager's own *memory element* and/or his *transformation skills* . . ."[6] Although cast in the context of "off-the-job training," which Greenlaw defines as "conferences, university executive development programs, and institutes and seminars sponsored by professional associations . . . ," the *intent* of the training appears to be extremely cogent to this discussion of combining training and education:

> That is, the manager: 1. May be furnished with information which hopefully will be stored in his mind for future utilization in making decisions or 2. May be provided in the training conference with some form of synthetic experience in actually transforming certain types of inputs and outputs—e.g., assuming the role of a supervisor in a mock performance appraisal interview, or playing a business game.[7]

---

[5] A typical summary statement on the training program directed by the author.

[6] Paul S. Greenlaw, "Management Development: A Systems View," *Personnel Journal,* 43, No. 4 (April 1964), 207.

[7] Ibid.

Combining training and education, as already noted, is for the purpose of managerial development programming that hopefully leads to transformation skills as well as increased memory. But does the combination lead to leadership? For that matter, is leadership training necessary?

MANAGERIAL DEVELOPMENT

In an astonishing paper read to the 1971 convention of the American Psychological Association, Fred Fiedler drew upon years of research in leadership training to observe:

> The fact that neither leadership experience nor leadership training appears to improve organizational or group performance is, not surprisingly, one of the more embarrassing and certainly one of the less celebrated findings in organizational psychology. But experience and training may simply not raise the overall effectiveness of leaders.[8]

Fiedler included in the implications of this observation the research findings that "sensitivity and T-Group approaches" reflect no evidence of "organizational improvement."[9]

Managerial development programming can scarcely ignore the implications of these observations if genuine effort is being expended toward development of managerial capability.

Fortunately for the systems model, neither leadership per se nor sensitivity training is significant in the role interfacing function approaches to achieving administrative results. Instead, emphasis is placed upon managerial role clarification and managerial function accountability, to the virtual exclusion of concern for personality changes among managers—results achievement is the single variable.

The significance of Fiedler's research may be substantially greater to other very respectable approaches to managerial development. Overtly and covertly, sensitivity training, and in some instances leadership training, is emphasized in varying degrees. Organizational development (OD), for instance, emphasizes a kind of process that at least implicitly calls for "sensitivity" throughout its rich and impressive literature.[10] The popular manage-

---

[8] Fred E. Fiedler, "On the Death and Transfiguration of Leadership Training," invited address of Divisions 8, 14, and 19 and Research Award winner Division 13, American Psychological Association, Washington D.C., Sept. 3, 1971 (revised October 1971, University of Washington Technical Reports 70–16 and 70–21, "Organizational Research Group"), p. 2.

[9] Ibid., p. 1.

[10] See in particular Jack K. Fordyce and Raymond Weil, *Managing With People. A Manager's Handbook of Organizational Development* (Reading, Mass.: Addison-Wesley Publishers, 1971). As a background for the proposed managerial change, see also the same publisher's OD series consisting on six books: *Strategies of Organizational Development; Developing Organizations; Process Consultation; Nature of Organization Development; Grid Organization Development; Third Party Consultation.*

ment by objectives (MBO) does not *require* sensitivity training, but the frequent absence of categorical positions on sensitivity in the typical MBO package[11] at times leaves an administrator feeling that some T-Group might help. There are a number of management consulting firms whose entire package consists of sensitivity training.

The fact that sensitivity training is not necessary for the systems model is in no way critical of the laudable goals of such training.

> As the name suggests, the goal is to make men more sensitive to themselves and others, to make them aware of how, consciously and unconsciously, they affect others and others influence them. Its role in management development is based on the assumption that a manager will do a better job of achieving results through efforts of others if he has a heightened sensitivity to others.[12]

Within the context of the line work of criminal justice, such sensitivity might be exceedingly useful to policemen in contact with the public, with probation and parole officers or prison staff relating to offenders, and possibly with prosecution-defense relationships with, say, juries—assuming of course that sensitivity training could be made successful enough to justify the great amount of time and money involved in large-scale programs.

But the isolation of management as a separate and significantly important criminal justice function suggests training with far greater yield than has already been noted and is further clarified by this observation:

> . . . quite a number of former participants have become enthusiastic advocates of sensitivity training. Almost no one, however, is able to say precisely how the experience has helped his work as a manager. . . .[13]

The systems model, however, emphasizes clarity of managerial roles and accountability for management functions to the exclusion of concern for either leadership training or sensitivity training as such—out of deference to a growing amount of empirical evidence that both emerge effectively when roles, functions, and programs interface systematically.

Combining education and training for the systems model, then, is somewhat less complex, and therefore an advantage.

> One can generalize that, in most management programs where conventional methodologies were utilized, the training resulted only in limited if any atti-

---

[11] As a refinement of Peter Drucker's original management by objectives concept, a number of excellent MBO "packages" have been developed. For example, Glenn H. Varney, *Management By Objectives* (Chicago: Dartnell Corporation, 1971). See also Malcolm E. Shaw, *Developing Communication Skills* from George Odiorne's fine television series on MBO, Educational Systems and Designs, Inc., Westport, Connecticut, 1968. (also Odiorne's *Management By Objectives* (New York: Pitman, 1965).

[12] Walter S. Wikstrom, "Sensitivity Training," *Studies In Personnel Policy*, No. 189 (New York: National Industrial Conference Board, Inc., 1964), p. 90.

[13] Ibid., p. 94

tude change; there is almost a total lack of evidence that what little attitude change did take place was of sustained duration; there is almost no evidence that management training resulted in on-the-job behavior changes of significant duration.[14]

Attitudes and even behavior are not the explicit goals of the systems model—results achievement through performance of specific functions of clearly defined *roles* is the primary goal. With this particular array of managerial development priorities the advantage of less complexity is amplified.

But even with this advantage, the systems model faces many of the same formidable challenges faced by any successful managerial development effort. Many types of resistance confront efforts to develop managerial potential for role performance in any systems model. Consider this typical list as it relates to dynamic, effective, results-oriented management:

1. We tried that before in criminal justice.
2. Our place is different from other subsystems.
3. It costs too much.
4. That's beyond our responsibility.
5. That's not my job, it's the judge's.
6. We're all too busy to do that.
7. It's too radical a change for the community.
8. We don't have the time.
9. Not enough help.
10. That will make other programs obsolete.
11. Let's research first.
12. Our department is too small for it.
13. Not practical for operating people.
14. The men will never buy it.
15. The union will scream.
16. We've never done it before.
17. It's against department policy.
18. Gums up our other program.
19. We don't have the authority.
20. That's too ivory tower.
21. Let's get back to reality.
22. That's not our problem.
23. Why change it? It's still working O.K.
24. I don't like the idea.

[14] Wallace Wohlking, "Management Training, Where Has It Gone Wrong?" *Training and Development Journal*, ASTD, 25, No. 12 (December 1971), 3.

25. You're right—but . . .
26. You're two years ahead of your time.
27. We're not ready for that.
28. We don't have the money and personnel.
29. It isn't in the budget this year.
30. Can't teach an old dog new tricks.
31. Good enough, but impractical.
32. Let's hold it in abeyance.
33. Let's give it more thought.
34. Top management would never go for it.
35. Let's put it in writing.
36. We'll be the laughing stock.
37. Not that again!
38. We'd lose in the long run.
39. Where'd you dig that one up?
40. We did all right without it.
41. That's what we can expect from the staff.
42. It's never been tried before.
43. Let's shelve it for the time.
44. Let's form a committee.
45. Has anyone else ever tried it?
46. Community won't like it.
47. I don't see the connection.
48. It won't work in our department.
49. What you are really saying is . . .
50. Maybe that will work in your department, but not in mine.
51. The executive committee will never go for it.
52. Don't you think we should look into it further before we act?
53. What do they do in other departments?
54. Let's all sleep on it.
55. It can't be done.
56. It's too much trouble to change.
57. It won't pay for itself.
58. It's impossible.
59. I know a fellow who tried it.
60. We've always done in this way.
61. You're not here to think.
62. Let me think about that and I'll get back to you.
63. Let's wait until conditions are more favorable.
64. You don't understand . . .

This only partial list symbolizes the significant problem in getting a managerial development program started. And the problem exists even though personality change is not a requisite of the systems model. Combining education and training in such a way as to cut through the resistance (and at times apathy) becomes the first order of business.

Still another consideration within the context of resistance to managerial development has to do with the influence of "what we've always done." Of course this variety of resistance may not even be conscious. But whether overt or covert it becomes a major consideration at the implementation stage of most managerial development programs. For this reason, the selection of a training consultant as discussed in Chapter Fourteen requires consideration of much more than merely the consultant's technical expertise.

A consultant, to be successful in combating resistance, must know the difference between *learning* and *doing*. In an indirect way, this difference in turn relates to combining education and training.

COMBINING EDUCATION AND TRAINING

The Literature

Ideally, the literature would be the place to examine various possibilities of combining education and training in such a way that any resistance to change could be negotiated. Regrettably, there is probably too much literature to be of help. Lyman Randall has synthesized an excellent eighteen-page Managerial Development bibliography for the Joint Commission on Correctional Manpower and Training to supplement the extensive literature.[15] The outstanding *Probation Management Institutes* of the National Council on Crime and Delinquency are no less prolific in fine, relevant literature.[16]

The inclusion of extensive, relevant bibliographies in most contemporary criminal justice books also reflects literature directly related to managerial development. For example, Clarence Schragg's extremely comprehensive *Crime and Justice American Style*[17] concludes with a relevant bibliography of seventy citations under "problems in administration," supplemented by eighteen citations under "manpower and training" and twenty-two under "personnel and training."

Compounding the problems of effective use of literature in combining

---

[15] Many publications of the Joint Commission on Correctional Manpower and Training, 1522 "K" St., NW, Washington D. C., 20005.

[16] The NCCD-administered Probation Management Institutes funded in late 1969 under the Dept. of Justice LEAA grant no. 065; see also the management literature of the related *National Probation and Parole* Institutes.

[17] Clarence Schragg, *Crime and Justice American Style*, U.S. Government Printing Office, Washington, D.C., 20402.

education and training is the extremely wide range of philosophical positions on management.[18] This author must confess a rather wide range of philosophical orientation reflected in the five-page selected bibliography compiled for the training program overviewed earlier in this discussion.

Combine these problems of volume and diversity with the virtual blizzard of relevant training materials (that are in effect literature),[19] and there is little wonder that literature is rarely incorporated in serious efforts to deal with the resistance that has been noted.

Approaching resistance while combining education and training for managerial development might well, then, be approached not from literature but from the wisdom of Galileo: *"You cannot teach a man anything; you can only help him find it within himself."* Combining education and training is not a matter of teaching, but of creating possibilities to *learn*.

Creating Possibilities to Learn

A managerial development program that attempts to negotiate the implicit resistance inherent in most established organizations is in need of a motive to learn.

From old experience I know that amateur productions, offered ostensibly for one's honest cold judgement, to be followed by an uncompromisingly sincere verdict, are not readily offered in that spirit at all. The thing really wanted and expected is compliment and encouragement.[20]

Managerial development programming that equates success with managerial productions that "are offered ostensibly for one's honest cold judgement" (i.e., results measurement) might do well to provide motive to learn through "compliment and encouragement"—recognizing that scientific measure and achievement alone may prove grossly inadequate to deal with organizational resistance. When compliment and encouragement are transmitted through the genuine satisfaction of achieving results through learning, a rather powerful motive to learn hopefully begins to emerge.

[18] As examples, Robert L. DeSatnick's *A Concise Guide to Management Development* (New York: American Management Association, 1970) affords an optimistic blueprint philosophy not unlike the systems model presented in this book. Anthony Jay's *Management and Machiavelli,* (New York: Holt, Rinehart and Winston, 1967) translates organizations into "states," some "feudal, Tudor, eighteenth-century Spain or Renaissance Italy." The *Administrative Revolution* by George Berkley (Englewood Cliffs, N.J.: Prentice-Hall, Inc., 1971) is not far from the dramatic philosophies of Alvin Toffler's *Future Shock* (New York: Bantam Books, 1971) in forecasting the total collapse of current organization structure.

[19] For example, J. William Pfeiffer and John E. Jones through University Associates Press publish a fine series under the title of *Handbook of Structured Experiences for Human Relations Training* (Iowa City, 1969) so impressive and inexpensive that many training directors who do not utilize sensitivity training purchase the series.

[20] Mark Twain, "Mark Twain Speaks Out," *Harper's,* December 1958, p. 36.

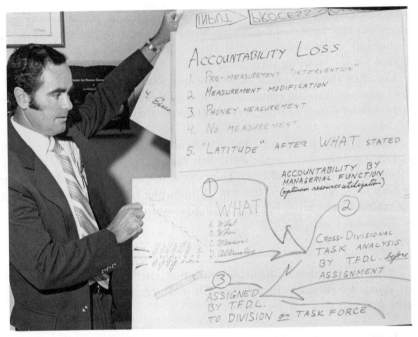

The combination of training and education required for managerial development changes
constantly in criminal justice. Here the author conducts an executive level session on cost
effectiveness in probation.

Photo courtesy of Dick Cox and Charles A. Taddo.

Further enhancement of the motive to learn is gained from the systems
model's accountability matrix. The creation of possibilities to learn is the
intent of managerial development, but compliment and encouragement combine with accountability if the intent reaches fruition.

TOP MANAGEMENT

From the frame of reference that providing possibilities to learn, rather
than literal "teaching," is the intent of education and training, the findings
of certain managerial research might be an excellent starting point for moving past resistance into managerial development programming.

> These results suggest that directors of training and development may be well
> advised to attempt to influence the attitudes with which managers *approach*
> training and development. . . .[21]

[21] Vera Kohn and Treadway C. Parker, "The Value of Expectations in Management
Development," *Training and Development Journal*, ASTO, 26, No. 6 (June 1972), 29.

Combined with the further observation that "a manager develops his expectations about a development program on the basis of communication from his superior,"[22] the most effective starting point for managerial development appears to be top management, i.e., starting with attempts to influence the attitude of managers through the top man. The attitude of top management about managerial development probably affects organizational resistance to development more than any other factor.

Moreover, on a common sense basis, top administrators are better equipped to support the development program if they understand it while it is in progress—and a side factor is the curiosity of most top administrators about how the organization for which they are responsible is being managed.

How to Start

Perhaps the most appropriate starting point in formulating programs for top managerial development is to reemphasize the priority of results achievement and once again to deemphasize the "personality change" approach. The broad and diverse literature that is not particularly useful in focusing on a specific starting point conceptually may clarify this difference. For example, the excellent OD series alluded to earlier in this discussion clarifies a number of significant differences.[23]

Once there is clarity regarding what training and education is *not*, the literature can be used to clarify what the systems model *is*. For example,

Teaching by talking is a good method, but other methods have been developed which are more appropriate at particular times than talking. When members of the group, trainees, function as active rather than passive participants, the learning process is enhanced. . . .

One of the dominant concerns of training departments in recent years has been to find ways to improve the content as well as the mtehods of training managers. . . .[24]

Top administrators often find themselves pondering the nature and the process of training and education. When this happens, extremely useful questions usually emerge:

---

[22] Ibid., p. 30.

[23] See footnote 10; also not previously cited Allen Zoll, *Dynamic Management Education*, 2nd (Reading, Mass.: Addison-Wesley, 1969); also S. S. Boocock and E. O. Schild, eds., *Simulation Games In Learning* (Beverly Hills, Calif.: Sage Publications, 1968); R. G. Graham and C. F. Gray, *Business Games Handbook* (New York: American Management Association, 1969); Rolf Lyndon and Udai Pareek, *Training for Development* (Homewood, Ill.: Dorsey Press, 1967), J. L. McKenney, *Simulation Gaming for Management Development* (Boston, Mass.: Harvard University, 1967); N. G. McNulty, *Training Managers, The International Guide* (New York: Harper and Row, 1969).

[24] Donald P. Crane, "Involvement Techniques for Manager Training," *Training and Development Journal*, ASTD, 26, No. 5 (May 1972), 26.

Q: Doesn't this development program produce *change?*

A: Yes.

Q: Then why say personality change is not a goal?

A: Because the manager is held accountable only for achieving results—any changes that he finds necessary to do this are *his* responsibility, not the responsibility of the organization.

Q: But doesn't training and education by definition suggest change?

A: Yes, change *either* in the manager personally *or* change in the system over-all—both varieties of initial change leading to change in the other.

Q: Are you saying that it doesn't matter which change occurs because each will eventually change the other?

A: Yes.

Q: Well, why not set the goal of changing the manager in the first place if the system follows?

A: *Effectiveness*—people vary so much even after they've been "changed" that continuity is possible only through system continuity.

Q: Does "system" intimate rigidity or inflexibility?

A: On the contrary, reflexive synergetics and role interfacing are *far more flexible and adaptable* than group "consensus" or "open personality"—and role interfacing provides this flexibility on a *continuing predictable* basis.

Q: But aren't there certain managerial styles that work better than others?

A: For certain managerial personalities there are—but changing all managerial personalities would take a great deal more effort *even if it were possible.*

Q: When do we start?

A: Your last question started us.

Although top management is by definition a small group for receiving education and training, the dependence of all other managers on top management for the expectations about the program discussed earlier justifies emphasis on the value of small groups. This hopefully can be integrated into the administrative acceptance of the program on a rather simple basis such as suggested in the following:

A group of 4 or 5 is generally the best size, although other sizes can serve a specific purpose. A group of three is appropriate when case material leads to role playing. . . .

. . . more than 5 introduces the problem of control. The larger the group, the harder it is. . . .[25]

Once the small size of the managerial groups that are to become involved in the program has been negotiated, the concepts of "fail-safe" and

[25] P. F. Suessmuth and M. Stengels, "Staging Case Studies for Results," *Training in Business and Industry*, 9, No. 6 (June 1972), 39.

"track record" require consideration before moving into the systems model itself.

Implementation: Fail-Safe and Track Record

Perhaps the context in which the fail-safe and track record concepts operate in the systems model could be clarified with a comparison with management by objectives. MBO and the systems model face essentially the same problem initially:

> Too many managers look upon MBO either as a gimmick or a cure-all, without giving careful thought to the objectives they want to accomplish—or to the adjustments which must be made. . . .[26]

Facing this realistic problem squarely in the initial stage will hopefully generate a top management commitment to make the necessary adjustments in order to achieve results. Ideally, this commitment would take the form of an organizational elaboration of results achievement within this simple definition:

> A successful manager must know how to work profitably with the attitudes, feeling, and motivations of those around him. He must be able to maintain good relationships at every level. . . .[27]

Ultimately, of course, these relationships are a systematic consequence of functional role interfacing and reflexive synergetics. In the meantime, top administration may do well to retain an index of its track record in order to avoid failure during the managerial development program.

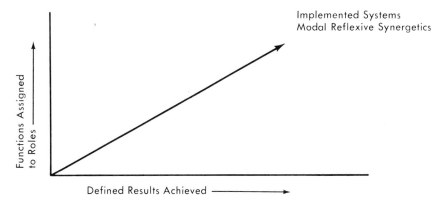

Track Record and Implementation

[26] George Strauss, "Management By Objectives: A Critical View," *Training and Development Journal,* ASTD, 26, N. 4 (April 1972), 21–28.

[27] *Training Directors Handbook* (Waterford, Conn.: Bureau of Business Practice, 1970), p. 65.

As performance of these functions establishes a track record, various people in management assume accountability for the functions. Where performance is not forthcoming, top management retains a "fail-safe" position in any particular function. Implementation, then, is gradual and on the basis of empirical evidence.

Managerial Skills

Recalling the managerial program skills, conceptual skills, human skills, and political skills, some concern must be given these before proceeding directly into a discussion of the education and training of the systems model itself. These skills are collectively a part of the education part of the development program and, as such, they are part of the systems model itself.

But because the *political* skills are limited functionally to the results definitions of the model, it is probably advisable to isolate them for top administration prior to proceeding with the systems model education and training program.

The nature and intensity of concern with political skills varies widely with the jurisdiction and organizational structure involved. But without exception, definition of viable results in a criminal justice organization is a managerial function that requires political skill, along with the three other managerial skills required of all managerial roles in the systems model.

The Systems Model: Organization Wide

Having negotiated top management's commitment and support for implementation of the systems model, the development program implementation begins on the track record and fail-safe basis as discussed. If a track record cannot be established for results definitions, there is little purpose in proceeding to the *what* level of the development program, another example of the fail-safe mechanism.

By emphasizing the *purpose* of this sequence through levels, all managers receive advanced word about the nature of the program, while at the same time placing the boss in the position of wanting to perform at his best for two reasons: (1) modeling administrative commitment and (2) not wishing to appear incapable.

Administrators who are reluctant to put it all on the line as suggested here usually modify their reluctance when asked to weigh the morale problems of a mystique preceding implementation and the doubts that could emerge regarding the boss's ability to perform his function.

Within this framework, the systems model development program proceeds with top management in whatever locally available format that can combine the broad education of managerial principles with the pragmatic training of the function performance of the model.

Coordinated efforts of college graduate schools with departmental training may be the approach, or consultants may participate with a departmental training director—any or all can participate in any and all stages of the
development program in the combination of education and training that
produces managerial capability to achieve results.

EXECUTIVE MANAGEMENT

Recalling that the *what* function tends to lend itself to executive roles
in the model, this stage of the development program is not only separated
from but follows top managerial training in larger organizations. Ideally, if
large numbers of executives are assigned to a number of small groups (as
suggested earlier), all groups receive education and training at the same time
even though not together. A number of advantages are afforded by simul-
taneous implementation of the development of *what* functions—primarily
in terms of uniformity and continuity of the overall development program.

Systems Model

As in the case of the results phase, the entire systems model is incorporated in the education and training at the executive level. Of course, emphasis is placed upon the relationship of the *what* function to the managerial
skills: conceptual, program, and human (recalling political skills as a part of
the results function).

The entire range of the management information system through the
personnel matrix approach of the model is covered, but within the context
of managerial role interface definition: *enough function overlap to permit
communication but not enough to distort roles.*

MIDDLE MANAGEMENT

Once the education and training reaches the planning phase, a track
record will have been sufficiently developed. This in turn evolves the fail-safe
mechanism's need to undertake development of the *who* function.

The popular "management case study"[28] as well as the managerial role-
playing methods seem to be singularly useful in learning resource and energy
assessments involved in the *who* function. But any combination of education
and training that produces the functional capability of system energy assessment through reflexive synergetics is appropriate.

[28] See for example Fred Luthans, *Cases, Readings and Review Guide for Principles
of Management* (New York: John Wiley & Sons, Inc., 1969), supplement to Albers' *Principles of Management* from the same publisher.

In smaller organizations, in which one manager combines the *how* function with the *who* function, it may be useful to begin with the supervisorial use of system energy assessment—the distinction between task definition and the energy to perform a task. When this is done, emphasis is needed on the structure of the role interface: results definitions do not include concern for what is operationally needed to achieve the results; *what* definitions do not include concern for who is operationally appropriate to achieve results, and *who* definitions remain separated from how results are achieved. Of course emphasis is also placed upon the participatory influence of all organizational staff on the definition of results through the system energy assessment process. Recalling previous mentions of the quasi-military nature of many criminal justice organizations, this emphasis on the participatory advantages of reflexive synergetics cannot be overstated, at least in terms of managerial development.

LINE MANAGEMENT

The supervisory determination of methods to achieve goals may require more emphasis on training (as defined) than upon education because of the nature of the line manager's activities in the model. The task/problem chart called for at staff meetings suggests this. Fortunately, the literature in this area is expanding sufficiently[29] to indicate development of the same complementary balance between education and training and the line supervisor's concerns with task energy as exists between training and education at all other managerial functions of the model. Indeed, there appears to be emerging a sense of direction in this newer literature on task energy. Hopefully, this will not only help create a balance between training and education for this managerial function but also increase the overall effectiveness of the management team.

Permeating every phase of the managerial development program is the ever-constant possibility that managers will confuse the functions that must be learned with the complex technology of the management information system of the model. Enthusiasm and challenge is predictably replaced with dread and panic if a manager mistakenly believes he is expected to learn any more about technology than is necessary to make it work for him.

One approach to preventing technology from intimidating managers is to establish an early relationship, at least in the larger organizations, be-

[29] See for example C. Bennett, "Toward Empirical, Practicable, Comprehensive Task Taxonomy," *Human Factors*, 3 (June 1971), 229; and E. Poulsen and E. Asnussen, "Energy Requirements of Practical Jobs from Pulse Increase and Ergometer Test," *Ergonomics*, January 1962. See also K. Murrell, *Human Performance in Industry*, (New York: Reinhold Publishing, 1965), and I. Streimer, "Energy Considerations as Determinants of System Design," *Human Factors* (February 1968), pp. 53–56.

tween managers and Electronic Data Processing (EDP) programmers for familiarity, but not so early that the manager doesn't know that a computer should meet his needs, and not the converse. Indeed, it should be stressed that a manager does not even need to have enough technical knowledge of how the "hardware" works. (Many people couldn't drive a car if they had to understand the theory of internal combustion engines.) In any case, the supportive role of science and technology is worth emphasis—particularly within the context of the initial organizational resistance covered earlier in this discussion. Later discussion of the role of technical consultants within managerial development will elaborate the supportive potential of science and technology. But necessary training and education depend relatively little on science and technology for support. Successful managerial development depends far less on science than on positive expectations.

> It cannot be emphasized enough that trainers and supervisors must genuinely believe that all employees are capable of more than they have shown. . . .[30]

More to the point, administrators need not panic in the presence of technology if they believe all *managers* are capable of more than they have shown.

SUMMARY

Managerial development was discussed as that combination of education and training which produces the capability of achieving results. Managerial education was presented as broadly inclusive academic and theoretical principles of applied science and systems. Managerial training was defined as the methods, strategies, techniques, and systems of applying managerial education.

Emphasis was given to flexibility in format for combining education and training in managerial development, including training directors, college curricula, consultants, and so forth, with the only criterion of success being the achievement of results.

Leadership training and sensitivity training were represented within the context of results-oriented management, with role interfacing of the model having the advantage of not depending on either.

Organizational resistance to change was dealt with as a significant concern in efforts to combine education and training. The vast literature was discussed as being too varied to be of assistance in clearly focusing on a starting point. A starting point was then suggested as providing possibilities to learn, including motivation to learn through encouragement combined with model accountability to learn "as a function."

[30] Albert S. King, "A Review: How Supervisor's Expectations Affect Trainee Performance," *Training In Business and Industry*, 9, No. 8 (August 1972), 31.

Top management was isolated as the beginning of any such learning program, followed by managers lower in the management hierarchy, all learning the entire systems model, each sequence having established a track record and a fail-safe mechanism.

QUESTIONS

1. Discuss managerial training as opposed to managerial education.

2. Discuss managerial education as opposed to managerial development.

3. Define education and training within the context of managerial development.

4. How does skill and concept training differ from management training?

5. Contrast training that seeks to change the personality of management with training that focuses totally on results achievement.

6. Discuss the managerial implications of any five of the reasons it won't work.

7. How does the systems model cope with resistance in training?

8. Discuss the combination of managerial training, education, and development.

9. Relate top administration to managerial development.

10. Discuss fail-safe and track-record implementation.

ANNOTATED REFERENCES

AVOTS, I., "Why Does Project Management Fail?" *California Management Review,* Fall 1969, pp. 77–82. An excellent analysis of a number of variables relating to the discussion of problems in managerial training that depends on such methods as T-Groups. See also "Matrix Management: A Tough Game to Play," *Dun's,* August 1970, pp. 31–34.

BIENVENU, B. J., *New Priorities In Training.* New York: American Management Association, 1969. An excellent criticism of short-range training programs around the theme that the objectives of training should be geared to the organization, direction and administration, and *development* of human resources rather than simply the conduct of courses.

DRUCKER, PETER, *The Practice of Management.* New York: Harper and Row, 1954. An excellent background for the educational aspects of the systems model written by the "father" of the popular management by objectives method.

HAMMERTON, J. C., "Management and Motivation," *California Management Review,* Winter 1970, pp. 51–56. A fine elaboration of the discussion of motivation.

LEVINSON, HARRY, "Management By Whose Objectives," *Harvard Business Review,* July–August 1970. Focuses on objectives with emphasis on top managerial ability to define results on "track record" and "fail-safe" basis.

ODIORNE, GEORGE, *Management By Objectives.* New York: Pitman, 1965. One of the many excellent extensions of Drucker's MBO, but particularly relevant to this discussion relating MBO to the systems model via common problems.

WARR, P., "Evaluating Management Training," *Personnel* (English), 2, No. 2 (February 1969), p. 26–29. Fine elaboration of the continuity required in the evaluation of managerial development and in the development process itself.

See also the training director material, especially: CRAIG, R. L., BITTEL, L. R. eds., *Training and Development Handbook,* ASTD. New York: McGraw-Hill, 1967, particularly Robert Burr's "Management Development," Chapter 19.

The Training Director's Handbook. Waterford, Conn.: Bureau of Business Practice, 1970, particularly the early sections on the mechanics of training programs.

"Transferring Space-Age Management Technology," *Conference Board Record,* October 1970, pp. 50–55. Good elaboration of this discussion's approach to a distinction between technology and science and the managerial use of technology and science.

PART THREE

ORGANIZATIONAL
CONSIDERATIONS

CHAPTER 9

Administrative Structure and Systematic Organization

GLOSSARY

RESULTS—administratively defined department goals ; **WHATS**—operational determination of what is needed to achieve results along with precise measurement ; **WHO**—managerial determination of operational staffing ; **HOW**—supervisory determination of methods.

This chapter will examine systematic organization as it relates to administrative structure. Approaches to systematic organization will be considered in terms of the systems model presented in the four chapters of the preceding section. Before moving ahead, however, we will discuss a background of the current organization structure in criminal justice.

There is an extremely wide variation in administrative structure from one police department or probation department to another, in spite of a widespread belief that criminal justice organizations are, for the most part, very similar. This variation has a number of technical dimensions that will be deferred to the discussion of scientific system analysis in Chapter Fourteen. In focus here, specifically, is the administrative structure as it allows or prevents managers to *manage,* rather than merely supervise.

Improvement of administrative structure at any time is, in terms of the systems model, improvement in the systematic management. Administrative organization has many other influences on management aside from systematic considerations, however. Of specific relevance to the systems model are those direct influences of the style of management adopted. For example:

> Another type of merger of police operations involves the integration of police and fire services into one department—the Department of Public Safety, with a number of modifications or variations in this basic concept.[1]

> There is no single pervasive reason why integrated protective service should be adopted. However, it is apparent that a number of elements will certainly encourage additional city administrators to consider unification as a potential solution to their public-safety problems.

> First, public employees engaged in protective activities constitute a major portion of all those engaged in municipal operation; therefore, a large share of the average city budget is directed toward the support of public-safety service. Proposals for additional police-fire mergers are in various stages of study and development in a substantial number of other communities.[2] Police and fire protection are usually the two largest items in municipal budgets outside of the retirement of bonded indebtedness, and the resulting economics of integration have attracted the interest of taxpayers and public officials alike.

> In Sunnyvale, California, which has had a combined department, the Department of Public Safety, since 1957, the City Manager estimated that the unification of the two forces was saving the city more than $3,000,000 per year in comparison to what it would cost to maintain two separate departments. Although most of this saving comes from greater efficiency in the use of manpower, some of it is the result of not having to maintain two communication systems, two sets of buildings and two records facilities, as well as freedom from the duplication of other services.[3]

Variation in administrative structure of this kind definitely impinges directly upon management. For this reason, further consideration will be given efforts to improve management through changes in organizational structure.

VARIATION AND ADMINISTRATIVE STRUCTURE

Improving the administrative structure of an organization in terms of

---

[3] Harry W. More, Jr., *The New Era of Public Safety* (Springfield, Ill.: Charles C. Thomas, 1970), p. 195.

[2] *Police-Fire Integration—A Survey,* Cleveland Bureau of Governmental Research, November 15, 1961.

[3] V. A. Leonard and H. W. More, *Police Organization and Management,* 3rd ed. (Mineola, N.Y.: Foundation Press, 1971).

its mission and size begins with recognition of the nature of its variations. As an example of such variation, the public safety approach to organization will now be further considered.

Any of the jurisdictions that use the name "Department of Public Safety" would probably clarify the concept of organizational variation. But a Department of Public Safety that combines police function with fire-fighting clarifies organizational variation best. Proponents of this approach note that the "public safety" is in jeopardy from both law violation and fire, and that successful fire-fighting requires the coordination of police traffic control and emergency fire equipment. Firemen, when they are also policemen, theoretically carry this coordination on every fire call. In addition, firemen who must remain on call can, as police officers, increase the police patrol function by driving prowl cars between fire calls. Critics of this approach point out that an armed robbery or burglary in one part of town can be accomplished with greater ease if a fire is set on the opposite side of town, and that the various remedies for this problem customarily resort to police specialization, which is simply a return to a separate police department without the benefit of career orientation for personnel.

Advocates, nevertheless, go on to cite still another advantage of the public safety administrative structure—that of staffing and training. Operation of emergency equipment in particular and a number of other general training areas are noted in this regard. But underlying all of these considerations is a belief that the *safety* of society is a single function.

In a discussion of variations in administrative structure, and with local considerations aside, though, what ultimately precludes defining public safety as including flood and rabies-animal control, along with criminal justice functions within one administrative structure? This question is not intended to be facetious; it brings into focus the role of public opinion in organizational structure—another source of great variation. Organizational structure that proposes to provide more service for less tax money is never an impossibility—particularly when it combines a number of governmental services that could easily be made to *appear* related.

The variations of administrative structure relating to public safety concepts are significant, to say the least. And yet they represent only one of many variables influencing administrative structure in criminal justice. This remains consistent with the systems approach to management—an approach that is geared to dealing with the many variables that do indeed influence organizations:

> What appears to be occurring is that our conception of the organization is changing from one of structure to one of process. Rather then visualize the organization in its traditional structural, bureaucratic, and hierarchial motif, with fixed sets of authority relationships much like the scaffolding of a building, we are beginning to view organization as a set of flows, information, men,

material . . . time and change are . . . critical . . . change in construction
will become more pronounced in the future. . . .[4]

Against the background of continual change in criminal justice organizations, consider the value of the continuity afforded by the systems model, by the function interfaces and reflexive synergetics that remain relatively constant in their functions even during major program or even organizational changes.

Working Chiefs. But even with the systems model, many influences impinge on the administrative structure of the organization. Public safety is indeed only one of many such influences. Another is the wide variation of involvement of administrative staff in line work. By placing the consideration of line work involvement within administrative structure, it becomes possible to examine not only "who reports to whom," but also what it is that should be reported.

Placing consideration of line work involvement within administrative structure begins with a series of questions about what an administrator does or does not do. Does a chief probation officer actually appear in court? Does he prepare court reports? If so, who reviews them? What size does a department have to be before the chief reports only to government, and then only on administrative matters—and reports to the complete exclusion of line work matters? At what point is a department large enough to permit administrative programming that can be measured totally by results accomplishment (results defined in such a way that line work is included in its measurement)?

Does a police chief make arrests? If so, does he report to anyone on the basis of his participation in line work? If he participates in line work without being directly and personally responsible to anyone, does it make good managerial sense to have line work being done on this basis? Does it make good managerial sense to have a manager judged on nonmanagerial work as well?

Local jurisdictions vary so widely on these matters that what will be presented later in the chapter as tables of organization rarely gives so much as a clue on how the administration is structured in this regard. Even flowcharts occasionally fail to clarify this issue in any way. Indeed, such information is at times even left out of job descriptions for administrative and managerial staff.

The point being made here is that involvement in line work varies from jurisdiction to jurisdiction at least in degree—and in some cases by strict requirement for or against involvement. A related influence bearing directly on variations in "working chiefs" has to do with the influence of tradition.

Tradition. Some jurisdictions with precincts would like to reorganize

[4] Stanley D. Young, "Organization as A Total System," *Proceedings of the 9th Annual Midwest Management Conference* (Carbondale, Ill.: Business Research Bureau, South Illinois University, 1966), p. 20.

into centralized administrative structures, while others would like to decentralize the administrative structure. Presumably both preferences are founded on good research. But the tradition of the department is likely to mitigate against fundamental adjustments in the administrative structure.

The administrative structure of a police or probation department formed when the jurisdiction was small may find the structure cumbersome when population growth increases the work loads. The addition of personnel may merely compound the problem unless the administrative structure is reorganized into functional divisions of service and restructured into terms of systems as discussed in Chapters One and Three.

In the case of centralized versus decentralized administrative structure, and in the case of reorganization required by growth, as well as dozens of additional concerns about administrative structure, tradition has a great influence on any changes. And extremely wide variation exists in administrative structure even within regions of similar tradition.

The vastly complex influences that produce these organizational variations are not likely to change significantly. It appears necessary, then, to devise methods of combining administrative structure with systematic organization in spite of the influences discussed thus far. Fortunately, certain avenues are open to combining systematic organization with administrative structure—geared to provide greater administrative continuity and effectiveness.

But, as will be noted shortly, variations continue to exist even in the most systematic organization and administrative structure, so coping with variation is an *on-going* managerial task.

But also noted shortly will be the organizational capability to cope systematically with variation—variation that can be conceived of in criminal justice as follows:

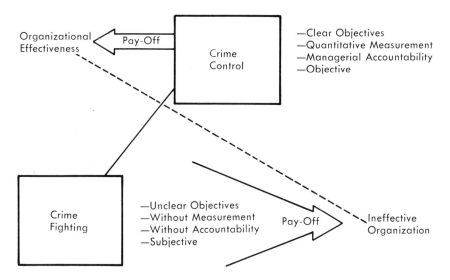

The intent of the systems model, of course, is to make organizational effectiveness possible in spite of variations, depending primarily upon systematic interfacing of management functions, but also depending upon systematic organization.

Recalling the discussion of systems in Chapters One and Three, the main parts of a systematic organization can be thought of as input, process and output.

The principle of focusing administrative concern on output, or *results,* remains. Input and process, however, are also parts of an administrative structure even though the "actual management" of both remain the job of a first-line supervisor—at least in the ideal.

Top administrators, then, *are* concerned with input and process—concerned with the organizational structure of all three components.

But all too often when top administrators recognize this concern and attempt appropriate reorganization, the new administrative structure has more to do with assessment of various personal capabilities of managers than it has to do with analysis of the system.

The problem here is that even if this particular approach to reorganization is carried out as well as possible, the administrative structure is still apt to depend on a particular person instead of on a *system.* Reorganizing after each retirement is bothersome at best.

This is not saying that organizational adjustments can or even should be avoided. Indeed, a systems model obviously requires systematic change on a continuing basis, but on the basis of system needs rather than personnel changes. This argues for the clarity of specific roles and functions that can be organized into a systematic administrative structure.

Organizing input and process into systematic structure brings the administrator to grips with the nature of his organization—"nature" proving still another source of major variation in criminal justice administrative structure. The nature of the criminal justice system can be determined in part by analyzing its process. Criminal justice process is made up of law enforcement, courts, prosecution-defense, and corrections. For example, knowing that settling family fights and patrolling around the township are the only part of the process of a small-town constable system is enough to suggest the particular nature of that organization. It probably varies slightly from a constable system that includes some traffic control and operation of a jail in addition. However, both systems have the same purpose: law enforcement.

This is not to say that the size of an organization determines its nature, although it is true that it is a great influence. It is the *complexity* of functions that influences the nature of an organization. The California Highway Patrol, for example, is a large system in which process is virtually limited to traffic. Compare this extremely large organization to any number of smaller police systems that have many more functions in addition to traffic control. Their variations begin to emerge with this kind of comparison.

Once the nature of the organization has been clarified beyond simply stating its purpose, the systems approach to combining administrative structure with systematic organization becomes possible. To further clarify what has been presented thus far in this volume as the systems approach, the following article is reprinted in its entirety. The article also affords a context in which the management information system and program evaluation review technique, along with planning and managerial flexibility, can be explored.

MANAGEMENT BY SYSTEMS[5]

A large amount of information has been expounded by authorities on the subject of management. Much of this information has not been disseminated by the average Chief of Police because it is not within his particular field of training. Daily, however, it is becoming increasingly important for the Chief to select the best way to build strong organization and also have good management. He must utilize and adapt new available management information to the field of law enforcement.

A possible solution in this area is a new discipline called *systems*. This theory of management is being used more and more and is proving to be an efficient and effective solution to management problems. As in any other form of management, no statement in this treatise should be defined as being a hard and fast rule; rather it should be used to investigate further use.

Several basic objections arise to the use of other forms of management in police work. The primary objection is that police work, by actual definition, is and must be flexible enough to cope with any situation that arises in any given period of time. In business and government, where other methods are used, management itself requires, in order to prove effective, that rules be fixed and followed by all members of the organization. Police work, too, must follow certain rules, but it is facetious to say that a rule can be set for every situation that the police manager will face. However, he must be able to plan, based on prior knowledge of certain events, and understand how the systems of which he is a part will react or should react.

Management by systems has a basic rule. *Each system must be understood and considered a separate entity within the overall structure of the organization.* Basically, the systems as a group make up the organization. Knowledge of this will afford the manager the ability to follow the span of control, the chain of command or communication and enable him to assign like tasks to related work groups in the time and area that they are needed. Without this knowledge, he must search for these things, costing the department time which it cannot afford.

It is important that the use of data processing be completely understood and the application of the hardware into the systems be regulated if it is to be a useful tool and not a burden. It also must be understood that the application of management by systems does not depend on the output of a high-priced

[5] E. G. Columbus, "Management By System," *The Police Chief*, 37, No. 7 (July 1970). Reprinted by Permission.

device that computes. The computer and the related components are a tool. A similarity may be drawn in this regard to an adding machine. It would be foolish to base and operate a management technique on an adding machine—and so it is with a computer. The adding machine may be considered a tool, a part within a cycle. Without the tool, it may be more difficult to establish a base of operation or a required output. So it is with a computer. Another analogy may be drawn by stating that it would be foolish to base the operation of a squad of men on one sergeant. What would happen if the sergeant should become ill? Would the men all go home? No. This is the same application as a computer. The system then is not based on the device, rather, the device is a tool within the system which aids in the many complex computations that are made to assist the manager in making a decision.

This decision-making process is assumed to be necessary on all levels of supervisory command. No device will answer all the needs of management. Some areas of information such as personal traits and characteristics may be programmed into a computer to establish who is the best suited person to complete a task. This would, however, be a very involved program and would not be completely accurate. The human mind, in the long run, must come into play because a human being, namely the manager, will make the final decision in any given problem. Systems can aid in this decision by contributing all of the necessary facts available in the proper sequence to permit the decision to be made with some mathematical or scientific probability. Masses of data can be assimilated by machinery and rapid, accurate answers obtained which are based on probabilities more accurate than the human mind. No personal feelings are involved and the machinery can operate much faster. Speed is thus gained. This application to police work is apparent. Besides routine administrative duties, the police manager at all levels is required to answer questions requiring immediate attention, many of which are of multiple variety and some involving human life. The speed necessary is evident. These decisions will be made on a background of experience, facts known, data and human emotions. The ability to eliminate the areas of facts and data by relying on a machine to produce these allows the police manager to balance his final decision with his experience and human judgment. This lessens the actual burden on the manager and allows for accuracy never before obtained. In some cases this type of decision making is referred to as quantitative analysis.

What then are the steps to be taken to organize and operate a management approach of this type? Several basic rules are needed.

The rules may be divided into the following categories: surveys, analysis of results, synthesis of system, the documentation of systems, implementation of systems and the continuing necessary planning and research. These are described below. The assumption is made that these functions will be performed by an experienced technician. No attempt should be made to accomplish these tasks without proper training.

SURVEY

A survey must be made of all phases of the administrative duties of the department. This survey must include, in detail, processing techniques of all documents and forms presently in use. Also included should be the organizational structure with the titles, authority, and responsibilities of the groups that comprise the entire organization. Job descriptions for all employees, indicating their responsibility as they see it, should be obtained.

There are several ways and methods by which a survey may be conducted. Walking through the operations is one and collecting data that has been produced earlier is another recommended method. Other ways include personnel interviews and research of existing policies and procedures. During this time, the surveyor must be careful not to recommend any changes in the existing operations. He must act as a fact-finding agent only.

ANALYSIS

Collation of the collected data is the next logical step. The data must be categorized and studied to determine the basic operations of all phases of the organization. In order to expedite the overall job, part of the analysis should be done as the survey is being conducted. Caution must be exercised not to make any conclusions with this limited amount of data, however. Flow charts should be made during this period to explain the present operations. This will aid in the measurement of effectiveness of the new operations when they are operational.

SYNTHESIS

After completion of the survey and analysis of all phases of the organization, the synthesis begins. The synthesis must be complete in detail to avoid overlooking any phase. It will require considerable time and effort in planning and coordination. The organization's interaction must be taken into consideration and the existing management should be consulted at each step to gain cooperation and to promote understanding. Failure to gain this cooperation can mean fatality at the time of implementation for even the best plan. All of the new concepts that can be employed should be fully discussed and understood. Programs for retraining should be established where necessary. In the course of this synthesis, the entire organization is "reassembled," so to speak, using the proper techniques, hardware and personnel. New forms and procedures must be created and secured.

DOCUMENTATION

After the synthesis has been completed, all new concepts along with any of the old methods that were retained must be documented. Documentation may take several forms. The line personnel will require documentation necessary for completing a task, using proper techniques and forms. The operating personnel will require enough documentation to show clearly the entire operation and the processing necessary of any forms or other documentation involved in the system. Flow charts showing the processing steps of any system will also be included. These must be clear and concise. All documentation should be assembled in proper sequence with allowances made to correct or change any area that may later develop.

IMPLEMENTATION

When the preceding steps are completed, implementation is the next step. This should be done on a carefully planned timetable to assure slow phasing into the overall operations. A close review is necessary at this stage to assure compliance with the rules and the new techniques developed. It is recommended that a PERT program (Program Evaluation Review Technique) be developed and followed. Some changes will be required as the systems go into operation. These changes should be made with all members of the department understanding how and why. This will foster cooperation and, in many cases, excellent suggestions will be received. Emphasis must be placed on the care needed in the initial phases of implementation.

PLANNING AND RESEARCH

Continuing research must be done to improve the systems. The good manager will assign one person to be responsible for any necessary planning and research. This endeavor will encompass a review of all systems as a collateral by-product of the research. Failure to continually review will cause an impasse and the organization will lapse into a state of suspended animation and become ineffective. New methods and procedures must be reviewed in order to implement them where useful and effective.

ADDITIONAL BENEFITS

Many by-products will be realized from this form of management. Forms design and control may be accomplished easily. This will create more usable forms for the man on the street and thus it will reduce his time spent with forms. Forms control can be a major factor in reducing operational costs in time and material. Further, more complete reports for estimating tasks and better statistical information will be available.

USE OF DATA PROCESSING

Data processing is a tool of the manager. If properly used, this tool can afford him much help. For this to be done, the rules shown earlier must be followed. After completion of the survey and analysis, the synthesis begins and at this point consideration of the use of data processing must be made. Key questions will arise and must be answered. For example, how much will it cost? What will it do that a human cannot do? What equipment will be needed and how much training will it require to operate? Is it worth while?

It would be difficult to consider these questions in this paper because we are speaking of generalities and not any specific department or organization. It is enough to state that the benefits of data processing equipment have been found to be economical and justified in a large majority of installations. The question we are required to answer here is, What value is this to the public administrator or manager?

Assuming that key equipment will be available to the manager, we may proceed to explain in what areas he may use the equipment. Today, the average police department is saturated with paper work. Much of this has been brought about by the demands of the public for better and more reliable services. If measures can be taken to assist in the processing, filing and retrieval of data, they should be used. Some of these measures actually allow for better distribution of manpower in a given area at a set time. To do this, facts of events must be properly processed. Case record reporting, daily activity reports of the officers, budgets and personnel accounting are but a few of the many areas that may be utilized within the scope of this method.

Other uses are many and varied. A citizens group comes to the police and asks what the accident rate is near a given intersection. A large school or housing development is being planned for this area and they feel that it would increase their local problems because of the additional traffic load. They need the accident information to aid in argument against this development. Most departments would state that they cannot supply this data. Why not? Isn't this a public service? Shouldn't the police know what the accident rate is at any given place within their jurisdiction? They should, not only to supply information but to know their own problems! The use of machine searches for this type of data is very simple. It is not simple without the data in machine form.

Another use would be in the securing of adequate manpower. How many chiefs can go to their governing body and state *exactly* why they need more men? Most will say their problems have increased; they do not have enough men to do the job requested. The members of the body listen politely and think of the number of times they have seen a policeman sitting in a coffee shop drinking coffee. What they don't know is that the officer they have seen may very well have been working for twelve hours without relief to complete his task. Data processing can and does give facts on manpower expended in hours and on cases and other related factors that cannot be argued with. Without such information the administrator is not prepared to debate a budget problem. Data processing can give him this material.

I believe that police as a group may expect management by systems to come more to the front when it is realized that this area will give answers, unavailable at this time by other methods, to many questions.

Combining systematic organization with administrative structure, then, depends in part on the ability of criminal justice administrators to recognize that the organization itself is a large system, made up of individual smaller systems, or subsystems, functioning within the overall organization. Systematic organization also requires a flexible responsible managerial process such as proposed in the reflexive synergetics of this model.

In spite of this requirement of flexibility, and the requirement of recognizing subsystems, administrative structure is necessary for continuity—a structured *table of organization* from which management systems can operate with continuity.

TABLE OF ORGANIZATION: ADMINISTRATIVE STRUCTURE AND FLEXIBILITY COMBINED

The table of organization, even in a systems approach that includes flexible updating of administrative structure, may never again occupy the significance in bureaucracy that it once did. Indeed, there is increasing literature to the effect that the classical use of these tables in management has already outlived its usefulness.[6]

Even if this assessment invites debate, most would agree that TO's will need to do a great deal more for modern systems management than has been the case in the past. For a TO to be useful, it must provide systematic flexibility in which role interfaces can occur—recalling that role interfaces were defined as enough role interlap to afford communication but not so much as to distort roles. In this regard, the TO has been placed in a context that relates to the informal organization.

> Company organization charts are used to depict the formal organization, but the informal organization typically is not charted in business firms. One reason is that the system of relationships among the members of an organization is always changing, so that any such chart would soon be too outdated for any managerial use.[7]

If informal organization is made up of organizational relationships that change too rapidly for managerial use, taking the TO beyond the purpose it has served in the past should not be in the direction of the informal, which ultimately suggests that people *are* the organization rather than that they merely contribute activities to the organization.[8] Instead movement should be toward coordination of the contributing activities of individuals—of their roles and functions. Indeed, in design of the administrative structure, it might be well to include in the TO the following definition: "An organization is the coordination of different activities of individual contributors to carry out planned transactions with the environment."[9]

---

[6] Alvin Toffler, *Future Shock* (New York: Bantam Books, 1971), p. 128. See also G. E. Berkley, *The Administrative Revolution* (Englewood Cliffs, N.J.: Prentice-Hall, Inc., 1971).

[7] Leonard J. Kazmier, *Principles of Management,* 2nd ed. (New York: McGraw-Hill, Inc., 1969), p. 163.

[8] In addition to the model presented in the preceding section, see C. I. Bernard, *The Function of The Executive* (Cambridge, Mass: Harvard University Press, 1950).

[9] Paul R. Lawrence and Jay W. Lorsch, *Developing Organizations: Diagnosis and Action* (Reading, Mass.: Addison-Wesley, 1969), p. 3.

Combining Flexibility and Structure: Differential Accountability

Recalling that systematic organization must be flexible, the TO must be designed to allow flexibility. But it must provide structure to the organization along with its flexibility—at least if it is to prove useful on a continuing basis. In other words, the TO must combine structure and flexibility.

The problem facing efforts to combine structure and flexibility are twofold: first, as noted earlier, flexibility gained through plotting the informal suggests that people *are* the organization, rather than that the organization is made up of only contributions from the people. The second part of the problem is that when structure eliminates informal organization entirely, it also prevents the needed flexibility because role interfaces and managerial communication (as well as the management information system) require just enough informal overlap to permit relevant communication, but not enough to distort roles.

Resolution of this problem is possible through differential accountability for managerial role and function.

By *differential accountability* is meant a TO that clearly delineates the roles as the traditional accountability chain (in other words, roles are placed on a "who reports to whom" basis); it also delineates *functions* of these roles in terms of differences in accountability—accountability being linked to other parts of the organization in addition to the command links of accountability for roles.

Imagine, for example, that the entire American criminal justice system were to be placed on a single table of organization. Recalling that a system is made up of input, process, and output, the first task is to determine what part of the system is to be depicted on the TO.

Criminal justice input is the selected law violation referred to in Chapter One. But though significant, it does not appear on the TO. Criminal justice output is the reduction in crime and those committing crime. Extremely significant though it is, it does not appear on the TO either—at least not directly. Criminal justice process is the combined activities of police, courts, prosecution-defense, probation, prisons, and parole systems. It, then, *does* appear on the chart:

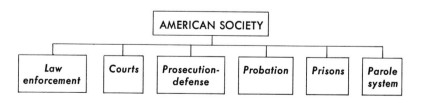

In terms of role, each segment of process becomes a subsystem of the overall criminal justice system. The role of any given subsystem is what society holds the subsystem accountable for performing—at least in this theoretical example. The accountability for the functions of these various roles, however, is not always totally to society, although some of the accountability flows along with the roles. The role (as defined in Chapter Four) of police, for example, may be to keep the streets safe. The role of the prosecutor may be to seek convictions for every police arrest. Presumably, society could hold these two subsystems respectively accountable for the performance of these two criminal justice system roles.

Some of the functions (as also defined in Chapter Four), however, might have a different accountability in addition to the command chain for roles. For instance, one function of the police role might be gaining sufficient policemen per 10,000 population to arrest everyone who makes the streets unsafe. Society holds police accountable for their making the streets safe, and to some degree for the function of proportionate staffing. But a major accountability for the proportionate staffing also goes to the prosecutor, who may in turn hold police accountable for this function for more than the police role.

Should the police subsystem gain massive manpower increases by implying that this increase would eliminate the crime problem, the understaffed prosecutor would not be able to cope with the caseloads and volume produced by the greater police activity. Moreover, a public led to believe that it was through worrying about the crime problem is less enthused about the prosecutor's staffing pleas.

Society continues to hold each subsystem accountable for its respective roles, but one subsystem holds the other subsystem accountable for many of the functions of that role.

The TO using this differential accountability, then, gains the desired combination of structure and flexibility. Structure, even rigid structure, is possible through accountability for roles on a command chain basis. Flexibility is possible, indeed demanded through accountability for function requiring reconciliation of one subsystem influencing another.

Reconsider the TO for the American criminal justice system, this time using differential accountability. To simplify interpretation, role accountability will be represented by solid lines, function accountability by dotted lines.

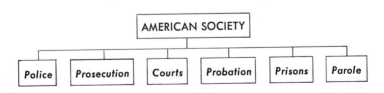

Note that accountability for functions, whatever they may be, exists between even the furthest points of separation of subsystems. For example, the role of the parole subsystem may be to prevent further arrests. Although society holds parole accountable for this role and to some degree the related functions, the police subsystem is also holding parole accountable for its *specific* functions—particularly when they prevent further arrest on some basis other than prevention of crime. Unlike the single direction of accountability for role, accountability for function includes mutual or reciprocal accountability to other subsystems.

Differential accountability, then, might be thought of within the framework shown in the following diagram: the outside circle represents the role. Each of the middle sections are subsystems to which the *function* of the *role* relates—six in this example, but more or less depending on the complexity of role. The inner circle represents the function or functions involved.

Of course this approach is substantially different from that traditionally proposed in the literature of criminal justice administration.[10] As a matter of fact, it differs substantially from nontraditional approaches as well.[11]

But this approach does have things in common with the traditional and nontraditional approaches. For example, there is a great deal of agreement with some of the traditional postulations regarding functional organization, such as specialization. Indeed, in terms of the TO, the only essential difference with traditional approaches to any segment of functional organization (not just specialization) is the systems method of adding the lateral accountability to other subsystems (as the "horizontal TFDL function).

In common with the many nontraditional approaches to functional organization is this very same systems method of relating subsystems to each other subsystem by function.

Table of Organization and Subsystem Relationships

In the four following chapters, the management of each criminal justice subsystem will be presented—police, probation and parole, correctional institutions, and the special cases of courts, prosecution-defense, and elected criminal justice officials. Of course the nature of the particular subsystem along with its particular societal role and mission will be covered. This is what will distinguish one subsystem from the other. But the TO of each subsystem necessarily has a great deal in common with all other criminal justice subsystems if criminal justice is to function as a system.

---

[10] See particularly O. W. Wilson's *Police Planning*, (Springfield, Ill.: Charles C. Thomas, 1952), chap. 5, pp. 40–64, in which he lists 28 cogent management decisions to be made in the process of organizing by function. They relate to vertical accountability presented in 9 principles listed on the first two pages of his discussion. Even the excellent coverage of variables influencing the structural form of the TO is cast totally in vertical accountability chains.

[11] See, for example, the entire Addison-Wesley Series on Organizational Development; in particular, Richard Beckhard, *Organization Development: Strategies and Models*, chaps. 2 and 3, and Paul R. Lawrence and Jay W. Lorsch, *Developing Organizations: Diagnosis and Action*, chaps. 3 and 4.

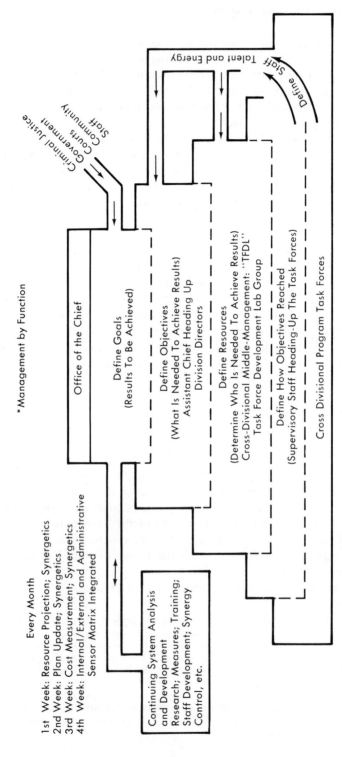

*Management by Function

Every Month

1st Week: Resource Projection; Synergetics
2nd Week: Plan Update; Synergetics
3rd Week: Cost Measurement; Synergetics
4th Week: Internal/External and Administrative
         Sensor Matrix Integrated

Office of the Chief

Define Goals
(Results To Be Achieved)

Define Objectives
(What Is Needed To Achieve Results)
Assistant Chief Heading Up
Division Directors

Define Resources
(Determine Who Is Needed To Achieve Results)
Cross-Divisional Middle-Management: "TFDL"
Task Force Development Lab Group

Define How Objectives Reached
(Supervisory Staff Heading-Up The Task Forces)

Cross Divisional Program Task Forces

Criminal Justice
Government
Courts
Community
Staff

Define Staff
Talent and Energy

Continuing System Analysis
and Development
Research; Measures; Training;
Staff Development; Synergy
Control, etc.

*Function interface is enough overlap of management functions for
communication but not so much as to distort management roles

Administrative Structure of Differential Accountability. As the nature of reflexive synergetics is further elaborated, it will become increasingly important to recognize the significance of interfacing between management functions (rather than roles)—interfacing the overlap of function sufficiently to permit managerial communication, but not enough overlap to distort management roles (as presented in Chapter Four).

In addition to the differential accountability approach, all subsystem TO's will, ideally, have in common a service reference rather than a product reference. In other words, "sales," "merchandizing," and "marketing" are not managerial concerns and are not reflected on the TO. The public relations system, although similar, however, is a separate and crucial matter. Indeed, it is critical to the point of personal responsibility of criminal justice personnel—in this case, police.

> The officer must remember that there is no law against making a policeman angry and he cannot charge a man with offending him. Until the citizen acts overtly in violation of the law, he should take no action against him, least of all lower himself to the level of the citizen by berating and demeaning him in a loud and angry voice. The officer who withstands angry verbal assaults builds his own character and raises the standards of the department.[12]

Having in common the absence of product orientation, then, does not relieve any criminal justice subsystem of concern for the image of his own subsystem, or the entire criminal justice system. The bulk of this responsibility, rightly or wrongly, falls upon the police officer.

> Relatively few citizens recall ever having seen a judge; fewer still, a prosecutor, coroner, sheriff, probation officer or prison warden. The patrolman is thoroughly familiar to all. His uniform picks him out from the crowd so distinctly that he becomes a living symbol of the law—not always of its majesty, but certainly of its power. Whether the police like it or not, they are forever marked men.[13]

In terms of the TO of a criminal justice subsystem, *all* criminal justice subsystems must ultimately accept the consequence if any of them ignore public relations. This is not a proposal for commercial image-building, but for emphasizing what all criminal justice TO's should have in common beyond differential accountability: a structure that encourages improved image. This task begins with the assumption that there exists an ever-present possibility of poor image for criminal justice as a whole.

> Law enforcement and the equal administration of justice have become major national concerns in recent years. The rapid growth of our cities, with attendant problems in housing, education, employment and social welfare services has accentuated these concerns and have been high-lighted by the increasing urban concentration of minority groups.
>
> Crime rates have generally been higher in those areas where poverty, family distintegration, unemployment, lack of education, and minority group frustra-

---

[12] O. W. Wilson, *Police Administration* (New York: McGraw-Hill. 1963).

[13] B. Smith, "Municipal Police Administration," *Annals of American Academy of Police and Social Science,* 40, No. 5 (1968) 22.

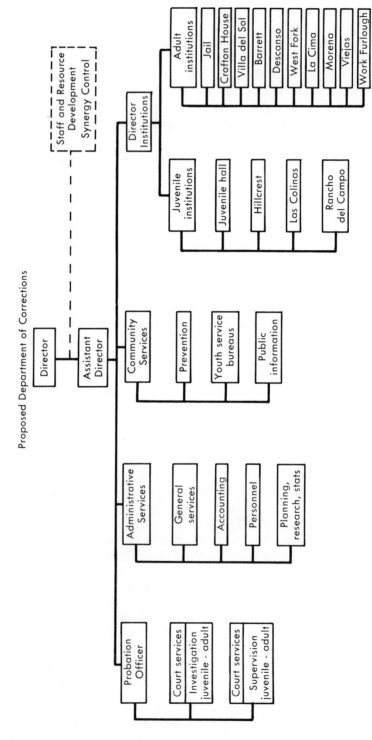

Proposed Department of Corrections

This is the third and final developmental stage of a total correctional organization at the local level.

Courtesy of Kenneth F. Fare, Chief Probation Officer, San Diego, California.

tion and resentment in the face of social and economic discrimination—the ghetto syndrome—are manifest. The expectations, excitement and additional frustrations engendered by the Civil Rights movement have compounded the difficulties inherent in the entire process of law enforcement and the administration of justice.[14]

The very tenor of our society amplifies the possibility of a poor image emerging suddenly—and again, emerging for criminal justice in total and not a single subsystem.

These are extremely difficult times for police, especially in the cities. Race riots have exposed them to personal peril and public controversy. And court decisions that have limited the use of confessions and have otherwise restricted police procedures, have greatly hampered the police in making cases against suspects.

In riots, the police duty is to try to keep order. In many disturbances, they have been under orders for long periods to endure snipers and fire-bombers without retaliating. When the police do shoot back, some denounce them as murderers. When they use force to subdue rioters, some raise the cry of "police brutality."[15]

Although the dramatic impact of public concern in these instances focuses directly on police, the crime problem remains extremely relevant to administrative structure.

The administrative structure through the TO either seeks to make possible improvement of "image," or it does not. While the implications of "image" obviously go far beyond the TO itself, the TO and the administrative structure it describes nevertheless combines with *differential accountability* to permit "image" to improve and to stay improved.

Consider, for example, the TO of a probation department in a large jurisdiction, as illustrated on the opposite page.

Now, take as an example the TO position Director of System and Staff Development added in dotted lines to this TO.

In terms of *differential accountability*, the function of this position may be an on-going systems analysis to insure optimum resource utilization. The Chief holds this position accountable for this function and, to some degree, the "executive role" as well. But this Director, accountable directly to the Chief, is in charge of program development as a *measurable* function.

Note that the functions relate to all activities on the TO—in this particular case, every activity on the TO including the Chief.

Note also the ease with which the systems model can be integrated into

[14] Coffey, Eldofonso, and Hartinger, *Human Relations: Law Enforcement in a Changing Community* (Englewood Cliffs, N.J.: Prentice-Hall, Inc., 1971), p. 4.

[15] Coffey, Eldefonso, and Hartinger, *Police-Community Relations* (Englewood Cliffs, N.J.: Prentice-Hall, Inc., 1971), p. 15.

a *differential accountability* context by simply isolating the *function* of each role.

Substitute police or prison titles and it works just as well.

The function of defining results could then be thought of as the function of the Office of the Chief. Operational whats might be conceived of as the function of those roles designated as responsible for each major division. The who function of course is the middle managerial staff performing the function of the role of cross-divisional resource utilization for what implementation.

The how function of course occurs in the role of supervisory staff.

SUMMARY

This chapter introduced the relationship of administrative structure to systematic organization. In the introduction, emphasis was placed on the wide variation in organizational structure within criminal justice.

Administrators involved in line work were also cited as a source of variation in administrative structure, as was the influence of various traditions.

Systematic organization was cast in the systems approach presented in earlier chapters. Consistency purpose was dealt with as separate from variations in nature of the organization—"nature" defined as a combination of organizational complexity, size, mission, and jurisdiction.

The Table of Organization was dealt with from the frame of reference that it must combine administrative structure with systems flexibility to survive various criticisms that were reviewed. A method of combining structure and flexibility was presented, with *differential accountability* perceived as the basis of roles and functions. Once again, the relationship between all subsystems in the criminal justice system was emphasized, this time in terms of image. The role function distinction of differential accountability was elaborated and presented in a sample TO as a background for the remaining chapters in this section on organization.

QUESTIONS

1. Define organizational variation.

2. Contrast the police criminal justice role with the fire-fighting public safety role, and relate this contrast to effective criminal justice management.

3. What have "working chiefs" to do with administrative structure?

4. What has tradition to do with effective management?

5. Relate administrative structure to the systems approach presented earlier in this volume.

6. Discuss organizational nature in terms of mission and purpose.

7. How does the TO relate to combining administrative structure and systems organization.

8. Discuss differential accountability.

9. Discuss the relationship of the TO and criminal justice subsystems.

ANNOTATED REFERENCES

Addision-Wesley Series on Organizational Development, Reading, Mass., 1969. The entire set, marketed as a series, is singularly germane to this chapter even though *differential accountability* is a substantially different administrative structure than proposed by OD. In particular in the series, see RICHARD BECK-HARD's, *Organizational Development: Strategics and Models.*

BERKLEY, G. E., *The Administrative Revolution.* Englewood Cliffs, N.J.: Prentice-Hall, 1971. Clarifies the criticisms of the traditional use of the T/O.

BERNARD, C. L., *The Function of The Executive.* Cambridge, Mass.: Harvard University Press, 1950. Good elaboration of what was referred to in this chapter as "traditional approaches."

SMITH, B., "Municipal Police Administration," *Annals of American Academy of Police and Social Science,* 40, No. 5, 1968, 22. Covers the broader ranges of complexities that influence variations in organizational nature.

TOFLER, ALVIN, *Future Shock.* New York: Bantam Books, 1971.

WILSON, O. W., *Police Administration.* New York: McGraw-Hill, 1963. Elaborates in great detail the implications of T/O in traditional administrative criminal justice structure. See also Wilson's excellent *Police Planning.* Springfield, Ill.: Charles C. Thomas, 1952.

CHAPTER 10

Managing Law Enforcement

In this and the next three chapters, management of each subsystem of criminal justice will be considered. By way of review, a subsystem is a vital segment of an overall system; a system's effectiveness depends on all the subsystems functioning.

WHY POLICE FIRST

The law enforcement subsystem of criminal justice is the first to be considered for good reason. Managerially, there are far more police and law enforcement agencies to be managed. Appropriately, police outnumber the personnel of all other criminal justice subsystems combined, but the understaffing and underequipping of police is of much greater concern and therefore higher priority as a problem than the same problem in any other criminal justice subsystem.

Of far greater significance managerially, *the administrative practices of the police subsystem virtually determine the management of the entire system of criminal justice.* The input of the criminal justice system is "selected law violation." Although police do not *make* the laws, they are forced to be "selective" regarding which laws are enforced.

The understaffed department cannot enforce all laws nor enforce all laws equally at all times. This regrettable comment on the consequence of understaffing remains true in spite of the obvious ideal of *uniform* law enforcement. Selective enforcement policies then become necessary.

Selective enforcement policies are influenced by administrative interpretation of public support which in turn often is related to the department's relationship with the press. Policy dealing with the types of laws to be enforced is particularly sensitive to public opinion as well as political influence and, of course, the severity of manpower shortages. The unique problems of the community, which often include the availability of taxes, frequently create still further influences on the setting of selective enforcement policies.

Often the influences interpreted by the administrative leaders in setting policies relating to the fiscal budget are precisely the same or at least related to influences interpreted in setting policies on selective enforcement.[1]

The administrative practices relating to this selection of course determine which offender, and how many offenders the other subsystems of criminal justice will process. And because administrative practice depends on the nature and volume of offenders involved, the administrative practices of the police subsystem determines the administrative practices of American criminal justice in general—local and isolated exceptions such as in the case of juvenile referrals notwithstanding.

In terms of this selectivity, the police in recent times have been forced to modify many of their traditional guidelines to the selective process on which the rest of criminal justice depends.

A traditional role of law enforcement in Constitutional forms of government is *apprehending* law violators, while leaving *punishment* to the judicial process. Philosophically, at least, such a role permits crime prevention to be a mutual, although secondary, responsibility of both police and courts. In recent times, police and courts are increasingly faced with "crimes" stemming from growing demands for social reform, rather than merely from the violation of criminal statutes. One apparent reaction by the courts, particularly the Supreme Court, has been a number of decisions tending to have great impact on police procedure in general, and on the relationship of police to social change in particular. In effect, the Supreme Court has handed down rulings that judge not only the lower courts' functions but the police function as well.[2]

---

[1] Eldefonso, Coffey, and Grace, *Principles of Law Enforcement* (New York: John Wiley & Sons, Inc., 1968), pp. 152–53.

[2] Coffey, Eldefonso, and Hartinger, *Human Relations: Law Enforcement in a Changing Community* (Englewood Cliffs, N.J.: Prentice-Hall, Inc., 1971), p. 60.

Increasingly deprived of many of the customary latitudes in approaching the selection of laws to be enforced, there is little wonder that police administrative practice in selectivity varies widely from one jurisdiction to another. And the problem is by no means diminished by the tenor of the current social era.

> According to police executives, physical assaults on officers, vilification of policemen, snarling spitting rioters defying police orders, and the law-breaking activities of campus anarchists are all symptoms of a lack of respect for law and order and for the policemen . . . a symptom of community ignorance and indifference to the problems of the lawman. A Task Force of the National Commission on the Causes and Prevention of Violence directed by Jerome H. Skolnick, a noted author and member of the Center for the Study of Law and Society at the University of California at Berkeley, viewed the police situation with particular alarm in a 262-page report entitled Task Force on Demonstrations, Protest and Group Violence. The report stated, "We find that the policeman in America is overworked, undertrained, underpaid, and undereducated."[3]

Although extremely favorable signs are beginning to emerge,[4] the social era in which police administrators currently work appears to retain a great deal of the negativism that O. W. Wilson found between police and public.[5]

Selectivity is by no means an easy responsibility to handle—especially within the awesome recognition that police selectivity actually is the input of the entire criminal justice system. Indeed, even James Q. Wilson's distinction between *maintaining order* and *enforcing law*[6] relieves little, if any, of the huge burden of selecting that part of the crime problem with which criminal justice will deal with overall. Not surprisingly, Charles McCloskey began an article with the statement:

> The administrative and operational problems of law enforcement are many, varied, and increasing.[7]

The problems of managing any criminal justice subsystem are varied and increasing, but in the case of police, there is the additional responsibility

---

[3] Ibid., Preface.

[4] See for example *Life,* June 30, 1972, "A Plan to Cut Crime," pp. 51–59, in which the editor makes such comments on police as: "Virtually all experts speak out for more officers, better paid and trained, who will seek and receive support from the community." This kind of public message also appears from time to time in the media and seems to support some of the local programs referred to in the *Life* article.

[5] *C. F. Parker on Police,* O. W. Wilson, ed. (Springfield, Ill.: Charles C. Thomas, 1957), pp. 135–46; also O. W. Wilson, "Police Authority in A Free Society," *Journal of Criminal Law, Criminology and Police Science,* 54, (June 1963), 175–77. For background, see O. W. Wilson, *Police Administration* (New York: McGraw-Hill, Inc., 1963).

[6] Wilson, *Varieties of Police Behavior: The Management of Law and Order in Eight Communities* (Cambridge, Mass.: Harvard University Press, 1968), pp. 16–20.

[7] Charles C. McCloskey, Jr., "Police Administrative Services," *FBI Law Enforcement Bulletin* (September 1969), pp. 9–11.

for virtually choosing what it is that will be managed by the rest of the system.

Of course some police administrators simply ignore this responsibility and cope with selectivity solely on the basis of internal organizational problems. Assuming a mutual dedication to increasing the effectiveness of criminal justice within a democracy, every subsystem depends upon the success of every other subsystem to succeed—beginning with law enforcement because it is the input of the system.

SELECTIVE LAW ENFORCEMENT

So far in this volume, the concept of role has had a specific, managerial definition: the performance of expected managerial functions. By modifying this definition slightly, the same concept can be used to examine what it is that gets managed in the police subsystem: the performance of expected police functions. Just as in the case of expectations influencing managerial functions, they also influence the functions that make up police role.

The difficulty, of course, is that police functions are not as easy to clarify in terms of expectations as are managerial functions. For example, managerial functions are simply a determination of what is expected in the way of special-purpose duties by rank or status to achieve managerial results. They interface through clearly defined roles for both sides of the interface. In contrast, the range of possible police functions varies as widely as the public with whom the police interface—there is no clearly defined role for this public. Police may be clear on their own role, but cannot assume role clarity on the part of the public. And with "performance of expected functions" a part of role definition, the question remains, *which* function is expected? With the relatively broad and generalized definition of police role that will be presented later in this chapter, the expected functions of police become critical. Police administration, then, is at least in part responsible for defining police role by specifying the expected functions—of operating the input of the entire criminal justice system. In essence, the selectivity of enforcing law is a major part of defining the role that is to be managed.

Before moving on to a clear definition of police role, we will consider some of the things that influence it.

Organization. Recalling the discussion of systematic organization in the preceding chapter, the impact of administrative structure on selecting which functions make up police role becomes evident. In addition to this, the pattern of police organization is also significant to the police role.

The most significant patterns of police organization that has emerged in the United States and cities with populations in excess of 10,000 are as follows:

1. Controlled by a state-appointed administrator as in Baltimore, St. Louis, Boston, Kansas City, and a number of New Hampshire cities;

2. A department of public safety that integrates various protective services, as in Philadelphia or Sunnyvale, California;

3. Control by a member of a city commission, designated the police or public safety commissioner, as in Newark, Birmingham and numerous cities throughout the country utilizing the commission system;

4. An independently elected chief, as in Laredo, Santa Ana, California, West Palm Beach and many smaller cities;

5. A city legislative body controlling police, as in Atlanta, Charlotte, North Carolina, Jacksonville, Corpus Christi and numerous other cities;

6. Police responsible to a "strong mayor" as in New York, Chicago and other mayor "oriented" cities;

7. Responsibility to city manager elected or chosen by city councils as in Cincinnati, Oakland, California, Fort Worth, Miami and most manager-cities;

8. Police responsible to a board under a "weak" mayor as in Los Angeles, San Francisco and a number of smaller cities.[8]

The obvious implications of this wide variation in patterns of organization are significant, but so are many other influences—such as the concept of police discretion.

Police Discretion. Beyond the selectivity involved in administratively determining which laws are to be enforced is the discretion of any officer enforcing the law.

> The use of discretionary prerogatives by individual police officers is a positive and on-going practice that exists in modern law enforcement. The novice officer must become aware of this process as his senior counterparts are; he must be guided throughout his career by fair-minded and socially aware administrators and educators who are conversant with the mores of society, the intent of the law, and the letter of the law. The officer must perform his job in such a manner that his performance will later be judged by others to have been correct under the circumstances.[9]

> "Who is this man," Alice wonders. "Is he a murderer, a burglar, an escaped convict, or only a diabetic wandering aimlessly in shock for lack of insulin?" Perhaps he is none of these—nothing more than an irate neighbor intending to wreak vengeance upon a tomcat that has been keeping him awake half the night.

> And whoever he is, what will he do? Will he shoot? Will he slash at the officers with a knife? Will he run? Or will he merely beg their pardon for having done something foolish?[10]

---

[8] Eldefonso, Coffey, and J. Sullivan, *Police and The Criminal Law* (Pacific Palisades, Calif.: Goodyear, 1972), pp. 26–27.

[9] Thomas F. Adams, *Criminal Justice Readings* (Pacific Palisades, Calif.: Goodyear, 1972), p. 231.

[10] Dwight J. Dalbey, "Alice Would Have Questions Traveling In A Police Patrol Car," *FBI Law Enforcement Bulletin,* July 1966, p. 10.

Social Change. To further illustrate the many influences on police role, consider the following quote:

> Perhaps the greatest clarity of the concept of change can be gained by first noting that change is not optional. The Grand Canyon is becoming deeper at the rate of one inch a year, whether people approve of such change or not. Scotland moves toward Ireland about eight feet annually, and Europe and the United States are moving about one foot apart each year. London sinks a fraction of an inch annually, while the North Pole moves southward one-half foot.
>
> When you note such changes in the tangible physical world, then changes in the social world should be no surprise. Any difference in human behavior over a period of time is change, and differences in human behavior are constantly observable. But change may not always be of a positive nature. A brief discussion of leisure may illustrate this.
>
> Many, if not most, would agree that leisure has a great number of positive factors. Discovery of tools and the use of animals along with numerous other sources of energy placed prehistoric man on a path ultimately leading to enough free time for the creation of the arts and sciences—neither of which was conceivable until sufficient leisure was available.
>
> In this context leisure tends to gain a favorable connotation, probably because it can be equated either with *recreation* or productivity. But not all leisure is recreational or productive and herein lies a source of community tension. Among the unemployed and underemployed of the ghetto leisure may mean only having more time in which to get into trouble.[11]

In this context, *change* is a constant in which the management of police role remains perplexing, to say the least. This is particularly true when the perplexity is compounded by the requirement that police roles and functions be as clear as possible in spite of ever-constant social changes.

> Law enforcement officials must make a serious and realistic attempt to outline a role that will be accepted by all segments of society; above all, it must be made fully understandable to the public. Some authorities feel that the police must not be imbued with moral self-righteousness which reflects the attitude that the sole purpose of law enforcement is to "enforce the laws." An analysis of actual police performance, however, clearly shows that this is not what actually happens. In structuring a viable role for law enforcement, emphatic consideration should be given to the police function in the slums. It must be acknowledged that the police serve more than one "public." This lends to the difficult question of whether the police should enforce suburban norms in urban communities where the standards differ.[12]

[11] Coffey et al., *Human Relations: Law Enforcement In A Changing Community,* pp. 146–47.

[12] Harry W. More, Jr., *Critical Issues in Law Enforcement* (Cincinnati, Ohio: W. H. Anderson, 1972), p. 1.

Bearing in mind that these examples represent but a small part of the many influences influencing police role, and recalling why the police subsystem is being considered first, police role itself will now be considered.

POLICE ROLE

The role of the police subsystem is important not only to criminal justice but also to society.

> The police comprise one of the most important occupational groups in the nation. They are important because they keep our complex society together. They keep its citizens living, working and prospering within the framework of civilized law and acceptable social conduct. Consequently it is to the advantage of every citizen that the importance of police work be recognized and that the performance of police work be made as efficient, sensible and satisfying as possible.[13]

> In this present period of social unrest, when crime, lawlessness and civil disorder and violence have intruded into all our daily affairs and have threatened our personal well-being, the role of police, as protectors of the public welfare and as the primary means of exercising social control, has become justifiably a matter of wide-spread social concern.[14]

Police role, then, is of importance far beyond the clarification of an occupational career. Police role has to do with the *primary* social control—the fundamental means of maintaining an orderly social environment.

In part, police role can be conceptualized in terms of who performs it. Better yet, what kind of person *should* perform the role? This question is not easy to answer.

> While it may have been difficult to determine the nature of restrictions and the extent of control needed, probably it is more difficult to determine those best qualified to act as enforcers and maintainers of the peace. It is one thing to establish rules; another to maintain them and to impartially apply them.[15]

More specifically, in terms of determining "those best qualified to act as enforcers," what is the nature of the *qualifications*?

> It should not be very hard to persuade a policeman to agree that his job requires him to have the ability of a superman. As a matter of fact, in choosing

---

[13] Richard H. Blum, "The Problems of Being a Police Officer," *Police*, 5, No. 2 (November–December 1960), 10. [Full article completed in *Police*, 6, No. 2 (January–February 1961), pp. 10–16.]

[14] T. A. Fleet and T. S. Newman, "The Role of the Police in Modern Society," *Police*, 9, No. 2 (March–April 1969), 21.

[15] Dorothy P. Humphrey, "Why A Cop?" *The Police Chief*, 36, No. 7 (July 1969), 38.

his profession, he has elected to be a superman. What he has said is that he wishes to announce himself ready to act more forcefully, more wisely, more calmly, more bravely and more law-abidingly than the average man.[16]

Beyond the difficult question of who is best suited for the police role, it is even more difficult question of defining the *objective* of performing police role.

> In terms of actual performance, the police objective of crime prevention defies definition. Is it the same as "the control of crime" or "the repression of criminal activities" or is it something that is unique and distinct? Is it something peculiar to the police function or do other components of the criminal justice system have primary, secondary, or even tertiary responsibility in this area? . . . Another area of current dispute is "control of conduct" or "maintainance of the peace." This nation is currently besieged by acts of violence, civil disturbance and riots. On the one hand, there is a cry for "law and order," and on the other hand some espouse a policy of "absolute permissiveness." The police are currently the scapegoats of this dichotomy, therefore it is imperative that standards be established that will protect us from anarchy, and at the same time, allow for reasonable dissent.[17]

Of course these two problems do not in themselves answer the question regarding *objectives* of performing police role. They do, however, emphasize the need for an answer to two questions of singular importance in clarifying the role that police administrators are to manage—what are the objectives of police roles, and who is best suited to perform them?

The Law

Perhaps these questions can be combined through a brief discussion of law *as an instrument of social control.*

Law, it should first be acknowledged, can be broken by those who enforce it.[18] From this acknowledgement, at least part of the first question is automatically answered: *Those best suited for police role are, among other qualifications, unwilling to break the law in order to enforce it.* As Jerome Skolnick points out, "If the police could maintain order without regard to legality, their short-run difficulties would be considerably diminished."[19]

Bringing the law as an instrument of social control to bear on the dilemma suggests considering its influence on the entire criminal justice sys-

---

[16] Karl Menninger, "Are Policemen Supermen?" *The Police Chief*, 32, No. 9 (September 1965), 26.

[17] Harry W. More, Jr., *Critical Issues in Law Enforcement*, p. 7.

[18] See, for example, Alan Barth, *Law Enforcement versus The Law* (New York: Collier Books, 1963).

[19] Jerome H. Skolnick, *Justice Without Trial: Law Enforcement In Democratic Society* (New York: John Wiley & Sons, Inc., 1967), p. 6.

tem. In this context, the law itself is the cohesive force of criminal justice as a system. The law is the only reason that criminal justice has either input, process, and, most important, output. The input is selected law violation—everything else the system does (or should do) relates to that, regardless of which particular subsystem is involved.

This of course does not answer the specific problems posed with regard to crime control versus criminal activity repression. These problems were raised in the specific context of crime prevention and will be related to police functions to be considered later in the chapter. But conceptualizing the law as a cohesive force between criminal justice subsystems permits further consideration of crime control versus criminal activity repression in terms of police role overall.

Seeing the law as the common denominator of all criminal justice subsystems permits an answer to the question posed regarding whether other components of the criminal justice system have primary, secondary or tertiary responsibility. If this responsibility is equated with the role of the subsystem, *every criminal justice subsystem ultimately depends upon every other subsystem.* From an administrative viewpoint, this requires every criminal justice manager to accept at least tertiary responsibility for managerial success of all criminal justice subsystems functioning in relation to the same law.

Indeed, the fundamental intent of differential accountability discussed in the preceding chapter for top administrators is to put an end to the ridiculous notion that the problems of any one subsystem using law as an instrument of social control are not the problem of *all* subsystems using the law.

Although this admittedly changes the context in which the problem of clarity of objectives was introduced, relating all criminal justice subsystems through the use of law provides an avenue to define police role in relation to criminal justice. Moreover, it affords an avenue from which the expected functions of police role can be isolated to answer the question regarding the *objective* of police role—crime preventive and otherwise.

Some expected functions deal with controlling crime, some deal with repressing criminal activities, and certain combinations of functions deal with preventing crime—all three varieties hopefully part of the police role.

Police Role Defined

Recalling that for purposes of this book role is *the performance of expected managerial (and police) functions,* performance of police role is defined as repression of law violation combined with control of crime and crime prevention. The expected functions of this role are those that meet the objectives of the role: *an orderly environment through rule of law.*

Police role, then, as is true in all other criminal justice subsystems, has the objective of using law as an instrument of social control in order to perform the combined functions of repressing law violations, controlling crime, and preventing crime.

In a sense, confining police role to simply performing these three functions makes the police of this society less significant than police around the world:

> Examination of the activities of police agencies around the world makes it apparent that they perform five basically different kinds of functions. These are:
>
> 1. Combating violation of the traditional criminal law (murder, rape, robbery, arson, etc.).
> 2. Combating violation of temporary convenience norms (traffic and health regulations, etc.).
> 3. Performing a miscellaneous group of service functions (operating an ambulance service, operating a jail system, escorting bank messengers, etc., activities assigned to the police because they are usually the only governmental agency on duty 24 hours a day, 7 days a week, 365 days a year).
> 4. Controlling or suppressing opposition to the government in power.
> 5. Maintaining forces for the possible repelling of military aggression against the nation-state.[20]

But being able, at long last, to focus police role and resources on the problems involved in repressing law violation, controlling crime, and preventing crime, and doing all three within the law, is (or should be) the dream of every police administrator dedicated to effective law enforcement.

Consider for a moment the relative ease with which innovative, creative, and skilled police administrators could manage a results-oriented program if totally relieved from the additional duties implied in the following:

> In addition to these responsibilities for achievement of conformity both to the traditional criminal law and to convenience norms, the police have been assigned or voluntarily assumed responsibility for a wide variety of service functions. The following list of just a few of these will doubtless remind the reader of many more:
>
> 1. Operating an ambulance service
> 2. Operating a jail system
> 3. Operating a dog pound
> 4. Collecting delinquent taxes
> 5. Furnishing chauffeurs for executive officers of the government
> 6. Operating recreational facilities
> 7. Performing clerical functions for courts
> 8. Escorting funerals and parades
> 9. Licensing and regulating certain businesses (taxi-cabs, pawn-brokers, night clubs, etc.)
> 10. Serving as censors for movie houses and book stores.[21]

[20] Richard A. Myren, "The Role of Police," reference document for the President's Commission on Law Enforcement and Administration of Justice, 1967.

[21] Ibid.

This by no means suggests that the actual activities of police in performing the expected functions of their three-part role are not widely varied. Administrative programming in the area of community relations alone clearly diversifies the activities involved in police work.

> The need for strengthening the relationships of police with the communities they serve is critical. Negroes, Puerto Ricans, Mexican-Americans, Indians, and other minority groups are taking action to acquire rights and services which have historically been denied them. Law enforcement agencies, as the most visible representative of the society from which minority groups are demanding fair treatment and equal opportunity, are faced with unprecedented situations today which require that they develop new policies and practices specifically for dealing with the problems of these groups.
>
> Even if fairer treatment of minority groups were their sole consideration, police departments would have an obligation to attempt to achieve and maintain a positive public image and good police-community relations. In fact, however, much more is at stake. Police-community relations have a direct bearing on the character of life in the cities and on the community's ability to maintain stability and to solve its problems. At the same time, a police department's capacity to deal with crime depends to a large extent upon its relationship with the citizenry. Indeed, no lasting improvement in law enforcement is likely in this country unless police-community relations are substantially improved.[22]

Substantial improvement has numerous categories of activities involved. But regardless of the diversity of these and other police activities that are involved in the performance of expected functions of police role, the role itself must remain focused on its three objectives within the framework of using law as the instrument of social control.

Having considered police role in terms of its objectives, consideration is now given the many police functions that administrators selectively bring to bear in precisely defining police role. It is these functions that not only define the role of the police subsystem but clarify the nature of managing the police subsystem.

POLICE FUNCTIONS

Police functions that repress law violation and control crime do so on the basis of two fundamental expectations: first, that police will retain order in such a way as to prevent crime and, second, that police will function within the law. What the law *is* needs, therefore, to be considered at this point.

> There are actually two major divisions in American law, the *Common Law* derived first from the Germanic regions and then from England, and the *Civil*

[22] Coffey, Eldefonso, and Hartinger, *Police-Community Relations*, p. 5–6.

Law, derived first from Roman influences and then from France. The Common Law system is a process of developing law "continuously" by reference to precedence, whereas Civil Law is based on specific codes that are written and "legislated." Put another way, Common Law seeks to "remain common" by using court rulings and similar cases in the past as a guide for current dispositions. Civil Law, on the other hand, concerns itself with precise interpretation of an appropriate, but legislated, statute. A further distinction might be made in the "accusatorial" nature of Common Law, and the "inquisitional" nature of Civil Law. But technical distinctions between Common Law and Civil Law are no longer crucial, since American courts have come to function under a combination of both systems. In this combination there is what some consider excessive dependence on precedence and constitutionally dictated due process which tends to relate more to Common Law than to Civil Law. Nevertheless, American jurisprudence, particularly the Criminal Law, combines both law forms.[23]

For purposes of this chapter, however, use will be made of the simple but cogent definition of law given by St. Thomas Aquinas in his *Summa Theologica*:

Law is a regulation in accord with reason, issued by a lawful superior for the common good.

Emphasizing both "lawful" and "common good," police functions within the law are expected to be in the interests of social rules. Police functions and activities that do not serve this lawful common good are not functional in terms of the police role.

Managing and administering police programs, then, is actually pursuing the lawful common good; administrative results either reflect lawful common good or are inappropriate results. With this in mind, some of the specific police functions and activities using law as an instrument of social control will now be presented.

Police Investigation

Criminal investigation is an activity that is closely related to arrest or apprehension of offenders. Weston and Wells relate these police activities as follows:

1. A crime is reported, discovered or detected.
2. Police officers respond.
3. A search is conducted for the perpetrator of the crime—a "hot" search of the crime scene, a "warm" search in the general vicinity of the crime or a "cold" search.
4. Throughout the search suspects appear and are questioned.

[23] Eldefonso et al., *Police and The Criminal Law*, p. 6.

5. In a successful search, sufficient evidence to support a charge is assembled and a suspect arrested.

Criminal investigation encompasses a lawful search for people and objects which can be used to reconstruct the circumstances of an unlawful act (or omission) and the accompanying mental state. An investigation probes from the known through the unknown, backwards in time, to determine the truth as far as can be discovered by inquiry after the fact.[24]

From an administrative point of view, managing programs which include investigation activities are clarified even further by the following:

The ultimate objective in the investigation of a crime is the conviction of the perpetrator. Its achievements necessitate proof in court that the crime was committed and that the perpetrator did in fact commit it. All efforts should be directed toward this end. The police, therefore, must ascertain the facts of the crime (the answers to the questions who? what? where? when? why? and how?) and the identity of the criminal. They must identify and arrest the perpetrator and discover witnesses and physical evidence that may be used to prove the charge in court. Recovered stolen property provides additional evidence of guilt; the return of stolen property to its rightful owner is a further police responsibility quite separate from its use as evidence.[25]

The police patrol division is usually the first representative of law enforcement to arrive at the crime scene. The patrol officer, therefore, plays a vital role in the preliminary investigative process. Administratively, cross-divisional coordination and reflexive synergetics are a vital link in connecting the patrol division to detective specialists. Evidence and information gathered by the patrol officer responding to the initial call is, more often than not, critical to a successful investigation program within an agency. This is particularly true in terms of interviewing witnesses with fresh recall of incidents.

Also critical to the investigative process is *timing*—getting the investigation under way. Administrative programming that emphasizes immediate action upon assignment of investigation has gained a great deal of managerial advantage. *How* the investigation itself begins ranges from examining information already available (which at times is sufficient to close the investigation) to exhaustive effort to gain further information from other sources.

Recalling the personnel functions in the systems management model and the reflexive synergetics dealing with staff resources, of crucial administrative concern is the assignment of officers with ability to obtain, analyze, and communicate investigative information. Frequently the administrator

---

[24] Paul B. Weston and Kenneth M. Wells, *Elements of The Criminal Investigation* (Englewood Cliffs, N.J.: Prentice-Hall, Inc., 1971), p. 1.

[25] *Municipal Police Administration*, 5th ed. (Chicago, Ill.: Municipal Management Series, The International City Managers' Association, 1967), p. 263.

will find, from a personnel point of view, that this ability entails a good knowledge and understanding of the law, court decisions, the rules of evidence, and court procedures, all combined in an analytical kind of talent for sensing incongruence. In addition, this ability depends on certain intangible attitudes and mental habits that successful investigators soon develop. There are a number of these attitudes and habits, but most important of these are observation, suspicion, curiosity, and memory.

Administratively, the use of informers is a particularly significant segment of investigation—indeed, it appears to be the best method of obtaining investigative information, and therefore is a primary tool in police investigation. This particular segment of police investigation continues to draw criticism from a number of different sources; nevertheless, an investigator is only as good as his information, and an informer is often able to circulate and gain information in areas that are closed to an investigator.

Also of significance in police management is the criminal record system—a valuable information source for the investigator attempting to obtain information regarding a suspect, an apprehended violator, witness, or personal identification and other data. The record division of any police department is its information center, and the success achieved in dealing with the many facets of a complicated criminal investigation often depend on the coordination of record operations as a sophisticated police activity.[26]

The exchange of information between police officers, investigators, and prosecutors is of course vital to the interfaces between the various subsystem administrations. It is also important administratively, for achieving the apprehensions and convictions that mean effectiveness in this segment of criminal justice.

To aid and better meet the need for rapid communication and exchange of information within criminal justice, the field of modern electronics has been used in many innovative ways. The computer and other forms of automated data processing have already substantially expedited the flow of information within criminal justice—particularly the PIN system (Police Information Network) in use in California for the past few years.

As an administrative example, PIN consists of fundamental processes made up of input, retrieval, updating and deletion—affording an excellent criminal justice tool in its operation. PIN operates from centrally located computers that are fed law enforcement information from cities and counties connected to the system, and arranges it into categories of, for example, wanted persons, stolen vehicles, outstanding warrants, and so forth. This information is available on a moment's notice to all agencies connected to the system and the system allows participating agencies to communicate directly with each other through inquiry terminals, thus bypassing the main infor-

---

[26] O. W. Wilson, *Police Records, Their Installation And Use* (Chicago, Ill.: Public Administration Service, 1951), p. 9.

mation center and saving time in receipt of information. This system will soon be supplemented with an additional network called SPIN (Southern Police Information Network) which will, in effect, connect the entire state of California in a law enforcement information network.

Also in the area of sophisticated law enforcement information is the program undertaken by the Federal Bureau of Investigation in 1965 known as NCIC (National Crime Information Center).[27] Headquartered in Washington, D.C., NCIC has been put into operation to complement the development of electronic information centers throughout the nation and to coordinate the setting of standards that will enable all systems to readily interchange information. Administratively, the ultimate goal is for the system to encompass the entire nation and provide every police subsystem desired criminal justice information within seconds.

With these various systems at federal, state, and local levels, the advantage of mobility on the part of offenders will hopefully be modified in the favor of the police function.

The sources of information available to law enforcement remain many and varied. It is impossible for a single investigator, or indeed, a single record system to know everything. Indeed, this is part of the rationale for separating the management information system of the management model from the police record system. From the investigative point of view, however, the more sources of information possessed by the police agency, the less complex this part of police function. The most frequently used sources of information are records and other data available in city halls, county court houses, financial institutions, public utilities, transportation and delivery companies, local directories, state and federal agencies, commercial sources, schools and colleges, hospitals, newspapers, journals, magazines, churches, doctors, attorneys and accountants, special agencies and committees of the federal government and the Congress, real estate agencies, Better Business Bureaus, and Chambers of Commerce.

Less concerned from an administrative programming point of view, but nonetheless directly related to the investigative process, are the various *techniques* of investigation. Effective investigative results require information and facts. These are obtained for the most part by talking to people who have some knowledge of the particular situation being investigated. Police *interview* and *interrogation* are crucial techniques.

The interview is the interface between the public and the police subsystem and in this context is of administrative concern. Frequently the conversation concerns an individual's knowledge, information, background, character, or testimony. It may be concluded readily that the process of interviewing as defined covers a large area and could include that of speaking

---

[27] Federal Bureau of Investigation, "A National Crime Information Center," *FBI Law Enforcement Bulletin,* 35, No. 5 (May 1966), 2–6.

with suspicious persons on the streets, talking with witnesses to gain information, or obtaining information with reference to the background of police applicants, criminal suspects, informants, or any number of people. Through interviewing, the investigator learns a great deal of information, hopefully bearing directly on the successful completion of the police mission.

Interrogation, in contrast to interviewing, is an enforced conversation between the investigator and a person suspected of a crime, or one who has confessed to a crime. A great deal of training and experience, along with certain personal skills, are prime requisites in this technique of information-gathering.

Administrators can distinguish between interrogations and interviews in terms of the atmosphere in which they are conducted. An atmosphere for interviewing is more relaxed and a person is more likely to open up and supply the desired information. In most cases it is just a matter of the officer asking the right question in the right way that makes this technique successful. On the other hand, an interrogation is usually conducted with a person who is reluctant, for any number of reasons, to converse with a law enforcement official. The atmosphere and tenor of the conversation is not as relaxed as in an interview, and the success or failure of the interrogation depends in large part on the skill and ability of the interrogator to get at the information possessed by the person being interrogated.

A particular administrative concern with regard to interrogation has to do with the Supreme Court rulings in recent years. The ability to distinguish between admissible and nonadmissible statements, admissions, and confessions is critical—for example, confession of a murder suspect has little value if, by some legal error, it is excluded from admissible evidence in court.

Administratively, the greatest problems seem to relate to statements made by persons arrested for a criminal offense. The many rules in reference to these statements are continually being changed, interpreted, and revised and are often so complicated and even contradictory that trial judges have difficulty in understanding them.

Police must of course emphasize these legal variables—regardless of how complicated they are. In the past, the police subsystem had simply to ask: "Is this confession true?" Increasingly, however, emphasis is being placed upon whether or not the statement was offered voluntarily and without coercion of any kind, and was made in the full and complete awareness and understanding of the defendant's constitutional rights. In other words, emphasis by the courts is being placed on the Fourth, Fifth and Fourteenth Amendments of the United States Constitution, all of which directly influence the administrative design of the police function.

Interrogating a person who is already in custody requires the same procedures to be followed in the investigative techniques. Essentially, the person being interrogated must be advised of and understand his constitutional rights as follows: (1) he has the right to remain silent; (2) any statement he makes may be used as evidence against him in subsequent criminal court proceedings; (3) he has the right to the presence of an attorney during any questioning and at all stages of the proceedings; and (4) if he cannot afford the cost of an attorney, a lawyer will be appointed immediately to represent him.

Administrators are aware that advising people of their rights often involves language difficulties. The U.S. Supreme Court decisions involving *Miranda versus Arizona* and *Massiah versus the United States* are of particular administrative concern in programming appropriate approaches.

Still another area in the investigative process of administrative concern is undercover work. Because it is one of the oldest investigative procedures, it is employed by private industry, business, and government, as well as criminal justice, for a variety of purposes. This technique requires that the person performing the work discard his identity and assume another in keeping with the goals and objectives of his particular police subsystem. The purpose of the technique is three-fold: (1) to conduct surveillance, (2) to obtain information, and (3) to obtain evidence that will be admissible in a court of law.

The success of undercover work depends on how well the officer can penetrate a group or organization, obtain the desired information, and avoid identification. The administrative programming involved here is a specialized operation within the police subsystem, used particularly in crimes involving illegal sales, smuggling, narcotics, prostitution, abortions, alcohol, blackmail, fraud, gambling, stolen property, subversive activity, and so forth.

Occasionally blended into the same police subsystem operation is general *surveillance*. This investigative process is, like interrogation, learned through training experience and improvement of personal skills. The common misconception that the policeman simply walks or drives behind the car of a suspected person is rarely the main part of surveillance, although it may be some part. A surveillance is simply the secret observation of a suspected person. It can be either "moving," meaning that a subject is being followed, or "fixed," meaning that a subject is being observed from one or more stationary points. In terms of investigation, police administrators are also faced with the necessity of programming methods of identification. The identification of persons is an extremely important part of the police function and the police subsystem. Of the many methods used, the most frequent are portrait parle, photography, the artist's sketch, Ident-kits, use of modus operandi information, eye-witness, fingerprinting, voiceprints, and reports from the crime laboratory.

Scientific "field aids" such as microphones, recorders, cameras, binoculars, telescopes, chemicals, ultraviolet light, fluorescent powders, inks, infrared light, x-rays, geiger counters, radios, television, and electronic alarm systems, aid the investigative process. Administratively, each of these must of necessity be subjected to strict policies and, indeed, are frequently regulated by specific law.

Final administrative concern in the investigative process of police function is *physical evidence*. Each piece of physical evidence at a crime scene is important to the solution of that particular crime. To the investigator it tells a story of who was present, what happened, when, where, and sometimes why the crime occurred. Hopefully, it eventually tells *how* the crime occurred. Therefore, administrative programming has policies zealously guarding and protecting this evidence through interpretation by the investigator or technician in the processes of photographing, marking, collecting and otherwise analyzing evidence to be *preserved*.

There are many methods and procedures in which an investigator may be trained for the *preservation* of evidence. Administratively, these are of lesser consequence than the establishment of a policy of high priority for this preservation.

Search and Seizure

One of the more critical procedures of police function from an administrative program point of view is the search and seizure operation. Peace officers may use many techniques to secure evidence to be used at the trial of a criminal suspect. The evidence obtained during the investigation of a crime must not be lacking integrity or an innocent man may be convicted. Search and seizure, then, is extremely significant.

Unrestrained police tactics may endanger individual rights and freedoms that are fundamental in our society and the American system of criminal justice. Concern for this type of action has, in some instances, excessively increased limitations upon police. Nevertheless, the limitations exist and must be dealt with administratively.

The district attorney relies heavily upon adequate police work in obtaining evidence, as will be noted in the chapter that follows covering the management of the prosecution subsystem. The work of the police officer in obtaining such criminal evidence provides the basis upon which the district attorney prosecutes his case successfully or unsuccessfully.

When evidence upon which the case relies is challenged, the prosecutor has little choice but to defend the procedures followed by police in obtaining the evidence. In order to provide him with evidence upon which he can depend with or without challenge, the police must operate within the sanctions of approved procedures that the court imposes upon the prosecutor in presenting the evidence.[28]

The area of search and seizure, both with and without warrant, con-

---

[28] E. Warren, "Search and Seizure," *Police Work: Concern; Criminal Evidence*, December 1969, pp. 9–12.

tinues to cause consternation among law enforcement administrators. The law of search and seizure (with or without warrant) throughout the history of jurisprudence has never remained stagnant; rules pertaining to it are continually changing. It is a necessary part of police work to have a working knowledge of the more important constitutional and statutory limitations on search and seizure, and for the administrators of police subsystems to program this knowledge into operation. The Fourth Amendment states:

> The right of the people to be secure in their persons, houses, papers, and effects, against unreasonable searches and seizures, shall not be violated, and no warrant shall be issued, but upon probable cause, supported by oaths of affirmation, and particularly describing the place to be searched, and the persons or things to be seized.

The Fourth Amendment was obviously designed for the protection of individual privacy. This means security for both the individual's person and his property. This amendment allows the individual to conceal himself and his property from the view of his government. The framers of the constitution, however, recognized that this right must at times give way to other societal requirements. Focusing on this awareness are the words "unreasonable," "probable cause," and "particularly"—these are the clues for unravelling most of the police administrator's programming concerns with respect to search and seizure.

The Fourth Amendment prohibits unreasonable searches and seizures; the problem is in deciding what is "reasonable." Though the search is usually deemed reasonable if a valid search warrant is first obtained, the courts have allowed searches without warrant when consent was given by the subject, when the search was incident to a lawful arrest, and when only vehicles were searched. Such court tests are, however, at best general and there are many facets to each type of search.

Administrators coping with "probable cause" face further problems. Determination of whether or not there is probable cause to justify search must be decided on the basis of each specific set of facts—not on the basis of the methods used—thereby making a more difficult administrative program.

The standard for determining probable cause has been established by the Supreme Court as "A reasonable ground of suspicion, supported by circumstances sufficiently strong in themselves to warrant a cautious man in the belief that the party is guilty of the offense with which he is charged." The court further comments on probable cause as being a "non-technical standard." The Supreme Court adjudged the problem in the light of everyday experience rather than giving a legal formula. Moreover, reasonableness is tested according to what a "cautious man," not an ordinary citizen, would consider to be probable cause—and in this case a "cautious man in belief that the party is guilty," meaning an experienced peace officer. This allows persons involved in law enforcement to weigh the circumstances in the light of their training and expertise. The rule is helpful to administrators in that legal standards invariably affect department activities, and clarification of such standards permits clearer policy.

The third key word is "particularly." Unlike problems involved in testing and evaluating reasonableness and probable cause, problems relating to *particularity* as to the person seized or the premises searched generally arise under a search warrant. A warrant must be specific, not only as to who or what is to be searched but also as to the items that are to be seized. A case that supports the rule of "specifics" or "particularity" follows:

> Defendant was convicted of forgery and receiving stolen goods. On appeal, defendant contended that trial court erred in denying his pre-trial motion to vacate a search warrant and to suppress evidence, and in receiving as evidence, over his objections, material seized pursuant to a defective search warrant. The Court of Appeals of New York *reversed* the conviction and dismissed the indictment. Since the search warrant described an entire building, one part of which (for which probable cause was shown) was occupied by defendant and another part (for which probable cause was not shown) by an innocent third party, the warrant was obviously constitutionally deficient for not *"particularly describing the place to be searched."* The court noted that the innocent third-party's failure to complain about the search of her apartment was immaterial, since the pertinent issue was whether or not the warrant was constitutional when issued.[29]

The requirement of particularity not only restricts the items or places that may be searched, but also limits the type of search that may be conducted. A search of "Warehouse A, 1000 James Street, for illegal liquor stills" restricts officers to that location and that purpose. They cannot go into the warehouse and search for evidence in the office because the warrant specifies the *particular* place and items involved.

Of related concern to police administrators is the "exclusionary rule." When the constitution was written, there was added to it the Fourth Amendment, guaranteeing that searches like those carried out under the notorious Writs of Assistance during colonial times would cease. The language of the Fourth Amendment, as well as the Fifth Amendment bears this out: "No person shall be compelled in any criminal case to be a witness against himself, nor be deprived of life, liberty or property without due process of law." From the Fourth and Fifth Amendments, the Supreme Court has evolved several basic principles of strategic importance to administering a police subsystem: first, searches may not be made for certain classes of materials such as "tools of crime," the "fruits of crime," "contraband goods," or "goods on which an excise duty is due." Second, American courts have held that searches

[29] *People versus Rainey*, 197 NE 2nd 527 (NY 1964).

may only be made with either the consent of the person to be searched or the proprietor of the premises, or with a search warrant, or in the absence of these, searches can be made only incidental to a violent arrest. The constitution clearly forbids the use of "general warrants" or dragnet searches.

As a consequence, the exclusionary rule emerged in a 1914 Supreme Court holding that evidence obtained by "unreasonable" search and seizure would be *excluded* from court—eventually from every court and in every circumstance. In 1961, the Supreme Court moved to establish the exclusionary rule in every court and in every circumstance in a ruling on *Mapp versus Ohio*, 367 US 643. The court held that the Fourth Amendment guarantee against unreasonable searches and seizures is an essential part of the Fourteenth Amendment, which restrains the actions of the states and their officers —bringing the exclusionary rule into direct concern of administering every police function in the United States.

> The police play a vital part in the process of prosecution in that they are in the best position to assure that evidence needed by the prosecutor will not be excluded by the court because it was obtained by improper methods. In the area of search and seizure, recent decisions have greatly increased the necessity of obtaining a search warrant. The decisions in Chimel (*Chimel versus California*, 1969) and Morales (*Morales versus California*) complement each other in requiring and then providing a workable warrant system. In terms of police workload, this imposes an added burden on the officer . . . when the context of prosecution, however, the warrant requirements encourage the police officer to fulfill his role in providing dependable admissible evidence.[30]

The Law of Arrest

Administering a police agency, regardless of the managerial complexities presented thus far, faces no greater challenge than directing the policy on arrest. Administratively, establishing the *validity* of arrest is important for two critical reasons: first, because only a valid arrest will justify the arresting officer in conducting a search for evidence incident to the arrest; and second, because an officer can be sued for damages for making an illegal or false arrest. Underlying both of these concerns, however, is the much greater concern of successful operation of one of the criminal justice subsystems in a democratic society. False or invalid arrest concerns the American criminal justice system in total more than any other consideration. With this in mind, some of the administrative ramifications of the law of arrest will now be considered.

Constitutionally, an officer may make an arrest only on the basis of "probable cause" in the context of the Fourth Amendment just discussed. Going beyond, probable cause must consist of evidence sufficient to "warrant

[30] E. Warren, "Search and Seizure," pp. 10–11.

a man of reasonable caution" to believe that a crime has been committed and that the person to be arrested committed it. Administratively, probable cause when executed properly protects both the arresting officer and the police department from civil suit even if it turns out that the arrest was made in error.

A warrant is also a method of seeking an arrest in a manner that protects both officer and department. Police need not have personally witnessed an act to seek a warrant, but may instead rely upon information obtained from others as discussed under the investigative activities—provided the information is conspicuously reliable. Such information would suffice even if it would be excluded from a criminal court as hearsay. In addition, police must set forth the information that gives probable cause in sufficient detail and particularity to enable a magistrate, judge, or other official to make an independent appraisal before issuing the warrant. The point here, from an administrative context, is that both the police subsystem and criminal justice in general profit when arrest activities related to police functions are conducted either within the boundaries of probable cause or warrants.

Of crucial concern to arrest is the right to make telephone calls. Most states provide that a suspect, once arrested, has the right to make at least one telephone call—other states allowing two or more calls to be made. Booking is merely a clerical process, inasmuch as many if not most people booked are not brought to trial. Nevertheless, the right to make telephone contact is far more than incidental administratively.

Bail, also incidental to arrest, is of equal significance to the phone call —frequently the phone call is for the purpose of arranging bail. Increasingly throughout the land, release on "own recognizance" is replacing bail in cases of minimal risk—"risk" in terms of an arrested party leaving the jurisdiction of the court and failing to appear on the court date. Bail continues, however, to be incidental to many if not most arrests throughout the land. Bail could be defined as "security given for the due appearance of a prisoner in order to obtain his release from imprisonment"—commensurate with the derivation of the word "bail" from the French word meaning "to deliver." Used as both noun and verb, bail is the method of securing the release of a party charged with either a misdemeanor or felony while assuring his attendance in court at a future date—meaning that even when bail is granted, the person charged with the offense remains under the jurisdiction of the court.

Administratively, bail is cumbersome only when the police function includes operation of the jail system. In some instances, an additional administrative complication can occur with "station-house bail"—a method of posting bail on misdemeanor complaints in large metropolitan cities. This, in effect, requires a jail commander, using an established table to simply collect the appropriate bail for the particular misdemeanor offense. Regrettably, there are as many bail schedules as there are counties in the United States. One police station may release a person on $50 bail for petty theft, whereas another police station may require $250 bail. Station-house bail, cumbersome administratively for several reasons, is intended to prevent a degrading experience for defendants charged with infractions that do not warrant more than a nominal fine—such as traffic cases.

In some jurisdictions in which the police function overlaps into the surrender of people who have skipped bail (the person posting bail returns the person having skipped bail to police), awkward programming compounds the police subsystems activities.

For the most part, however, telephone calls and bail remain incidental and of no great concern when arrest policies are administered from the reference of probable cause or well-executed warrants.

ADMINISTERING THE FUNCTION

The police administrator who is able to come to grips with the role and function of the law enforcement subsystem has narrowed the vast range of problems confronting police in an ever-changing community. For one thing, he has reduced the problems of adopting the management model discussed in the preceding section (or *any* management model, for that matter). Admittedly, a great number of problems remain and will be explored in the chapter on managerial training and development. Nevertheless, recognizing the role and function of the law enforcement subsystem greatly reduces the problems facing modern law enforcement administrators.

Local exigencies from one jurisdiction to another no doubt will forever plague police administrators in attempting to implement an effective managerial model. Problems beyond those that will be discussed under managerial development and training later in this book will doubtless continue to challenge the police administrator. But once the police role and function in relation to an entire criminal justice system is conceptualized, a constant sense of direction is available in all managerial spheres of the police subsystem.

Placing the functions and activities just discussed in the context of a role that relates to the entire criminal justice system enables the adoption of a management model geared specifically to the crucial interface between the top administrators of police departments and other top administrators in criminal justice—the prime requisite of removing the odious label of "non-system" from criminal justice in America.

SUMMARY

The rationale for presenting the police subsystem before other criminal justice subsystems was discussed in terms of the fact that police constitute the actual input of the overall criminal justice system. The input function was elaborated in terms of selective law enforcement.

Management was cast in the framework of police role, and representative influences that influence role were considered, including selective law enforcement, organization, police discretion, and social change.

Police role itself was presented as important not only to criminal justice but to society in general. Two questions were raised in terms of who is best suited to perform role functions and what constitutes the objectives of police role; the law as an instrument of social control that unifies all criminal justice subsystems was used to answer both questions.

Police role was defined as performing functions that repress law violation and control crime in such a way that crime is prevented. This definition was discussed in terms of international comparisons and in terms of focusing resources available to police.

Functions were discussed as the classical police activities performed in all police subsystems. Administrative concern with the investigative function of police was covered in several contexts and further consideration was given some of the technical considerations involved, such as surveillance, undercover work, and so forth. Records and identification were cast in the framework of police functions of significant administrative concern. Evidence and the preservation of evidence were discussed as a background to search and seizure functions of police subsystems. The Fourth, Fifth, and Fourteenth Amendments were analyzed as a background for relating the police subsystem and its management to the use of law as an instrument of social control. Supreme Court rulings were related to administrative concerns about the police function.

The law of arrest was dealt with as a particularly significant administrative concern in managing the police subsystem. Related administrative concerns incidental to arrest such as telephone call and bail and release on "own recognizance" were also considered.

As general context for managing the police subsystem of criminal justice, the terms *role* and *function* were discussesd as simplifying the monumental task of bringing police resources to bear effectively on crime in a democratic society.

QUESTIONS

1. Discuss the rationale for presenting the management of police subsystems before discussing the other criminal justice subsystems.

2. What is "selective law enforcement?" Why does it exist?

3. Discuss organization, police disgression and social change as influences on police role. Are there other influences?

4. Discuss the question of who is best suited for enforcing law.

5. How is stating the objective of police role a problem?

6. Discuss this chapter's approach to the "role-objective problem."

7. How does the law as an instrument of social control relate each criminal justice subsystem to all other criminal justice subsystems?

8. What advantage exists in the relatively narrow police role defined in this chapter? Contrast narrowed role with broad police activities.

9. Discuss police function as presented in this chapter.

10. Relate the investigative process to laws of arrest.

11. Discuss probable cause and warrants in terms of problems for administering a police subsystem.

ANNOTATED REFERENCES

BARTH, ALAN, *Law Enforcement Versus the Law*. New York: Collier Books, 1963. Good background for this chapter's discussion of the law as an instrument of social control.

BLUM, RICHARD H., "The Problem of Being a Police Officer," *Police*, 5, No. 2 (November–December 1960) and 6, No. 2 (January–February 1961). An embellishment of performing the expected functions of police role.

COFFEY, A. and V. RENNER, *Criminal Justice: Readings*. Englewood Cilffs, N.J.: Prentice-Hall, 1973. A comprehensive collection of articles on police within a context of articles on the entire criminal justice system.

COFFEY, ALAN, E. ELDEFONSO, and W. HARTINGER, *Human Relations: Law Enforcement in a Changing Community*. Englewood Cliffs, N.J.: Prentice-Hall, 1971. Ideal background for the context in which police programming is administered.

MORE, HARRY W., Jr., *Critical Issues in Law Enforcement*. Cincinnati, Ohio: W. H. Anderson, 1972. Scholarly synthesis of cogent issues influencing police programming.

WILSON, JAMES Q., *Varieties of Police Behavior: The Management of Law and Order in Eight Communities*. Cambridge, Mass.: Harvard University Press, 1968. Excellent coverage for the serious student of criminal justice.

WILSON, O. W., "Police Authority in a Free Society," *Journal of Law, Criminology and Police Science*, 54, (June 1963), 175–77. Good background for further understanding the implications of orderly environment through law in democracy.

POLICE OPERATIONS

ALLETTO, W. C., "Public Safety in State Government: A Procedural Guide to Organization," *Police*, May–June 1970. Vol. 12, No. 2, pp. 131–139.

BANK, MORTON, "The Role of Law Enforcement in the Helping System," *Mental Health Journal*, 7, No. 2 (June 1971), 432–445.

REISER, M., "A Psychologist's View of the Badge," *Police Chief,* September 1970. Vol. 37, No. 9, pp. 25–29.

WARD, R. H., "The Police Role: A Case of Diversity," *The Journal of Criminal Law, Criminology and Police Science,* 40, No. 2 (December 1970), 112–118.

ARREST

BURKE, E., "Probable Cause, Warrants and Judicial Innovation," *FBI Law Enforcement Bulletin,* April & May 1971 issues. Vol. 39, No. 5, 6.

CARRINGTON, F., "Speaking for Police," *The Journal of Criminal Law, Criminology and Police Science,* June 1970. Vol. 40, No. 1, pp. 10–17.

COHEN, S., ed., "The Chimel-Vale Decision: An Analysis," *Police,* January–February 1971. Vol. 13, No. 1, pp. 12–14.

McLAUGHLIN, D. J., "Misdemeanor Arrest—The Presence Requirement," *FBI Law Enforcement Bulletin,* September & October 1971 issues. Vol. 39, No. 9, 10.

POLICE SCIENCE

"Cable TV: Does It Have Law Enforcement Possibilities?" *Law and Order,* September & October 1970 issues. Vol. 15, No. 12, pp. 8–9.

"Science and Technology and The Criminal Justice System," Chapter One in *Task Force Report: Science and Technology,* The President's Commission on Law Enforcement and Administration of Justice.

SHAW, W., "The Role of the Computer in the Coming Decade," *Law and Order,* February 1970. Vol. 15, No. 9, pp. 40–44.

CHAPTER 11

Managing Probation
and Parole

In the National Council on Crime and Delinquency Training Center publication, Dennis Sullivan states:

> . . . it is questionable whether bureaucratized probation organizations with their stress on routinization and their centralized decision-making processes are flexible enough to meet the change occurring within the environment of the community. . . .[1]

Whether or not this position is totally accepted, Sullivan's next point is exceedingly convincing.

> . . . Having been created in periods when the rate of change was relatively a slow, bureaucratic type, organizations such as probation departments are accustomed to functioning in a fairly undifferentiated and stable environment and under conditions of predictability. Today, however, the very texture of the

[1] Dennis C. Sullivan, *Team Management In Probation: Some Models for Implementation* (Paramus, N.J.: Training Center, NCCD, 1972), p. 6.

236

social as well as the physical environment has changed. The rate of change itself has changed, accelerating at an ever-increasing rate. . . .[2]

Against the background of the "inevitable and pessimistic fate" forecast for bureaucracy by Bennis,[3] Sullivan does an outstanding job of establishing the legitimacy of his concerns.[4] Indeed, he establishes not only the legitimacy of his concerns within the context of Argyris' "individual versus organization" theory,[5] but the same concerns discussed in Chapter Two as *Likert influence*[6] are also given constructive attention—particularly productivity.

The management of probation through the systems model is an effort to acknowledge the legitimacy of the kinds of concerns expressed by Sullivan. More appropriately, the management of probation and parole as a single subsystem is such an effort. But if police functions form a single subsystem, why don't the functions of probation form a different subsystem from parole roles and functions?

The answer to this question differs on the basis of input, process, or output of the criminal justice system.

When process is isolated, a great number of distinctions become evident between probation and parole; these differences will be considered in this chapter. However, when the specific administrative concern of output is isolated, at least part of the results are exactly the same: corrective rehabilitation through noncustodial treatment. And because this volume deals with managing and administering the subsystems of criminal justice as a system, the administrative concern with output is chosen.

The process distinctions are, nevertheless, managerially significant and will now be considered.

PROBATION AND PAROLE: ADMINISTRATIVE DISTINCTIONS[7]

Probation and parole are, of course, not without important distinctions. Probation evolved as an alternative to imprisonment, while parole

[2] Ibid.

[3] W. G. Bennis, "Organizational Developments and the Fate of Bureaucracy," in *Organizational Behavior and Human Performance* (Homewood, Ill.: Richard Irwin, Inc., 1969), pp. 434–49.

[4] Sullivan, *Team Management*, pp. 7–37.

[5] Chris Argyris, *Integrating the Individual and the Organization* (New York: Wiley & Sons, Inc., 1964). See also Argyris references in chaps. 2 and 3 herein.

[6] R. Likert, *The Human Organization: Its Management and Value* (New York: McGraw-Hill, Inc., 1967).

[7] Much of the information in this section was adopted from F. Cohen, "The Legal Challenge to Corrections: Implications for Manpower and Training," a consultant's paper prepared for the Joint Commission on Correctional Manpower and Training, U.S. Government Printing Office, Washington, D.C., March 1969, pp. 26–27.

evolved as an alternative to *continued* imprisonment. But probation is generally administered at a local level as a component of the judicial system, and parole is generally administered at the *state* level and by the administrative agency that is part of the executive branch of government. There are broad differences in the characteristics of probationers and parolees—probationers tend to have committed less serious or at least fewer offenses than parolees.

Despite these differences, it is clear that probation and parole now share precisely the same goals and use precisely the same techniques. Both pursue the goals of rehabilitation, surveillance, and economy; both assist the agencies of law enforcement, prosecution, and institutional confinement; conditions are attached to the grant of either; the community is involved in both probation and parole; and the individual is in each case under the supervision of someone who has access to coercive authority.

Taken from this perspective, probation and parole fill identical needs. Therefore the following theoretical needs that are fulfilled by probation would be applicable to parole.

Probation functions to fill three social needs:

1. There is a social need created by mere acceptance of the idea that the "eye for an eye" philosophy should be tempered by the "reasons" an act occurs. Clearly there is no way to completely reconcile the philosophy of government by "laws not men" with the philosophy of mitigated circumstances. Probation is the instrument by which the society attempts to sustain these incongruent and often conflicting doctrines. Here there is a need to note that probation should not, indeed cannot, combine these conflicting doctrines entirely. It is said that there is a theoretical basis comprised of interpretive behavior in terms of statutes on the one hand, and recognizing that identical acts have different causes on the other. Beyond this, probation does not relate to the opposing philosophies.

2. There is a social need filled by probation in the somewhat unique therapy that it contributes to those individuals deemed to be in need of "correction." The role of probation within a range of corrective measures can be considered unique in that the "second chance" philosophy prevails. Contrasting against the generally punitive overtones of other treatment techniques, even the most restrictive measures of probation are definable as mere support for the probationer's own efforts to justify his "second chance." Few authorities would defend incarceration on these grounds, semantic confusion notwithstanding.

   Probation provides the potential to modify behavior without the attack on dignity that is associated with liberty deprivation. Unlike the prison inmate facing the social reality that his personal behavior forces his removal from the group, the probationer needs only focus on modifications required to remain with the group.

   Clearly the need served by probation in this respect is most significant in treating offenders whose criminal activities fail to justify liberty deprivation.

3. The final need filled by probation relates primarily but not exclusively to adults. This is the assumed personality support gained by saving the community the costs and responsibility of the offender and his dependents. When an offender is spared the psychological need to rationalize the burden imposed on his unacceptable behavior, he should be able to approach his "missing insight" with less interference. But the financial savings here is only a fortunate by-product and not the main advantage. Indeed, if the probation program fails within the theoretical framework presented, the later cost of corrections would erase any such savings. The single need served in this connection remains the psychological variable of an offender not forced to feel he is not responsible for himself or his dependents.[8]

The decision-making that occurs within the subsystem process of both probation and parole occurs within a similar statutory framework. This framework, however, is somewhat vague as to basic objectives and specific criteria; this is true of both subsystems' supervisory process concerning decisions to grant or deny either probation or parole. In Texas, for example, probation may be granted "when it shall appear . . . that the ends of justice, and the best interests of the public, as well as the defendant, will be served thereby." Parole, on the other hand, may be awarded "only for the best interests of society."

Probation decision-making, which is simply a specific aspect of sentencing, is typically restricted by statutory exclusions related either to the nature of the offense or the prior criminality of the accused offender. Parole decision-making, on the other hand, is limited not only by the statute but also by the leeway left after the sentencing authority has acted within legislatively defined limits.

In some jurisdictions, parole is prohibited for persons sentenced for specific felonies or a life term. Typically, however, eligibility is based upon serving some portion of the sentence.

Probation is now the most frequent penal disposition, just as release on parole is the most frequent form of release from prison. The most accurate view of either probation or parole is not as acts of mercy, but as supervised releases that have become an integral part of the criminal justice process.

With these initial and somewhat cursory distinctions between probation and parole, the organizational structure of probation will now be considered.

Probation Organization

The present nature of virtually all correctional organizations is somewhat military. What is meant here by "military" is the line-and-staff method of organizing an agency around various levels of authority. Of course, au-

---

[8] Alan Coffey, "Correctional Probation: What Use to Society?," *Journal of the California Probation, Parole and Correctional Association*, 5, No. 1 (Spring 1968), 28–30.

thority can be defined in various ways. As will be recalled, the systems model depends on accountability for specific roles and functions to a larger degree than does authority per se. Nevertheless, the quasimilitary structure remains a part of the systems model as well. This is true if for no other reason than the availability of administrative control if managerial functions "fail."

As related to probation organization, the definition of authority is simply the degree to which organizational policy influences probation activities or line functions.

Correctional Policy: Offender vs. Community. But also with or without the aid of a systems model, correctional policy implies effective long-range programming. Although the role of administrative policy has been discussed in many contexts within the systems model and discussed in terms of influence on line functions, there is still another organizational context for correctional policy: offender versus community.

Vincent O'Leary and David Duffee have devised an impressive method of conceptualizing various categories of correctional policy based upon organizational concern for the offender as opposed to concern for the community.[9] Without exploring in detail the value of their approach, it is noteworthy that seeing correctional policy on the basis of concern for offenders suggests many powerful influences over organizational structures totally concerned with "the community" . . . correctional policy ideally being a combination of *both* concerns.

Courts. An additional consideration in organizational structure that will be considered in a management context shortly has to do with the relationship of a probation department and the court subsystem. Organizationally, some probation functions are performed before the court process, some as part of it, and some afterward. The point is that probation, regardless of organizational structure, is strongly interrelated to the courts and the court process—there is an extremely strong interface between the two subsystems.

A wide range of influence flows from the courts to the probation system; this will be considered shortly in terms of the managerial model. There are very few probation activities, however, that are not in some way influenced either by the court or the court process.

As probation agencies continue to grow in size, the administrative and managerial complexity of long-range programming produces an increasing body of evidence that discourages direct judicial involvement in the administrative fiscal process. From this frame of reference, we will explore some ramifications of the interface between the courts and probation.

Notwithstanding the growth of managerial science within probation agencies themselves, the courts remain an extremely significant variable in the present nature of probation organization.[10]

---

[9] O'Leary and Duffee, "Correctional Policy—A Classification of Goals Designed For Change," *Crime and Delinquency*, 17, No. 4 (October 1971), 373–86.

Variations. Although "line and staff" probation is the most prevalent form, there are a number of jurisdictional variations in organizing a probation agency that relate directly to our proposed systems model. The most common approach to organizing a probation department is to form the county department, in which the state writes the law but the county administers the roles, functions, and activities. The variation from this approach is the centralized state probation system, from which a "super agency" administers role and function throughout all counties of the larger jurisdiction.

As will be noted shortly, the federal government in particular combines probation and parole functions in a single organization. In other instances, cities and towns form probation units independent of the county in which they are located, and, except for the law, also independent of the state in which they are located. The advantage of local autonomy is usually cited by those in favor of the county plan and the fiscal advantages of state control are usually cited by those preferring a "super agency."[11]

Operations. The operations of a probation agency include functions that involve juveniles and adults, males and females, misdemeanants and felons, and even certain civil investigations related to divorce and the custody of children. Customarily, these operations include appearance in court —adults for the determination of guilt or innocence, juveniles for the determination of whether or not they are in need of probation assistance. In most jurisdictions the law requires that probation operations include investigations not unlike those discussed in the preceding chapter. Even in certain restricted instances when this is not a requirement, judges as a group seem to have adopted the practice of seeking probation assessment. Determination of probation eligibility, when not clearly defined in statute, is often a matter of the probation officer's recommendation, particularly in juvenile cases, but in adult cases as well.

In terms of conditions of probation itself, the court has the authority to select for probation, and the bench establishes the conditions, the judge having broad and fairly unrestricted powers.

In terms of the general nature of probation, the processing of both adult and juvenile cases has great similarities, which are likely to increase as greater emphasis is placed on providing juveniles the rights of adults— this will be discussed shortly within the specific managerial context of administering the probation subsystem.

The operating procedures involved in adult probation activities consist of investigation (with a similar framework as discussed for police in the pre-

[10] The President's Commission on Law Enforcement and the Administration of Justice, *Task Force Report: Courts,* U.S. Government Printing Office, Washington, D.C., 1967, pp. 4–106.

[11] D. Dressler, *Probation and Parole* (New York: Columbia University Press, 1959), pp. 27–28.

ceding chapter) and supervision. The traditional investigative function is limited to providing the court with information about an accused person prior to sentence. A presentence investigation report is geared to assisting the judge in arriving at an appropriate disposition of the case.

Current trends in justice and its interpretation continue to modify the specific activities of the investigative area of adult probation. There is an increasing screening and diverting of people with special kinds of behavior problems that might best be dealt with in a noncorrectional mode—as in the case of juvenile probation programming. This necessarily increases the range of alternatives for court dispositions and further increases the significance of the interface between the court subsystem and the probation administrator.

The traditional adult supervision has in the past emphasized surveillance to the virtual exclusion of case-work in some instances. As a corollary of the increasing avoidance of punishment as a part of correctional treatment, this approach to adult supervision is changing significantly enough to become of managerial interest.

Parole Organization

In dealing with the organization and structure of probation, the essential considerations of parole organizations have also been covered. To review, the classic difference is that probation is referred to as a correctional program used *before* a criminal law violator is institutionalized (and "appended" to the court) and parole is a similar type of correctional program used after a person is released from prison (and "appended" to a prison).

Legally there is a difference in status in that a person on parole is felt to be more or less on leave from an institution. This distinction at times is of managerial significance. However, from a philosophical point of view, there are not many differences. As for evidence that probation and parole are similar, a statement in a publication of the federal government indicates that "Parole is the post-incarceration equivalent of probation.[12]

Again reviewing, a realistic distinction between probation and parole that directly affects organizational structure has to do with the severity of the offense involved—probation customarily dealing with offenders earlier in the correctional experience than in the case of parole. The criminal experience of the person removed from the community in the case of parole is customarily of a more severe nature. This also will be discussed in the context of managing the parole subsystem.

Parole has on a number of occasions been defined as a type of leniency. It probably could be better described as a means of public protection, at

---

[12] The President's Commission on the Administration of Justice, *The Challenge of Crime in a Free Society*, p. 164.

least when properly used; offenders are returned to the community from correctional institutions either on parole or without supervision of any kind. The staff of the National Council on Crime and Delinquency discussed the rationale for parole as follows:

1. Release of each person from confinement at the most favorable time with appropriate consideration to requirements of justice, expectations of subsequent behavior and cost.
2. The largest possible number of successful parole completions.
3. The smallest possible number of new crimes committed by released offenders.
4. The smallest possible number of violent acts committed by released offenders.
5. An increase of general community confidence in parole administration.[13]

Public confidence in parole administration is probably the most significant of these five concerns.

Thinking of parole as an extension of the institution from which the offender is released conditionally permits a further administrative concept to emerge—the interface between prison and parole that will be discussed as part of managing the parole subsystem.

Operations. Inasmuch as the structure and organization are essentially the same in both probation and parole, their main distinction in terms of the nature of parole perhaps lies in the treatment following rather than preceding institutional care.

Although the various methods successfully utilized by probation officers are also used in parole programs, such distinguishing features as the "Half-Way House" cast the treatment approach in a different setting.[14] This difference, combined with the fact that parole agents deal with offenders who usually have a wider range of criminal experience, continues to remain significant in the operations of probation and parole. The "Half-Way House" idea and similar parole-related matters tend to direct attention to the interface between police functions and parole functions—the suspected criminal activities of parolees being the focal point of concern.

PROBATION MANAGEMENT

In managing probation role and function, it is important to recognize the great similarities with the parole subsystem, as well as the distinctions

[13] M. Matlin, ed., "Corrections in the United States," *Crime and Delinquency,* 13 (January 1967), p. 210.

[14] P. Keve, *Imaginative Programming in Probation and Parole* (Minneapolis: University of Minnesota Press, 1967), pp. 222–52.

just discussed. As already noted, the *nature* of both probation and parole are virtually the same.

Role and Function

To clarify the similarities of role and function in parole and probation consider the questions: What is probation and what is parole? Social work? Sociology? Psychology? Education? Psychiatry?

In an attempt to answer these questions as a prelude to developing a massive national program aimed at alleviating current manpower problems in probation and parole, six national organizations began a series of discussions in mid-1963. These included the American Correctional Association, the American Sociological Association, the Criminalogical Association, the Council on Social Work Education, the National Council on Crime and Delinquency, and the Western Interstate Commission for Higher Education —all used the following conference definition:

> This conference was called to launch an offensive on the furthering problem of crime and delinquency. For purposes of this conference on the manpower and training for corrections, the term correctional personnel refers primarily to those persons and public or private agencies who work in the field of probation, parole, institutions and related sources dealing with offenders as well as those persons in related occupations, insofar as their responsibilities include efforts to change the behavior of offenders. The term shall also extend to all personnel employed in comparable tasks with potential offenders.[15]

It should be pointed out that the conference did not arrive at the definition of "correctional personnel" easily. The agreement pertaining to the above definition was the focal point of most of the conference discussion. From an administrative point of view, however, any definition pointing out similarities in roles and functions is of great advantage. As related to probation and parole, this common definition of role and function introduces the possibility that many of the vexing problems of the past may be at the threshold of resolution. At the very least, administering the two subsystems can now be within the same theoretical framework—one that will afford practical approaches. If nothing else, managing the subsystems of probation and parole can utilize similarities in role and function to pursue the objectives implicit in the following:

> The general underlying premise for the new directions in corrections is that crime and delinquency are symptoms of failures and disorganization of the community as well as of individual offenders. In particular these failures are

[15] C. S. Prigmore, "Correction Blueprint for National Action on Manpower and Training," *Federal Probation*, 28, No. 3 (September 1964), 4.

seen as depriving offenders of contact with the institutions that are basically responsible for assuring development of law-abiding conduct, sound family life, good schools, employment, recreational opportunities, and desirable companions, to name only some of the more direct influences. The substitution of deleterious habits, standards and associates for these strengthen influences that contribute to crime and delinquency.[16]

The necessary tasks of probation and parole, therefore, are quite simple: build or rebuild solid ties between offender and community, integrate or reintegrate the offender into community life, restore family ties, obtain employment and education, and secure a place for the offender in the routine function of our society.

Administratively, managing a probation or a parole agency can be given a sense of direction at all times when results are defined, or when the systems model is used to update long-range planning. When both probation and parole administration are carried out with regard to these mutual roles and functions, continuity is maintained in the correctional area of criminal justice.

Philosophy

The probation or parole administrator pursuing program management on the basis of these mutual roles and functions has access to a functional philosophy: that the fields of probation and parole find their roots and substance in forces of spiritual and intellectual enlightenment throughout their history. All areas of human knowledge contribute to the field when conceptualized on this basis. Managers of both probation and parole subsystems recognize the influences of social, economic, and emotional problems in terms of deviant behavior and seek, through the application of professional skills, to deal with all of them. Certain human needs are acknowledged, and the impact of negative, as well as psychological factors from the culture can be dealt with and modified.

Principles

Administrative programming operating within such a philosophy can be aided by the adoption of principles directly related to both role and function of probation and parole:

1. Criminally oriented individuals or delinquent youths may be helped to become useful law-abiding persons within their families and their communities.
2. Constructive change in the individual may be effected by an understanding of the social and personal causes of crime and delinquency.

[16] The President's Commission on the Administration of Justice, *Task Force Report: Corrections,* p. 6.

3. Appropriate use of individual and group relationships is a crucial factor in accomplishing the satisfactory constructive change.

4. Family relationships should be utilized whenever possible.

5. The use of community resources enhance the rehabilitation process.

6. Appropriate use of legal authority as strength, stability, and reality is of correctional value to the individual and group relationships.

7. An interdisciplinary approach reflects and develops the core of the profession.

8. The combined subsystem of probation and parole ultimately depends upon the success of the police subsystem, the court subsystem, and the prosecution-defense subsystem of criminal justice.

Objectives

Once a philosophical position with principles has been adopted for administering the combined subsystem of probation and parole through the systems model, managerial definition of results is facilitated still further through certain subsystem objectives:

1. Protection of the community—to safeguard the community from the repetition of offenses through the use of scientific methods of diagnosis, control, and treatment.

2. Prevention—as in the case of the police subsystem—to assume responsibility for discharging role and function in such a way that prevention occurs; to identify and correct behavior likely to result in crime and delinquency; to assist in and support programs to alleviate social and economic conditions that are conducive to crime and delinquency.

3. Rehabilitation—to restore the offender to a useful and law-abiding life through the use of scientific methods of improving behavior and attitudes.

4. Administration of justice—to support enforcement of the law and provide full and objective information to the subsystems of police, courts, and the prosecution-defense.

5. Protective services—to provide protection and assistance upon order and under authority of the court to children who have been neglected, abused, or abandoned.

6. Treatment practices—to utilize the best skills and knowledge, including those from related disciplines, in treating offenders.

7. Employee standards and development—to recruit technically qualified employees of high morale and ethical standards; to provide them with maximum challenge and opportunity for a continuing development and service through training.

8. Effective management practices—to achieve maximal use of departmental resources through systematic applications of advanced managerial techniques; utilize systematic managerial role interfaces and reflexive synergetics to bring to bear optimum subsystem resources on criminal justice input.

9. Program research—to evaluate current methods; to explore, develop, and improve methods of practice.

10. Public understanding—to inform the community of the problems facing the entire criminal justice system—the problems of crime, delinquency, and dependency, and the role of the combined subsystem of probation and parole along with the other criminal justice subsystems.

With these common grounds between probation and parole, probation management need not differ significantly from parole management except in organizational structure as indicated earlier in this chapter—probation appended to the court subsystem and parole appended to correctional institutions or prisons.

From the process analysis of the criminal justice system, a great deal of difference exists in the nature of the "clientele" of these two subsystems, probation deals with people the court deems appropriate risks, whereas a parole program focuses on the problems of people having been found by courts to require imprisonment.

From the output analysis of the criminal justice system, managing both subsystems remains essentially the same.

Recalling the systems model chapter on organization, the example of a table of organization used that of a probation department (see Chapter Nine, page 206).

Obviously the TO was designed to illustrate organizational structure within the systems model. Although the systems model by design fits *any* organizational structure, certain combinations of flow process lend themselves to the reflexive synergetics, the managerial role interfaces and managerial functions emphasized by the systems model. For this reason, the TO and the system model appear to be an excellent combination in administering a probation department (or a police department, or a parole agency).

But just as the police administrator may be challenged by problems unique to the police subsystem (for example, managerial staff performing nonmanagement functions), so also does the probation administrator face unique challenges—specifically, many top probation administrators serve at the pleasure of the court.

A great number of jurisdictions conceive of probation process as an arm of the court—a specific court service. As such, probation functions are at least technically court functions. In terms of the clear, tangible accountability for managerial functions emphasized in the systems model, conceiving of probation management as a court function disrupts not only the continuity of output but frequently of process as well—and continuity on the basis of long-range managerial planning is essential to effective management by any model.

The problem facing many probation administrators, then, is to design a top-level interface with the court subsystem that permits the accountability called for in the systems model. Once the continuity of the planning, updating, and implementation can be established, this interface becomes administratively useful for program continuity.

Administrative Program Continuity

In terms of this top-level interface becoming administratively useful for program continuity, recall the Chapter Six discussion of cost benefit facets of administrative budget.

Hopefully, cost benefit procedures produce evidence at the end of each fiscal year that budgeting, like planning, is far more effective when managed over longer periods than one year—long-range plans with corresponding long-range budgets.

The sometimes managerially erratic influence of some judges in their interfacing activities with particular probation administrators is far less likely to occur when neither is forced to come up with a new budget every year. Indeed, both systems are likely to strive to maintain any well-thought-out scientific plan and budget once the benefits begin to accrue. Moreover, such striving can occur without the slightest risk to the integrity of either the judicial or the probation administration.

Once continuity is insured, managing the probation role and function through the systems model is essentially the same as managing any subsystem with a results orientation. The precise definition of results may vary as well as the process of achieving results, but isolating management as a process permits the systems model to function essentially the same in all of the subsystems of criminal justice—this is significant because all subsystems must succeed for any to succeed ultimately.

Administering Programs for Juveniles

As discussed earlier in this chapter, another administrative concern in probation has to do with the handling of juvenile matters. This is a particular administrative concern in view of the steady increase of juvenile crime and public focus on the handling of juveniles within the criminal justice process—called by many the juvenile justice system. Although public attention tends to have a more direct impact on the process of probation subsystem than on output, it nevertheless remains a managerial concern.

Changes in process are related to output through the interface between probation administrators and the court subsystem. For this reason, some of the dimensions of process changes should be examined.

Edward Eldefonso cites an outstanding summary of the underpinnings of this administrative problem:

> One of the confusing and unanswered questions in juvenile court law is whether proceedings are to be continued as a civil hearing or to operate as a crimi-

nal hearing. Much discretion is allowed through the statutes; and, as the following illustrates, the courts have generally upheld the statute in the past.

The proceeding is civil in nature and not a conviction, nor the order adjudging the minor a ward or committing him to the youth authority a sentence.

In an earlier case, however, the statute was criticized.

While the juvenile court law provides the adjudication of a minor to be a ward of the court shall not be deemed to be a conviction of crime, nevertheless, for all practical purposes, this is legal fiction, presenting a challenge to the credulity and violence to reason.

The United States Supreme Court has indicated discomfort with the proceedings being held civil in a case referred to from New York in 1970.

In effect, the Court of Appeals distinguished the proceedings in question here from a criminal prosecution by use of what Gault called a "civil" label of convenience which has been attached to juvenile court proceedings . . . we made clear in that decision that civil labels and good intentions do not themselves obviate the need for criminal due process safeguards in juvenile courts. . . .

Arrest

Although the California Welfare Institution Code allows for the arrest of juveniles without a warrant, regardless of whether a misdemeanor or felony is committed in the officer's presence, an arrest must be lawful and based on more than hearsay.

Police officer's testimony that defendant's name had appeared on a board at police headquarters after being named by various people in some undescribed way was not sufficient to justify defendant's arrest without a warrant. The legality of an arrest must be measured by information possessed by the arresting officer at the time of the arrest, and not by the total information gained later.

Bail

Presently, juveniles undergoing delinquent proceedings are not generally considered eligible for bail. In California, bail has not been much of an issue, and the matter was resolved several years ago.

An order adjudging a person to be a ward of the juvenile court is not a conviction of crime, and proceedings to have wardship declared are not criminal proceedings. It follows that provisions relating to bail contained in Article I, Section 6 of the California Constitution and Sections 1271 and 1262 of the Penal Code do not apply to such proceedings.

However, when the court interprets the Constitution differently, bail has been granted. In 1968, the U.S. Supreme Court considered bail as one of the issues and remanded the case back to the Ohio Court of Appeals for "reconsideration in light of Gault." Bail thus far is a matter of state law and is provided for in nine states: Alabama, Arkansas, Colorado, Georgia, Massachusetts, Michi-

gan, North Carolina, North Dakota and West Virginia. The U.S. Supreme
Court has not seen fit to make any changes in this area.

Moreover, tribunals of this nature were established with the view of
showing more consideration to the juvenile and were not designed to
deprive him of any of his constitutional rights. A finding of delinquency
usually demonstrates the necessity for making a change in the custody
of the child, but prior to such a finding, he is entitled to his constitutional right to bail.

Right to Counsel

The matter of representation by counsel was made clear by the U.S. Supreme
Court in the Kent decision of 1966.

The right to representation by counsel is not a grudging gesture to a
ritualistic requirement. It is the essence of justice. Appointment of counsel without according an opportunity for hearing on a "critically important" decision is tantamount to denial of counsel.

Since the Gault case in 1967, most states require that "Miranda warnings" be
applicable to juveniles. The Miranda decision requires that certain legal requisites be fulfilled when an officer engages a suspect on the street and questions
him. The officer must advise the suspect of his right to remain silent; of his
right to speak to an attorney; that if he wishes an attorney but cannot afford
one, the state will provide him with one; and that anything the suspect says
may be held against him.

Jury Trial

Like bail, jury trial in juvenile proceedings is not granted in most states. A
Nebraska case was declared inappropriate by the U.S. Supreme Court and the
Writ of Per Curiam was dismissed. The issues presented to the court in this
case included the right of juveniles to a jury trial. California had two cases
appealed on the subject. In the first case, the court stated:

Juvenile court proceedings are not primarily criminal in nature; therefore, trial by jury is not a constitutional requirement.

The second case made reference to the Gault decision.

To adopt trial by jury in juvenile court would "introduce a strong tone
of criminality into the proceedings," destructive to the beneficial purpose of the juvenile court law, not warranted as due process of law safeguard of individual rights.

There are certain exceptions, since some states have statutes providing for jury
trial. However, the juveniles must demand trial by jury, or the juvenile judge
on his own motion must call for a jury trial.

The record discloses that counsel made no demand for jury trial at the
time of the hearing before the county court. It appears that the county
court had jurisdiction of the person, jurisdiction of the subject matter,
and jurisdiction to render the particular judgment which was rendered
and that the petition for habeas corpus should be denied.

States that allow for jury upon demand in juvenile cases include Oklahoma, Texas, Tennessee, Nevada and Georgia.[17]

The probation officer who drafted this overview was concerned primarily with criminal justice process related to juveniles. But from the administrative point of view of subsystem output dealing with the interfaces between probation and courts, it is hopefully clear that this summary bears directly upon results-oriented management.

PAROLE MANAGEMENT

Parole management, as has been shown, is no different from probation management once output or results are isolated. The differences in organizational structure, however, are significant enough to merit a brief discussion.

As noted earlier in this chapter, the federal probation structure is organized as a combination of the probation function and parole function within a single organization. Probation officers for the federal government serve for both the federal courts and prisons. But the majority of jurisdictions segregate the parole function from the probation function, establishing a managerial need for an interface between the two administrations. An additional consideration is that, in some jurisdictions, parole administrators and prison administrators are one and the same—thereby establishing an extremely difficult interface between probation and parole in that the customary probation-prison interface has to do with probation failures (and administrative programming functions accordingly).

A related concern is the managerial interface between parole administrators and parole boards or other "release-determining" bodies. The accountability chain of the systems model is severely strained when the release-determining body is either totally unrelated to management of parole, or they are one and the same.

The systems model has one additional challenge in parole management that to some degree relates to the probation system: mutual or reciprocal parole supervision between various states.[18] More and more, persons on parole are permitted, even encouraged in selected cases, to move to other states for the parole programming removed from earlier influences upon the parolee. The output concerns of a results-oriented parole administrator relate to the differences in the definition of results from state to state. Of

---

[17] Eldefonso, *Youth Problems and Law Enforcement* (Englewood Cliffs, N.J.: Prentice-Hall, Inc., 1972), pp. 55–59.

[18] See for example, *The Handbook on Interstate Crime Control* (Chicago: The Council of State Governments, 1966), pp. 3–31. See also California Youth Authority, *Operations Manual: Interstate Compact For Juveniles*.

course the parole practices or the results definitions of the accepting state parole administrator prevail. Hopefully, however, the differences between state parole subsystems (and between all criminal justice subsystems, for that matter) will diminish enough to reduce this as an administrative concern.

SUMMARY

This chapter dealt with managing a criminal justice subsystem made up of the combined subsystems of probation and parole. The rationale used for combining the two was the administrative output or results definitions of rehabilitation through noncustodial treatment—the role and to some degree the functions of the combined subsystems.

From emphasis on similarity in subsystem output, the differences in process of probation and parole were explored. Probation management was discussed first in terms of similarity in role and function between parole and probation, and then in terms of differences in organizational structure. Probation management was isolated in terms of specific subsystem administrative concerns relating to the systems model, and then in terms of the unique administrative exigency: many top probation administrators serve at the pleasure of the court. This particular problem was discussed in terms of a resolution through effective administrative interfacing between the probation subsystem and the court subsystem.

Various programming concerns peculiar to probation were discussed. Administrative concerns relating to the handling of juvenile programs were related to other criminal justice subsystems and then discussed in terms of particular administrative problems.

Parole management was presented as essentially the same as probation management once output and results have been isolated. The organizational structure differences between probation and parole subsystems was related to the interfaces of probation and courts and parole and prison.

Problems confronting the management of a parole subsystem were discussed in terms of jurisdictional situations in which the parole administration and the prison administration is one and the same, creating an interface difficulty in that probation relates to prisons in terms of coming before commitment and parole after commitment. Various jurisdictions, such as that of federal probation, were discussed because they combine both probation and parole in one organizational structure. Further administrative concerns with parole boards or "release-determining bodies" were examined in terms of managerial interface.

The administrative parole programs involving interstate agreements to supervise persons on parole was reviewed and related to the probation subsystem.

QUESTIONS

1. Discuss the rationale for considering systems output (as opposed to process) for combining probation and parole into one subsystem for purposes of an administrative discussion.

2. Discuss the differences in process.

3. Discuss the similarities of role and functions of probation and parole; relate these similarities to managing either subsystem.

4. What is meant by probation being "appended" to the court? Of parole being "appended" to prison?

5. Discuss the position taken in this chapter in terms of the managerial consequence of probation functions being considered court activities.

6. Relate probation management to the systems model.

7. In what way could a managerial interface between the probation administrator and the court subsystem influence continuity of probation management? Relate long-range managerial planning and continuity to your answer.

8. How do the essentially process-oriented juvenile programs of a probation agency relate to the managerial output functions of probation management?

9. What are the main problems with administrative interfacing in parole management? How do parole and prison specifically relate? How do prison and probation interfaces specifically relate?

10. Discuss the philosophy, principles, and objectives of the combined probation and parole criminal justice subsystem in terms of a relationship to other criminal justice subsystems.

ANNOTATED REFERENCES

AMOS, WILLIAM E., and CHARLES F. WALFORD, *Delinquency Prevention Theory and Practice*. Englewood Cliffs, N.J.: Prentice-Hall, 1967. Chapters 5 through 11 afford an excellent discussion of the preventive nature of the subsystem function discussed in this chapter.

BARNES, HARRY ELMER, and NEGLEY K. TEETERS, *New Horizons in Criminology, 3rd ed.* Englewood Cliffs, N.J.: Prentice-Hall, 1960. Chapters 33 through 36 provide an excellent context for the process of parole.

DRESSLER, DAVID, *Practice and Theory of Probation and Parole*. New York: Columbia University Press, 1959. An outstanding coverage of the combined subsystems of probation and parole.

KEVE, PAUL W., *Imaginative Programming in Probation and Parole*. Minneapolis: University of Minnesota Press, 1967. An ideal elaboration of process in probation role and functions.

Nelson, Elmer K., Jr., and Catherine H. Lovell, *Developing Correctional Admin-istrators.* Washington, D.C.: Joint Commission on Correctional Manpower and Training, 1969. Chapters 1 and 7 relate to further consideration of administrative role in the managerial change process.

O'Leary, Vincent, and David Duffee, "Correctional Policy—A Classification of Goals Designed for Change," *Crime and Delinquency,* 17, No. 4 (October 1971), 373–86. Elaboration of the contrasting influences of community protection and offender treatment in correctional policy, with a 4-part schema for conceptualizing the variables involved.

Sullivan, Dennis C., *Team Management In Probation: Some Models For Implementation.* Paramus, N.J.: NCCD Training Center, 1972. Presentation of influences influencing the administration of probation departments experiencing the stress of social change.

Tappan, Paul W., *Crime, Justice and Correction.* New York: McGraw-Hill, 1960. A virtual encyclopedia for the criminal justice system. Chapters 19 and 23 elaborate in depth the relationship between treatment process and the overall administration of justice.

CHAPTER 12

Correctional Institutions and Jails

As has already been noted in the subsystems of police and of probation and parole, managing criminal justice subsystems is virtually identical once output or results have been isolated. This is true of managing the prison subsystem as well. It is the process, not the principles of managing criminal justice subsystems that change.

As in the case of police, probation, and parole, a kind of military organizational structure remains in the institution even after the systems model is adopted. The table of organization relates to managerial roles and functions as well—the warden is customarily ultimately accountable for results definitions, divisional commanders for defining what is needed to achieve the results, program managers under various titles for who will be the operational staff, and the shift or "watch" commanders for the supervisory determination of methods, which of course ultimately involves the guards, counselors, and other line staff.

Other similarities exist between managers in all correctional subsystems of criminal justice.

Three pervasive themes which run through correctional management may be identified.

First, the goals of restraint and reformation have helped to reinforce correctional administrators' perception of offenders as morally, psychologically, physically and educationally inferior human beings. They must be upgraded and in the meantime they must be controlled. As a result of this perception, correctional administrators focus the resources at their command primarily upon the individual offender. . . .

A second persistent attribute of correctional management has been a particularly useful approach to program development change. This approach has been characterized by fadism, a somewhat frivolous subscription to "new" ideas and generally non-rigorous, non-scientific rule of thumb for determining what to delete from the old system and what to add to it. The predominant conversation of system managers has militated against deviations from familiar ways and has led to tokenism in the launching of new measures. . . .

A final theme which has its roots in the "prison culture" of the past and still runs through correctional management today is the syndrome of isolationism and withdrawal. This condition has helped conceal the realities of life in institutions and probation and parole agencies from the public, and has thus acted to perpetuate stereotypes and myths. . . .[1]

But while the correctional subsystems and particularly the institutional subsystems are managerially similar to each other and to all other criminal justice subsystems, in other respects criminal justice institutions are also very different.

An institution is managed more like a city than a service organization; in an institution, the services are only one part of the process, whereas in probation and parole, services are the *entire* process. Beyond correctional services, an institutions feeds, houses, clothes, and protects the health of the clientele—this represents a great deal of functional activity beyond correctional services. When an institution such as a jail is operated by the police subsystem, the functional activities beyond services per se are immediately felt by top administrators in terms of budget, staffing, planning, and organizational problems.

However, it is not the purpose of this chapter to emphasize this particular additional managerial concern of institutional administrators, but to discuss institutional management against the background of significant and functional activities substantially different in depth and scope than activities managed by other criminal justice subsystems.

INSTITUTIONAL MANAGEMENT

The philosophy, principles, and most of the objectives of the probation and parole subsystem discussed in the preceding chapter apply to defining

[1] Elmer K. Nelson and Catherine H. Lovell, *Developing Correctional Administrators* (Washington, D.C.: Research Report of Joint Commission on Correctional Manpower and Training, 1969), pp. 5–6.

administrative results in correctional institutions as well. In a sense, then, the roles and functions of correctional institutions are almost the same as probation and parole, but within the context of rehabilitation through custodial, rather than noncustodial, treatment. This difference is of such importance in programming the activities of the institutional subsystem that output-oriented managerial consideration is now directed temporarily toward institutional process—recalling of course that management principles remain the same in all subsystems.

Efforts to describe the process of correctional institutions in relation to managerial principles is somewhat difficult because institutions differ not only in their physical facilities but in the various approaches to care and treatment of inmates as well. Moreover, there is great diversity in the quality of the services they offer.[2] In terms of volume, correctional institutions house about 1⅓ million inmates and during a typical year, handle over 2½ million admissions, and spend over a billion dollars.[3]

Although correctional institutions are responsible for large amounts of money and a great number of people, the diversification of their administrations leaves a number of questions unanswered in terms of their relationship to the criminal justice system. Administratively, the corrections system is fragmented into facilities run by the federal government as well as by all the states, by the District of Columbia, Puerto Rico, most of the counties, and many of the cities throughout the nation.[4] Almost invariably, each level acts independently of the other levels; the federal government has no control over state prisons and the state governments have no control over county and city jails. This situation is quite different from correctional systems in most other industrialized countries, in which all correctional activity is usually the responsibility of the central government.

Typically, administration of the American system of correctional institutions is divided within a jurisdiction *and* among various levels of government. There are various explanations for this, among which is the historic tendency for adult and juveniles to be separated. This development may have come about because the idea of reform and rehabilitation occurred at different times in different jurisdictions—some retaining the idea of punishment to the exclusion of rehabilitation longer. Distinctions between older and younger offenders create a number of classification problems even when their correctional systems are separated.[5]

---

[2] Much of this information is covered in greater depth and scope in Hartinger, Eldefonso, and Coffey's *Corrections: A Component of the Criminal Justice System* and Eldefonso and Coffey, *Criminal Justice Process: A Human Approach* (Pacific Palisades, Calif.: Goodyear Publishing Co., 1972).

[3] The President's Commission on Law Enforcement and the Administration of Justice, *The Challenge of Crime in a Free Society*, p. 159.

[4] The President's Commission on Law Enforcement and the Administration of Justice, *Task Force Report: Corrections*, p. 5.

[5] Ibid., p. 5.

Three major categories of correctional institution systems can be discerned:

1. Those that use boards to manage their correctional programs;
2. Those that have placed corrections in some larger, existing department;
3. Those that administer corrections in an independent department.[6]

These approaches are customarily considered unequal in terms of efficiency. Generally, local boards are the least effective, being appointive or ex officio types composed of such persons as the governor, certain appointees, or former board members—all usually busy and committed to other duties or businesses, which leaves them little time for the board functions. In spite of remarkable exceptions, this customarily leaves the functions to be performed by whoever chooses to take the initiative, and in effect creates a "rubber stamp" board.

Placing corrections within larger, already existing departments is generally an improvement and makes for more efficient management. For example, a department of corrections can be combined with a department of mental health forming a "super agency." Although this violates some of the function and role interfaces of the management model, it appears to be a definite administrative improvement over the local board approach.

For most states, a correctional system with a single chief administrator is preferred. The administrator within such a system can, from the systems model point of view, have role and function accountability specifically related to correctional problems, as opposed to the ineffectual role accountability of a local board or the diffused accountability of the super agency just discussed. Presumably, an administrator whose role and function are directly related to correctional concerns has the increased capability to manage effectively.

Administrative differences in correctional institutions have been elaborated in considerable detail.[7] The differences, at one extreme, indicate that there are five states wherein each juvenile institution and three states wherein each adult institution has a *separate* administrative board. At the other extreme, there is one state wherein all the correctional services are organized in a single department. Between these two extremes there are only six states in which more than three functions are administered by a single state administration.

In forty-one states, certain correctional services are administered by departments such as welfare, mental health, hospitals, and public safety—this is substantially removed from the criminal justice synergetics proposed in our systems model. Criminal justice subsystems attempting to relate to the

[6] G. Heyns, "Patterns of Corrections," *Crime and Delinquency,* 13, No. 3 (July 1967), 422.

[7] Heyns, "Patterns of Corrections," pp. 199–200.

correctional subsystems operated by welfare, mental health, and hospitals find themselves coping with interfaces that have neither role nor function in common. Claims to the contrary notwithstanding, continuity in criminal justice in such structure is of necessity hampered.

A cursory examination of criminological history establishes the jail or "gaol" as an institution that, until fairly recently, housed men, women, and children, together, and virtually without supervision, in penal programming. Early classification of institutions began with male-female and adult-juvenile distinctions, and has eventually developed into three broad categories that will be considered as part of the correctional process: (1) the degree or amount of security provided by the institution; (2) special or specific types of institutions; and (3) the jail in both the detention and the correctional context. (Jails will be considered under a separate heading.)

Degree of Security

The primary responsibilities of correctional institutions are custody and control of inmates, followed hopefully by rehabilitative programs. These responsibilities are usually explicit in the law establishing the jurisdiction of the institution, even though public expectations vary widely.

Although emphasis on security may appear somewhat divergent from rehabilitation philosophy, it is obvious that a correctional institution ignoring security is likely to find itself operating a rehabilitation program without an inmate clientele. A wide range of variation in security operates along lines other than pure custody and control of inmate population; but though conspicuous in some jurisdictions, these variations are not the focal point of this discussion, which is restricted to managerial concerns with major administrative distinctions in subsystem process of correctional institutions. Although program differences exist for juveniles and women institutionally, they are not significantly different from managerial programming in all institutional contexts.

The degree of security being considered here relates directly to the degree of risk involved in retaining custody of an inmate population. A term frequently used to describe a correctional institution handling a high-risk inmate population is the *maximum security* prison. Typically, such an institution is enclosed by brick or stone walls from 18 to 25 feet high, augmented by guard and gun towers. Variations of this exist with double fences 12 feet high, screened by gun towers, but, in any event, extreme caution is taken to retain custody of the inmate population. In the extremes, walls combined with additional fences and barbed wire are used in some jurisdictions.

The institutional process occurs in an atmosphere in which inmates are housed in interior cell blocks which, in the ideal, house no more than one inmate per cell. The overwhelming majority of prisons built in the United States before World War I were of the maximum security type. Many fewer security institutions have been built since that time, possibly because of the increasing evidence that most prisoners require far less security—and security costs are proportionately high to the degree of security provided.

The so-called *medium security* institution often uses the double fence enclosure and retains many of the characteristics of a maximum security prison. Sometimes it utilizes the "Pennsylvania model," with up to 150 units in cell block buildings, and dormitory housing a frequent compromise with the penitentiary philosophy of individual rooms.

In most instances, the medium security facility houses a larger proportion of a given jurisdiction's prison population than the maximum security institution.

The *minimum security* institution may or may not be fenced. Frequently, as much as 70 percent of the inmate population is housed in dormitories supervised on a minimal basis reflecting the nature of the overall institution.

Obviously, the minimum security institution is far less expensive than a maximum security institution not only in terms of construction but in terms of the number of personnel the administrator requires to direct the program.

In a similar range of security, the camp or ranch facility operated as a correctional institution is of administrative concern. Acknowledging that a great number of persons committed to prisons do not require guarded enclosures, this type of facility flourishes. Through sophisticated classification procedures, the better camp systems find programming functional with a minimum of personnel. Armed guards and other forms of restraint are customarily considered unnecessary—inmate supervision conducted by unarmed officers and treatment personnel.

Special Types and Specific Institutions

In addition to the ranges of security classifications of correctional institutions, certain specialties exist: reception classification centers, institutions for offenders with severe psychiatric problems, private institutions, and the Half-Way House.

Reception Classification Centers. The reception and classification center, whether it is a separate institution or part of an existing institution, is administratively operated on the basis of an offender being committed by a court to the correctional process rather than to a specific prison. It is used as a method of individualizing the offender, with the treatment program and the specific correctional institution designed to fit the specific needs of the offender. Although the court making the commitment has frequently been exposed to an exhaustive study of the offender through the probation department's presentence report (as mentioned in the preceding chapter), few judges are completely acquainted with the various institutions and programs to which an individual can be committed, including the reception classification center.

One of the keys to having a good correctional program within the state is provision for an orderly diagnosis and treatment of offenders by classification into appropriate treatment categories. Administratively, this can best be effected by statutes permitting the courts to commit convicted offenders to the process of corrections rather than to a given institution or program.

Institutions for Severe Psychiatric Problems. For a number of years, persons in the correctional field have felt that the establishment of special medical institutions for mental cases would be entirely justified, but *within* the criminal justice system. Medically, the nature of the mental disorder may be essentially the same as that of a person in a mental hospital. The criminal behavior for which a person is committed to prison nonetheless remains the ultimate responsibility of the criminal justice system, eloquent arguments from social work and mental health advocates notwithstanding.

The correctional institution geared specifically to psychiatric treatment has as its primary purpose the reception, segregation, confinement, and treatment of inmates on the basis of their psychiatric problems, but with the administrative results definition of criminal rehabilitation—results being considered accomplished only when criminal behavior has been eliminated whether or not the mental health problem has been corrected.

Categories of inmates in a psychiatrically oriented institution are (1) mentally ill inmates, (2) mentally defective inmates, (3) epileptic inmates, (4) inmates strongly addicted to drugs, (5) physically or mentally abnormal inmates, including sex offenders, and (6) inmates suffering from chronic disorders or conditions.

In addition to these categories, certain other inmates are often committed to this type of facility, such as pronounced homosexuals or those with a history involving sexual problems.

Private Institutions. From an administrative point of view, correctional institution process involving private institutions has a substantially different managerial program than the prison. Nevertheless, correctional administrators are increasingly involved in managing programs that include private institutions.

Private institutions, as well as "Half-Way Houses are often referred to as "non-institutions." This is because many of them are not under direct administrative control, but have their programs coordinated by the correctional administration utilizing their service.

Private institutions have been significant in the treatment of youthful offenders since the time when institutional segregation of juveniles from adults first emerged. Probably as much as 25 percent of juveniles who are institutionalized in the United States are placed in private facilities.[8]

The number of youngsters handled in private institutions is significant when it is noted that most of the private institutions operate on extremely

[8] D. G. Blackburn, "Institutions for Juvenile Delinquents—a Review of Recent Developments," *NPPA Journal,* 4, No. 1 (January 1958), 12–21.

limited budgets, and that they often must compete with numerous other programs for charity donations such as the United Fund or Community Chest.

Although financing private institutions may pose problems, a great number of advantages exist for the results definitions of the administrators. Among these is the ability to remain comparatively small, selecting only those who truly fit the institutional program. Dealing with youthful offenders in small groups and within classification systems that are relevant has been frequently established as far more conducive to rehabilitation than are programs in larger, overcrowded, understaffed public training schools.[9]

The Half-Way House. The Half-Way House and its program has probably established itself as a permanent fixture of the correctional institutional subsystem—or the correctional "non-institution" subsystem. For a number of obvious reasons, the Half-Way House frequently brings institutional subsystems into an interface with the police subsystem, particularly in jurisdictions in which police believe a great number of the crimes committed are committed by persons within these programs. Administratively, this negative interface is of major managerial concern to efforts to synthesize criminal justice as a system.

Initially, Half-Way House programs were used as a means of easing inmates out of correctional institutions, to facilitate their transition from the rigid control of a prison to the relative freedom of a community (in reference to parole supervision). Recently, the program has come to be used as an alternative to formal institutionalization. Although the Half-Way House approach is conceived of by correctional practitioners as a "non-institution," it has nevertheless proved a useful interface between probation and prison as well as between prison, parole, and probation.

From a process point of view, there are many essential differences between prison and a Half-Way House. But in terms of administrative results, the output of the system shows a number of similarities between them.

A residence program is used that establishes the institution, but it is customarily operated by either probation or parole personnel, which technically justifies the label "non-institution." In some instances, however, Half-Way House are staffed by persons who are neither parole nor probation officers but equally trained in behavior science and qualified as counselors—counseling programs being the essential ingredient in most Half-Way House programs.

JAIL MANAGEMENT

Although frequently administered by the police subsystem, the functions system and roles involved in a jail system often place the administration

---

[9] H. J. Palmicri, "Private Institutions," *NPPA Journal,* 4, No. 1 (January 1952), 51–56.

closer to the correctional institutional subsystem. This is true particularly when jails are used for treatment or rehabilitation, but even when they are used totally for detention. This also holds true with regard to housing, feeding, and generally caring for inmates. Although it is unlikely that the proportion of police subsystems operating jails will change significantly, it is worth noting that so long as "enforcement" does the "correcting," the synergetics of the criminal justice subsystem suffer somewhat. This suffering is in terms of administrative interfaces between the criminal justice subsystems of police and corrections.

With this in mind, the jails will be discussed in the context of the correctional institution subsystem, acknowledging the existence of many police oriented and administered jails—jails for "correction" is well as police-detention.

From an administrative point of view, the issue is not whether a person taken into custody is to be punished or dealt with constructively, but concern for the safety of society regarding the ability of the accused to escape before his guilt or innocence can be established. From this particular frame of reference, administering jails as part of the police subsystem is amply justified, the assumption being that an arrest would not be made unless the community was in some danger requiring the custody of the accused.

Of course many arrests are not followed by a court action. And even when court action follows arrest, an individual may be released from custody through bail procedure or his on own recognizance pending the trial.

But in cases in which are arrested party is detained pending court, the period of incarceration is particularly significant and relevant, notwithstanding the argument that the incarceration pending trial is not intended to either punish or treat. Remaining in custody has essentially the same impact in several psychological areas regardless of intent.

Compounding the administrative difficulty of jail being used purely for detention are the cases in which people having been detained for some time are found innocent and released. It is extremely important that these people be convinced of the fairness of the criminal justice system.

If he is guilty it is even more important that he, who has acted "unjustly," be impressed with the contrast between his own behavior and that of the state which is theoretically the embodiment of justice. Yet sometimes the impression of the detained is rather one of injustice. Sometimes he is detained in jail when others he knows have arranged a fix or release; his bail is high, while another man's is low; he is offered assistance in return for a bribe he cannot pay; the well-to-do returns home while he languishes in jail; the jail is foul and full of vice and corruption at which the jailer connives or in which he participates; he is punished more severely in jail before he is proved guilty than many are punished in prison afterwards. Under such conditions, it is fair to assume that his anti-social attitude will be confirmed, and that he will feel that his own crime is a racket not unlike that in which government agents are engaged.[10]

Authorities in the correctional field agree that in spite of the short periods that thousands of men and women are detained in jails pending trials every year, the experience itself is significant. The rate of recidivism among those found guilty and incarcerated is extremely high.

> From many points of view, the jail is the most important of all our institutions of imprisonment. The enormous number of jails alone is sufficient . . . to make [one] realize that the jail is, after all, the typical prison in the United States. . . . From two-thirds to three-fourths of all convicted criminals serve out their sentence in jails. But this is not all. The jail is with small exception, the most universal detention house for untried prisoners. The great majority, therefore, of penitentiary and reformatory prisoners have been kept for a period varying from a few days to many months within the confines of a county or municipal jail. Then, too, there is the class, not at all unimportant in number, of individuals who have finally established their innocence, have been set free, spending some time in the jail awaiting trial. Important witnesses also are detained in jail, and it is used at times for still other purposes, even serving occasionally as a temporary asylum for the insane. The part, therefore, which the jail plays in our scheme of punishment cannot be over-estimated. Whether for good or for evil, nearly every criminal who has been apprehended is subject to its influence.[11]

The President's Commission on Law Enforcement and the Administration of Justice noted that even in this decade, the above commentary, along with further comments on filth, neglect, and maladministration regrettably describe the status of many jails throughout the United States.[12]

As a place of detention for accused persons, the jail traces its lineage back to Biblical times. Of interest to most jail administrators would be the heritage of the workhouse developed in the sixteenth century to deal with unemployment, vagrancy, petty thievery, prostitution, and disorderly conduct. So successful was it in clearing the streets and public places in the economically depressed that the English Parliament ordained the establishment of such an institution for minor offenders for every county in England. The innovation of this type of imprisonment spread during the seventeenth century to Holland, Belgium, Germany, and finally to America.[13]

In a sense, given the particular heritage of the jail and the frequency

---

[10] D. R. Taft, *Criminology*, 3rd ed. (New York: The MacMillan Co., NY, 1956), p. 414.

[11] L. N. Robinson, "Penology in The United States," cited in *Task Force Report: Corrections* (The President's Commission on Law Enforcement and the Administration of Justice), p. 162.

[12] Ibid., p. 162.

[13] Ibid., p. 162.

with which it is run by the police subsystem rather than the correctional subsystem, jails are "orphans"—at least orphans of the criminal justice institutional subsystem. As such, the administration of the jail system is often faced with the problem of concern for correctional institutions not applying to jails. From a societal point of view, jails often remain "out of sight and out of mind."

Every year, approximately 141,000 American men, women, and children are locked up in jails, convicted or awaiting trial for offenses ranging from shoplifting to murder, from political demonstrations to treason.[14] In the course of their confinement they will undergo an astonishing variety of experiences—frequently negative. They will wait, drunk or sober, in the vomit-covered drunk tanks in countless city and county jails. They may put in twelve-hour days picking cotton in some states, be thrown nude in totally dark isolation cells in other states, be raped by members of their own sex in still other cities and counties.

> In Washington, D.C., jails, for example, any young white man under 150 lbs. is likely to be the unwilling host of a "blanket party." As soon as the guards leave the barracks-like dormitories, a blanket is thrown over the new arrival's head, dozens of hands pummel him and a series of unseen men commit homosexual rape upon him.
>
> The guard force is inadequate to control the situation. Usually there is one guard posted outside each 50-man dormitory: "he's not going to enter that dorm at night even if he thinks 10 people are being murdered," . . .
>
> Washington's prisons, of course, have no monopoly on the gang homosexual rape. It goes on all across the country. . . . The investigation uncovered other chilling facts, two-thirds of the aggressors in these attacks were in jail for serious, assaultive crimes, on the other hand, the victims were usually charged with minor offenses.[15]

Although the process of a jail system remains, in terms of system, a different concept than output, it is so dramatic that the managerial output concern must of necessity focus in this area.

> No part of corrections is weaker than the local facilities that handle persons awaiting trial and serving short sentences. Because their inmates do not seem to present a clear danger to society, the response to their needs has usually been one of indifference. Because their crimes are considered petty and the sentences served are relatively short, the correctional system gives them low status. Many local jails and misdemeanant institutions are administered by the police or county sheriffs, authorities whose experience and main concerns are in other fields. Most facilities lack well-developed recreational and counselling

[14] Ibid.

[15] N. Horrock, "Our Jail Jungle," *San Francisco Examiner,* San Francisco, Calif., January 16, 1971.

programs, sometimes even medical services. The first offender, the innocent awaiting trial, sometimes juveniles and women, are imprisoned with confirmed criminals, drunks, and mentally disturbed or retarded.[16]

During the past fifty years there have been a number of graphic descriptions of the immorality and physical decay that is prevalent in most jails across the nation. Descriptions are made of indiscriminate mixing of all types of prisoners—felons and misdemeanants, hardened offenders and first, offenders, ill and the healthy, young and the old, mentally defective and psychotic along with the alcoholic.

Enlightened jail administrators are coming to recognize that though jails have been a part of western society's law enforcement establishment for a great length of time, the tremendous social changes have not been accompanied by significant changes in jails. Frustrating them is the fact that many if not most of the critical problems have little or nothing to do with the managerial program. Instead, many of the difficulties flow directly from the system of which the jail is a part. Jails, intended as places of "safekeeping" for persons awaiting trial, are at the same time utilized (deliberately or unwittingly) as rehabilitation facilities for convicted offenders. Regardless of the adequacy of the managerial program, performing these two separate and distinct functions simultaneously in precisely the same physical facility generates many problems. Needless to say, the detention of material witnesses, or mentally ill persons within the same facility is totally destructive to a functional managerial program.[17]

Expecting jail administrators to perform mutually exclusive functions simultaneously within the same physical plant and with the same personnel ultimately produces frustration; both the federal government and the National Council on Crime and Delinquency feel that these functions must be separated. To accomplish this, a separate type of institution from the one commonly referred to as a jail must be built within the community to accommodate either one function or the other.[18] Some communities that have partially implemented this are San Diego; Multnomaha County, Oregon; Westchester County, New York; and St. Paul, Minnesota.

To emphasize the urgency of a remedy for the problems of jails, administrators need only conceive of the jail as a "port of entry."[19] The pretrial period itself is a port of entry into the correctional system—either favorable

---

[16] The President's Commission on Law Enforcement and the Administration of Justice, *The Challenge of Crime in a Free Society*, p. 178.

[17] M. S. Richmond, "The Jail Blight," *Crime and Delinquency*, 11 (April 1965), 132–41.

[18] M. Matlin, ed., "Corrections in The United States," *Crime and Delinquency*, 13 (January 1967), 153–56. See also M. S. Richmond, pp. 134–35 in the same publication.

[19] L. T. Empey, *Studies in Delinquency: Alternatives to Incarceration*, Department of Health, Education & Welfare, U.S. Government Printing Office, Washington, D.C., 1967, p. 9.

or unfavorable—rarely neutral, frequently negative. It is a crucial period because there is increasing evidence that the mere incursion of a person into the system, especially through detention or jail while awaiting adjudication of guilt or innocence, may *increase* rather than lessen the likelihood that he will remain in the system and continue posing a criminal problem to society. The deeper the defendant has been plunged into the correctional process, and the longer he has been held under punitive (even humanely punitive) restraints, the more difficult is the road back to social restoration.

From this administrative perspective, criminal justice as a system might profit through a concentration of collective effort at this specific point on the continuum of criminal justice process overall. In effect, this proposes an intensified managerial interface between jail administration and virtually all subsystems of criminal justice. Conceivably, administrative effort could produce coordinated programming in which detention jails (presumably remaining within the police subsystem) have the benefit of the most sophisticated and effective treatment available from the entire correctional institution subsystem as an investment in reducing the severity of the cases ultimately arriving in the penal institutions.

Such a coordinated administrative interface might also produce a far more effective form of jails for the rehabilitation of those convicted of minor offenses. But in any event, the strategic position of the jail on the criminal justice continuum is worthy of the greatest efforts of the administrators of different subsystems. In this broader context, jails, along with the suggested separation of jails for local correctional purposes, remain the *reception centers* for the major criminal justice institutions.[20] Within this administrative context, the classification of offenders by the seriousness of the offense is of managerial concern.[21] Two broad categories have developed: felons and misdemeanants:

> The distinction between misdemeanants and felons is, in general, a distinction between less serious and more serious crimes, but it does not always hold. The line that exists between a misdemeanor theft and a theft that is a felony is drawn by the value of the property, a distinction that may be totally irrelevant in determining the sentence.[22]

The inaccuracy of the popular conception of misdemeanor distinctions has a direct influence on the management of jails when they are used for

[20] The President's Commission on Law Enforcement and the Administration of Justice, *Task Force Report: Corrections*, pp. 162–63.

[21] For in-depth elaboration of characteristics and numbers of offenders, refer to Hartinger, Eldefonso, and Coffey, *An Introduction to Corrections: Part of the Criminal Justice System*, chapter 11. See also President's Commission, *Task Force Report: Corrections*, pp. 163–64.

[22] S. Rubin, *The Law of Criminal Correction* (St. Paul, Minn.: West Publishing Co., 1963), p. 170.

rehabilitation. It has been established that out of 215 correctional institutions studied, 49.6 percent admitted felony cases and 50.4 percent excluded felony cases—about half and half.[23] These figures suggest the value of one day determining how many prisoners serving misdemeanor sentences in institutions that exclude felony cases were actually serious offenders who happened at the time of arrest to have been arrested for a lesser offense or had a felony reduced to a misdemeanor. In any event, the possibility definitely exists that a jail administrator operating a rehabilitation program for misdemeanants may in fact be operating a rehabilitation program for many criminal problems of equal severity to that handled by large criminal justice institutions.

Even in situations in which this distinction is clear, studies have indicated that indiscriminate mixing of prisoners occurs. In the area of "non-victim crimes," the mixture continues.

> Fully 50 percent of all commitments . . . [are] for drunkenness or other offenses directly related to alcohol. Multiple commitments are the rule and not the exception—10, 20, and even 50 commitments of one alcoholic are commonplace.[24]

Although record-keeping practices virtually eliminate the possibility of determining how many persons account for over one million commitments a year, it seems a safe estimate that the number of persons incarcerated is considerably lower than the number of commitments. It is evident that the vast majority of those presently confined to jail institutions will return after release or subsequent short terms, or will "graduate" to major institutions as they become more criminally sophisticated.[25] Placed in the context of administrative results definitions, this is most discouraging.

Jail Organization:
Uniqueness of Institutional Structure

Recalling the similarity of the quasi-military organizational structure of jails and other criminal justice subsystems earlier in this chapter, only a cursory examination of the uniqueness of jail organizational structure will be considered—and considered in a specific context.

The uniqueness of jail organizational structure might be thought of in terms of how a correctional institution frequently "organizes dilemma."[26] By "organized dilemma" is meant the inherent irrelevance of life styles for

---

[23] President's Commission, *Task Force Report: Corrections*, p. 163.

[24] M. E. Alexander, *Jail Administration* (Springfield, Ill.: Charles C. Thomas, 1957), p. 311.

[25] President's Commission, *Task Force Report: Corrections*, p. 165.

[26] D. Cressy, ed., *The Prison* (New York: Holt, Rinehart and Winston, 1961). chaps. 3 and 7.

which there are no community models. In other words, the life styles learned in a correctional institution have no place in the community situation to which the offender is returned. The dilemma is compounded by the infrequent public concern generated at certain intervals after accusation of corruption or fraud, bribes, dramatic escapes, killings, or other newsworthy activities.

The administration of larger correctional institutions, through the interfaces with probation and parole, and through the use of such programs as Half-Way Houses, tends to work toward solving this problem of training an inmate in a life style that is irrelevant in the community. The jail, however, rarely has the advantage of this kind of transitional organizational structure. Fortunately, dramatic innovations such as the work furlough and jail structures specifically earmarked for rehabilitation are beginning to alleviate some of this regrettable strain on the criminal justice system. Nevertheless, jail organization retains for the most part an inherent dilemma because it combines the necessity of public initiative and public assistance with the virtual necessity to retain the jail as a negative symbol to be rejected by the public—and does so without many of the mitigating operations available to larger correctional institutions.

INSTITUTIONAL SUBSYSTEM ADMINISTRATION

Hopefully, the gross differences in subsystem process have emerged through this discussion, particularly in terms of the "'organizational dilemma." Notwithstanding these great differences, however, managing the institutional subsystem is not significantly different than managing any other criminal justice system, as long as management is the consideration involved. The process differences are so great, however, that remaining focus on management is by no means easy in the various administrative interfaces.

Recalling the problems of parole administrators interfacing with both prison and probation, it should be clear that the prison administrators' problems are compounded in the same way, but with the additional interface problem of parole process influence on prison process. In other words, parole process is desirable and attractive to those under prison process—a difficult managerial interface in terms of when one program exceeds the value of the other in any given point in time in a particular case.

Perhaps the toughest obstacle in isolating managerial principles as the institutional administrator's main function is best described in the succinct comment made by Cressy:

Institutional necessities include a continuous flow of prisoners, personnel, and money; statutory permission to operate and to maintain a physical plant and program.[27]

[27] Ibid., p. 5.

Police administrators celebrate reductions in reported crime. Reductions in the caseloads of judges, prosecutors, probation officers, and parole agents is of administrative advantage. The entire history of corrections, it has been suggested, can be summarized as simply passing through three stages, each categorized by a particular emphasis in the handling of offenders: first, *revenge*; second, *restraint*; and finally, *reformation*.[28] It is possible, with the possibility emerging that criminal justice may be administered as a *system*, still another stage will occur: *continuity with other subsystems.*

SUMMARY

This chapter dealt with management of the criminal justice system of correctional institutions and jails. The similarity of managerial principles involved in managing this and other criminal justice subsystems was emphasized. The major differences in institutional process, however, were also stressed; against the background of complete custody and care in addition to services, the institutional process was explored in the major areas of concern to management.

Jurisdictional variations were explored, as were variations in designations given institutions, that included the nature of inmates, the degree of severity of crimes involved, and security required.

Camps and other special institutional programs were discussed, as was special programming for psychiatric problems and private institutional programs.

Jails were discussed in the institutional administrative context as having a two-fold function, the first dealing with detention, which appropriately enough is likely to remain in the police subsystem, and the second as being rehabilitative in nature and better suited for the goals, roles, and functions of the correctional institution subsystem. The context of jails as the "port of entry" into the overall correctional system was elaborated.

The problems of artificial life styles were discussed as part of institutional organization in general, and stressed as a particular problem in the context of jails.

Against this background of major process differences, institutional management was cited as being the same as management of all criminal justice systems, as long as it is isolated from process.

Some of the problems in remaining focused on management as a concept in the correctional institutional subsystem were also discussed.

---

[28] Daniel Glasser, "The Prospect for Corrections," mimeograph for the Arden House Conference on Manpower Needs in Corrections, 1964, p. 203.

QUESTIONS

1. Discuss the application of the systems model to institutional management as presented early in this chapter.

2. How is institutional programming beyond the service level of other criminal justice subsystems?

3. Discuss the jurisdictional variations of correctional institutions.

4. Contrast the various designations given certain institutions (nature of inmate, security, etc.).

5. Relate private and psychiatric programming to the "Half-Way House" idea in terms of organizational structure and programming.

6. Discuss the disparity in institutional role and police role in terms of police subsystems operating jails that include rehabilitation. Discuss the justification of police subsystems retaining operation of jails designed solely for the purpose of detention.

7. Discuss jails as "ports of entry."

8. What is meant by "organized dilemma?"

9. Why is focus on management principles more difficult for institutional administrators than administrators of other subsystems?

ANNOTATED REFERENCES

ALEXANDER, M. E., *Jail Administration.* Springfield, Ill.: Charles C. Thomas, 1957. Synopsis of the singular management problem of administering an institution not designed for corrections per se.

CRESSY, DONALD, ed., *The Prison.* New York: Holt, Rinehart and Winston, 1961. Outstanding collection of readings on the sociology of prisons.

FOX, VERNON, "Why Prisoners Riot," *Federal Probation,* Vol. 41, No. 2, March 1971. A penetrating exploration of the problems of focusing on managerial principles.

GRUZEN, J. L., "Developing a Design for a Medium Security Prison," *Police Chief,* November 1970.

HARTINGER, W., E. ELDEFONSO, and A. COFFEY, *Corrections: A Component of the Criminal Justice System.* Pacific Palisades, Calif.: Goodyear, 1972.

HEYNS, G., "Patterns of Corrections," *Crime and Delinquency,* 13, No. 3 (July 1967).

MATLIN, M., "Corrections in the United States," *Crime and Delinquency,* 13 (January 1967). Good overview of jurisdictional variations.

CHAPTER 13

Courts, Management of Prosecution, and Defense

Were this text concerned primarily with the pure line-and-staff form of what was identified earlier as command management, the discussion of courts, prosecution, and defense in terms of administration would prove exceedingly difficult. For, unlike the early structured state and federal correctional systems, the courts, including prosecution and defense, present subsystems that are greatly removed from the line-and-staff structure.

The systems model, however, conceives of managerial roles and functions as having priority over structure. For this reason, it is possible to discuss *any* subsystem in criminal justice in a management context.

The relative simplicity with which the conceptual model of systems management can be applied has to do with the ease with which problems can be resolved in the criminal justice subsystems of police, probation and parole, and correctional institutions. The difficulties of the police subsystem managing jails were essentially resolved by modifying jail function into two parts: detention for police role and rehabilitation functions for correctional institutions. The conceptual difficulty for the probation system functioning prior to imprisonment, and parole functioning after imprisonment were essentially resolved through the common administrative role of rehabilitation through noncustodial treatment.

Courts, prosecution, and defense, the remaining subsystems of criminal justice, present different conceptual problems, equally resolvable but somewhat more difficult to deal with.

The process and output of courts do not lend themselves to easy assignment of managerial role and function as in the case of police, probation-parole, and correctional institutions. Elected officials serving as top administrators in prosecution may find the long-range planning function of the model difficult to retain as a priority when plans exceed the term of elective office—a significant enough variable to be isolated as an individual problem later in this chapter. Indeed, elected sheriffs, chiefs of police, judges, and appointments made by elected officials may conceive of their roles as being totally without planning responsibility inasmuch as they terminate at the time new appointments are made.

In short, the long-range planning requirement of the model may face difficulties related to the unique nature of their process, these difficulties compounded by the additional difficulty of elected status in many instances.

With the background in mind, the subsystems of courts, prosecution, and defense will be considered.

THE COURTS

In order to gain the administrative advantage of the systems model for the court subsystem, it must first be recalled that (1) role and function in the management model are separate, and (2) one role can be accountable for more than one managerial function (as in the case of a chief of police in a small jurisdiction).

Differences in the managerial administrative effort of courts no longer obtain once the distinction between role and function have been clarified, the uniqueness of judicial process notwithstanding. This obviously is of great managerial advantage in subsystem management, but would be greatly facilitated by certain reforms, as suggested in the following:

> The complex problems of court administration will not yield to any one simple solution, but a well-structured and efficiently organized system is a condition prerequisite to further change. Rebuilding the structure and organization of the administration of criminal justice has two aspects; the creation of a unified, simplified court structure within a state and the establishment of clear and direct administrative responsibility within that system.
>
> *A unified court system.* Proposals for the unification and simplification of court structures have long been part of programs for court reform. The Model State Judicial article which has been endorsed by the American Bar Association em-

bodies the most recent statement of these principles. Other model constitutional provisions have been drafted by the National Municipal League and the American Judicature Society.

Integration of all courts in a state interested in a single state court system which consolidates courts at the same level is a recurring element of reform. The unseemly and potentially venal institution of the profit-making court, which is seen primarily as a source of local revenue, is eliminated, and all fines and fees are paid to the state treasury. At the same time local inability to finance adequate courts and related facilities is alleviated.

. . . Traditionally jurisdictional lines have primarily followed county lines, with the county court as the unit of judicial management. In an era of rapidly shifting population, however, jurisdictional lines must accurately reflect community growth so that there will be enough judges to handle cases and so that all sitting judges will be kept busy. In some states the county court has been superseded by judicial districts which may include several counties or cut across county lines. . . .[1]

Specific concern in terms of organizational structure reforms is reflected in the following:

. . . Development of clear authority and responsibility for court management have been considered essential for effective administration. Under the Model Judicial Article the Chief Justice is executive head of the judicial system. . . . In any event it is important that power be vested in a single group, preferably in one person, to insure that decision-making does not become unwieldy, responsibility disbursed, and accountability lacking.

On the local court level there is a parallel need for administrative power, including superintendence of calendars, assignment of physical and personnel resources, and control over budgets. The most common solution has been to vest this power in a presiding or administrative judge within the court.

To supplement the administrative responsibility and authority, the judiciary in most states has been given varying degrees of rule making power over the procedures for handling its business. This power is needed because legislatures cannot deal with these problems effectively. . . .

. . . For centralized administration of the court system to prove effective, the need for careful selection and proper training of those who are to exercise administrative responsibility must be recognized. Administrative judges, and judges of one-man courts should be specifically trained. . . .

. . . Resistance to change commonly found in the judiciary and in related institutions must be overcome. To some extent this can be brought about by education. In many states administrative positions go to judges strictly on the basis of seniority, rather than on the basis of interest or talent in management. Administrative capability and innovation should become a key element for

---

[1] The President's Commission on Law Enforcement and Administration of Justice, *Task Force Report: The Courts*, U.S. Government Printing Office, Washington, D.C., 1967, pp. 82–84.

selection and advancement of judges and court administrators within the state court system.[2]

Perhaps the reference to "resistance to change commonly found in the judiciary" is more significant than it first appears, particularly in the context of combining a change in organizational structure with a change in managerial approach.

But whether or not change is resisted, the relationship of the crime problem to trial delays (compounded still further by increasing delays in civil matters heard by the same judges in many instances) leaves little doubt that changes will occur—hopefully on the same logical, rational basis in court management and output as applied by courts to judicial process.

Managerial Functions

With the incredible variety of jurisdictional sizes and organizational structures that currently describe the overall American court system, it is virtually impossible to explore all the possibilities in relating managerial functions to court roles.

In many instances, the presiding judge, as indicated in the preceding quote, is in effect the top administrator—he may or may not have the prerogative to define results or perform any other managerial function depending in some instances on how his appointment was accomplished. In other instances, a court administrator actually performs some administrative function—he may be in charge of little more than the acquisition of furniture in judge's chambers. In some jurisdictions, a jury commissioner in effect manages some of the managerial functions of court output—enough to permit total focus of judges on their judicial process. In other jurisdictions, a jury commissioner is a kind of social secretary to members of the bench.

Dysfunction Magnified

Of course these types of variations are not restricted to the court subsystem—very wide ranges of varieties in organizational structure and process exist in all criminal justice subsystems, as already noted. But in the case of the court subsystem, a kind of magnification of any systematic dysfunction occurs. Courts represent, after all, the most prestigious and certainly the most influential subsystem within criminal justice—at least in terms of the impact of court process on all other subsystems.

System dysfunction of the court subsystem costs criminal justice even more than dysfunctional subsystems in law enforcement, prosecution-defense, or corrections. The weight of the courts' prestige and influence magnify dysfunction substantially.

[2] Ibid., p. 84.

Systems Model

Yet even within the somewhat chaotic organizational structure of the overall American court subsystem, a great deal of managerial advantage can be gained through application of the systems model. Of course, as already noted, organizational modifications would help a great deal. But even without reorganization, significant improvement in managerial continuity is possible.

First of all, the systems model distinction between efficiency and effectiveness could be brought to bear. Recalling that effectiveness is the achievement of results, and efficiency is the expedient, economical use of resources in achieving results, the court subsystem is at once arrayed into at least one of the necessary managerial functions—that of results definitions.

The conservative (and at times preservative) nature of the court role suggests a substantially less measurable results definition. Nevertheless, results for courts are clearly definable within the context of the systems model, as is indicated by the richness of the literature on sentencing alone.[3]

As in the case of all subsystems, courts have input, process, and output. In terms of these components, consider the seven points of the model timetable for the processing of criminal cases:

> At least seven points in the process deserve special attention:
> 1. Arrest
> 2. First judicial appearance (presentment or preliminary hearing)
> 3. Formal charge (indictment or filing of the information)
> 4. Pre-trial motions and applications
> 5. Trial
> 6. Sentencing
> 7. Appellate review[4]

Arrest is obviously input, process is represented in points two through five, output in points six and seven (at least in the absence of appeal). Points six and seven, then, are part of an internally structured measurement of results achievement.

Managerial Roles for the Judiciary

As reflected in the citations from the Task Force Report on Courts, managerial status and roles for administrative judges are highly recommended. Without impinging on court process in any way except to get rid of managerial problems that impede results achievement, the presiding or senior

---

[3] The reader is referred to the annotated references at the end of this chapter, in the section headed "Court Process."

[4] President's Commission, *Task Force Report: Courts*, p. 84.

bench member serving as the administrator can assume results definition as a part of his role, or this function can be given an assisting senior or assisting presiding judge—perhaps functionally augmented by court administrators or jury commissioners in larger jurisdictions.

In effect, resource utilization of the managerial determination of operational staffing, simply a scheduling activity in most instances, is accomplished in two ways: (1) annual rotation of the presiding judge, and (2) rotation of calendar assignments at least in part on the basis of current interest—a primary goal of the management model as well as an answer to the criticism expressed in this regard in the Task Force Report.

Organizational Modification and Subsystem Interface

Fortunately for the overall criminal justice system, approaches to at least the scheduling problems such as the approach just discussed seem to be gradually emerging in judicial awareness, if not in judicial practice. Improved methods of calendar assignment by no means eliminate the problems posed in the Task Force Report—but they represent a start that at least tempers the harsh assessment of the Task Force Report when it cited the resistance to change existing in the judiciary.

Hopefully, organizational modification and application of managerial science can be facilitated through effective administrative interfacing between courts and other subsystems that are geared to results-oriented management that recognizes a difference between efficiency and effectiveness.

There are monumental problems facing efforts to modify the procedures that tend to delay court process. To make such modifications within the law and constitution may tax criminal justice talents so severely that efficiency and expedience could possibly emerge with priority rather than effective judicial process. Again, effective managerial interfacing between the courts and other subsystems can help retain judicial effectiveness as the priority.

The interface with the subsystems of prosecution and defense is perhaps the most strategic in answering increasingly vocal criticisms of the following variety:

American justice is in turmoil. After 180 years of neglect, there is need of a major overhaul. In spite of the lofty principles propounded in the Bill of Rights, the system presents numerous obstacles to effective crime control, and it sometimes threatens the very ideals it was designed to preserve and promote. There is evidence that instead of preventing crime, the system of justice—as it is now embodied in our police, courts, and correctional agencies—is a significant factor in crime causation.

In theory the system operates under a few clear and simple precepts, of which the following are fair examples. All law violations are to be reported to the police. The reports are investigated, and if there is sufficient evidence the offender is arrested. Whenevr an arrest is warranted there should be a court conviction. Conviction is followed by an appropriate punishment which, in turn, should serve as a deterrent against further offenses.

According to this model the case of an offender progresses by highly visible procedures from arrest to conviction to punishment. There is little opportunity for officials to exercise discretion and their decisions are presumably founded on conclusive information. Public participation is assured by the requirement that a jury of peers determine if the evidence warrants conviction, leaving the judge's decision regarding an appropriate punishment as the main point of discretionary authority.

In practice, however, the cycle of arrest → conviction → punishment is more the exception than the rule. Most offenses remain unreported. Many of those reported cannot be investigated. The lack of sufficient police personnel is the most obvious reason for this. In addition, the investigated cases are often screened to avoid the filing of official charges if conviction seems improbable. Moreover, our overcrowded court calendars encourage both prosecution and defense to engage in "bargaining justice" aimed at sparing the time and cost of a trial. Frequently this results in a plea of guilty to reduced charges or in outright dismissal. Even after conviction, most offenders receive fines, probation, or jail sentences instead of imprisonment in State or Federal institutions. The unavoidable conclusion is that our police, court, and institutional resources are too limited to sustain the arrest → conviction → punishment model, even if that were the desired course of action.

To illustrate, consider the report of the President's Commission on Law Enforcement and the Administration of Justice concerning criminal statistics for 1965, the most recent year for which detailed estimates are available. In that year approximately 2,800,000 major felonies—including murder, robbery, aggravated assault, burglary, grand larceny, and auto theft—were reported to the police. These reports resulted in 727,000 arrests, with the juvenile courts assuming jurisdiction over 260,000 of the individuals arrested. Among the remaining 467,000 cases arrested, more than 60 percent had their charges reduced or terminated, leaving 177,000 individuals who were formally accused in court as initially charged by the police. Of these, about 160,000 were found guilty by plea or court verdict and sentenced: 63,000 received felony commitments to correctional institutions; 35,000 were placed on probation in other local facilities; 56,000 were placed on probation; and 6,000 were given fines or unsupervised sentences.

The best estimate, then, is that there was one felony commitment for every 45 major offenses reported, or—if fines, probation, and jail terms are included—one application of court sanctions for every 17 offenses. While this estimate excludes the cases handled by juvenile courts—which cannot result in criminal convictions anyway—and fails to consider adequately the fact that a single offender can be responsible for several reported violations, it nevertheless suggests the extent to which the arrest → conviction → punishment model is circumvented in current practice.

Relatively minor offenses no doubt have an even lower incidence of official sanctions. This may be especially true of "crimes without victims," such as certain liquor and drug violations, gambling, the numbers racket, prostitution, homosexuality, and abortion, along with a number of other offenses that are often categorized under the rubrics of disorderly conduct and vagrancy. Notoriously resistant to the repressive tactics of law enforcement, such offenses are not likely to arouse official reaction unless they seriously disturb public conceptions of order and decency. Indeed the authorities may sometimes try to regulate these activities so as to minimize their public visibility. Yet the offenses mentioned are responsible for about half of the approximately six million arrests that occur annually, exclusive of minor traffic violations.

Such findings have obvious implications for the administration of justice. They show, for one thing, that most criminal cases are diverted from the traditional arrest-conviction-punishment sequence. Diversionary procedures are therefore an essential, though frequently overlooked feature of the justice system. However, the findings also indicate that much of our crime control effort may be mediated by social mechanisms having only an incidental connection with our police, courts, and correctional institutions. Of special importance in this regard are the community's alternatives to official punishment, the opportunities it provides for the achievement of goals by legitimate as compared with illegitimate methods, its expectations with reference to deviant behavior, the attitudes of its people towards their own deviance as well as the deviance of others, and the resulting sanctions (rewards are as significant as penalties) that accrue to the law violator by informal means. Informal controls are often more salient than formal ones.[5]

PROSECUTION

Many jurisdictions have a sufficiently large prosecutor staff to conceive of the subsystem of prosecution as an "organization" in the same sense as a police or probation department. The staff activities reach volumes, in such jurisdictions, to justify divisions—investigative, business, professional (i.e., the attorneys), fiscal, and support—all complex enough to justify training and personnel specialists along with a host of ancillary services not unlike the large police or probation department.

Applying the systems model to a prosecuting organization of such size and structure poses virtually no managerial problems beyond those encountered by any other organization. Even the frequent status of elective office is no more managerially hampering to a prosecutor than to an elected sheriff or an elected police chief—both have essentially the same problems in coping with the continuity of long-range planning. This elected status will be discussed later in this chapter in a different context.

Managerially, a reasonably large prosecuting organization readily lends itself to the systems model. The prosecutor (district attorney or prosecuting

[5] Clarence Schrag, *Crime and Justice: American Style* (Rockville, Md.: National Institute of Mental Health, Pub. No. HSM–72–9052, 1971), pp. 1–4.

Managerial functions are as significant in many areas of prosecution as other criminal justice organizations. Here a district attorney confers with his top level staff on managerial matters.

Photo courtesy of Dick Cox and Charles Taddo.

attorney) defines results and perhaps includes determination of what is needed to achieve results in his role; assistant district attorneys include either the latter function or the determination of operational staffing in their role; senior deputy district attorneys determine the *methods* needed to achieve results; and the staff determines how much is performed by deputy district attorneys—supplemented by line work from some or all of the managerial staff in certain cases (involvement being no less a managerial problem with prosecutors than with police).

However, this relatively easy application of the systems model to a prosecuting organization refers to a large jurisdiction in which managerial need is amplified by daily, tangible managerial problems. Smaller jurisdictions may find it difficult to sort out the managerial functions from the process of the prosecution subsystem.

To clarify the distinctions between managerial functions and all prosecution subsystems, consideration is again given to process, but again emphasizing managerial concern for output.

Prosecution Process

The process of a prosecution administrator is geared, among many other things, to managing a program of persuasion.

> There are two crucial considerations in persuasion. First is the nature of the evidence itself. Also, in terms of persuasion determining the "hard legal" considerations in criminal court, persuasion frequently becomes a function of logic.
> To understand the persuasive quality of criminal evidence, we must consider the concept of logic.

Persuasion and Logic. From a legal point of view, logic is simply a method (or system) of reasoning. The method can be either inductive or deductive. In either case, a "logical conclusion" is sought. In other words, to be "persuasive," there is at least an implied demand that the "persuasion" be "logical"—whether the logic is inductive or deductive.

The *deductive method* means reasoning from something general to something specific. An example is the specific conclusion that "this defendant is accused," drawn from the general observation that "all defendants are accused." An even more dramatic example is the specific conclusion that "this murderer is a killer," drawn from the general observation that "all murderers kill."

The *inductive method* is simply the reverse of deduction. It involves reasoning from "specifics" to the "general."

The "logical conclusion" sought in both methods has the same goal—persuasion.[6]

As already indicated, the process of prosecution covers a great deal more than the court activities in which logical persuasion occurs.

Essentially, the office of prosecutor is an agency of the executive branch of government charged with the responsibility of prosecuting *all* law violations, except in instances in which the interests of justice may be served by lesser prosecutions, or, as will be seen shortly, in some instances, no prosecution. Enforcement of law can be thought of as a three-fold operation involving police, court, and prosecutor, with prosecution as the key to the overall success. The discretion of the prosecutor hopefully places those trials in the court that are necessary for successful enforcement—the decision to prosecute left to the independent discretion of the prosecutor.

If the prosecutor does not act, or acts unwisely or wisely, corruptly or honestly, there is little the courts may do about his decision—or for that matter little the police can do. The exercise of prosecution discretion may operate to either frustrate or facilitate the efforts of police in bringing about achievement of their defined results. Conversely, a poorly managed police subsystem may have its deficiencies, such as inefficient preparation of cases, continually exposed to public view by an effective prosecution subsystem.

Discretion within the process of the prosecution subsystem covers both the decision to prosecute and the nature or level of the offense on which prosecution is based. This latter digression is exercised through what is commonly called "plea bargaining."

Plea bargaining, in effect, permits the prosecuting subsystem to negotiate with accused persons in terms of what can best be described as risks and odds. If the prosecutor has an exceedingly good case, he may, for the sake of court expedience, present it to the defense lawyer, stating a willingness to reduce the charge in return for a guilty plea. Although over half the persons arrested on felony charges are formally charged with commission of a felony, the remaining half are released on the prosecutors' own motion.

[6] Eldefonso, Coffey, and Sullivan, *Police and the Criminal Law*, pp. 138–39.

Seventy to eighty percent of the formally charged defendants plead guilty. This plea is normally entered after the negotiations—the plea bargaining. This method has not been constitutionally tested and continues in practice throughout the criminal justice system. Though courts are divided in their opinion of this approach, the majority approves of this method of disposing of criminal cases, the rationale behind such disposition usually relating to the philosophy that an admission of guilt is the first step toward rehabilitation.

Plea bargaining usually covers three issues: (1) sentence recommendation, (2) reduction of the charge, and (3) dismissal of other counts relating to the same incident. Of course plea bargaining takes place because of the high incidence of crime and the low number of prosecutors available—the "economics" of the criminal justice subsystem. Other considerations have to do with the frequency with which citizens would be called to jury trials if plea bargaining were not available.

In terms of subsystem process that relates directly to managerial interfacing between subsystems, however, the decision to prosecute remains the most significant of the district attorney's role functions. In many instances, in making the decision to prosecute, he frequently has only a report dictated by the patrol officer who made the arrest and spoke to the victim and witnesses, if any. Ideally, the decision should be based on a more exhaustive investigation, including evidence gathered by detectives or special prosecution investigators. In effect, then, a great deal of what the court subsystem encounters as judicial process depends entirely upon a some times weakly managed interface between the process of police and prosecution—of considerable concern to the administration of both subsystems.

The remaining process considerations in prosecution have little to do with the management of the overall subsystem, regardless of how interesting, and how very significant.

But even with this brief overview of the managerially related segments of prosecution process, it can readily be seen that prosecution encompasses far more than simply presenting logical persuasion to the court. Nevertheless, the ability of the prosecutor to bring this to bear when it is needed influences and even at times determines the course of the prosecution process.

Moving away from concern for personal characteristics involving the ability to logically persuade, there remain a number of managerial concerns that relate to this ability: (1) a viable ratio of attorneys to cases; (2) investigative resources within the organization or administratively coordinated with police; (3) criminalistic resources; (4) medical and other resource expertise.

Programs that permit continuity in the management of prosecution are ultimately the only way to achieve the prosecution subsystem role and func-

---

[7] The reader is referred to the section headed "Prosecution Process" in the annotated references at the end of the chapter.

tions reflected in the literature.[7] Moreover, managing the prosecution role permits the critical interface with the criminal justice subsystem of criminal defense, which has increasing influence on the overall system of criminal justice.

DEFENSE

In a sense, defense lawyers are not (as a group) a subsystem. In terms of image, many criminal justice personnel regard the defense attorneys as not only outside but *against* the system. Regrettably, the conduct and apparent ethics of some defense attorneys do little to improve this image. Nevertheless, criminal defense is not only a criminal justice subsystem, it is as vital to the ultimate success of the system as any other subsystem—at least in the democratic use of law as an instrument of social control.

Within this context of defense performing a criminal justice subsystem role and function, some consideration will now be given the definition of defense.

Under certain circumstances, an act that is defined as a crime may not lead to criminal liability. Among these circumstances are insanity, self-defense, or the defense of close relatives, necessity, prevention of crime, and insufficient maturity. Such defenses, or justifications, are usually presented during a trial along with a plea of not guilty.

There are complications in determining criminal liability with justifications of this nature since American law traditionally provides two standards: the first standard is *proximate cause*—a standard which required the courts to establish the *proximity* of the accused behavior to the crime. In essence, proximate causes exclude predisposing influences or justifications, such as social influence, character and personality. Simply stated, the accused either "did it" or he did not.

The other standard for determining criminal liability is the *necessary cause*—the cause "but for which the particular result would not have occurred." Known as the principle of *sine qua non,* this standard requires that the behavior of the accused be 'causally' related to the crime. *Sine qua non* can be an extremely simple concept as when the accused decapitates his victim with an axe. The difficulty with the *sine qua non* standard emerges when the accusation involves something like selling a weapon to an assailant or renting a hotel room to a prostitute.

To simplify the task of defining criminal defense, an assumption will be made that all defenses relating to inappropriate accusations can be reduced simply to allegations of injustice. . . .

. . . When an illegal act is committed with malice and premeditation, the accused is held responsible for the crime. If the person commits the illegal act through negligence, he is accountable for the illegal act. In either case, defenses against the accusation introduce the question of justification which in turn focuses attention on attempt to commit the illegal act.[8]

Public Defense

To further elaborate the role of defense, an outstanding article on federal probation by Sheldon Portman, Public Defender, Santa Clara County, California, is now quoted in its entirely.

THE DEFENSE LAWYER'S NEW ROLE IN THE SENTENCING PROCESS[9]

Gideon's trumpet sounded the opening note of the criminal law revolution and heralded the beginning of a new era for the role of counsel. Following in the wake of Gideon has come a long line of constitutional giants—Escobedo, Miranda, Gault, and Wade—to enlarge upon the significance of the right to counsel. Concurrent with that development has been the extension of other constitutional rights, involving the fourth, fifth, and sixth amendments.

Not very long ago, the conduct of a criminal case was a rather simple process of merely determining guilt or innocence. Today, however, the criminal courtroom has also become a constitutional battleground wherein lawyers must be prepared to defend a multitude of constitutional rights as well as life and liberty. In addition there has been activation of the right to counsel in the juvenile court, signaled by Gault, thus creating a whole new area of responsibility for the defense lawyer.

One would easily suppose that in a field of endeavor such as the law—long criticized for its snail's pace—the changes affecting the responsibilities of counsel which have been wrought thus far would have been enough to digest in one decade. Not so, however. From yet another source, not the Supreme Court this time, comes a clarion call for more action by defense lawyers in the sentencing and rehabilitation areas. In practically a single voice during 1967, two important authorities, the American Bar Association Committee on Sentencing and Review and the President's Crime Commission urged upon defense lawyers a far "more meaningful role" in the sentencing process.

There is certainly nothing new about the assistance of counsel at sentencing. In fact, the right to counsel at this "critical stage" has been recognized for some time as being constitutionally impelled. Despite this traditionalism, however, the Crime Commission and the ABA's Committee had some harsh things to say about the activities of "many" lawyers with regard to sentencing. Both called for renewed emphasis and even an expansion beyond the traditional concepts of the role of counsel at the sentencing stage. This article presents a summary of these criticisms and recommendations together with a review of

[8] President's Commission, *Task Force Report: Courts,* pp. 153–54.

[9] Sheldon Portman, "The Defense Lawyers' New Role in the Sentencing Process," *Federal Probation* (March 1970), pp. 3–8. Reprinted by permission.

the sentencing fundamentals. Hopefully this may inspire corrective measures where needed and lead to the implementation of the new programs which have been suggested.

THE CRITIQUE

Justice Sutherland's classic description of the disabilities of a layman without the assistance of counsel in a criminal case serves as a constant reminder to lawyers of their important responsibilities:

> Left without the aid of counsel (the layman) may be put on trial without a proper charge, and convicted upon incompetent evidence, or evidence irrelevant to the issue or otherwise inadmissible. He lacks both the skill and knowledge adequately to prepare his defense, even though he have a perfect one. He requires the guiding hand of counsel at every step in the proceedings against him. Without it, though he be not guilty, he faces the danger of conviction because he does not know how to establish his innocence.

The true honor and nobility of the profession are encased by these words. Competent lawyers everywhere devote their best efforts to the careful preparation of all factual and legal defenses. Furthermore, the constitutional right to "effective representation by counsel" has been interpreted by the California Supreme Court in an oft-quoted opinion to impose the duty to investigate carefully all defenses of fact and of law that may be available to the defendant. With the advent of increased emphasis upon the right to counsel, this subject has also been frequently discussed in law review commentaries.

These authorities, however, and the classic conception of the role of defense counsel omit mention of the vitally important duty of the attorney in the sentencing process. Most law schools wihch have gone beyond the rudimentary common law-of-crimes course (once the only criminal law subject taught in law schools) have yet to offer a course on sentencing. Is it any wonder, then, that lawyers have generally neglected sentencing aspects, and thus have come under attack from the ABA's Committee on Sentencing Standards and the President's Crime Commission for not giving adequate representation to clients at the time of sentencing?

Upon reflection, any lawyer who has had even a modicum of experience in the criminal field must agree with the point made in the ABA's recommended standards that the sentencing stage is frequently the most important insofar as many defendants are concerned. This importance, however, is frequently overlooked by many lawyers who the ABA Committee complains "view their functions at sentencing to involve superficial incantations of mercy . . . [and] seek the lightest possible sentence without much concern for the real needs of the defendant."

Insofar as adequacy of preparation for the sentencing stage, lawyers also come under heavy attack by both the ABA Committee and the President's Crime Commission. According to the Committee, "few" lawyers undertake the type of preparation required, and the Crime Commission describes the little that is done as "perfunctory."

THE RECOMMENDATIONS

What are the proposed remedies? Attorneys must, first of all, recognize that the sentencing stage is the one at which "for many defendants the most important service of the entire proceedings can be performed" and that the attorney's duties do not end upon a finding of guilt.

With that as a starting point, the ABA Committee proceeds to list the "bare minimum" duties of counsel with regard to the sentencing process. These are discussed as follows:

1. Educating the Lawyer

This consists of making an early, detailed inquiry into all of the possible sentences including parole eligibility (legal and de facto), facilities available at different types of institutions, the judge's control over the choice of institution, and the availability and terms of probation.

The importance of this inquiry and its complexity cannot be underestimated. It can be a herculean task in states having a hodgepodge of different sentencing statutes and a probation eligibility provision such as California's Penal Code Sec. 1203 which reads like something from Alice in Wonderland. (In a recent California case, an attorney who apparently was confused by this statute erroneously represented to the court that his client was not eligible for probation on a robbery conviction. This was ruled to be incompetent representation).

Study of the narcotics statutes with their geometrically increasing penalties for recidivists is a must in handling any drug case. In California, for instance, a heroin possessor with two prior narcotics convictions—even if the priors were for possession of small amounts of marihuana—will incur a sentence of 15 years to life with the minimum being a mandatory term without eligibility for parole until completion of 15 calendar years. This sentence exceeds the median time spent by first-degree murder life termers. In a recent case, a California Court of Appeal described this sentence as one involving a "Dantesque abandonment of hope."

Counsel must also be aware of the effect of such things as arming clauses and injuries to the victim which can profoundly aggravate a particular sentence. For example, in California an injury in a kidnap-for-robbery case will transform a life sentence into a death penalty or life without parole.

Habitual criminal laws are also a prime concern whenever dealing with a repeater. The "little bitch," as it is called in California, involves two prior felonies and can result in a mandatory term of 9 years; the "big bitch" with three prior felonies will result in a 12-year mandatory minimum.

Other sentencing provisions which counsel must be informed about are those relating to treatment of addicts and sex offenders. For the addict who has been repeatedly involved in narcotics offenses, a treatment program such as the one available in California may avoid an exceedingly harsh sentence as well as provide the defendant with the hope of rehabilitation. Eligibility for this program, however, is surrounded by a labyrinth of legal and de facto conditions which counsel must comprehend if he is properly to advise his client.

Sex offender cases are fraught with the gravest consequences in view of the prospect for an indeterminate medical commitment. In California, regardless of the designation of the offense, no matter how trivial, it can result in a mentally disordered sex offender proceeding if there are any sexual overtones which the judge deems peculiar. For example, in one reported case a defendant found the name and number of a woman written in the wall of a phone booth with the suggestion that a call to her would result in intercourse. After several calls he arranged to go to her home where he attempted to force his attentions on her; he was shot by the woman's husband. He pleaded nolo contendere to a simple battery and was thereafter certified and ultimately committed to the state hospital as a mentally disordered sex offender. At the hospital, the defendant became embroiled somehow in an internal quarrel between the ward doctor and the psychologist, and thereafter he was re-certified to the court as being not amenable to treatment. The trial court "rubber stamped" the superintendent's opinion and ordered the defendant committed for an indeterminate period as an incurable sex offender. He would still be languishing in a prison facility were it not for the subsequent reversal of the commitment order.

Knowing the legal and de facto limits on parole eligibility is important when advising a client on the practical consequences of a given plea which may result in a prison sentence. In California, this information can be obtained from the Adult Authority which annually publishes a chart showing the median time served for each offense and the minimum and maximum time served for the middle 80 percent of prisoners during the previous year. Comparison figures for an earlier period are also supplied.

In representing juvenile cases, the attorney is in another ball park, so to speak, and must acquaint himself with different procedures and a variety of sentencing alternatives which are foreign to the adult field but which can have an even more profound effect as evidenced in the Gault case. Before Gault, attorneys felt thoroughly frustrated in the juvenile court in fulfilling any meaningful role. This situation was certainly changed by Gault, and the defense attorney must now become thoroughly acquainted with the practices and procedures of that court if he is to be effective.

2. Conferring with the Defendant

The next step is for the attorney to convey the information about the sentencing alternatives to the client and to ascertain the client's desires. The defendant will often want this information at the very beginning of the case, and the sentencing consequences will surely influence the attorney's advice concerning a given plea.

Counsel must be concerned about the sentencing prospects from the time of the initial interview and direct his inquiry accordingly in order to determine just what the exposure is. If, for example, the defendant faces recidivist penalties because of prior convictions, the attorney will want to know whether the defendant had counsel or what the circumstances of waiver were in order to contest the constitutional validity of those priors. If there are sexual connotations, the attorney will want to advise the defendant concerning the possibility of a sex offender commitment proceeding. The attorney must be prepared at the very outset to discuss these and other considerations which may influence the handling of the case.

After the defendant has been informed of the sentencing alternatives, the attorney must ascertain the client's desires and endeavor to carry them out. The defendant, after all, is the one who must do the time—not the lawyer.

The act of explaining the sentencing procedures and consequences serves a useful collateral purpose. The defense lawyer is often the only one in the criminal justice system to relate the details of the sentencing process to the offender and his family. If the defendant understands what is happening to him he is more likely to respond positively to the correctional process and to be left with the impression that he has been fairly treated.

Another "rehabilitative" consequence of the informed attorney's discussion with the defendant on sentencing alternatives is the influence which the attorney can bring to bear by his recommendations concerning available correctional services. The "best deal" may not always be the lightest sentence, and the attorney should be ready to make other appropriate suggestions to his client.

3. Verifying the Factual Basis for the Sentence

The third duty of the attorney at the sentencing stage is to insure that the factual basis for the sentence is accurate and adequate and that all relevant circumstances of the offense and characteristics of the defendant are in the record. The accuracy of the presentence report, if it is made available, must be checked and supplementary information presented where necessary to correct errors, misleading impressions, or to supply omitted data.

This function of the defense lawyer cannot be underestimated. An error in a presentence report can, for example, haunt a defendant years later at a parole board hearing. Professor Newman cites an example of this is his study of the process of conviction without trial. In a Wisconsin case, a defendant's parole was deferred because of a statement in the presentence report that he "had a knife" during the commission of a sex offense. A subsequent investigation showed that this was a small pocket knife which the defendant usually carried and had nothing to do with the offense.

The facts of the crime presented in the presentence report are usually taken from the police report furnished by the proscution. These reports can be replete with inaccuracies or wholly one-sided. An example of this was experienced recently by the author in an assault case. During a fight, a bystander was struck and severely hurt by a hammer head which fell off the handle when the defendant attempted to strike another person who had provoked the fight. The circumstances of the provocation were wholly omitted from the police report which was based entirely on the complaint of the person who had provoked the fight. The circumstances of the provocation had prompted the prosecutor to reduce the charge to a simple battery, but on the basis of the presentence report, the judge was prepared to "throw the book" at the defendant. A much more lenient sentence was imposed, however, when the court was fully informed by counsel at sentencing about the matters not contained in the report.

Sometimes counsel can anticipate situations in advance and communicate the pertinent information to the investigating probation officer before the presentence report is prepared. Likewise, other favorable or mitigating facts concerning the offense or the defendant's background can be conveyed to the investigating probation officer for later inclusion in the report.

In those jurisdictions which permit the defendant himself to prepare a statement to be placed in the presentence report, the client should be counseled on the advisability and contents of such a statement. It is not uncommon for a defendant to be his worst enemy when trying to say something on his own behalf.

In California, defense counsel may file a written statement of views in the case of a state prison commitment. Copies of similar statements by the prosecution and the court must be furnished to defense counsel and the defendant. The statement for the defendant is an excellent method for placing into the record any factual or background information gathered on his behalf during the defense investigation of the case. Members of the California Adult Authority appreciate receiving these views from defense counsel and have found them to be very useful in evaluating a defendant for parole.

4. Disclosure of Terms of Plea Agreement at Sentencing

In a case of a plea resulting from an agreement that the prosecutor would take a position on the sentence, the ABA Committee recommends that defense counsel should disclose the terms of that arrangement to the court.

Not only does this procedure avoid the pretense which otherwise attends covert plea agreements when defendants must state for the record that "no promises" were made, but it also provides an important safeguard against later claims by disgruntled defendants that certain promises were in fact made but never kept. By being open and above board and stating the terms of such arrangements for the record, there can be no question about the matter later on.

RECOMMENDATION FOR AN EXPANDED ROLE

Thus far, the traditional duties of counsel at sentencing have been reviwed. Beyond these, however, a new, expanded role has been proposed which would combine the field of social work with that of the advocate and enlist the forensic skill of the attorney in the process of rehabilitation.

This concept is described in Section 5.3(f) (v) of the ABA Committee's Standards on Sentencing and reads as follows:

> In appropriate cases, the attorney should make special efforts to investigate the desirability of a disposition which would particularly meet the needs of the defendant, such as probation accompanied by employment of community facilities or commitment to an institution for special treatment. If such a disposition is available and seems appropriate, the attor-

ney, with the consent of the defendant, should make a recommendation at the sentencing proceeding that it be utilized.

The President's Crime Commission has also made a similar recommendation with a more detailed description of the duties of the defense attorney:

> When counsel believes that probation would be appropriate disposition for his client, he should be prepared to suggest a positive program of rehabilitation. He should explore possibilities for employment, family services, educational improvements, and perhaps mental health services and attempt to make specific and realistic arrangements for the defendant's return to the community.

In making these recommendations, both of the above authorities rely upon the example of the rehabilitative service provided by the District of Columbia Legal Aid Agency. Hampered by the anachronistic view current in some jurisdictions that defense attorneys are not to be trusted with probation reports, the Agency has established its own probation-type investigation division to gather facts about a defendant and to present a positive program for rehabilitation to the court through defense counsel.

This rehabilitative approach for defense lawyers at sentencing was also recommended by the Conference on Legal Manpower Needs of Criminal Law held in June 1966. The report of the Conference stated:

> . . . part of the job of counsel is to act on behalf of his client in cooperation with the court to work out a favorable disposition program. In many cases, careful development of a plan, including living arrangements and a job, may persuade the court to a disposition of the case which enables a convicted defendant to avoid imprisonment and yet enables society to avoid another crime in the future. The need for counsel includes these aspects of a defense as well as the more traditional functions of counsel.

The ABA Committee's commentary in support of this recommendation is particularly enthusiastic and suggests that by this activity the "lawyer can perhaps perform his greatest service, not only to the defendant but to the society that will be benefited by one less potential recidivist." The Committee further predicts that with a positive program of rehabilitation to offer to the court there is a greater likelihood that the judge will listen and that in many cases the defendant will be able successfully to support his family and obtain the help he needs without languishing in jail.

These are laudatory goals to which defense counsel should address his best efforts. Unfortunately, the many demands being placed upon defender services in the indigent field at the present time as a result of increased caseloads and new responsibilities imposed by Supreme Court decisions makes expansion of such services in yet another direction very difficult now. Considering the rewards, however, the effort seems merited.

Obviously, the lawyer cannot undertake this work alone. He must have the assistance of professional social workers in preparing dispositional programs which can be articulated to the court. To provide such additional staffing for defender offices serving the indigent, the value of this program will have to be clearly demonstrated to the agencies which will be asked to finance this expansion. Research is needed in the form of demonstration projects which could be established in selected defender offices located in various parts of the country. Carefully designed programs could measure the effectvieness of the expanded service both in persuading the court and in aiding the rehabilitation of the offender. Grant funds would be required to supply the financing for such demonstrations.

CONCLUSION

Competent representation by counsel in criminal cases extends far beyond the trial phase. Recent Supreme Court decisions have extended the right forward to the lineup and interrogation rooms and backward to the sentencing and probation violation hearings. In an important decision by the Supreme Court of Pennsylvania, the right has recently been extended in that state to parole violation proceedings also.

With increased emphasis upon the procedural right to counsel, the substance of that right must necessarily come under closer scrutiny. So it has, not only by courts examining into competency of representation, but by nonjudicial sources such as the ABA's Committee on Sentencing Standards and the President's Crime Commission. Addressing themselves to the quality of representation provided at sentencing, these authorities have concluded that much improvement is necessary. Their call for an upgrading and even an expansion of the role of counsel in the sentencing process should not go unheeded.

As in the case of prosecution, defense subsystem process may serve to clarify the output—"output" defined here as the defending of a person against accusations as discussed above. To insure a managerial context however, consideration of the defense process will be from the frame of reference of organizationally structured defense—the department of public defender.

Isolating the public defender is in no way intended to imply that the private attorney has any less responsibility and accountability for the process of defense. Indeed, most jurisdictions depend totally upon private attorneys for the process of criminal justice, and even where the defense subsystem is organized into the public defender's office, private attorneys handle a large proportion of the defense activities.

But within the context of managing the defense subsystem, the office of public defender affords the only organizational structure that can be administered. It is here noted that by isolating the managerial functions of the public defender's office, other subsystems, particularly the courts and prosecution, are better able to compensate managerially for the absence of managers held accountable for the output of defense as a subsystem.

The role of the public defender is in part precisely the same as that of the private defense attorney: performance of the function of defense against accusation as already discussed. Managerially, however, the roles and functions are essentially the same for a public defender as for any criminal justice subsystem.

Defense as a Unique Criminal Justice Subsystem

The public defender organization is the only criminal justice subsystem that by role definition is not committed to an output of reduced crime. Even the courts, and all their impartiality, attempt to operate a subsystem that permits the conviction of offenders through proof and evidence.

Once enough evidence produces the decision to prosecute, the overall system is geared to coping with the possibility of conviction—with the exception of the defense subsystem.

Public defender organizational management, unlike the management of any other subsystem, interfaces administratively on the subsystem output definition of overtly preventing all three correctional subsystems from becoming involved, and implicitly challenges the validity of the involvement of police and court subsystems. This unique orientation is by no means inappropriate—it is absolutely necessary in effective systems management of law as an instrument of social control as reflected in the literature of defense.[10] Indeed, were this volume concerned with the criminal justice system per se rather than the *management* of the criminal justice system, considerable attention would be given the absolute necessity of the defense subsystem retaining this unique orientation.

Managerially, the unique orientation tends to minimize the distortions of management roles when the top administrator of a public defender department is also handling cases. Because of the unique orientation, administrative results and determination of what is needed to achieve results relate to the process of other subsystems. Instead of being oriented toward planning the reduction of crime and criminal behavior, results definitions for the defense subsystem are geared specifically to the process of other subsystems. With regard to who will implement the plans and how they will be implemented, the defense subsystem remains the same except that measurements of results achievement do not relate to long-range managerial planning as in the case of other subsystems.

Although the functions of defense interface in the same manner as other subsystems, the unique orientation and the nature of the defense process reduce the significance of interfacing because output and results interface with the process. This differs, managerially, from other subsystems that interface on the basis of results or output. In effect, long-range planning is not possible in defense results definitions managerially, inasmuch as the results sought continually react to the process of other subsystems.

---

[10] The reader is referred to the "Defense Process" Section of the annotated references at the end of the chapter.

This unique orientation of defense virtually defines results as providing as much certainty as possible that the process of other subsystems is appropriate in each case.

Beyond the reviewing that occurs in the functions of a prosecutor, judge, or probation officer after a police arrest, and beyond all other systematic safeguards, the defense subsystem output and results are the overall system's method of retaining law as the instrument of social control in a democratic society.

So significant is this unique position that it is suggested here as a part of the role definition of defense as a subsystem—to retain this uniqueness as part of the subsystem role. Managerially, other subsystems can then interface with defense even where private attorneys handle defense entirely.

In jurisdictions in which the defense subsystem has been organized, the administrative interface of the systems model affords the promise of incorporating effective defense within the long-range planning of the overall system, and of including plans for this incorporation within the long-range planning of other subsystems.

ELECTIVE OFFICES

In terms of long-range planning, the elective office status of various top administrators within the criminal justice system is all too frequently a serious problem. The quasi-elective status of administrators who change each time a new mayor, city council, governor, senator, congressman, or president is elected also poses formidable problems in long-range administrative planning.

Ideally, the same level of commitment to improving the effectiveness of criminal justice exists for the administrator whether or not he is going to be present at the time of successful results achievement; he should have full commitment to successful results achievement even if another administrator will benefit from good managerial planning. However, few criminal justice administrators would argue that this ideal is realized with any consistency throughout the land.

Perhaps the only viable approach to a remedy begins by first acknowledging that elective offices are unlikely to be significantly changed in a democratic society, regardless of managerial advantage. The approach to solution then focuses on the influence of subsystems with career-orientetd administrative continuity.

Using subsystem interfaces to assist newly elected or appointed administrators, management of subsystems enjoying administrative continuity can hopefully reduce the problems of such fragmented planning as may occur when the sheriff or elected police chief hires more officers for more arrests without an awareness of the impact on caseloads of judges, prosecutors, and the correctional subsystem. Planning need not exceed the influence of these subsystems interfaces—interfaces restricted by definition of the systems model for *enough overlap for communication but not enough to distort the roles of each subsystem.*

The chapter that follows will introduce the area of "Training and Other Special Problems." Subsystem interfacing is deemed important enough to give specific attention to the managerial training needed to make subsystem interfacing possible. The vital role of the college in educating criminal justice managers will be presented as an important prerequisite to successful training of criminal justice managers within the system. Subsystem interfacing depends as much upon the broad conceptual model of education as it does on specific managerial expertise and techniques developed through training.

The point here is that subsystem interfacing is required for all those reasons considered prior to the discussion of elected offices, but is even more significant because of these elective offices; indeed, it is significant enough to portray managerial training as including interfacing between career subsystem administrators and elected administrators.

SUMMARY

This chapter isolated three subsystems in terms of special managerial approaches: courts, prosecution, and defense. Against a background of acknowledging that managerial methods are simpler to apply in the subsystems of police, probation-parole, and correctional institutions, the unique managerial characteristics of courts, prosecution, and defense were considered.

Certain organizational reforms of court organization were considered and the managerial functions of the model related. The intense magnification of systems dysfunction was reviewed in terms of the prestige and influence of the courts.

The strategic value of managerial interface between courts and other criminal justice subsystems was emphasized in the retention of judicial effectiveness as a priority over system efficiency, although both are needed.

Prosecution was presented as managerially no different than in other criminal justice subsystems in large jurisdictions when structurally organized with management roles. The process of prosecution was used to clarify managerial output in smaller jurisdictions; this in turn was related to the systems model, with emphasis on subsystem interfacing of the prosecution role.

Defense was presented from the frame of reference of being a unique role reinforcing a unique orientation. In relating the defense subsystem to the systems model, it was pointed out that the defense output or administrative results relate more to the process than to the output of other subsystems, thus reducing some of the managerial problems involved when top administrators from the defense role also perform the functions of process.

The public defender was discussed as being the only structured organizational approach to defense, but presented in such a way that other criminal justice subsystems can relate managerially to private attorneys performing the unique defense role.

Elective offices and appointments based on elected officials were discussed as problems for long-range planning in criminal justice. The problem of maintaining interface and continuity between criminal justice subsystems when some of the subsystems have rotating administrators was dealt with.

QUESTIONS

1. Discuss the position that systems management is easier to conceptually apply to the subsystems of police, probation, parole, and correctional institutions than to the subsystems discussed in this chapter.

2. What are some of the existing management problems of court organizational structure? Relate these problems to the rest of the criminal justice system; to society.

3. Discuss the magnification of system dysfunction when it occurs in the court subsystem.

4. Why was judicial effectiveness emphasized over system efficiency in courts?

5. Discuss the interface between prosecution and courts; between prosecution and defense.

6. Relate prosecution process to defense output.

7. Discuss the system function performed by relating defense output to the process of all other subsystems; relate this function to the use of law as an instrument of social control in a democratic society.

8. Discuss remedies for problems created in managerial planning through elective office status of many criminal justice administrators.

ANNOTATED REFERENCES

COURT PROCESS

For a fuller discussion of the judicial process see, for example, the following:

The Hon. W. C. Biddle, "A Legislative Study of the Effectiveness of Criminal Penalties," *Crime and Delinquency,* 16, No. 3 (July 1969), 135–40.

The Hon. E. M. Curran, "Lenient Courts Cause Crime," *FBI Law Enforcement Bulletin,* 29, No. 2 (December 1970), 17–21.

Kleps, Ralph N., "The Triple S Program: Judicial Administration of Court Calendars," *Journal of State Bar of California,* 46, No. 3 (May–June 1971), 345–54.

Hosner, C. T., "Group Procedures in Sentencing: A Decade of Practice," *Federal Probation,* 41, No. 5 (December 1970), 32–35.

PORTMAN, S., "The Defense Lawyer's New Role in the Sentencing Process," *Federal Probation*, 41, No. 2 (March 1970), 18–23.

GEIS, GILBERT, Ph.D., and CHARLES W. TENNEY, Jr., LLM, "Evaluating A Training Institute for Juvenile Court Judges," *Community Mental Health Journal*, 4, No. 6 (December 1968), 461–68.

MILLER, JAMES NATHAN, "Reprieve for New York's Criminal Courts," *National Civic Review*, 2, No. 2 (March 1972), 2–6.

MAISEL, ROBERT, Ph.D., "Decision Making in a Commitment Court," *Journal for the Study of Interpersonal Processes*, 33, No. 3 (August 1970), 352.

The HON. D. J. YOUNG, "Juvenile: Is the Juvenile Court Successful?" *Federal Probation*, 42, No. 4 (June 1971), 12–16.

DEFENSE PROCESS

Further elaboration of the article "The Defense Lawyer's New Role" cited in this chapter can be found, for example, in:

BRODROOK, ADRIAN, "Double Jeopardy and the Law," *Journal of Family Law*, University of Louisville School of Law, 11, No. 3 (1972), 603–14.

CATSINILOS, LLB, "Meeting the Prosecution's Case: Tactics and Strategies of Cross Examination," *Journal of Criminal Law, Criminology and Police Science*, 62, No. 2 (June 1971), 142–52.

———, "The Criminal Practitioner's Dilemma: What Should A Lawyer Do When His Client Intends to Testify Falsely?" *Journal of Criminal Law, Criminology and Police Science*, 61, No. 1 (March 1970), 50–56.

ELDEFONSO, E., A. COFFEY, and J. SULLIVAN, *Police and The Criminal Law*, Pacific Palisades, Calif.: Goodyear, 1972. A comprehensive examination of the interface between prosecution, defense, and courts within the criminal justice context of using law as an instrument of social control within a democratic society.

POPKIN, ALICE BRANDEIS, and FREDA JANE LIPPERT, "Is There a Constitutional Right to the Insanity Defense in Juvenile Court?" *Journal of Family Law*, 10, No. 4 (1971), 421–42.

President's Commission on Law Enforcement and the Administration of Justice, *Task Force Report: Courts*, U.S. Government Printing Office, Washington, D.C., 1967. One of the most comprehensive documents in existence on the court process.

SULLIVAN, THOMAS P., "Presentation of the Defense," *Journal of Criminal Law, Criminology and Police Science*, 62, No. 2 (June 1971), 153–72.

PROSECUTION PROCESS

For a fuller examination of the process of prosecution see, for example:

PETTINE, R. J., "The Police Witness," *FBI Law Enforcement Bulletin*, 28, No. 2 (February 1969), 10–12.

The Prosecutor, Journal of the National District Attornies Association, "Officers of Justice," 211 East Chicago Ave., Chicago, Ill. Vol. 2, No. 2, pp. 10–13.

SAGARIN, E., "The Problem of Entrapment," *Crime and Delinquency*, 18, No. 2 (October 1970), 100–108.

SEICHNER, I. B., "According to Law," *Law and Order*, 9, No. 5 (September 1970), 12–21.

TASK FORCE REPORT: COURTS

NEDRUD, E., "The Career Prosecutor," Part I, *Journal of Criminology and Police Science*, 51 (1960) and Part II in 51 (1961).

AMERICAN BAR FOUNDATION STUDIES:

JONES, F., ed., *The Courts, the Public and the Laws Explosion*, Englewood Cliffs, N.J.: Prentice-Hall, 1965.

PART FOUR

MAKING THE MODEL
GO SYSTEMATICALLY

CHAPTER 14

Criminal Justice Management and the Consultant Specialist

The chapters of the preceding section covered the management model itself. The chapters of this, the final section of the volume, are addressed to making the systems model go systematically. In terms of "making it go," the two chapters that follow will explore first the criminal justice administrative concern with community and political relations, then the optimistic outlook for any criminal justice jurisdiction that seriously pursues managerial development. In this chapter, the use of consulting specialists will be considered as a part of the context of "making it go."

Sophisticated management, more often than not, becomes so at least in part through the use of consultants—outsiders who assist far-sighted administrators to make plans become reality in many crucial areas such as *research, training, budget, communication, organizational structure, cost effectiveness,* and a number of other managerial functions. Moreover, consultants are frequently responsible in part for refined approaches to process areas such as criminology, automated crime-record retrieval systems, and similar activities. Concern here, however, is focused solely upon managerial development and the use of consultants in this regard.

Who Should Consult?

How does an administrator select the appropriate consultant? There are many kinds of specialists available, but the problem is that each may have a different focus on managerial needs. For example, a psychiatrist's conception of management direction may be totally different from that of an industrial engineer or an "efficiency expert" (specializing in the time and motion variety of consultation); a fiscal expert's views on the same organization may demonstrate still greater differences. A gifted budget analyst may have difficulties with organizational communication analyses—difficulties that he may be unaware of; a training consultant may be inadequate in recruiting.

Even among members of a particular specialty such as research consultants, great variation frequently occurs. Indeed, in many instances the philosophy of the consulting firm or the personal opinions of the specialist involved seem to have as much or more to do with the views of the consultant as the influence of academic discipline.

Later in this chapter, consideration will be given the principles and guidelines in making such a selection—of determining the talent and potential of a consultant. But even when a consulting specialist has great consulting potential, it may not fit precisely the particular managerial need. In other words, part of the problem is selecting not only a talented consultant, but a consultant with the *needed* talent.

Consulting: Why?

Knowing *why* a consultant is needed permits focused effort to find the *precise* specialist talent that is called for. Regrettably, however, the complexities of managerial development rarely allow an administrator the luxury of isolating, before consultation is engaged, the precise area in which special expertise is needed. When premature determination of the problem area does occur, it is apt to cause more managerial problems than are solved. Not the least of the problems generated in this unfortunate cycle is the very label of "problem."

Even when the managerial expertise called for is obviously within a specific area such as research, budget, personnel, training, or whatever, the implications of outside advice continue to significantly influence the remainder of the management system and development.

What is needed in most instances where specialty expertise will be sought in criminal justice is advice on the kind of advice needed—a "system analysis."

System Analysis

With so wide a range of professional services performed under the label "system analysis," a definition of the context in which it is being used here is called for: by *system analysis* is meant a combination of taxonomy (i.e., science and laws or principles of classification) of organizational structure combined with ergonetic (study of energy in relation to tasks or work) examination in order to develop a profile of all influences on the outcome of organizational activity. In other words, a system analysis is an effort to obtain a picture of how the organization really works (or really doesn't work).

The year 1972 witnessed the beginning of many excellent managerial development programs undertaken in criminal justice, the better programs starting with a system analysis (referred to by many administrations as *operations analysis*). Comprehensive overall development programs were undertaken in many criminal justice jurisdictions, with every function of every division programmed for sufficiently thorough analysis to provide a knowledgeable basis for further development of the organization. When analyses of such scope are aided by consultation, the effort usually requires more than one consultant working with a management task force. More often than not, an effective initial system analysis is a team effort.

Team Effort

Within the context of team effort, even when the problem areas are known, the impact of one suggested correction upon other segments of the system introduces the need for a variety of expertise and talents that are not usually available to an individual consultant. Moreover, the complexity of the analysis task changes continually in most criminal justice organizations, thereby raising the concern for completing the end before the beginning changes. Though this is only one of the justifications for a team effort, it is nevertheless significant enough to consider a major priority.

More often than not, the most expedient approach not only in private industry but within criminal justice as well is to select a team already formed. In some parts of the country, consulting teams are virtually nonexistent and must be either formed locally, or called in. In other areas, however, excellent consulting teams abound.

The implications of the contrast between favorable and unfavorable outcomes in consultation might be clarified by considering an analogy: Within the human body, there are several types of tissue that look very much alike to the untrained (or unconcerned) eye. Differences are difficult to detect without a concern for the function performed, by each tissue, in the overall system; however, *excessive* concern for these functions can cause one to lose sight of their dependency upon one another. This analogy lends itself to analyzing any system, and perhaps to analyzing the system analyst as well.

Like the similarity in tissue, many parts of a criminal justice organization look alike—when one is trying to determine the various functions (and dysfunctions) that spell out the differences, care must be taken to avoid overlooking the dependence of the system on all functions and dependence of all functions upon each other.

Of course the design of the systems model itself, once established, promotes a continuing clarity of the interfacing dependencies of system parts. But during the period of getting started, much depends upon the analysis of the existing system, and perhaps upon the philosophy of the system analyst.

Philosophy

Regardless of the level of expertise and sophistication, the consulting team that works from an initial philosophy of what must be done rather than how it can best be done has little motive to retain concern for the interrelationships of functions. If the consultant team approaches the criminal justice task as though the client must be *changed* (rather than *improved*), there may be motive to ignore the relationships of existing functions.

Of course, in many instances the client will *want* to change certain things as a result of the system analysis. But the point is that the client makes the decision—not a group of consultants exploiting the leverage of their position.

Regrettably, the expertise and credentials of the consultants that make up a team frequently gain far more attention than the philosophy from which it works. In this regard, an important question might be asked: Who remains accountable for effective administration after the consultation—the consulting team or the administrator?

Criminal justice administrators who seek sophisticated analysis of the system with an eye to improvement are not likely to be unaware of the social problems demanding modification in criminal justice practice.[1] It becomes then a matter of the judgment of the administrator who must live with how the system analysis is used.

Perhaps the views of one of the many consulting firms that serve criminal justice, here printed in toto, may clarify the relationship between consulting specialists and criminal justice even further.

THE ROLE OF THE CONSULTANT IN CRIMINAL JUSTICE[2]

As the problems of criminal justice become more critical, society allocates greater resources in an attempt to find solutions. Expertise and technology developed in other areas find application in criminal justice. Problems become better defined, and new approaches that began hesitantly and unsurely be-

---

[1] See for example, Coffey, Eldefonso, and Hartinger, *Police-Community Relations* or Coffey et al., *Human Relations: Law Enforcement in a Changing Community*, elaborating the need for *responsible* modifications of the criminal justice practice.

[2] Courtesy of E. A. Unwin, Director, Systems Evaluation, Public Systems, incorporated, and S. E. Kolodney, Director, Statistical Systems, Public Systems, incorporated.

come more directed and sophisticated. As technology and scientific inquiry becomes accepted, more and more talent and expertise is needed. Because it is impractical to attempt to duplicate technical specialists in all agencies of criminal justice where they might occasionally have impact, other methods of targeting these resources must be developed.

Consulting groups provide a pool of special necessary talents which are available selectively and intensively as problems arise. The following paragraphs explore the situations in which these groups are valuable, the services that they are capable of providing, and the ways that these consulting services should be secured.

WHEN CONSULTANTS ARE NECESSARY

Criminal justice agencies and organizations are established to carry out specific functions in an ongoing, routine way. Their staffs, therefore, are recruited to include the talents necessary to successfully fulfill the organization's responsibilities. Occasionally, problems arise that are beyond the expertise of the existing staff: thus, the need for additional help is established, and the use of a consultant is considered.

Because criminal justice agencies are staffed to perform well-defined operations, they are usually unable to divert resources to the solution of "one-time," special problems. Excess manpower, if available, would often not possess the requisite skills to effectively tackle the problem. Two courses of action become available. Hire individuals as part of agency staff to meet these needs, or purchase consultant assistance.

Governmental structure is such that hiring new staff is time consuming, once the positions have been authorized. The specific talents required may be difficult to find and entry salary levels may make it impossible to secure individuals with sufficient experience and training. Moreover, hiring staff to deal with special problems is counter-productive, for once the problem has been resolved the individuals may not be useful to the routine business of the agency.

The second course of action, consultant services, is an attractive alternative. The consultant can augment agency staff by providing specific expertise directed at the solution of the special problem. There is no commitment to maintaining the job position, nor to redirecting staff after problem solution. Full-time staff is free to continue to perform normally in the assurance that their efforts will not be diluted or inefficiently diverted.

Another dimension of augmenting staff through consultants is time. Consultant services can be secured relatively quickly; certainly more expeditiously than justifying new permanent positions and attempting to fill them. Because the consultant brings the essential expertise and has had experience with similar problems, his start-up time involves becoming familiar with the problem and the agency, but not with the various techniques of problem solution. He can bring sufficient resources to bear on the problem, unencumbered by the bureaucratic structure of reviews and approvals. The eventual outcome is likely to be timely and responsive to the agency and its activities.

Often, special problems arise out of a disagreement between an agency and some other involved organization in the criminal justice system. A consultant brought into this kind of situation can accomplish his work as a disinterested third party and present his findings impartially and objectively. For example, a police department may request ten new patrolmen as part of their yearly budget submission to the city council. Cursory review by the council may indicate to them that the request is not really necessary, given an reorganization of the police department and new allocations of existing manpower. Consultant services can productively be used to help resolve this situation. A study of the police department and its manpower uses can be undertaken objectively with some assurance that the results will have strong impact on the resolution of the dispute. The consultant, as impartial expert, can help minimize decisions based on politics or personality conflict.

Finally, consultants can be used effectively in the role of coordinator or integrator. Occasionally, projects are undertaken which affect more than one agency or governmental body. Project coordination provided by one of the interested parties may bias the direction toward a special interest. Similarly, other agencies may not fully trust the leadership vested in one of the participants—the project may flounder or proceed slowly due to lack of cooperation. A consultant as coordinator can serve as staff to a policy board representative of all those involved. He can "systematize" the project to assure that all interests are fairly represented and that the results will satisfy basic requirements. Recent federal projects involving many states, and criminal justice agencies within the states, have been very successful with this model. When offered the opportunity to hire permanent staff, these projects opted for contract consultant services because of the diversity of expertise available and the success of the consultant as coordinator of diverse interests.

WHAT CONSULTANTS DO

Merely knowing the situations in which consultants can profitably be used is insufficient—it is also necessary to understand the kinds of things that consultants are capable of doing. These divide into three separate though overlapping areas.

First is the area that can most truly be called consulting. This work is characterized by close contact with the customer in which the consultant acts as staff. Most of the work is performed at the site of the agency, interacting with agency personnel and administrators. When you buy this kind of assistance, you buy expertise—the "full-service bank" concept. The consultant is there to advise on a broad range of subjects. He must be aware of the position of the agency on criminal justice system questions, and must be sensitive to the politics that surround various decisions and courses of action. In this role, the consultant will often participate in presentations to management, advisory boards, and other interested bodies. He will speak for the agency and articulate its position. Final products developed from such relationships must be implementable within the practical and political constraints imposed on the agency. In many cases, it is advisable to use the consultant during implementation.

A recent example of this area of consulting involves a state planning agency (SPA) whose grant money for criminal justice information systems was frozen by the LEAA region until a master plan could be developed. Consultants were hired to work closely with the SPA to produce the plan. Other agencies had to be contacted, many administrators were briefed, and the decisions had to be presented to the Governor's Council. The final master plan was implementable because the realities and politics of the state were carefully considered and reviewed before the final draft was produced.

In another mode, consultants perform objective operational analysis which usually contains a strong fact-finding phase in which the consultant interacts with the agency to collect data by observation, interviews, etc. The consultant role is objective and disinterested; he is responding to a problem, not augmenting existing staff under the direction of the agency head. The conclusions and recommendations developed from the analysis are apolitical and reflect the correct way to approach the solution to the problem. Such analyses may take the form of design or of implementation.

The previous example of the police department study to determine manpower needs would fall into this area. The outcome is objective and carries the weight of a professional study performed outside the special interests of involved parties.

Finally, the last consulting area might be called system design/research. In these cases, broad policy questions have been framed, translated to hypotheses, and studied using scientific techniques and methodology. The research relies on scientific, quantitative analysis. Data is usually taken as the basis for accepting the hypotheses. Most of the consultant's work is carried on at his own office location, using his facilities and computer systems. Specific expertise is provided by the consultant—expertise not normally available in the organization posing the questions. The product consists of a document which details the hypotheses, describes the methodology, and draws conclusions. As a result, the full impact of the conclusions on the operations of involved agencies is usually beyond the scope of the effort.

The question of the relationship of incarceration to post-release outcomes is an example of the type of question that a consultant might attempt to study. Follow-up data about post-release outcomes of individuals released from prison would provide the data base on which various statistical techniques would be used. The results, the relationship in question, would be documented. It is then up to the legislature and corrections to understand the implications of these findings to the things they will do in the future.

HOW TO SELECT THE CONSULTANT

In selecting a consultant, four distinct considerations must be made: the problem/task statement must be defined; the source of funding must be identified; the criteria for selection must be delineated; and a contract must be negotiated. Depending on the experience and expertise of the agency requiring the consultant, each of these selection phases has a different significance.

Problem Definition

Once an agency or organization has recognized the need for the assistance of a consultant, the substance of the need should be carefully examined to define the problem and scope of the task to be performed. The level of detail required at this stage depends on the type of consulting work which is required. If the effort is classical consulting—i.e., a requirement for expert assistance in a staff role—the problem need not be articulated concisely. In fact, many times when this type of assistance is required, it is required because the problem cannot be well defined by the agency and the consulting assistance is used to define the problem. If, on the other hand, the consulting effort required is in the form of a more structured, objective project, the detail required will be greater since probably more expenditure will be required and better estimates of the scope and value of the effort are needed for project approval.

Funding Source Identification

If the services of a consultant are required, the source of funds to pay for the services must be identified. This should be done before an excessive amount of effort is expended on defining the problem, although some problem definition must be completed in order to estimate the anticipated expenditures.

Various funding sources are available to criminal justice agencies. If the agency itself is unable to provide funds, grant funds may be available. The Law Enforcement Assistance Administration (LEAA) of the Department of Justice disperses funds through the authorization of the Omnibus Crime Control and Safe Streets Act of 1968. The majority of the grant monies available from LEAA is allocated in blocks to the State Planning Agencies (SPA), who in turn provide project grants to component agencies within the criminal justice system. These grants typically result from fiscal plans being submitted by an agency to the SPA. Other grant monies are available directly from the LEAA. There are several other sources of funds for criminal justice agencies. These include: The Police Foundation of the Ford Foundation; the National Science Foundation; Health, Education and Welfare; Housing and Urban Development of Transportation; and Department of Labor. The appropriateness of each depends on the type of criminal justice agency and the objectives of the project for which funding is desired.

Selection Criteria

Having defined the problem and identified a source of funding, the next question is: how do I decide which consultant is best for me? If a particular consultant seems to be the most appropriate—or perhaps, the only one qualified—is it necessary or desirable to consider several others before making a selection? The answer to this question hinges on the work to be performed, the agency's knowledge of potential consultants, and any constraints which may be imposed by the organization or funding source. If the work to be performed is essentially follow-on work to a previous effort and if the working relationship is technically and politically sound, it may be the most expedient to forego any competition, providing there are no constraints—such as funding agency requirements—which prevent this. Although selecting a single contractor as the sole source may take some work to justify the action, it is often the most realistic way to hire a consultant. When an agency can determine in advance that a particular consultant is *the one* to perform the work—for whatever reason, be it technical, prior experience, or political—then it is patently unfair and costly to solicit proposals from several other firms. Unfortunately, this "sole source" practice has been badly abused at times. Hence, more and more constraints to force competition of one form or another are being imposed. Competition may turn out to be advantageous for the agency, in that one or more additional, perhaps better qualified, consultants will be found.

In considering a competition to determine the best choice of consultant, a list of interested and potentially qualified vendors must be compiled. Typically, this list is generated through previous experience and interest shown by contractors. In some cases a formal notice of intent may be issued, although much of this notification is provided through grant requests having been submitted to State Planning Agencies. The list of contractors to be considered should be as inclusive as feasible.

The actual selection of a consultant will be based on his proposed approach to the agency problem. The basis for these contractor proposals is a Request for Proposal (RFP) issued by the agency. The RFP contains a succinct statement of the problem and work to be performed. It should also include a clear definition of the problem scope, constraints, schedule, related interfaces, and the date on which the proposals are due. The evaluation criteria and methodology which will be used in selecting the consultant should also be delineated. Often the amount budgeted for the project has been fixed—this information, along with any estimates of manpower required, will help to assure that each potential contractor considers the same problem in proposing a solution. As a part of the formal proposal receipt and evaluation phase, it may be expedient or necessary to schedule a "bidders' briefing." This is a scheduled meeting between the criminal justice agency and any potential consultants who wish to attend. The purpose of the meeting is to provide additional data to the bidders and to answer questions regarding the project. Since there are always some questions, the decision to schedule a formal briefing depends on the amount of time which may be expected to be consumed with and without a briefing. If the RFP is relatively comprehensive and if all of the potential contractors are knowledgeable it is not necessary to hold a formal bidders' meeting.

When the proposals are received they must be evaluated. Typically, this selection process is done by a selection committee. An evaluation methodology is prescribed which assigns various weights to the relevant aspects of the proposals: technical approach, experience, personnel, and cost. If one proposal does not stand out as the best, it may be desirable to eliminate some of the weaker proposals and invite the better consultants—at most three or four—to make an oral presentation to the selection committee.

Contract Negotiations

After a contractor has been tentatively selected as being the most appropriate consultant for the agency for this particular project, the details of the contractual agreement must be worked out. Typically, this involves some clarification of the work statement, schedule, personnel, and method of payment. The proper type of contract—cost reimbursable or fixed price—depends to some extent on the type of consulting services desired and on how well the final product of the effort can be defined.

WORKING WITH THE CONSULTANT

The most important aspect of the utilization of a consultant by any governmental organization is the performance of the consultant during the project. The effectiveness of this performance will—in most cases—depend heavily on the relationship between the consultant and the agency project personnel.

After the consultant has been selected, it is imperative that each of the involved agency representatives accept the contractor as *their* selection. If prior biases—either technical or political—are not put aside, the possibility of a successful project may be seriously jeopardized.

The most effective consultant-agency relationships exist when both sides maintain close liaison. A specific, detailed work plan, along with a schedule and definition of milestones, constitutes the basis for the project performance. Both the agency and consultant personnel should clearly understand all of the requirements of the contract as well as any constraints or limitations which exist. Although it is often difficult to delineate pseudo-political constraints, they must be considered if any implementation is involved.

Remember that the consultant has been retained to work on a specific problem. Requesting services that go beyond the contract agreement puts the consultant in an awkward position. Although one of his primary concerns is a harmonious relationship with the contracting agency, the consultant should not be expected to perform tasks or undertake duties that he has previously not agreed to perform.

During the period of performance of the project, the agency should be monitoring carefully the milestone performance of the consultant; studies which are allowed to progress toward their final product without interim progress (technical and cost) reviews all too often provide undesirable surprises to one or both parties of the contract. If the consulting project is somewhat open-ended, in that actual choices exist for further effort during the course of the project (most are at least to some extent), then all agreements reached at these decision making milestones should be documented. The effort required for this is minimal, yet it may save considerable confusion later.

Finally, the results of the consulting effort should be presented to the agency in such a way that the study will be utilized to its fullest. The study will be most successful (from both the agency's and consultant's viewpoint) if it leads to an implementation of techniques and procedures which will be effective in solving the problem which was defined.

Before the consulting effort terminates, the contracting agency should be sure that it is in a position to effectively utilize the results when the consultant personnel are no longer available. In some cases, the consultant should be retained in an advisory role during the implementation phase. At other times, the agency should require that, as part of his work, the consultant hold training sessions for involved personnel and make explanatory presentations to administrators. At all times, it is advisable to have agency people actively involved with the consulting group during the course of the project. An agency that allows its consultant to work autonomously will often find that the final product serves them no good purpose.

SUMMARY

In summary, the consultant can and does play a significant role in the management of criminal justice agency operations. When special problems arise within an agency for which regular personnel are not available or trained, or when time is crucial, or when flexibility of travel is important, a consultant may be utilized very effectively. If objectivity is required, in the form of an impartial analysis, consultant services may be the only reasonable approach. And if a multi-agency project is being considered which requires coordination, integration, and systematization, again the objectivity provided by an outside, technically competent contractor may provide the desired leadership. The choice of consultant is crucial. The process through which the consultant is chosen includes a definition of the problem/services required, the identification of the source of funding for the project, the formal process of selection based on technical approach and experience, and the final task statement and contract negotiations. Finally, the most important aspect of utilizing a consultant is the relationship developed during the performance period of the project. Both the consultant and agency must know concisely what is to be done, when it is to be completed and what are the milestones at which decisions are to be made. The ultimate success and acceptance of the entire project—which is of concern to both consultant and agency—often hinges on the integrity and candor of the technical and political relationship developed during the contract.

The University and College as Consultants

In parts of the country that have not formed readily available consulting groups, or perhaps in cases which consulting groups that have formed are not clearly identifiable by philosophy, universities or colleges with criminal justice curricula may be of use in systems analyses. Regardless of how it is accomplished, once the system analysis is complete, effective managerial development frequently requires further consultation and further selection of specific consultants in precise areas of need. Because the primary intent of the system analysis was to make this kind of determination, hopefully selection of further consultants will become somewhat easier.

SELECTING A SPECIALTY CONSULTANT

Even though all consultation is a part of the managerial development program, the consultant needed may or may not be a management expert.

Indeed, a good system analysis may point up the excellence, or at least general adequacy, of the existing management program. But it may also pinpoint such things as a community problem or a training problem.

Once the area of needed expertise has been isolated, a few useful principles can be brought to bear:

1. The client should determine the nature and scope of the project to be undertaken prior to contacting prospective consultants.

2. The qualifications and experience of various consultants in relation to the project should be reviewed, and a short list of consultants qualified for consideration made.

3. Preliminary discussion should be held with each of these consultants in order to discuss the project and their approach to it; and they should be asked to submit proposals.

4. References of those consultants being seriously considered should be checked in depth.

5. The client should then study the proposals in terms of consultant understanding of the problem, approach, probable benefits, cost, and the particular experience and ability of each consultant to meet the requirements of the engagement. In weighing this experience, care should be taken to consider the qualifications of the personnel *who will actually be working on the project*.

6. The final selection should be based on careful weighing of the above factors. Final negotiation should follow the selection of one consultant.[3]

In some regards, it is unfortunate that the formula for federal and many state grants that subsidize management development programs creates the illusion that all of the steps listed above will occur automatically—at least if the grant formula is followed. Though the emergence of federal and state subsidies for managerial development programs has no doubt focused attention on the adequacy of consultation, the final responsibility for effective outcome remains the responsibility of the administrator.

Returning to the principles and guidelines involved in selecting a consultant, the following are also cogent to criminal justice administrators:

1. Does the consultant form sound interpersonal relations with the client? . . .

2. Does the consultant build dependence on his resources? . . . Need for people to develop their own competence and capabilities while he assists only when needed? . . .

3. Does the consultant focus on the problem? . . . A consultant who wants everybody to like him or to be happy at all times may be insecure. . . .

4. Is he non-judgmental and tolerant toward other consultants and response disciplines? . . .

5. Does the consultant treat the confidences of his clients? . . . Another sign

[3] P. W. Shay, "How to Get the Best Results from Management Consultants," Association of Consulting Management Engineers, 1967, pp. 19–20.

of a professional consultant is his ability to keep confidential his dealings with clients. . . .

6. Is the consultant clear about his financial arrangements? . . .
7. Does the consultant achieve influence appropriately in the organization? . . .
8. Does the consultant indicate the skills he possesses relative to your problem? . . .
9. Does the consultant clearly inform the client as to his role and contribution? . . .
10. Does the consultant express willingness to have his services evaluated? . . .
11. Does the consultant belong to a professional association and/or discipline? . . .[4]

Still more to the point in selecting a consultant-specialist are the basic decisions needed prior to hiring:

1. Whether the client wants to employ a
    A. Consulting firm or an individual,
    B. Large firm, a small one, or a new one,
    C. Firm giving a broad service or a more specialized firm.
2. Whether the client prefers a tested, standardized solution to the problem or a more creative approach.
3. What he wants to spend.[5]

In the event a group of consulting specialists is considered (as in the case of the system analysis), the following questions might be posed by the criminal justice administrator:

1. How long has the firm been in business?
2. What are the backgrounds of the principals?
3. Is the staff composed of men who view their jobs as a profession and are, therefore, reasonably permanent?
4. What standards of professional conduct and practice does the firm follow?
5. Do you think you would enjoy working with this firm?
6. Was the discussion sufficiently challenging to suggest that this consultant might stimulate you and your associates to see your problem in a new perspective?
7. What kinds of clients has it served?
8. How much of its business is repeat business?
9. How much time will principals of the firm spend on the assignment?
10. Has the firm had experience that is applicable to the problem?

[4] G. Lippitt, "How To Identify a Professional Consultant," *BNA Project*, 5, No. 2 (November 1969) 21–25.

[5] H. B. Maynard, "How To Select a Management Consultant," *Management Methods*, 1, No. 1 (February 1957), 76.

11. Is it the practice of the firm to make a proposal in writing, clearly defining the objectives of the assignment and the work to be done?

12. Does the firm provide an estimate of fees in advance?

13. Are the estimated charges reasonable, considering the difficulty of the problem and the time required to solve it?[6]

In the words of Beckhard, "Help is never really help unless and until it is perceived as 'helpful' by the person on the receiving end—regardless of the good intention or reputation of the helper or consultant."[7] The question of how helpful the help is may not be answered by a description of consulting, but such a description might nevertheless prove useful:

First, the consultant must be an expert in and have a thorough knowledge of his field. No one will retain him unless he shows that by experience and ability he will be of real service. This usually means that the budding consultant must have worked successfully and for a long period in the special field in which he proposes to advise others. He must have the financial means to hold out and wait for clients, which means he must be able to sustain himself either through savings, the earnings of his wife or children, or in some other way until his clientele is built up. He must have the persistence and tenacity to seek out clients. Many persons who seek to undertake such a career do not have the psychic waiting power or the emotional stamina to "wait it out." Unless the would-be consultant is prepared to persist over a long rather than a short period of time, he will probably not make a go of it.[8]

Unfortunately, even the presence of a growing number of experts willing to wait it out still finds the current state of consulting more of an art than a science. This may be changing as a result of emerging workshops and institutions specifically geared to consulting regardless of the particular expertise involved—whether it be management, research, community, communications, training, or whatever. In this regard, Lippitt observes:

In laboratories on consultation skills for professionals of all types, some of the problems most frequently focused on for practice include:
    Stimulate a need for help
    Give a taste of what it might be like to work together
    Develop a contract of collaboration
    Involve the appropriate client group
    Be supportive of working through resistance
    Stimulate change objectives or images of potentiality
    Give feedback to guide a consultation
    Conceptualize criteria for making choices among alternative interventions

[6] Shay, "How to Get the Best Results from Management Consultants," pp. 25–26.

[7] R. Beckhard, "Leader Looks at the Consultative Process," *Leadership Resources, Inc.,* Washington, D.C., 1965, p. 2.

[8] Irving Paster, "So You Want To Be A Consultant," *Personnel Journal,* 50, No. 11 (November 1971), 829.

It is a heartening sign that more and more professional helpers are accepting the idea that they also need help in practicing a specific interpersonal skill of intervention in designing consultation situations.[9]

As the pool of this help inside and outside the criminal justice system hopefully swells, the ease with which managerial development can occur will also increase.

In the following chapter, the administrative concerns with political and community relations will be considered as further background for the optimism of the final chapter.

SUMMARY

This chapter introduced the final section of the book by exploring the use of consulting specialists. Totally within the specific context of managerial development, the question of who should consult was discussed in relation to the nature and sequence of criminal justice consultation. The need to know *why* a consultant is needed was presented as the rationale for an analysis of the system.

Consulting teams were considered with emphasis on the philosophy of improving rather than changing. Adequacy of consulting groups was contrasted on this same basis, with a suggestion that universities and colleges operating criminal justice programs be considered when consultants are unavailable.

Philosophy of consultation was emphasized to the point of greater significance than expertise, although expertise of the consultant-specialist was also considered.

Against the background of a system analysis hopefully determining specific specialty areas, selection of specialty consultants was discussed and various guidelines and principles presented.

QUESTIONS

1. Discuss the problem of finding the precise consultant talent needed. Contrast early general systems analysis and later specialty consultation in terms of your discussion.

2. Contrast consultant expertise and consultant philosophy.

3. Why was administrative judgment presented as crucial in consulting?

4. Discuss who should consult. How is the college or university related to this question?

5. What is systems analysis? Why is it important?

[9] R. Lippitt, "On Finding, Using, and Being A Consultant," *Social Science Education Consortium Newsletter,* 5, No. 9 (November 1971), 2.

6. Distinguish between one consultant and a group of consultants in terms of complexity and time.

7. Discuss the reasons presented in this chapter that federal and state subsidy for management development in criminal justice does not relieve the administrator of responsibility for effective outcome.

ANNOTATED REFERENCES

LIPPITT, G., *Organizational Renewal*. New York: Appleton-Century-Crofts, 1969. An elaboration of the overall implications of organizational renewal from an existing pragmatic view.

MAASARANI, ALY, *American Management Consultants In The Middle East: Criteria For Success*. New York: St. John's University Press, 1971. Isolates a number of key variables in professionalizing consultation practices.

SCHEIN, EDGAR H., *Process Consultation: Its Role In Organizational Development*. Reading, Mass.: Addison-Wesley, 1969. Synopsis of the organizational development approach to consultation.

SCHMIDT, W., *Organizational Frontiers And Human Values*. Belmont, Calif.: Wadsworth, 1970. Overview of the general context of organizational consultation.

CHAPTER 15

Administrative Interfacing
with Politics
and the Community

Before the criminal justice administrative goals of good community and political relations are considered, let us take a brief glimpse at the private sector of management.

> Careful analysis reveals not only that Armco's tough-minded management development program teaches men to be managers—it brings back a healthy return on the training investment.
>
> For every $1 that Armco Steel Corporation puts into a training program for potential first-line supervisors at its Kansas City Works, it gets back $5 in cost savings from work improvement projects that trainees submit.
>
> One class, for example, set a goal of presenting the president of the corporation with $1-million in cost savings when he came to officiate at its graduation exercises. The trainees are within $100,000 of that goal right now.
>
> But beyond the immediate savings, graduates of the program scored higher on a performance rating that was based on productivity measures—costs, quality, number of units produced, installed savings, safety record, and the like—than did their fellow first-line supervisors who had *many* years of experience.[1]

[1] "A Profitable Management Development Program," *Training In Business and Industry*, 9, No. 7 (July 1971), 33.

Perhaps this comment on training managers seems more relevant to Chapter Eight, or the budgetary implications more relevant to Chapter Six; the discussion of consultants reflected in the preceding chapter may also appear to be a more relevant context for this quotation. In spite of these alternative contexts, however, this reference to fiscal attractiveness is placed here to provide a kind of background for the discussion of administrative interfacing with both politics and the community. The purpose of such a background is to replace cynical doubts with optimistic enthusiasm—to recognize that good administration pay-off includes good community and political relations as well as a fiscal yield.

> Law enforcement and the equal administration of justice have become major national concerns in recent years. The rapid growth of our cities, with attendant problems in housing, education, employment, and social welfare services has accentuated these concerns and has been highlighted by the increasing urban concentration of minority groups.
>
> Crime rates have generally been higher in those areas where poverty, family disintegration, unemployment, lack of education, and minority group frustration and resentment in the face of social and economic discrimination—the ghetto syndrome—are manifest. The expectations, excitement and additional frustrations engendered by the civil rights movement have compounded the difficulty inherent in the entire process of law enforcement and the administration of justice.
>
> Foremost among these difficulties are the relationships between police and minority groups and the general community. Deterioration in these relationships particularly between police and Negroes is increasingly evident. There are widespread charges of police brutality and demands for greater assertion of civilian control over police actions. Many police officials, on the other hand, decry the growing disrespect for law, the apathy of the public, molly-coddling of criminals by the courts, and political influence on the law enforcement process. Some policemen continue to view civil rights groups as trouble-makers who disrupt the law and order the police have sworn to uphold. At the same time, a stereotyped image of the policeman beclouds minority group attitudes, severely hampering potentially beneficial cooperative relationships.[2]

Although the emphasis of this quotation is on police and on the process of police activities rather than managerial concerns, the implications are significant to all criminal justice administrators in a managerial context. This chapter will relate these implications to the management model and to achievement of results through community and political relations.

Management, Law, Social Interests, and Public Apathy

The systems model equates effective management with results achievement—results that are predetermined, measurable, and compatible with both

---

[2] Coffey, Eldefonso, and Hartinger, *Police Community Relations,* p. 1.

law and social interests. This an extremely hard thing to accomplish, however.[3] As early as 1967, this author and colleagues attempted to isolate the essence of this administrative difficulty.

Unhappy is the department that functions in a community in which typical citizens expect law enforcement to *completely* eliminate crime and safety problems. Another extreme of equal detriment is a community expecting absolutely nothing from law enforcement insofar as crime and safety is concerned. Fortunately, *public opinion* usually falls somewhere between these two extremes. Of course, public support is a universal goal of law enforcement.

One of the more difficult tasks of administrative leadership is to judge public opinion accurately enough to set department policies that retain public support for the line officer while enforcing the law as consistently and efficiently as possible. Policies that guide officers toward public support are particularly difficult in a changing society.

Evidence of changes confronting both line and staff law enforcement personnel can be found in tragedies such as the one occurring in the Queens section of New York City in March of 1965. A 28-year-old woman named Catherine Genovese was attacked on three separate occasions over a span of 40 minutes by a knife-wielding assailant. During that time no fewer than 38 persons heard the woman scream for help or actually witnessed the attacks. Yet no one of them telephoned the police, let alone went to the aid of the victim. Finally, after nearly 40 minutes, a 70-year-old woman in the neighborhood called the police. A squad car was at the scene two minutes later but by that time the woman was dead. Public apathy of this nature must in all too many instances become a major influence on administrative leaders setting department policies with the goal of gaining public support. In this particular regard, the administrative leadership must often set policy with the knowledge that changing the public's attitude toward police often depends on personal contact which tends to be of less impact than the image of law enforcement generated in the press.

Judging public opinion sometimes requires administrative leaders to question whether the press reflects opinion or causes opinion. This question often arises when the local press consistently "headlines" crime to the point of stimulating what may seem to administrators to be greater citizen discussion of police activities than occurs in other communities with even higher crime rates but where the press is less inclined to "sensationalize" crime. The press of course argues that the public is entitled to all possible information on crime and any other social problems. And administrators customarily agree but only so long as public pressure as reflected or caused by the press does not totally divert police energies away from less sensational yet necessary activity.[4]

---

[3] See, for example O. H. Ibele, "Law Enforcement and the Permissive Society," *Police,* 8, No. 5 (September–October 1965), 15 and P. A. Devlin, "The Police in a Changing Society," *Journal of Criminal Law, Criminology and Police Science,* 57, No. 2 (June 1966), 123. See also J. J. Skehan, *Modern Police Work* (New York: Francis Basuino, 1951); E. Adlow, *Policemen and People* (Boston: William Rockfort, 1947); R. L. Derbyshire, "The Social Control Role of the Police in Changing Urban Communities," *Excerpta Criminalogica,* 6 No. 3 (1966), 315–16.

[4] Eldefonso, Coffey, and Grace, *Principles of Law Enforcement* (New York: John Wiley & Sons, Inc., 1967), pp. 153–54.

Conflicting and even divergent goals between law enforcement and social interests are but one of the problems in defining effective results, even when public apathy is involved. When defining results that integrate both law enforcement and social interests, criminal justice administrators face still another problem: the ease with which "myths" can replace reason in the criminal justice sphere.

Mythology

In his *The Gang And The Establishment*, Richard Poston wrote an outstanding account of how easily myths are generated about criminal justice.[5] Drawing upon his background and research at Southern Illinois University, Poston narratively evolves the anatomy of a great myth about gangs, which probably began with the passage of the 1964 Federal antipoverty program—the Economic Opportunity Act. He focuses on the willingness of many to theorize that gang members are experts not only on crime but on eliminating crime as well. Under the label of "innovation," existing criminal justice organizations were virtually bypassed, and staggering sums of cash were turned over to gangs or gang leaders who constituted at the time some of the most serious law enforcement problems.

Poston's impressive account of the near absence of solid accomplishment in the massive giveaway, against a background of systematically pumping huge sums of federal as well as private monies into the great breakthrough, is in a sense an account of what most criminal justice administrators must face: the myth of the easy crime solution.

Top administrators who choose to ignore either community relations or political relations ultimately learn of the ease with which any philosophy can be woven into an acceptable myth of easy solutions—frequently solutions that reduce the effectiveness of the criminal justice system in general. For this and many other reasons, community and political relations are of vital administrative concern.

CRIMINAL JUSTICE REPUTATION AND COMMUNITY RELATIONS

The vital administrative concern referred to here is not the growing need for criminal justice programs of all varieties on a community basis. Community relations programming per se is indeed vital,[6] but is in a context removed somewhat from the managerial and administrative context to

[5] R. W. Poston, *The Gang and The Establishment* (New York: Harper & Row, 1971).

[6] See for example the author's views on nonmanagerial contexts for community relations in *Police Community Relations* and *Human Relations: Law Enforcement in a Changing Community*.

which this entire volume is addressed. In many ways, community relations programming overlaps the reputation considerations of the administrative concern with community relations. But the reputation of criminal justice is the precise interest being considered here as the specific administrative concern.

One sobering reality with which an effective administrator must come to grips is the reputation of ineffectiveness gained by the criminal justice system when myths replace reason in the community.[7] The ease with which myths can replace reason emerges as a separate administrative dimension involving not only illegal law enforcement, discussed earlier, but all other matters relating to the reputation of criminal justice as well.

Again focusing on the police subsystem but emphasizing the administrative relevance to all criminal justice subsystems, consider the reputation implications of the following:

Many police officers today sense that they are held in low esteem by the very communities they are serving. Responsible people are not likely to march up to a policeman and start listing, point blank, such and such reasons why they do not regard their police force with fondness. If they did, their complaints might range anywhere from annoyance over a traffic ticket they once got to vague, general charges about police corruption.

Historically, the police have always been used for political and social control. In the past they have done their work with almost unanimous support from the middle and upper class. Now this is not so. Many of those who oppose the police are children of the rich and the suburban well-to-do. These young people make up most of the amorphous cultural entity called the New Left. . . .

. . . The frequency of police contact with the whole population (usually through the mass media) has thrown enforcement of the law in sharp collision with general standards, to which neither police nor public has reacted well. The public has—because of occasional "lawless" enforcement of the law (police abuse of constitutional rights)—become cynical about its own police officers and its legal system. This, in turn, has resulted in an almost universal phenomena: peace officers have isolated themselves from the community they serve and have banded together in condemning anyone who levels criticism at them. Because of the policeman's possible aloofness and egotistical and arbitrary demeanor, each "collision" results, on the one hand, in a swelling of his authority complex, and, on the other hand, in a new birth of antagonism in some large groups.[8]

[7] By "reputation" is meant the image implications implicit in a wide variety of criminal justice literatutre—for example, C. Westley, "Violence and the Police," *American Journal of Sociology*, 59, No. 34 (1953); D. R. Rolph, "Police Violence," *New Statesman*, 66, No. 102 (1963); J. H. Skolnick, *Justice Without Trial* (New York: John Wiley & Sons, Inc., 1966); and the entire Task Force series accompanying The President's Commission on Law Enforcement and Administration of Justice, *The Challenge of Crime In A Free Society*, U.S. Government Printing Office, Washington, D.C., 1967.

[8] Coffey, Eldefonso, and Hartinger, *Human Relations: Law Enforcement in a Changing Community*, pp. 70–72.

Improving The Reputation

Of course, administrative interfacing between criminal justice systems as discussed earlier in this volume bears directly upon any reputation improvements. The stressful situation experienced by the police subsystem is by no means insulated from any part of the criminal justice system; administrative interfacing between subsystems virtually eliminates the gross dysfunctions that lead to charges and myths that criminal justice is for one reason or another ineffectual or fragmented into a nonsystem.[9] Effective administrative interfacing between subsystems additionally permits the common use of law as an instrument of social control.

Convincing the public that such myths or accusations are untrue or exaggerated has, thus far, produced little if any improvement in the reputation of any part of criminal justice. Sufficient improvement in criminal justice reputation to afford administrative definitions of results that integrate law and social interests appears more in the area of achieving results than in answering charges. This is particularly true because charges appear likely to continue regardless of any answer given. Indeed, if the social scene continues to change, charges are likely to increase in both frequency and severity—and it appears that the social scene will continue to change.

> The problems of crime control, in general, and law enforcement in particular, are always related to changes in the social scene. The dimensions and substance of community life are undergoing such wholesale and radical transformation in our time that it behooves us to pause and reflect upon the influences that are sharply modifying the conditions of contemporary community life and posing new problems for the agencies of law enforcement.
>
> There are basic changes going forward in the community, and these are transforming the problems which confront law enforcement officials. Cities are becoming the residence of lower class Negro groups, while Whites are moving to the Hinterland. This wholesale settlement has coincided with problems of housing, of income, etc.[10]

Moreover, even if constant changes were not occurring an administrator could scarcely conclude that the past decade or two has produced any evidence that criminal justice has been able to answer the various charges effectively enough to systematically reduce their number. Answering charges, then, is not the avenue to improving the reputation of criminal justice. Administrative results that are systematically and continually achieved are by far the more useful approach.

---

[9] As part of the very few positive examples of increasing concern for fragmented criminal justice process, see for example F. W. Howlett and H. Hunter, "A Systems Approach to Comprehensive Criminal Justice Planning," *Crime and Delinquency*, 17, No. 4 (October 1971), 345–54; and the entire Task Force series accompanying The President's Commission on Law Enforcement and the Administration of Justice.

[10] Coffey et al., *Human Relations: Law Enforcement in a Changing Community*, p. 28.

But even when improvement occurs through effective administration, reputation improves only to the degree that the public is aware of administrative effectiveness. Public awareness, then, emerges as a primary and critical administrative concern.

Public Awareness: Publicity Without Selling

The image of the glib "snow-job artist" capable of confusing and evading all pointed accusations persists for public relations personnel in spite of the fact that this reputation began to decline following the post–World War II motion picture *The Hucksters*. Public awareness of administrative results now depends not on selling but rather on *achievement*. Recalling the managerial function of defining results within the system model, the most significant rationale for establishing the determination of results as a function of top management role is the requirement that they reconcile whatever differences exist between government and community. This requires enough awareness of the differences to define the results.

Publicity of results, of course, is continuous and in two stages at all times: (1) results defined and (2) results achieved. Because of the nature of the systems model, this approach to public awareness could be thought of as publicized research.

Publicized Research: Link Between Defined and Achieved Results

Recalling the constant upgrading of managerial plans and operations within the systems model, continuous research is required into approaches to increase the effectiveness of how the results are to be achieved. Noteworthy here is that the actual line work—the most publicly visible evidence of criminal justice in action—is the immediate consequence of this.

In effect, then, publicity of research in the systems model emerges as an ideal focal point geared to improve the criminal justice image. In other words, an administrator choosing to make continual research the focal point of public awareness combines both the defined and achieved result with the most publicly perceptible segment of his administrative program. Beyond this, publicity framed within such research assaults the myths of simple solutions, and reminds us that effective criminal justice within an ever-changing and complex democracy is at best a very difficult and involved process.

Coordination With Existing Programs

Larger criminal justice organizations with existing community relations programs already have, in effect, the communication channels to develop this results approach to public awareness—even when the channels have been previously utilized to defend and to answer charges. Indeed, to whatever degree the results to be publicized are valid, the improvement in reputation enhances the mission of community relations programming: "participation in any activity that seeks law enforcement through respect rather than enforcement."[11]

Starting Without Existing Programs

Smaller criminal justice organizations and organizations without existing community-based programs of course do not have the ready-made channels referred to above. Nevertheless, no serious difficulty is anticipated in developing the needed channels to bring achieved results to the public's awareness—this is simply a matter of periodically calling news conferences.

Except for certain political ramifications that will be discussed later in this chapter, few if any administrative difficulties need be anticipated in gaining the interest of the media once the systems model is producing achievements and making valid plans for further achievements. Independent of the natural human interest that surrounds virtually all criminal justice subsystems and their activities, the tax implications of effective management combine readily with the novelty of calling a news conference. Reminding the public of money saved, and of what its money is being spent for is newsworthy, as are candid acknowledgements that the criminal justice system has not *always* been quick to respond to the need for cohesive and effective management. Such candor is likely to close the gap that has perhaps developed through the years between the answering of charges and the achievement of results.

Although the news conference is a readily available method of improving the reputation of criminal justice once results are forthcoming, it also tends to bring the criminal justice administrator to grips with an ever-constant reality: politics.

POLITICS

Within a wide range of variation among criminal justice subsystems and jurisdictions, there is a point at which administrative concern for improving the reputation of criminal justice intersects political concern for what the public believes. At this point, the political skills discussed in Chapter Four come to bear. Political skills are discussed against a background of a manager's conceptual skills, his program skills, and his human skills, and presented as his ability to weigh consequences—to distinguish between a solution per se and a feasible solution. Some decisions might solve far fewer problems than they create. The political skills needed by managers in the

[11] Ibid., p. 8.

systems model focus conceptual skills on pertinent theory and pertinent prag-matics, and the consequences of both. Political skills also influence program skills toward consequence-oriented behavior—toward concern for results. Perhaps of even greater yield are political skills as a guide—the manager's judgment about communication—particularly when political skills involve real politics. . . .

To whatever degree criminal justice remains attractive as a political symbol of virtue instead of a desperately needed societal system is the crimi-nal justice administrator faced with a need to cope with politics—politics that in effect oppose effective management. More often than not, when this problem exists, it exists primarily within the range of administrative activi-ties involved in budget appropriation.

The administrative trick is to make results politically attractive. Re-calling the Chapter Six discussion of budget and program modules, the sys-tems model affords the potential to manage this trick.

Module Programs

By emphasizing the availability of specific, concrete measurement of success in any given module, political concern is reduced for where the money is going. Moreover, an administrator must establish a specific level of expectations and isolate the fiscal limitations on results in advance. But far more important, module programming provides a legislative body an attrac-tive political leverage; in effect, taxpayers can be made aware of a legislator's affiliation with sophisticated tax dollar-stretching managerial programs. Vot-ing taxpayers with this awareness are presumably more impressed with legis-lators with these affiliations than with legislators exposing the public to a barrage of platitudes about criminal justice virtue. In this regard, the public, even the apathetic public, is far more likely to recognize the validity of some of the most expensive programs when the emphasis is on the measurement of outcome instead of the description of activities and problems. This, in effect, replaces the annual justifications for budget with an array of price-tagged modules that contain clear definitions of results to be achieved and measurements of achievement.

In idealistic theory, effective criminal justice could work itself out of existence. In an era of escalating social change, however, this possibility seems no more likely than the elimination of the need for medicine in an increasingly polluted environment. The point being made is that to what-ever degree effective management is politically impeded by the fear that crimi-nal justice might be lost as a political symbol (or more cynically, as a career), the module program of increased service permits a way to correct this as a problem.

Recalling the mechanics of the systems model, planning alternatives are continually updated within the definition of administrative results. When the various module programs that are derived from results definitions include alternatives to the commonly acknowledged criminal justice problems,[12] the political value of effective criminal justice emerges to replace the political value of symbolic criminal justice. Diverting vast numbers of people presently involved in the criminal justice process and virtually eliminating "victimless crime"[13] makes possible a large increase in the amount of service offered by all criminal justice subsystems without increasing the cost of criminal justice itself. Presumably, increased service without increased cost affords a rather convincing political argument. When the resources of police, courts, prosecution-defense, and corrections are drawn away from severe crimes by the handling of large volumes of "victimless crime" and family matters,[14] the criminal justice system is unquestionably hampered and becomes less effective. Viewed from this perspective, the criminal justice system in effect becomes less politically attractive as well. It is possible that, with good management and planning, particular criminal justice subsystems could focus their resources solely on crime and delinquency and on such things as booking, evidence gathering, and preservation of evidence, as well as testimony—this would be effective, efficient, help in the accomplishment of criminal justice goals, and be economically and politically attractive to the community.

Of course these administrative concerns are hardly the sole justification for criminal justice interest in such laudable goals. Nevertheless, administrative concern when isolated, remains significant in a different context. For this reason, criminal justice management modules that afford alternatives which in turn focus criminal justice on crime and delinquency are modules that afford the basis for effective political relations. That which remains in establishing political relations (at least of a significant nature) has to do with the complex alignment of various federal, state, and local government structures —an extremely involved consideration. Though no effort will be made here to cover the enormous range of complexity in covering each local exigency, a few typical considerations might serve to clarify the main concern of criminal justice administration in this regard: successful political relations.

---

[12] There is a great amount of professional and public literature about overworked police, excessive caseloads for probation and parole, clogged court calendars, etc. Typical of the public literature, for example, is the March 22, 1971 *U.S. News & World Report's* "Speeding Up Justice—President's Plan," in which the president proposed elimination of "victimless crime" and the Chief Supreme Court Justice found that "the American system of criminal justice in every phase. . . is suffering from a severe case of deferred maintenance."

[13] By "victimless crime" is meant the wide range of offenses handled by the criminal justice system in which the accused is also the victim.

[14] By "family matters" is meant primarily the commitment of significant criminal justice resources to juvenile offenses that would not be offenses if committed by an adult. Community clinics and outside family counseling for such matters afford criminal justice an opportunity to focus on delinquency rather than "family matters."

Government and Criminal Justice Management Modules

Recalling the Chapter Six discussion of cost benefit analysis and module program and program budget, the module approach to political relations is ideally suited for any relationship between criminal justice and government. Delineating the benefits to be derived and the measurements used to determine whether or not benefits are derived establishes the basis for an appropriate administrative interface with government. However, enough variety exists in government to focus briefly upon some typical structural variations before the clarity of this interface can be assumed. Many police, sheriff, court, prosecution, and probation jurisdictions might, for instance, find these remarks of interest:

A city-county consolidation or merger involves the unification of the governments of one or more cities with the surrounding county. As a result of the consolidation, the boundary lines of the jurisdiction involved become "coterminous." However, certain incorporated jurisdictions may opt to be excluded from these consolidations.[15]

Judges, and all other criminal justice personnel for that matter, will be able to relate to the following:

The county's financial responsibility for the court was a practical consequence to court administration. In the areas in which the court could not or did not receive specific legislative authorization, such as expenditures for travel and equipment, the court had to justify these expenditures to the county chief administrative officer (CAO) in the formulation of the county budget. The county's budgetary authority over the court put the court in the same position as county departments. The executive officer attempted to free the court from county budgetary control either by direct negotiation or by obtaining the necessary legislation.

When the county attempted to control the court's legislative program by restricting travel expenditures, the court, after urging by the executive officer, responded by having a bill introduced. . . .[16]

For administrative who believe that a clearly defined government structure will ever exist in standard form, the following quotation will be relevant.

We can find three types of special purpose governments of importance today for the counties and for general purpose governments in general. The first is

[15] Charlene Caile, "Bringing the City and County Together," *American County*, 37, No. 2 (February 1972), 9.

[16] Richard W. Gable, "Modernizing Court Administration: The Case of the Los Angeles Superior Court," *Public Administration Review*, 31, No. 2 (March–April 1972), 137.

what I call the Special District. The Special District is a unit of government operating outside of the General Purpose government framework, usually to perform one function of government and financed primarily by special tax levies, usually on property. The distinction is that a special district is a unit of government for a single purpose financed primarily by special taxes, usually property taxes.

The Special District resulted from unincorporated territory around the cities. Our cities were locked in by early charters. The only possible way we could expand our cities was by a kind of crude system of annexation where you just reached out and grabbed.

For that reason there was a lot of unincorporated area lying around the cities. When people moved out to these areas they wanted some service. So they resorted to this device called the Special District. They would simply organize themselves a district and agree to tax themselves for some particular service they wanted. In New Jersey, for example, they have Fire Fighting Districts, Lighting Districts, Road Districts and Water Districts. There were no great expenditures for heavy equipment but there were for the performance of services that they could not get through any government because they were unincorporated. This did give them incorporation because the special district is a legal entity, a legally state-chartered entity.

This is a characteristic of American local government. A group of people are willing to tax themselves to pay for a particular service that they themselves want. The only difference is that it is only one function that the government performs.[17]

Although criminal justice services were not reflected in the discussion of groups of people taxing themselves for services, the complexity of such arrangements is hopefully obvious. Most if not all criminal justice administrators (at least below the federal and state level) certainly will find the following commentary cogent with regard to the potential effectiveness of the wide range of governmental structure:

It is legitimate, if not novel, to assert that local government institutions must find ways to increase their effectiveness if they are to solve the pressing problems of the urban society. One of the aspects of government that needs improving is the administrative system. A variety of avenues to upgrading administration are being proposed and tested. These include accounting and decision making tools based on computer technology, infusion of professional and technical expertise in the problem areas, and federal support to create new ancillary organizations such as neighborhood organizations, metropolitan area coordinating groups, and pollution control agencies. The establishment of this latter variety of new organizations is apparently based at least in part

---

[17] Commentary of Dr. Robert G. Smith from "an abridged transcript of a discussion" between Smith, Alastair McArthur, George Otlowski, Joan Aron, and Richard Sullivan, "Special Purpose Governments," *American County*, 36, No. 10 (November 1971), 10–11.

on the assumption that existing local government structure cannot be relied on to do the job.[18]

In the article from which this citation was taken, Eddy and Saunders go on to examine the need for increased flexibility in government, with emphasis on with problem solving rather than control, collaboration between organizations within government, effective managerial approaches, and greater responsiveness to "external and well as internal factors." The beauty of this outstanding article is the manner in which it is cast within political issues, of critical concern to criminal justice and administrators of public programs in general.

Also bearing on the variations in governmental structure are the many patterns of citizen involvement, which are of specific administrative interest to criminal justice managers. Consider, for example, the following definition, which somewhat pessimistically discusses citizen involvement as "an exercise in futility."

System means a socio-politico-economic complex dominated by White-Anglo-Saxon-Protestant (WASP) values, but not necessarily by WASP individuals.[19]

This definition of system moves into a discussion that includes the following:

. . . among non-whites there is a rising level of expectations due partly to undelivered political promises and to mass media induced desires, in addition, of course, to real physical need. Measured against the expectations, the promissory rhetoric of the system is basically untrue. As a result, there is only one way that minority members can interpret these implicit facts: the system is unwilling to share any kind of significant power. Near absolute system control of scare resource allocation is at the heart of the matter. All that non-whites desire is a piece of the action, to live a decent life, and to control some aspects of their own lives. On the whole, the system to date has prevented this intentionally. All that has been accomplished has been the creation of false hopes and desires. . . .[20]

In terms of the variety of government structural variations confronting the use of module programs as part of political relations, these very few dimensions do scarcely more than provide the flavor of the significant ramifi-

---

[18] W. B. Eddy and R. J. Saunders, "Applied Behavioral Science in Urban Administrative Political Systems," *Public Administration Review*, 32, No. 1 (January–February 1972), 11.

[19] L. Chatman and D. M. Jackson, "Citizen Participation: An Exercise in Futility: An Action Program for ASPA," *Public Administration Review*, 32, No. 3 (May–June 1972), 201.

[20] Ibid., p. 200.

cations involved. But in spite of the endless variations in American government, there remains a unifying principle which all administrative modules could relate.

> Few men had more insight into America than John Quincy Adams, son of the President, himself a President, close enough to Thomas Jefferson to be called his adopted son. Adams visualized clearly the intricate balance between good and evil on which the United States as a nation rests. In referring to the country's democratic system, he once stated, "The American government is an experiment upon the heart."
>
> Most men were of the belief that human nature could not be trusted with freedom. They were certain that if the right to protest, to resist injustice, and to criticize the government itself were accorded to the citizens, the inevitable result would be revolt, violence and anarchy.
>
> During the last few years, there has been a great deal of anxiety on the part of a significant number of Americans who have expressed concern over whether the pessimists were correct after all. Riots have left their marks on our cities, and have disrupted our colleges; the tragic assassinations of John Kennedy, Martin Luther King, Jr., and Robert Kennedy, have, without a doubt, taken their toll on the confidence of many citizens in the ability of America to survive and continue as a free society. However, the problems confronted by the American people throughout their history serve as a reminder that contemporary violence is not a new problem. . . .[21]

It is not the violence that is being emphasized here, but rather the struggle to integrate the many variables of democracy; this integration is in effect the principle around which American government is built. Ever-shifting variation and experiment are in the very nature of this democracy, and its political and governmental structure as well. The principle of integrating the many variables is hopefully present regardless of any specific local version of government structure.

Criminal justice module programs are a part of this principle—this experiment. Modules, when executed with managerial excellence, tend to become a vital part of the democratic experiment. Indeed, administratively good program modules for criminal justice may well play a role in answering the questions that political philosophers ask every society (democratic and otherwise):

> 1. What are men's motives to come together under government; are these motives strong enough to keep them obedient to government orders?
> 2. What is the moral basis and ethical justification for obedience to these government orders?

[21] Coffey et al., *Human Relations: Law Enforcement in a Changing Community,* p. 23.

Years of wisdom have not provided durable consensus of answers to these vital questions. Perhaps a criminal justice system capable of adapting to the political changes that occur in defining deviation from government orders is the answer, and perhaps it is available only to criminal justice administrators.

The chapter that follows will conclude this volume with a discussion of the reasons that make us believe that criminal justice can play this increasingly vital role in a changing society. The only question remaining unanswered is whether criminal justice will indeed make the administrative adjustments necessary to play such a role.

SUMMARY

This chapter dealt with the relationship between the managerial administration of criminal justice and the political influences of the community. The law, social interests, and public apathy were discussed in terms of administrative results definitions.

A kind of mythological easy crime solution was posed as an administrative concern in establishing community relations. This myth of easy solutions to crime was discussed as contrasting the actual criminal justice process . . . a "difference" that forms the basis of community relations. This difference was also discussed in terms of the reputation of criminal justice as opposed to the actual program activities of community relations. A strategy for improving the reputation of criminal justice was proposed in terms of deriving an array of program modules from results definitions to replace the traditional defenses against accusations. Public awareness was emphasized in this strategy, along with the research component of the systems model results development.

Political relations were defined as including the criminal justice administrator's interest in public awareness of results achievement as it intersects political interests in what the public believes. Managerial political skills (as presented in Chapter Four) were related to political relationships.

The political symbolism of criminal justice was discussed as impeding effective results-oriented management. Making program modules politically attractive was proposed as a solution; the use of modules presented the possibility of diverting certain criminal justice activities, such as dealing with victimless crimes and certain aspects of procedure (booking, evidence-gathering, etc.), to particular subsystems, making for a politically and economically attractive system of criminal justice overall.

Several examples of considerations involved in the wide range of government structure were discussed. A unifying principle was cited in terms of the continuing effort to integrate the many variables in democracy—integration of these variables ideally being the common denominator in the staggering variety of governmental structures to which criminal justice must administratively relate.

Criminal justice was presented as a potentially cohesive force in a changing democracy, with the potential of becoming one of the most significant of the democratic institutions.

QUESTIONS

1. Relate law, social interests, and public apathy to criminal justice management.

2. Contrast the discussion of mythology with the discussion of criminal justice reputation. What strategy was proposed for improving criminal justice "reputation?"

3. Relate public awareness to the research component of results definition and achievement.

4. Relate the news conference proposed in this chapter to the discussion of political relations.

5. Distinguish between community relations programming and administrative interest in community relations as part of results.

6. Relate political symbolism in criminal justice to administrative problems in achieving results.

7. Relate module programming to both community and political relations; to increased criminal justice service through diversion of less severe offenses.

ANNOTATED REFERENCES

CHATMAN, L., and D. M. JACKSON, "Citizen Participation: An Exercise in Futility: An Action Program For ASPA," *Public Administration Review*, 32, No. 3 (May–June), 199–201. A provocative viewpoint on citizen involvement in government process. For a substantially different perspective, see in the same issue CLIFFORD GROVE's, "Citizen Participation in Metropolitan Planning," along with JOSEPH ZIMMERMAN's, "Neighborhoods and Citizen Involvement." (As a specialty issue, also carried are interesting articles by HOWARD SKINNER, "Citizen Participation and Racism," and by JAMES RIEDEL, "Citizen Participation: Myths and Realities.")

COFFEY, A., E. ELDEFONSO, and W. HARTINGER, *Human Relations: Law Enforcement in a Changing Community*, Englewood Cliffs, N.J.: Prentice-Hall, 1971. (See also *Police Community Relations*, same authors and publisher.) The authors' views on the process dimensions of community relations are elaborated in contrast to the administrative concern for community relations discussed in this chapter.

EDDY, W. B., and R. J. SAUNDERS, "Applied Behavioral Science in Urban Administrative/Political Systems," *Public Administration Review,* 32, No. 1 (January–February 1972), 11–23. On the systems approach to integrating political exigency with administrative approach.

GABLE, R. W., "Modernizing Court Administration: The Case of the Los Angeles Superior Court," *Public Administration Review,* 31, No. 2 (March–April 1972), 133–43. Account of the problems confronting efforts to coordinate local government and the court subsystem. In the same issue, see also EDWARD GALLO's, "The Court As A Social Force" and ERNEST FRIESEN's "Constraints and Conflicts in Court Administration," along with SENATOR JOSEPH TYDING's "The Courts and Congress."

NOTE:

The references of the preceding chapter, although in a different context, tend to clarify the relationship of criminal justice in general to the political and community implications discussed in this chapter. See also the annotated references of Chapters Four and Six.

CHAPTER 16

Any Jurisdiction Can Manage Effectively

This concluding chapter is devoted to an optimistic review of the possibility (and frequently the probability) that a major training and development effort will produce a high yield of effective management in any jurisdiction. This assessment is based on many factors, not the least of which is the total absence of concern for particular managerial personalities.

Within the criminal justice system in general, there appears to be a widely held belief that the management system can be changed but the managers themselves can't be. More often than not, discussion this leads to the conclusion that many criminal justice managers believe that profound personality changes must occur before improvements can be made within administrative practice.

As noted in numerous contexts throughout this volume, the systems model does not seek personality change, nor even view personality change as necessarily valuable. Indeed, the design of the managerial role interface and the reflexive synergetics are based on a premise that personality changes are not feasible and perhaps not even possible, extraordinary claims of many managerial communication experts notwithstanding.

Effective, continuing management that produces results is possible through systematic regard for the functional components of success—clearly defined managerial roles systematically related without insistence on a particular type of manager filling any given role. In the ideal, of course, the manager seems effective, as well as proves effective, through measurement. In reality, nevertheless, a manager who performs effective functions is effective whether he seems it or not.

The degree of difficulty in developing effective management varies between jurisdictions. The least significant reason that difficulty is encountered is the absence of particular types of managers. In other words, the management personality is simply not a requisite of the systems model. This by no means removes the major effort required to develop an effective results-oriented management system, but it at least makes such development realistically possible.

Because this is so, we believe that any jurisdiction can manage effectively.

Criminal justice does not encompass *all* social problems; the question is one of defining the scope of success. The parameters within which administrative results are defined do not include community mental health or economic security, *even if both are related to crime.*

In pursuit of effective criminal justice management, the systems model permits any jurisdiction to administratively succeed. Police management does not fail simply because family fights produce homicides; probation management does not fail simply because social unrest permeates caseloads and community alike. The jury that seems to ignore an excellent prosecution does not necessarily prove criminal justice management has failed. Those who criticize the mental health problems of prison and parole do not, by their criticisms alone, establish the inadequacy of criminal justice management.

And lest the fiscal implications be forgotten when administrators must cope with critics who fail to offer budgetary assistance along with their criticisms, reflect on this:

> From the moment of his arrest, if not before, the offender becomes the consumer of public resources, most of which are tax-supported. The cost of his apprehension and booking are the first expenses on the list. Unless he is released immediately on bail or personal recognizance, the taxpayers pay for his confinement in jail until his trial. And the costs of prosecution (and defense, if he cannot afford to hire counsel) and the expense of trial and related court services. In the event of his conviction, probation or imprisonment and parole will be paid for with tax money.
>
> . . . this situation can no longer be tolerated. Rising costs will eventually outstrip the availability of funds for meeting them. The ineffectiveness of the system is now seen as a major contribution to the alarming increase in the crime rate. . . .[1]

[1] Mark S. Richmond, "Measuring The Cost of Correctional Services," *Crime and Delinquency,* 18, No. 3 (July 1972), 243.

A wide range of criticism continues to flow from the mouths of many "experts." But in term of bringing about the managerial improvements necessary to meet the growing problems of criminal justice, the key is fiscal support and cost effectiveness as discussed in Chapter Seven. Even when criticisms are conspicuously valid, the criminal justice administrator must recall that his ultimate success does not depend upon the *variety*, but upon the effectiveness of solutions.

If criminal justice administrators recognize the true nature and scope of criminal justice success (as opposed to success that serves the purpose of a given critic), any jurisdiction can avoid the pitfall of trying to "do everything" when barely budgeted to do the things required for effective criminal justice.

Once the administrative goals are focused clearly within criminal justice, and the nature and scope of criminal justice success is recognized, *any* jurisdiction can move with the systems model.

With the certainty that any jurisdiction can develop effective management, a review of the systems model will be useful as a background for discussing the various avenues of such development.

MANAGEMENT MODEL: REVIEW

This volume began with a discussion of the entire criminal justice system. It was noted in particular that all subsystems of criminal justice are sufficiently interrelated to consider the overall system manageable. From this perspective, the concept of management was isolated and discussed as being uniquely different from the various specialities of line work. The historical perspective of management as a concept was developed and traced in terms of the continuing affinity between management per se and criminal justice since ancient times. Constant emphasis was given the contrast between the nature of a given work activity and the management required to insure productive continuity of work.

Many managerial philosophies were presented in terms of styles and approaches in order to reinforce management as an entity and to reinforce the legitimacy of management as a concept.

The evolution of a systems approach to management was discussed as an emerging method that combines all needed components to achieve success on a continuing systematic basis.

The classical management theories of X and Y were presented, but discussed as less significant than the clarity of role definitions—roles and functions being presented as the most crucial first step in the development of an effective management method. The presumed contrasts in managerial "style", it was indicated, have far less to do with effective management than was previously believed.

Human behavior was presented as extremely significant, but only insofar as it is integrated within a system of achieving specific, concrete results. In this regard, predetermined empirical measurement was emphasized over managerial judgments about behavior.

The systems model itself was presented as beginning with clarification of managerial roles and functions to clearly delineate accountability for performance. Great emphasis was given the contrast between efficiency and effectiveness in dysfunctional management—efficiency and effectiveness being synonymous only when managerial roles and functions are performed.

Clarity of interfaces between these clearly defined roles and functions was presented as the systematic approach to insure effectiveness as the management priority whenever efficiency and effectiveness differ.

Reflexive synergetics were presented as the dynamic approach to insure optimum synthesis of resources and resource utilization within a management model founded on the following:

> The *function* of defining results to be achieved is separate from the functions of what is needed to achieve results, who is needed to achieve them, and how results are achieved; the function of what is needed to achieve results is separate from who is needed, just as the function of who is needed is separate from how results are achieved.

These various functions were suggested for roles depending on the nature and size of the criminal justice organization.

Great emphasis was given the avoidance of an "end justifies the means" orientation. Measurement and explicit accountability were reiterated as the keys to such avoidance.

The requisite managerial information, planning, and decision-making were elaborated along with the budget process of the model. Personnel, labor unions, and managerial communication were also presented as critical concerns. The elaboration of the systems model concluded with a discussion of managerial education, training, and development.

Administrative and organizational structure was dealt with as a background for separate elaboration of management in each of the criminal justice subsystems: police, probation and parole, correctional institutions, and courts, along with elected offices of criminal justice.

In the chapter preceding this, final attention was directed to administrative concern with community and political relations.

Now, after having briefly reviewed the systems model approach to criminal justice management, attention is returned to the theme of this closing chapter: any jurisdiction can manage effectively.

EFFECTIVE MANAGEMENT

In effective management, what is important in dealing with any problem is an approach that focuses on the systematic dysfunction that *produces* the difficulty rather than on the difficulty, itself. This is properly giving attention to *management* rather than the *manager*—on measured achievement rather than on any specific person.

Paul Greenlaw writes:

> . . . The total organizational system is, in effect, comprised of a number of interdependent subsystems (and sub-subsystems), with the outputs of some serving as inputs to others. Whether one wishes to consider the individual members of an organization as constituting its subsystems, to view the organization's departments as subsystems, and their members as sub-subsystems, or to focus attention on still other sub-organizational elements will depend on the purpose of his analysis. . . .[2]

From this frame of reference, a focus on the manager as a sub-subsystem rather than on the system of management overall leads to the various myths about "ideal" management personalities. Unfortunately, these myths tend to discourage the use of managerial creativity and talent—at least among the many managers whose personalities do not fit the myth. Moreover, such mythology produces (albeit often unwittingly) far more concern for *who* the manager is than for *what* he could achieve within the results model in his own unique way.

Focus on management rather than upon the manager and his personality is then the key. This, however, is no easy task.

> A system is "an organized or complex whole; an assemblage or combination of things or parts forming a complex or unitary whole." The term system covers an extremely broad spectrum of concepts. For example, we have mountain systems, river systems, and the solar system as part of our physical surroundings. The body itself is a complex organization including the skeletal system, the circulatory system, and the nervous system. We come into daily contact with such phenomena as transportation systems, communication systems (telephone, telegraph, etc.) and economic systems. . . .[3]

As the systems model proposed in this volume evolved, concern with definitions for goals and functions that constitute the managerial interfaces within an organizational system became great. Once roles and functions are defined sufficiently to permit explicit measurement and accountability, who one is becomes less important than what one functionally achieves.

The implied criticism of personality simply need not arise in the training and education required for functional role achievement through effective managerial interfacing—through reflexive synergetics with accountability.

[2] Paul S. Greenlaw, "Management Development: A Systems View," *Personnel Journal,* 43, No. 4 (April 1964), 205.

[3] R. A. Johnson, E. Fremont, and J. Rosenzweig, "Systems Theory and Management," *Management Science,* 10, No. 5 (January 1964), 368.

Substantial training, of course, remains necessary, but with focus on management rather than on the manager.

The seeming paradox is that once emphasis is removed from the individual manager's personality, a great number of individual talents seem to emerge. In the earliest stages of governmental managerial development, talent seems to emerge as soon as clearly defined goals replace concern for individual managers. The following summary is quoted from an actual application for a federal grant that was prepared totally by full-time, available executive staff immediately after the administrative goal was set:

I. Project Summary

Criminal Justice Information Control (CJIC) in Santa Clara County is an integrated regional information system intended to improve daily criminal justice operations and to support comprehensive planning by utilizing modern data processing technology and administrative concepts. The proposed system represents the best alternative for meeting the real information needs of the criminal justice community. CJIC provides for gathering, retrieving and interchanging information on criminal activity, custody status and judicial processes. The data base thus developed and the analytical tools that are part of CJIC give law enforcement management the ability to plan and innovate and test alternative strategies.

CJIC represents a cooperative planning effort of local governmental agencies in a metropolitan area of one million population. It is extensive in scope but sufficiently detailed to meet local needs. Cooperating agencies have the necessary capability to develop and operate the system. The project is scheduled in phases over a period of four years at a total cost of $1,330,850 with a grantee contribution of $532,340. The Booking and In-Custody component, under design, can be implemented by early 1971. CJIC will document and evaluate use of the system, as well as changes in criminal justice procedures.

CJIC is consistent with the goals and priorities of the Omnibus Crime Control and Safe Streets Act of 1968 and the California Council on Criminal Justice. As amended, it is the Model County Criminal Justice Information System proposed in the Region V Plan for Information and Communications Systems. It includes formal provision for supporting transfer to other agencies.

II. Project Significance and Expected Results

The CJIC system proposed here will meet the known information requirements of various county and municipal law enforcement organizations, will coordinate all law enforcement information within the county, and will interface with regional, state, and national criminal justice information systems. Close collaboration of local agencies avoids duplication and inconsistency, and assures the inclusion of peripheral activities that are closely associated with law enforcement.

The CJIC plan will focus on the extent of criminal activity, causes of crime, crime prevention and control, analysis of criminal behavior, and improvement of judicial processes. The CJIC data base supports the following Task Force priorities:

(#1) Alternatives to institutionalization.
CJIC will provide the information base upon which various types of alternative plans can be modeled.

(#2) Training of local government officials.
CJIC can provide aggregate data for a more comprehensive overview of current practices and insight into improvements based on *real* information.

(#1) Reduction of delays in courts, etc.
CJIC booking, court recording and calendaring procedures provide current data before, during, and after judicial processes; CJIC information can serve as the base for instituting improvements in court scheduling and procedures.

(#1) Development and evaluation of youth service bureaus.
CJIC will aid in evaluating a bureau being established in July 1969.

(#3 and #4) Alternatives to detention.
CJIC will provide information needed to develop new policies.

(#1) Determination of existing deficiencies.
CJIC data base provides a comprehensive analytical framework for programs of problem identification and service improvement.

(#1 and #2) Coordination of agencies and support of information programs.
CJIC's countywide data facilitates interagency coordination and improves opportunities for timely action.

(#1) Strategic intelligence system.
CJIC provides interagency intelligence in a current and comprehensive package.

(#3) Prediction of organized crime activities.
CJIC data base provides the framework for crime pattern simulation and development of organized crime operating models for enhanced prediction.

(#2) Acquisition/dissemination functions for intelligence network.
CJIC has inherent value in acquisition and dissemination of intelligence for interagency use on a countywide basis.

The improvement of daily law enforcement operations will be facilitated through improvement in criminal justice data quality and accessibility. CJIC will retain the current status and record of persons involved in criminal processes. It will provide that status or record in concise, comprehensive reports, tailored to meet the needs of any law enforcement user, on a real-time basis if required. CJIC eliminates the maintenance of duplicate record files at each law enforcement agency within the county.

The availability of a large integrated data base in machine-readable form, developed as a by-product of normal operations, will provide a unique and innovative opportunity for top management to use advanced techniques to measure agency effectiveness and evaluate alternative policies and procedures.

CJIC will use information from county data banks of census, population, land use, transportation and other information partially financed by federal funds.

CJIC will provide information for a Youth Services Bureau that begins operation in July 1969, hopefully for a Community Correctional Laboratory (grant application from Institute for Study of Crime and Delinquency to National Institute of Law Enforcement and Criminal Justice, dated May 13, 1969), and possibly for a municipal information system project proposed by a local city government.

CJIC covers a large geographical area (1,302 square miles with one county government, 15 cities, a largely diversified urban population of slightly over one million, with a significant agricultural segment.

CJIC includes all of the components of the criminal justice system within the county, with a representative management team to guide the project.

CJIC serves an immediate need for an integrated county-wide information system that is prerequisite to many improvements in criminal justice processes.

CJIC can and will be implemented within a reasonable period of time; resources supplemental to county funds will shorten this time.

CJIC incorporates methods and plans for careful evaluation of the system.

CJIC satisfies, to a significant degree, the categorical goals of LEAA, and of CCJ task forces, as shown earlier in this section.

Although this is only one example of just one facet of criminal justice management, it nonetheless illustrates the basis of optimism about doing something significant—any jurisdiction can manage effectively, in many instances without the aid of the consultant specialists discussed earlier.

Any jurisdiction stressing functional achievement can define managerial roles and functions sufficiently to develop effective managerial interfacing. In doing so, the organization can remove most of the barriers to effective management that have to do with personality and any belief that "good" managers have a particular kind of personality. By removing these barriers, the frequent inclination to simulate a particular kind of personality is reduced, thereby leaving latitude to bring an individual's own, unique creativity and talent to bear on achieving results. Moreover, the emphasis on measurement and accountability reduces the value of sustaining certain myths about ideal managerial personalities that might encourage managers to perpetuate the myth that effective management is a matter of personality.

Removing the expressed or implied administrative priority of personality change also permits the setting of useful priorities—or at a minimum, determining where priorities are not useful.

Anything that implies an absence of focus on achievement or its measurement demands the immediate attention of a good manager. The various excuses given to avoid making changes within a managerial system, such as those discussed in the chapter on managerial training, education, and development, demonstrate a resistance to even consider using the administrative tools toward achieving an effective and efficient management. If achievement is the priority, all *positive* approaches—even criticisms—are worth considering. Of course there are positive approaches that would work to produce managerial results but that exceed the scope of a given criminal *justice administration*. But when managerial priorities are set correctly, the conclusion that any approach cannot produce or is not viable in particular circumstances is a conclusion reached through effective managerial interfacing. This is a use of reflexive synergetics rather than reflexive cynicism.

ANY JURISDICTION REALLY CAN MANAGE

Lest the reference to reflexive cynicism generate the belief that cynicism cannot be constructive, it should be noted that a modicum of cynicism is an absolute requisite to successful continuity in effective management—a "healthy reluctance to run off half-cocked." Cynicism, then, is more a matter of degree than kind. Only to the degree that interferes with effective management is cynicism worth being avoided.

In all too many organizations, there is actually more than one system— one or several existing in the minds of organizational members and one in reality. Developing effective management is enhanced substantially by recognizing this and trying to avoid it. When a person first joins an organization, there is the system as seen through the orientation procedure; there is, for long-term employees, the system that "old soldiers" know about. Then there is the system that top management sees as contrasted with the system that the supervisory staff sees. But with results-oriented management, there can be a single system.

In the "single system" with results priorities, clear articulation is required within managerial interfaces if results through functions are to be achieved.

> The task of the manager is usually thought of as getting things done through people. While it is something akin to this, there is always the danger that this will be interpreted by some as implying a kind of manipulation of people by a manager attempting to be an amateur psychiatrist. To avoid this misguided and hopeless approach, it appears to make more sense to regard the central role of the manager as one of effective and efficient operation of *individuals* working together in groups.[4]

Again with emphasis on the absence of concern with managerial personality, this definition of manager is possible only to the degree that there is managerial articulation within the interface of the model. Moreover, the very philosophy of reducing the many systems of an organization to a single, results-oriented system tends to aid administrative effort in eliminating the value of glibness as a substitute for accomplishment. Isolating measurable

---

[4] Harold Koontz, "Management and Challenges of the Future," *Advanced Management Journal*, 33, No. 1 (January 1968), 21.

accomplishment as a main priority not only increases the certainty that any jurisdiction *can* manage effectively, it also increases the likelihood that a jurisdiction will develop effective, continuous management—thus having his "own sweet way."

GETTING YOUR OWN SWEET WAY[5]

In his book on systematic management, Phillip Crosby does an outstanding job of clarifying the generic power of understanding and using any organizational system. Using International Telephone & Telegraph as a model, Crosby shows how the effective use of an organizational system achieves predetermined results.

Assuming the criminal justice administrator's getting his "own sweet way" would include results that integrate law as an instrument of social control with community and political variables, along with effective administrative interfacing between various criminal justice subsystems, the underlying managerial message of this book can scarcely be ignored—at least in a criminal justice system continually accused of fragmentation and "nonsystem" performance.

Crosby offers ten Laws of Situation Management that can be helpful to criminal justice management:

1. The primary concern of management is survival.
2. A person's loyalty is a function of how much he feels he is appreciated.
3. The amount of accurate information an executive possesses concerning the status of his operation varies inversely with his position in the organization.
4. The effectiveness of any program depends upon the amount of participation delegated.
5. The less systematic support a decision maker receives, the better decisions he will make.
6. Pride goes before all.
7. A job can only be as successful as the means supplied to measure it.
8. People are more important to situations than things.
9. Improvement is the only practical management goal.
10. Nobody really listens.[6]

Although the industrial orientation management philosophy of these ten laws may not fit criminal justice precisely, consider the following relationships:

[5] Crosby, *Getting Your Own Sweet Way* (New York: McGraw-Hill, Inc., 1972).
[6] Ibid., p. 9.

1. That of Law 1 to results definitions for the systems model.
2. Law 2 to the activities involved in how results are achieved, who does the work, and the actual definitions of what is needed to achieve goals.
3. Law 3 to the systems model rationale for clearly defined roles and functions with accountability.
4. Law 4 to the reflexive synergetics of the interface between the *who* and the *how* functions.
5. Law 5 to the systems model accountability design relating solely to results achievement.
6. Law 6 to requiring that functions be performed without regard to a manager's personality or methods in which pride can be taken.
7. Law 7 to the emphasis given measurement in each managerial interface of the systems model.
8. Law 8 to the rationale for focus on clarity of roles and functions.
9. Law 9 to the use of decision trees in planning, and to the entire range of activities involved in defining results.
10. Law 10 to the design of the management information system.

Of course, it would be inappropriate to assume that Crosby's laws consistently dovetail with a management model geared solely to criminal justice. Nevertheless, he has written a book of considerable interest to any criminal justice administrator who wonders if he should try managerial development.

TRY IT: YOU'LL LIKE IT

Even within an ideal administrative situation, there are certain things to aim for in good management philosophy.

> It is odd with all the emphasis today on developing managerial personnel that little effort is given to discovering who is progressing and regressing and at what rates. The large corporations invest millions of dollars each year on training and education of managerial personnel but do little to determine who are the real beneficiaries. The science of mobilography will bring a rare degree of precision and refinement to the process of managerial development. . . .
> . . . Mobilography is based upon [knowing] who are the most upward-mobile men in the corporation and [comparing] them to the least. . . .[7]

Presumably, reducing the potential complexity of "molilography" to a single, understandable dimension within a single results-oriented system would be desirable even in a system that is otherwise perfect. But this is actually what an effective management is all about.

---

[7] E. E. Jennings, "Charting the Difficulties to the Top: A Study of Executive Mobility Patterns," *Management of Personnel Quarterly*, 6, No. 2 (Summer 1967), 13.

The only variable in determining upward mobility of managers is achievement of results; this is true no matter how complex the variables developed by mobilography. Any jurisdiction can reach the point of asking only one question: Do all these complex variables produce desired results?

Try the systems approach to management—you'll like it!

SUMMARY

In this, the concluding chapter, an optimistic position was taken on the potential of every criminal justice subsystem to evolve continuous, effective, systematic management. As a background for the various avenues to increasing this possibility, the systems model was reviewed.

Emphasis was placed on achievement (or management) rather than on the manager. The examination of existing priorities and establishment of results achievement as the main priority was also emphasized.

The resistance discussed earlier as confronting managerial training and development was also reviewed, with a suggested strategy for using evidence of resistance as a systems diagnosis and starting point for managerial accomplishment.

Cynicism was discussed as valuable and healthy insofar as it does not impede effective results achievement. Reduction of excessive cynicism was approached on the basis of reducing the numerous organizational systems that frequently exist to one system that is results-oriented. Also stressed was the importance of articulate managerial interfacing.

The achievement of an administrator's goals was presented as readily available through the understanding and use of an organizational system.

Finally, mobilography was discussed as potentially reducible to one single variable: results achieved.

QUESTIONS

1. Relate the concept of managerial personality to the statement "The management system can be changed but the managers themselves cannot."

2. Discuss the distinction between the position that any jurisdiction can manage and the position that "any jurisdiction will manage."

3. Relate administrative priorities to the optimistic belief that every jurisdiction can develop effective management; discuss methods of determining existing priorities.

4. Contrast several typical existing systems within an organization in terms of new personnel, of "old soldiers," and various levels of management.

5. Discuss the value of evolving a single organizational system that incorporates all previous systems. Further discuss the value of a results orientation for the single system.

6. What is the single understandable dimension proposed for mobilography?

ANNOTATED REFERENCES

Reference here is made to the specific annotated references that appear within specific contexts at the conclusion of each of the fourteen preceding chapters.

Author Index

Subject Index